ONE WEEK LOAN

Java Programming with SAP NetWeaver®

 **PRESS**

SAP PRESS is a joint initiative of SAP and Galileo Press. The know-how offered by SAP specialists combined with the expertise of the publishing house Galileo Press offers the reader expert books in the field. SAP PRESS features first-hand information and expert advice, and provides useful skills for professional decision-making.

SAP PRESS offers a variety of books on technical and business related topics for the SAP user. For further information, please visit our website: *www.sap-press.com*.

Alfred Barzewski, Carsten Bönnen, Bertram Ganz,
Wolf Hengevoss, Karl Kessler, Markus Küfer,
Anne Lanfermann, Miroslav Petrov, Susanne Rothaug,
Oliver Stiefbold, Volker Stiehl

Java Programming with SAP NetWeaver®

Galileo Press

Bonn • Boston

ISBN   978-1-59229-181-6

© 2008 by Galileo Press Inc., Boston (MA)
2nd revised and extended edition

German edition first published 2008 by Galileo Press, Bonn, Germany.

Galileo Press is named after the Italian physicist, mathematician and philosopher Galileo Galilei (1564–1642). He is known as one of the founders of modern science and an advocate of our contemporary, heliocentric worldview. His words Eppur si muove (And yet it moves) have become legendary. The Galileo Press logo depicts Jupiter orbited by the four Galilean moons, which were discovered by Galileo in 1610.

Editor Stefan Proksch
Translation SAP AG
Copy Editor Lori Newhouse
Cover Design Silke Braun
Layout Design Vera Brauner
Production Katrin Müller
Typesetting SatzPro, Krefeld (Germany)
Printed and bound in Canada

Contents at a Glance

Contents

3 SAP NetWeaver Developer Studio — Step-by-Step to a Sample Application 113

9 Developing Composite Applications 379

10 SAP NetWeaver Development Infrastructure and the Component Model — Concepts 453

Preface to the Second Edition

Two years have passed since the first edition of *Java Programming with the SAP Web Application Server* was published. While the first edition described SAP NetWeaver 2004 and SAP NetWeaver 7.0 (equivalent to SAP NetWeaver 2004s) a complete revision became necessary due to the market introduction of SAP NetWeaver Composition Environment 7.1:

Content

▶ On the one hand, many programming techniques such as Web Dynpro Java or the SAP NetWeaver Developer Studio have undergone major changes. SAP NetWeaver 7.1 was the first enterprise platform to support the Java EE 5 standard that demonstrates the high speed of innovation of SAP NetWeaver. All aspects are covered thoroughly in this new edition.

▶ On the other hand, the positioning of SAP NetWeaver as a technology platform has evolved based on its strong market adoption. You can derive this from how SAP NetWeaver is used today: as a foundation for SAP's solutions such as SAP ERP and the SAP Business Suite on one side, on the other side as integration und composition platform for the Enterprise Service-Oriented Architecture (enterprise SOA) of SAP.

Because of this, new chapters have been added that introduce the composition technologies. Of great importance in this context is the interoperability between the different releases of SAP NetWeaver (7.0 und 7.1), including their varying speeds in terms of innovation. We still involved experienced authors of the different topic areas for the second edition as well.

The presentation starts in Chapter 1, *SAP NetWeaver*, with the positioning of SAP NetWeaver as platform for enterprise SOA as well as an introduction of the major SAP NetWeaver capabilities.

Structure

In Chapter 2, *Overview of the SAP NetWeaver Developer Studio*, the focus is on Developer Studio. The Java EE 5 programming model, the development, and the deployment of a sample application is shown in Chapter 3, *SAP NetWeaver Developer Studio — Step-by-Step to a Sample Application*. The focus here is not so much on a complete discussion of the Java EE 5 programming model (there are plenty of publications out there), but how the Java EE 5 model is supported by the many perspectives of the Developer Studio.

In Chapter 4, *Java Persistence*, the different approaches to Java persistence supported by SAP that are based on Enterprise JavaBeans 3.0 and the Java Persistence API are introduced. Chapter 5, *Web Services and Enterprise Services in the SAP NetWeaver Composition Environment*, leads into the world of enterprise SOA, based on standard Web service technology, and describes how to develop applications that consume Enterprise Services.

Chapter 6, *Developing Business Applications with Web Dynpro*, is dedicated to Web Dynpro because of the importance of the user interface. The Portal integration of Web Dynpro applications is described in Chapter 7, *Running Web Dynpro Applications in SAP NetWeaver Portal*. The Visual Composer as a tool for model-driven UI development is presented in Chapter 8, *SAP NetWeaver Visual Composer*. Further techniques for the creation of Composite Applications are discussed in Chapter 9, *Developing Composite Applications*.

The Java development process and the development infrastructure offered by SAP comprise three chapters. In Chapter 10, *SAP NetWeaver Development Infrastructure and the Component Model — Concepts*, the fundamental component model and the basic elements of the infrastructure are presented. Chapter 11, *SAP NetWeaver Development Infrastructure — Configuration and Administration*, explains the setup and administration of the Java Development Infrastructure. The Java EE 5 sample from Chapter 3 is revisited in Chapter 12, *SAP NetWeaver Development Infrastructure — Developing an Example Application Step-by-Step*, in order to demonstrate the development infrastructure.

In Chapter 13, *SAP NetWeaver Application Server Java — Architecture*, the architecture, scalability, and robustness of SAP NetWeaver Application Server 7.1, based on SAP's Java Virtual Machine, are discussed. The presentation concludes with Chapter 14, *Supportability of the SAP NetWeaver*

Composition Environment, which presents supportability aspects that are critical for the successful operation of applications.

On the trial DVD, you will find a test and evaluation version of SAP NetWeaver Composition Environment 7.1, including SAP NetWeaver Developer Studio. The samples that are discussed in the various chapters are stored on the DVD as well. You will find details about installation and configuration on the start page of the DVD that is displayed automatically when you insert the DVD into the drive.

DVD content

At this point, I would like to thank the authors. Without their passion the second edition would not have been possible: Alfred Barzewski for introduction of SAP NetWeaver Developer Studio (Chapter 2) and the basic Java EE 5 sample application (Chapter 3); Markus Küfer for the presentation of Java Persistence (Chapter 4); Susanne Rothaug und Anne Lanfermann for introduction and consumption of Enterprise Services (Chapter 5); Bertram Ganz for presentation of Web Dynpro Java (Chapter 6); Oliver Stiefbold for the creation of the DVD trial version of SAP NetWeaver Composition Environment as well as for the chapter on Portal integration (Chapter 7); Carsten Bönnen for his contribution on Visual Composer (Chapter 8); Volker Stiehl for the introduction to the development of Composite Applications (Chapter 9); Wolf Hengevoss for the presentation of SAP NetWeaver Development Infrastructure (Chapters 10, 11, and 12); and finally Miroslav Petrov for the overview of supportability (Chapter 14). You will find the bios of the authors at the end of the book. The chapters on the positioning of SAP NetWeaver (Chapter 1) and the presentation of the server architecture (Chapter 13) fall under my responsibility. Special thanks go to the translation team at SAP AG who created the English version: Paul Smith, Neil Matheson, Susan Want, Michèle Coghlan, and Abigail Haley. Last but not least, I would like to thank Stefan Proksch from SAP PRESS for his ongoing support and advice during the project.

Acknowledgments

Karl Kessler
Vice President, Product Management SAP NetWeaver

Preface to the First Edition

SAP NetWeaver is based on the SAP Web Application Server — the technological basis of all modern SAP solutions. Without the SAP Web Application Server (SAP Web AS), no Enterprise Portal, Exchange Infrastructure, Business Information Warehouse, or SAP enterprise software would be able to run. SAP Web AS is the platform on which applications can be developed and operated. The success of SAP's software depends largely on the efficiency and robustness of SAP Web AS.

As we reflect over the past decades, SAP's implementation of the application server at the end of the 1980s and the beginning of the 1990s was revolutionary. SAP's competitors — in so far as they existed at the time — were building two-tier applications. Some competitors moved the entire business logic to the frontend, creating the extremely cost-intensive *fat client*. This was difficult to scale as numbers of users increased, because every user process was assigned to a shadow process in the database. Other SAP competitors moved the business logic to stored procedures running directly in the database, but soon learned that with stored procedures an application couldn't be run on a database platform without recoding the entire application.

SAP's solution to this problem was to insert a separate tier between the frontend and the database: the *application tier*. This was when the application server — as we know it today — was born — even outside the context of SAP.

The application server from the days of R/3 still had all the features of a modern application server. It abstracted data from the underlying operating system and database platform, and optimized access to database resources using a sophisticated transaction and update concept. It provided a platform-independent programming language (ABAP) that was tailored to meet the requirements of professional enterprise software.

Many ideas from the world of Java, such as generating bytecode interpreted by a virtual machine, have been *state of the art* in the ABAP world for a long time. Another advantage of Java was that the development and runtime environments were interlinked. There's probably no other system in which you can perform all development work without ever having to leave the system. As the system compiles itself incrementally after changes, you no longer have the long generation times that were standard for classic C and Java development.

The swift success of the R/3 System on the market led to the application server being widely distributed. At the same time, the Internet and the World Wide Web (WWW) took off at an incredible speed. Proprietary worlds were no longer in demand; instead, people wanted open standards that were adopted by the Internet community. The primary standard was the Java programming language. Even though its core wasn't designed for business applications, it was popular because it was simple and platform-independent. Consequently, Java became widespread quickly (largely because of the Internet).

But not all concepts from those early years had any chance of success: Downloading entire applications on request from the Internet onto simple devices still remains an illusion. Endeavors to define a Java-based application server that different software providers could implement were taken more seriously, although it wasn't until well-known providers (including SAP) actually implemented the J2EE standard that Java had any real opportunity for success in the field of enterprise software.

However, implementing the standard came at a price. You had to implement many functions that were not imperative for business applications. Conversely, the J2EE standard could not sufficiently define many requirements essential for a business application, primarily the user interface, which is fundamental for business applications because an application's acceptance by end users depends largely on the user interface.

This is where SAP's many years of experience with enterprise software came into play. Even in the earliest versions of SAP's software, the user dialog was the focal point. This tradition is currently supported by Web Dynpro for SAP Web AS. Web Dynpro represents an application's user interface running in the SAP Enterprise Portal and, as such, is often the starting point for a development project. Powerful tools such as the SAP NetWeaver Developer Studio (NWDS) help you to design your applications as prototypes, while Web Dynpro supports a highly declarative, model-oriented approach. In addition to the user interface, elements and issues such as business logic, service-orientation, persistence, scalability, and maintainability are vitally important for the success of an application.

Karl Kessler
Product Manager SAP NetWeaver Foundation

This book focuses on SAP's Java programming model. To help you better understand SAP NetWeaver Application Server Java, this chapter introduces SAP NetWeaver as a platform for enterprise SOA, integration, and composition. The SAP NetWeaver Technology Map provides an overview of the central capabilities of SAP NetWeaver.

1   SAP NetWeaver

For more than 35 years, SAP has produced extremely successful enterprise software. SAP's enterprise software controls all business processes in many companies, and is therefore an important factor in business success.

However, SAP does not just develop enterprise applications, such as software for enterprise resource planning (SAP ERP), for maintaining customer relationships (Customer Relationship Management, SAP CRM), for optimizing production (Supply Chain Management, SAP SCM), or for maintaining supplier relationships (Supplier Relationship Management, SAP SRM). With SAP NetWeaver, SAP also offers a technology platform that, on one hand, is independent of the underlying hardware and system software (operating systems, database systems, networks), while on the other hand offers suitable tools, frameworks, and services for developing enterprise applications. Because all SAP applications were implemented on the basis of SAP NetWeaver, SAP NetWeaver is therefore the foundation for all SAP applications. However, SAP NetWeaver can also be used independently of the SAP applications as a stand-alone integration and composition platform.

SAP NetWeaver as the integration and composition platform for SAP applications

1.1 Platform for Enterprise Service-Oriented Architecture

Enterprise SOA and Business Process Platform

In a competitive environment, it is increasingly more important for companies to react as quickly as possible to new market requirements. SAP has therefore developed the concept of the Enterprise Service-Oriented Architecture (enterprise SOA). Unlike other middleware vendors, however, SAP does not just deliver a technology platform, but also the business content. When you combine these two levels, a complete Business Process Platform is created (Figure 1.1).

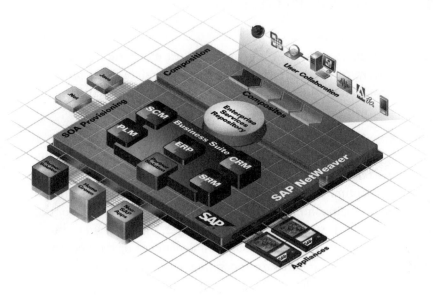

Figure 1.1 Business Process Platform

1.1.1 Enterprise SOA: A Definition

In this context, SAP NetWeaver acts both as the technological basis of SAP ERP and SAP Business Suite and as a functional kernel. Companies that deploy SAP NetWeaver and SAP Business Suite therefore have a concrete blueprint for service-oriented IT available, with which innovations such as process integration and composition can be implemented significantly faster than was previously the case. This is because business processes will be modeled in the future, and can be put together in almost any combination; SAP NetWeaver allows the integration of enterprise applications at different levels. The application must, however, have suitable interfaces.

In the context of enterprise software, these interfaces are also known as enterprise services. An enterprise service encompasses all of the semantic aspects that need to be taken into account in the use of the service. For example, if the "Cancel Order" enterprise service is called, it is not sufficient to delete the data record from the database in which the order was originally entered. At the same time, corresponding actions need to be triggered in all connected systems. For example, a connected vendor system might need to be informed about this change. If data from the order was transferred to a connected reporting system, the cancellation must also be taken into account there. The enterprise services ensure the semantic integrity of the associated applications.

Enterprise services

The more comprehensive and extensive the variety of enterprise services, the greater the opportunities for the company to make use of the newly gained flexibility. It is not enough to provide a technological platform with which pure Web services can be implemented. When SAP NetWeaver was launched in 2004, SAP announced the Enterprise Service-Oriented Architecture with the aim of providing enterprise software (SAP ERP, SAP CRM, SAP SCM, etc.) step-by-step with enterprise services (enterprise SOA by evolution).

Enterprise SOA Roadmap

It is important here to take a complete procedural view that does not isolate the services, but rather handles them in the context of a business process. For SAP ERP, this process is already largely complete: the enterprise services were published on the SAP Developer Network (*http://sdn.sap.com*) as enterprise service bundles. The process has already begun for the other components of SAP Business Suite, and the methodology has been successfully transferred from SAP ERP.

1.1.2 Advantages of a Service-Oriented Architecture

A new generation of applications can be created based on enterprise services: composite applications. Composite applications use services from

Composite applications

a number of underlying systems — you can combine services from SAP solutions and partner solutions — thus generating added value.

Classic integration scenarios are also based on a service-oriented architecture. These scenarios are normally technically asynchronous interfaces, because the communication partners involved cannot make any assumptions about whether the other side is currently technically available and accessible from a communications point of view. Higher technologies, such as the choreography and orchestration of integration processes, are then usually provided based on the service-oriented architecture.

Many technologies such as workflow or business process management require a service-oriented infrastructure. Event-oriented linkages, in which composite applications usually subscribe to events that are triggered by lower-level application layers, are related to this.

Enterprise Services Repository All service definitions, together with their underlying data type information and the use of the services in integration scenarios are centrally stored in the Enterprise Services Repository. The service definitions are specified in a standardized way with WSDL and XSD. It is then easy to generate proxy classes for the different runtime environments (ABAP and Java) based on the standardized definition.

The central storage of the services is very important, on one hand to ensure the consistency of a service-oriented infrastructure, and on the other hand to allow the SAP NetWeaver ecosystem to take part in the definition process. In the SAP NetWeaver ecosystem, partners and independent software vendors (ISV) can collaborate on the common definition of enterprise services in the context of the enterprise service community process.

1.1.3 Enterprise SOA by Design

When designing SAP Business ByDesign, an innovative solution for small business and midsize companies, SAP went a step further and created a complete service-oriented application platform.[1] This application platform consists of reusable business objects for which the Services

---

1 This book only discusses the technologies relevant for SAP ERP and SAP Business Suite.

were designed when the business objects were created, not the other way round as is the case with ERP. SAP Business ByDesign is also based on SAP NetWeaver as a platform and unifies core functions from all classic SAP solutions (SAP ERP, SAP CRM, SAP SRM) in an integrated approach. The enterprise SOA approach creates significant potential for pattern-oriented development of applications and in the deployment model, if business objects are implemented in different deployment units that communicate with each other using message-oriented interfaces. The flexible deployment allows you, for example, to run the process components for finances and logistics on separate computers, if needed.

SAP user interfaces are designed traditionally with professional users in mind and contain a large number of functions and features that allow a high degree of dynamic adjustment. However, this means that the use of the technology is reserved to the small group of highly specialized experts that have the necessary programming knowledge.

Pattern-oriented user interfaces

It is therefore very important to simplify and standardize the user interface for new users. Business process experts must also be able to configure user interfaces (UI) with standardized UI patterns, even if they have no programming knowledge. This configuration is only possible if the application has suitable standardized interfaces, meaning that you can define the generic UI patterns with actual application services. Of course, these services follow the conditions of the user interfaces and have a different granularity from the message-oriented services.

1.2 Platform for SAP ERP and SAP Business Suite

When designing the SAP NetWeaver Composition Environment, SAP strategically focused on the Java stack, because SAP and non-SAP services are to be increasingly combined here. However, it is important to remember that the business logic of SAP ERP and SAP Business Suite is predominantly implemented in ABAP. In the context of enterprise SOA, it is helpful to have some basic knowledge of the ABAP infrastructure. At the latest, if errors occur when calling enterprise services, this knowledge will be helpful in identifying the cause of the errors. However, you do not need detailed ABAP programming knowledge to work with SAP NetWeaver Java applications. In the context of enterprise SOA, ABAP plays the role of the service provider, while Java takes on the role of the service consumer.

Distinctions of this type are not always fixed, and in principle both language stacks are flexible. However, there are key focus areas for the content, for historical reasons, and for the current technology strategy.

ABAP infrastructure
A significant characteristic of SAP ERP and SAP Business Suite is the use of a platform-neutral programming language (ABAP) that has been optimized for the development of business applications. In addition to elementary language constructs and data types, ABAP has a sophisticated technique for accessing tabular data structures in main memory (internal tables). Database tables are accessed using a portable SQL Subset that is syntactically and semantically embedded in the language. ABAP supports both procedural and object-oriented programming styles. With ABAP, you can easily implement GUI-oriented or browser-based user interfaces (Business Server Pages, Web Dynpro ABAP).

The runtime environment for ABAP programs is optimized for a high degree of scalability. ABAP programs are generated in a temporary code and executed in parallel in large caches on the application server, which are assigned to users for the duration of a dialog step in each case (Figure 1.2). A dispatcher ensures that free work processes are correctly assigned to active user sessions. The user context is held in the roll area during the processing of a dialog step, and transferred between the work processes using the shared buffer. Each work process maintains a connection to the underlying database. The division into dialog steps produces balanced transactional behavior, because database resources (locks, open cursors, etc.) can only be held during a dialog step.

Tools, frameworks and services
Another significant characteristic of the ABAP platform is its integrated development environment. You can use the development environment to define database structures such as tables and views. Numerous data structures used in programs can be specified on the basis of these definitions (ABAP Dictionary). All dependencies between development objects are actively managed, which means that if an object is changed, all dependent objects are regenerated, if necessary. Changes to develop-

ment objects can be transported from one system to another. This results in a development and production landscape that allows distributed development in large teams.

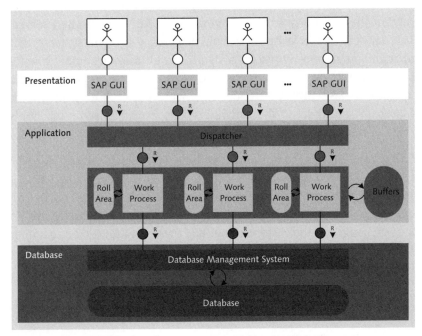

Figure 1.2 ABAP Stack

The ABAP stack provides countless services and frameworks, including central address management, public holiday and factory calendars, and change document management, all of which belong to the ABAP Reuse Library. They are used centrally by different applications, meaning that the code only exists once in the system.

The following sections build a bridge between SAP NetWeaver as the foundation for SAP Business Suite, which is overwhelmingly implemented in ABAP, and SAP NetWeaver as a platform for process integration and composition, for which the Java stack is primarily used. When doing so, we need to take into account the pace of innovation that SAP customers traditionally expect from SAP applications (long maintenance cycles), in contrast to the more aggressive innovation model that the market imposes of the Java stack.

1.2.1 Enhancement Packages

Since the launch of SAP R/3 in 1992, the ABAP stack has developed into the most robust application server for business applications. Worldwide, more than 50,000 installations in mission-critical environments rely on the scalability and robustness of the ABAP application server. The datasets of active ABAP systems have now become so large that upgrading a system represents a significant hurdle. Customers using a particular release (for example, SAP R/3 Enterprise) postpone the upgrade to SAP ERP due to the significant customization overhead. Moreover, the costs of the software maintenance consume the lion's share of the annual IT budget.

SAP is counteracting this problem with its new release strategy for SAP ERP. SAP ERP 6.0 is positioned as the target release for existing SAP R/3 customers, who are often still on release 4.6C. With SAP ERP 6.0, SAP delivers a stable ERP core. This means that the core processes are no longer changed, if the customer does not want them to be. The customer can, however, invest in innovation in a targeted way by implementing Enhancement Packages (Figure 1.3).

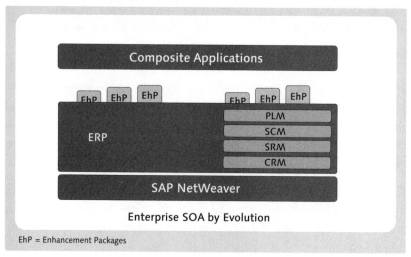

Figure 1.3 Stable ERP Core and Flexible Enhancement Packages

The Enhancement Packages contain new generic functions, such as simplified UI scenarios, and the associated enterprise services. Industry-specific functions are also delivered, and customers can activate new or extended functions as required. The activation process provides only the functionality that the customer actually requires to handle his or her processes. This significantly reduces the import cost, and could be called a minimal upgrade.

Because SAP ERP 6.0 is based on SAP NetWeaver 7.0, all of the technological innovations of the SAP NetWeaver platform, as well as the Enhancement Packages, are available to ERP customers; for example, portal content contains the role definitions for typical ERP processes.

Once SAP ERP has successfully introduced Enhancement Packages, the other members of SAP Business Suite (SAP CRM, SAP SCM, SAP SRM, and SAP PLM) will also use this technique to deliver enhancements that customers can selectively import on the foundation of a stable application core.

1.2.2   Switch and Enhancement Framework

The switch and enhancement framework provides the technical foundation for the Enhancement Packages. The fundamental idea of the switch and enhancement framework is to assign parts of ABAP development objects, or entire development objects, to a switch, with which the object is activated. The technique was initially created for the reintegration of the industry solutions (the industry solutions were previously developed in separate system environments), to maintain and deliver all industries within the ERP code basis. This concept was extended to the Enhancement Packages. The principles of the mode of operation are as follows:

Management and selective activation of enhancements

- ▶ An input/output field on a screen (analogous to Web Dynpro) is selectively activated. If the associated switch is activated, the field is displayed, and the input is processed.
- ▶ A module call is performed in the flow logic of a screen if the associated switch is active.
- ▶ Explicit or implicit enhancement points can be active in the business logic. In this case, additional sections of code run.

▶ Additional fields of a structure become visible with the corresponding switch setting. In database tables, these structures lead to additional columns.

▶ Parameters of a function module or of a method can be activated.

The application developer assigns the switch when defining the relevant development object in the ABAP Workbench. However, customers do not need to delve into the technical implementation: For the semantic assignment, the technical switches are assigned to a business function, and multiple business functions are combined into business function sets. A business function set corresponds to an industry solution (e.g., IS OIL, IS Media) or to an Enhancement Package. The customer administrator selects an industry solution and, if applicable, an Enhancement Package that he or she wants to activate. A background job then determines the required objects and activates them in the background.

Transaction SFW5 provides an overview of the active objects. It is currently only possible to select one industry solution in each case; however, it is possible, with the business functions, to use functions from another industry solution. The Enhancement Packages are cumulative, that is, higher Enhancement Packages include lower Enhancement Packages.

The Enhancement Packages therefore offer extensive functional options, which can be selectively used. Customers define the speed at which innovation is implemented in their existing landscapes. Without exception, SAP NetWeaver 7.0 is used as the technological foundation of the Enhancement Packages. Currently, small technical extensions required to operate the Enhancement Packages are delivered through the SAP NetWeaver Support Packages. However, in the future, they will also be delivered as SAP NetWeaver Enhancement Packages; this is currently in development. In both cases, the high cost of a complete SAP upgrade is avoided.

Independently of the Enhancement Package strategy, massive technological innovation is delivered based on SAP NetWeaver 7.0 in standalone SAP NetWeaver products, which are upward compatible and backward interoperable with the Enhancement Packages. Examples are SAP NetWeaver Process Integration 7.1 (see Section 1.3.4, *SAP NetWeaver*

Process Integration) and SAP NetWeaver Composition Environment 7.1 (see Section 1.3.5, *SAP NetWeaver Composition Environment*).

1.2.3 Web Dynpro ABAP

After the switch and enhancement framework, Web Dynpro ABAP is the second most important technological innovation of the ABAP stack in SAP NetWeaver 7.0. The programming model of Web Dynpro ABAP is identical to that of Web Dynpro Java, the main differences are in the development and runtime environment. While Web Dynpro Java applications are developed with the SAP NetWeaver Developer Studio, based on Eclipse®, and are deployed on the Java stack, Web Dynpro ABAP applications are developed in the classic ABAP Workbench (transaction SE80) and are executed directly on the ABAP stack. Due to the Enhancement Package strategy, Web Dynpro ABAP is positioned for SAP NetWeaver 7.0, and Web Dynpro Java for SAP NetWeaver Composition Environment 7.1.

User interface innovation with Web Dynpro

1.3 Platform for Integration and Composition

In addition to its role as technology stack and foundation for the SAP solutions, SAP NetWeaver provides numerous features for integrating processes and for composing new solutions from existing applications, based on flexible interfaces.

1.3.1 Integration Within a System

Traditionally, enterprise software has always optimized selected processes or sections of processes in companies. An ERP system optimizes order processing, integrated within a single system, and takes into account all aspects of the process that are significant for a company. From the receipt of the orders through the availability check and production management to the issuing of the invoice, all process steps are logged in the system. In the background, all relevant data is transferred to financial accounting and prepared for cost accounting. Technically, the consistency of the business data is ensured using a shared database, a comprehensive Dictionary, and appropriate function interfaces.

However, this approach reaches its limits whenever data cannot be stored in a shared database for technical or organizational reasons. There are many examples of this:

▶ Acquisitions and company mergers generally lead to heterogeneous landscapes.

▶ The applications involved each have their own database.

▶ The business processes across company boundaries. For example, company A is responsible for procurement, while company B performs the order processing (Figure 1.4).

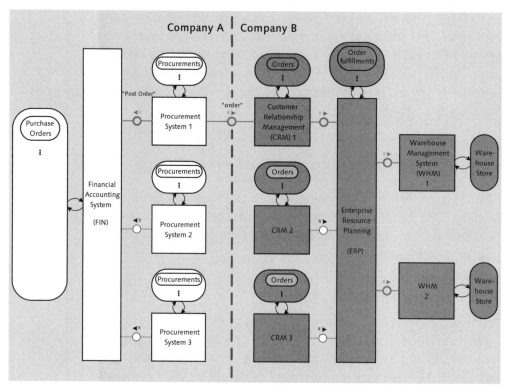

Figure 1.4 Business-to-Business (B2B) Integration: Procurement and Order Processing

However, it is not sufficient to optimize these processes within a system; these processes between multiple involved systems, which may belong to different companies, need to be reconciled with each other so that as many steps as possible can be automated.

1.3.2 Integration Using Standards

Internet technology and standardization are important prerequisites for taking full advantage of the integration potential. Standards offer a common language that is accepted and adapted by all participants. Examples of this are the Web services that allow services to be called over the Internet. In this case, the technological basis from which the service is called, or with which the service is provided, is irrelevant. Web services are important technological modules for implementing integration scenarios.

Web services

Another example is the use of a platform-neutral programming language such as Java, which many companies are involved in further developing (language, tools, frameworks). SAP NetWeaver is consistently aligned with standards, and SAP was the first enterprise vendor to implement the Java EE 5 standard, with SAP NetWeaver 7.1.

1.3.3 Invoice Verification Integration Scenario

We will use the simple, but critical, business process of invoice verification to explain the set of problems relating to integration. Invoice verification is a process with goals that are easy to formulate:

▶ Only goods and services that were actually ordered and received should be paid for.

▶ Invoices should only be paid once.

In the simplest case, all of the required information is stored in a single system. In this case, you only need to check for each invoice whether a corresponding, correct order has been entered in the system. It is more difficult, however, when multiple systems are involved. This is always the case if:

▶ Areas of the company have historically grown together.

▶ The company emerged from other companies.

▶ Procurement is organized in a decentralized way, but financial accounting is centralized, or has possibly even been outsourced to a service provider.

Component archi-tecture of invoice verification Invoice verification consists of a number of components; these are shown in Figure 1.5. To be able to perform the invoice verification on a uniform format, the incoming invoices are standardized by the Unifier component and stored in the invoice pool. There are different ways in which the invoices can be received.

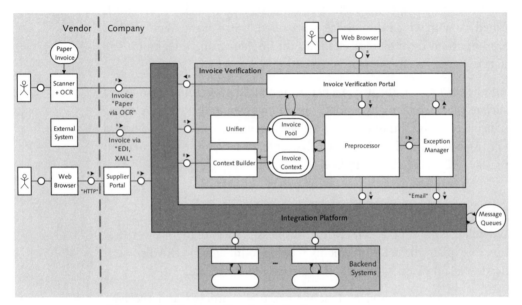

Figure 1.5 Architecture of Invoice Verification

Electronic exchange formats In addition to the universally familiar paper format, electronic exchange formats are also increasingly used to automate invoice processing. EDI or XML can be used for this purpose. For smaller vendors, the solution also provides a supplier portal, which vendors can log on to directly.

When the incoming invoices have been converted to a uniform format, it is important to provide as much context information as possible with which the invoice can be checked. The Context Builder component is responsible for this. If the invoice contains a reference for an order number, you can directly compare the invoice with the order. Otherwise, the system needs to find the open orders with the vendors involved and assign the invoices in each case. The Preprocessor component filters out duplicate invoices and, if necessary, triggers an Exception Management component.

If the invoice has been successfully verified, it is passed to a back-end system for further processing. The user interface for invoice verification is represented by the portal, through which the user has a complete overview of the process steps connected to invoice verification.

1.3.4 SAP NetWeaver Process Integration

To integrate processes such as invoice verification across system boundaries, the processes need to be defined in a design time tool, and executed in an engine intended for this purpose. There is a range of typical issues and problem fields that arise in this context that have to be solved and handled by the infrastructure for process integration.

For successful process integration, the following fundamental requirements need to be fulfilled by the infrastructure:

▶ **Messaging**
Messaging is the elementary task of reliably transferring a message (usually an XML document) from a sender to a recipient. There is usually a certain quality of service connected with this, such as an asynchronous link with the assurance of delivering messages precisely once in the correct sequence. The asynchronicity means that the recipient does not necessarily have to be available when the sender wants to send something.

▶ **Routing**
This decides to which recipient a message is to be transferred.

▶ **Mapping**
If the formats at the sender and recipient sides do not match, the message can be mapped and transformed so that the recipient side can successfully process the message.

▶ **Business Process Management**
Routing on its own is sufficient as long as messages can be forwarded independently of each other. To coordinate logical dependencies in the flow of the messages that applications want to exchange with each other, as well as the schedule and the subsequent steps, you need an executable process description that models the process flow of the communication between the systems involved. This process is exe-

cuted in the Business Process Engine, which provides the functions of the classic Business Workflow, extended with the control of cross-system processes. Only with Business Process Management is it possible to flexibly adjust the enterprise processes to changed conditions.

The infrastructure therefore needs to incorporate the following components:

▶ Design and configuration tools, which define processes and configure the landscape

▶ Integration Server, which is responsible for the tasks of messaging, routing, and mapping

▶ Process Engine, which executes Business Process Management

▶ Adapter, which adjusts the systems involved (e.g., log adjustment)

▶ Monitoring tools, which monitor the smooth operation in the Exchange Infrastructure

Architecture of SAP NetWeaver Process Integration

In the architecture of SAP NetWeaver, SAP NetWeaver Process Integration (PI) is intended for this purpose. It is easier to obtain an overview of the architecture of SAP NetWeaver Process Integration by considering the aspects of design, configuration, and Integration Server separately (Figure 1.6).

Design environment

The central tool for defining Process Integration content (message interface, mappings, etc.) is the Integration Builder. With release 7.1, the Integration Builder and the Integration Repository became part of the Enterprise Services Repository. All definitions are stored in the Integration Repository, which accesses structural information (e.g., software components) that can be managed in the System Landscape Directory (SLD). The SLD centrally describes the entire installed system landscape and also plays an important role in the SAP NetWeaver Development Infrastructure.

The central definition of message interfaces for Process Integration is performed in the Integration Builder based on XSD (data types) and WSDL (message types), and is therefore Web-service-compliant. What is unique, however, is that, through routing and mapping, Process Integration offers significant added value in comparison to a Web service infrastructure. It is then possible to generate proxies that the application can use for the ABAP and Java stacks from the message interface definition. The application is therefore separated from the technical implementation of the Process Integration.

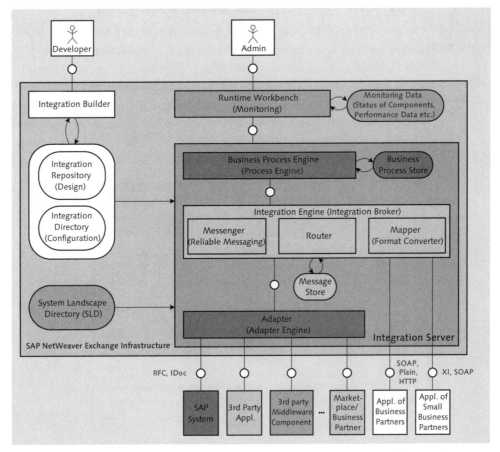

Figure 1.6 Architecture of SAP NetWeaver Process Integration

The actual configuration is stored in the Integration Directory. This includes rules that define the correct routing of messages in a specified landscape, and information about connected systems of business partners in Collaboration Profiles, which are required for business-to-business (B2B) communication.

Configuration environment

The runtime environment is implemented using the Integration Server, which is responsible for message delivery and the execution of the inte-

Runtime environment

gration processes in the Business Process Engine. The Integration Server is monitored in the Runtime Workbench.

1.3.5 SAP NetWeaver Composition Environment

Support for the Java EE 5 standard

SAP NetWeaver Composition Environment is a user-friendly development and runtime environment for composite applications (Figure 1.7), with which you can develop any Java applications. In the SAP context, however, the focus will mainly be on the simple usage and the composition of Enterprise Services provided by SAP ERP and SAP Business Suite, where any services from Partner and ISV software can be combined.

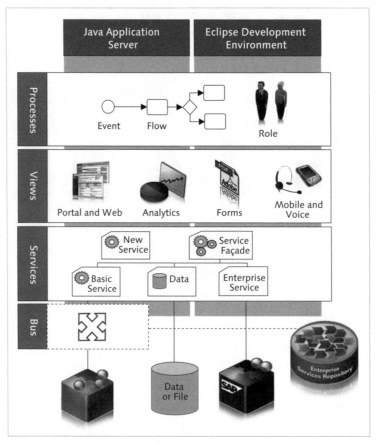

Figure 1.7 SAP NetWeaver Composition Environment

SAP NetWeaver Composition Environment is based on the SAP NetWeaver Java Stack 7.1, which supports the Java Enterprise Edition 5 (Java EE 5) standard. This offers many advantages and simplifications:

▸ Some simplifications of the Enterprise JavaBeans concept significantly simplify the programming. These simplifications are based on the use of annotations, which were enshrined in the Java language with the Java Development Kit 5 (JDK). You can use annotations to syntactically label code blocks.

The source code of an Enterprise JavaBean is then correspondingly syntactically annotated, which the development tools can efficiently evaluate.

▸ On the UI side, the JSF Framework (JavaServer Faces) has been integrated. Unlike the low-level Servlets and JavaServer Pages, JavaServer Faces provide control-based access to UI elements that can be declaratively embedded and assigned attributes in XML syntax in a JSP page. You can manipulate JSF controls using control classes in Java code.

▸ On the persistence side, Java Database Connectivity (JDBC) is used for low-level relational persistence, along with the persistence model of Enterprise JavaBeans 3 (EJB) (see Chapter 4, *Java Persistence*).

You can operate the Composition Environment in Java-only standard mode (Java EE 5 only) or in full Composition mode (including Composite Application Framework, SAP NetWeaver Visual Composer, and SAP NetWeaver Portal). The server is very slim, has a small footprint, and supports session isolation. If a session has errors, this does not cause the entire server to fail but only the sessions that are held by the same VM instance. The basis for this is the use of the SAP Java Virtual Machine (SAP Java VM), which is based on the Sun Hotspot VM, but stores the session information in shared memory. This means that the sessions can be better isolated from each other.

The following list gives an overview of the current programming models supported by the Composition Environment. You can, of course, also combine the different programming models.

▶ **Composite Views**

SAP NetWeaver Visual Composer is also delivered with the Composition Environment. You can use SAP NetWeaver Visual Composer to generate simple, schematic user interfaces (see Chapter 8, *SAP NetWeaver Visual Composer*). The definition environment of the Visual Composer is browser-based and offers data binding techniques that are easy to learn.

▶ **Composite Processes**

Composite Processes provide a workflow-oriented framework that supports simple sequential workflows and also branched workflows known as guided procedures (see Chapter 9, *Developing Composite Applications*). Guided procedures usually consist of Web Dynpro applications in which the Guided Procedures' runtime controls the assignment of the work items to the users involved. The definition environment is again browser-based.

▶ **Web Dynpro Java and SAP NetWeaver Developer Studio**

For sophisticated, dynamic user interfaces, the Visual Composer is usually not sufficient. Web Dynpro Java is available for this purpose. Web Dynpro Java is strongly model-driven and has a comprehensive set of tools, which together form the Web Dynpro perspective. They support the visual design, the modeling of the Web Dynpro components, and the data flow between the different elements. Chapter 2, *Overview of the SAP NetWeaver Developer Studio*, provides an introduction to SAP NetWeaver Developer Studio and the Web Dynpro perspectives.

▶ **Composite Application Framework**

The Composite Application Framework (CAF) allows you to define a separate persistence layer for Composite Applications (see Chapter 9, *Developing Composite Applications*). This is necessary if the data is not stored in the back-end systems.

▶ **BPM Features**

For future versions, capabilities for process definition and execution in SAP NetWeaver Composition Environment are planned. *Business Process Management Notation* (BPMN) will be used as a standardized notation.

1.4 Technology Map

The previous sections illustrated, in a problem-oriented way, some uses of SAP NetWeaver that will, above all, be meaningful for the programming model in the upcoming chapters of this book. In the following sections, the Technology Map (Table 1.1) is used to give you as complete an overview as possible of the capabilities of SAP NetWeaver, Application Development, Business Process Management, and Service-Oriented Architecture. Middleware is not explained here because it was already discussed in detail in the previous sections.

With such an extensive technology platform, which has, of course, diverse roots, a detailed description would be beyond the scope of this book; additional information is available in relevant SAP PRESS publications. A brief presentation of the topics is provided here, however, for your information.

User Productivity	User Interface Technology	Portal and Collaboration	Search	Mobile
Information Management	Master Data Management	Content Management	Business Intelligence	Data Management and Integration
Business Process Management	Business Process Modeling	Human Interaction Management	Business Process Monitoring	
Composition and Application Development	Composition	ABAP Development	Java Development	
Lifecycle Management	Landscape Design and Architecture	Application Management	Software Logistics	Operations
Security and Identity Management	Identity and Access Management	Compliance and Software Life-Cycle Security	Secure Collaboration and Interoperability	
SOA Middleware	Repository-Based Modeling and Design	Service Bus-based Integration	SOA Management	

Table 1.1 SAP NetWeaver Technology Map

Capabilities of SAP NetWeaver This capabilities view should not be confused with an architectural view. Architecturally, SAP NetWeaver is based on the Java and ABAP stacks, with the respective software components and the interplay of the two stacks. Even the famous "SAP NetWeaver fridge" was never intended as an architecture diagram (and is not very useful as one).

1.4.1 User Productivity

User interface In the context of SAP NetWeaver, User Productivity means the user interface and access to the system. The integration aspect is based on the fact that all users have uniform, role-based access to all of the systems that they need to access in the context of their activities using the Web browser through the SAP NetWeaver Portal. Alternative front ends are therefore no longer required because the portal allows logon-free access (Single Sign-on) to back-end systems.

In a typical SAP environment, a user needs to access a range of different systems. For example, a manager requires access to an HCM system that contains all personnel-related information, such as applications, performance feedback, salary data, and so on. The current business performance, on the other hand, is usually recorded in an Financials system. Development and production, in turn, are controlled from other systems. The task of the portal is now to harmonize access to these very different systems, which may come from different vendors, so the user does not need to know in detail in which systems the different information is stored.

Portal Content Portal integration is made possible using the role concept. Every user has a particular role within the company, for example, an accounting clerk, a manager, a salesperson, a purchaser, an invoice verification clerk. All functions and information that a user needs to access are stored in the role. The role concept in SAP NetWeaver Portal has been created in such a way that the administration effort remains at a manageable level. The portal provides the external frame; the actual portal content usually comes from back-end systems connected to the portal.

Portal content is not just static Web content, but in the SAP context actual, interactive applications. One of the reasons for the introduction of the Java platform in SAP NetWeaver was so that standard-compliant content for the SAP NetWeaver Portal could be developed. The techniques for doing so form the fundamental content of this book.

The elementary unit for content in the portal is the iView (integrated view). The iView represents a self-contained application in the portal, which can be placed in relation to other iViews in many different ways. iViews can be technically implemented in very different ways. Prominent examples include Web Dynpro applications, BSP applications, and HTMLB-based applications, but also include SAP transactions that are started using the Internet Transaction Server and BW-Reports.

iViews

If different iViews are semantically closely related, you can combine them in a portal page. The portal infrastructure supports the exchange of information between different iViews through portal eventing at the front end. iViews and pages are the modules for worksets, which are, in turn, the modules for portal roles. Both worksets and roles are represented by folder structures, which are then also used for navigation in the portal (top-level and detailed navigation). Through the role assignment, each portal user has individual access in the portal to a large number of applications in very different systems.

Instead of browser access, access is now also possible through the SAP NetWeaver Business Client, which displays the role menus in the navigation area (known as the L shape, because the geometric form is of an L rotated 90 degrees), while the iView is displayed in the character area (known as the canvas area). For the application, it is not important if the user is navigating using the browser or the SAP NetWeaver Business Client; in either case, it is just a formatting of the role information.

SAP NetWeaver Business Client

The topics Collaboration and Knowledge Management are closely linked to the portal technology. In its early phase, the Internet primarily offered simple access to documents. However, in companies, in addition to the structured information that is provided by portal applications and BW reports, there is a great deal of unstructured information (documents of any type) that is important to the success of the company. It is therefore vital that every user can access documents in the portal.

Knowledge Management and Collaboration, Search

Knowledge Management in SAP NetWeaver is not a document management system (in the same way as the Portal is not an application system), but rather a parenthesis around existing document and content management systems, which are integrated into Knowledge Management through generic interfaces. This allows common full-text indexing and search (Enterprise Search), a comprehensive classification and taxonomy system, and feedback functions.

Because the primary purpose of documents is the exchange of information between people, it should be possible to access shared documents in a simple way. SAP NetWeaver provides a range of Collaboration techniques to allow this. In this case, the communication takes place in Collaboration Rooms, which are similar to Internet forums. A room is technically a document container, with the possibility of including project-specific data such as calendars, task lists, and so on. The browser-based interface of the rooms is completely embedded in the Portal. Users receive access to a room through an invitation mail. Room templates help users to define new rooms and support different usage scenarios. A room can also be a starting point for Real-Time Collaboration (e.g., WebEx). Collaboration is not restricted to static documents. Users usually also want to exchange the results of a BW report or of a portal application. In this way, the components, SAP NetWeaver Portal und SAP NetWeaver Business Intelligence (BI), are closely linked in the cross-NetWeaver scenarios (such as Information Broadcasting).

1.4.2   Information Management

Information Management includes all SAP NetWeaver capabilities that are related to the integration of structured and unstructured information. These include, above all, Business Intelligence, Master Data Management, and Content Management.

Business Intelligence
In addition to the ABAP stack, SAP NetWeaver BI is an extensively developed component within SAP NetWeaver. This is no surprise when you consider that reporting in companies is an important basis for making strategic decisions, such as:

▶ Identification of customer and market potential

▶ Optimization of warehouse stock

▶ Selection and optimization of purchasing

Because business intelligence is distributed across a large number of systems in very different formats, SAP built a Business Information Warehouse in the 1990s. In contrast to the systems in which data is mainly recorded (Online Transaction Processing, OLTP systems such as SAP ERP or SAP CRM), the data in SAP NetWeaver BI is available exclusively for analysis and evaluation (Online Analytical Processing System, OLAP).

To structure the analysis and evaluation in as flexible and comprehensive a way as possible, and to achieve performance that is optimized for reporting, the data is extracted from the OLTP systems, processed (information that is not required in the reporting is hidden), and physically stored in the Business Information Warehouse (Figure 1.8) in data structures that are suitable for OLAP applications (InfoCubes).

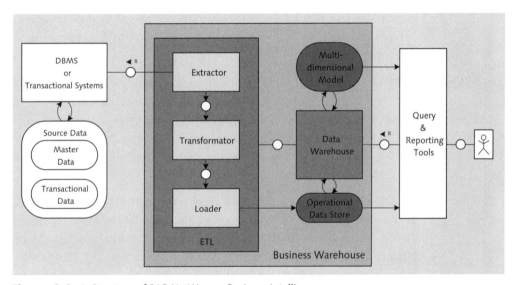

Figure 1.8 Basic Structure of SAP NetWeaver Business Intelligence

The back-end of the Business Information Warehouse is technically based on the ABAP stack, onto which BI Content is imported. The front-ends usually used in this context are the Web browsers to display the reports, Microsoft Excel to define queries and reports, and for the postprocessing of report data and the classic SAP GUI for administrative purposes.

Within SAP NetWeaver, Business Intelligence is interwoven with the other SAP NetWeaver components in many ways. The SAP NetWeaver

Portal allows central, role-based access to the reports and analyses. The Collaboration techniques allow team-oriented collaboration.

An OLTP system is usually not suitable for analysis and reporting for a number of reasons:

▶ The data in the OLTP system is heavily normalized. For reporting purposes, normalization significantly reduces performance, because the data needs to be aggregated with expensive join operations.

▶ OLTP applications are geared to established business processes. It is difficult to perform ad hoc queries and analyses.

▶ OLTP systems do not usually support universal, multidimensional reporting. In contrast, with the universal data structure of InfoCubes, OLAP allows the aggregation of data by different categories. For example, you can analyze sales revenues by categories such as region, business area, and customer group. It is also easy to display combinations.

OLAP systems

OLAP systems fall into different categories, depending on how the data is stored. With Relational OLAP (ROLAP), the InfoCubes are stored in tables of a relational database. Alternatively, you can use tree structures (MOLAP) to store multidimensional data. Although this type of access can be implemented very efficiently, it has disadvantages if the data structure has to be set up.

With the ROLAP model, the star model is frequently used to represent the data. In the center of the star model, there is a fact table that contains the elementary facts (basic, aggregated information that can usually be totaled), and radiating from this in each case, there is a dimension table. In the previous example, the fact table contains the sales revenue dat a, while the dimension tables contain detailed data about customers, regions, and company areas. The fact table is linked with the dimension tables using foreign key relationships. A multidimensional query first searches in the dimension tables for matching records. It then uses the foreign key relationship to filter out the matching facts. To balance the disadvantages of the star model, due to the lack of standardization, there is also a range of other models in use that combine the star model with the normalized display.

Unlike SAP NetWeaver BI, SAP NetWeaver Master Data Management (MDM) is a very new SAP NetWeaver component. Master Data Management is primarily used to consolidate master data (customers, suppliers, employees, materials) that plays an important role in companies. Starting from SAP NetWeaver Master Data Management, you can then usually distribute master data to other components and systems using Process Integration functions.

1.4.3   Lifecycle Management

With an architecture that provides as many functions as SAP NetWeaver, it is vital to have powerful tools and frameworks for Lifecycle Management. These include considerations about the architecture of the elementary design of an SAP or SAP NetWeaver landscape and tools for monitoring (SAP NetWeaver Administrator) and for maintenance (Software Lifecycle), patch, and upgrade. Developers will usually not work very intensively with these tools but rather leave their use to system administrators.

There are, however, a number of interplays in particular if you want to integrate your own application into the SAP NetWeaver Administrator, for example. It will also sometimes be necessary to patch the development work center to a particular level to be able to correct errors. If you are operating applications on a larger scale, consistent application management is required. With the SAP Solution Manager, SAP offers a comprehensive solution for this.

1.4.4   Security and Identity Management

The capabilities for Security and Identity Management are primarily concerned with functions such as user management, Single Sign-On, authorizations, procedures for secure authentication, and so on. These topics are, like the Lifecycle Management topics, more administration-related.

The SAP NetWeaver Security Guide, available in the SAP Developer Network (*http://sdn.sap.com*) under **SAP NetWeaver • Security • SAP NetWeaver Developers Guide • Secure Programming**, provides you with support for technical security, both from administrative and development perspectives.

1.5 Outlook

SAP NetWeaver is SAP's strategic platform: It is the foundation that forms the basis for SAP solutions. SAP will adjust the speed of innovation to the requirements of SAP customers' long-term maintenance cycles. SAP Business Suite will be based on SAP NetWeaver 7.0 in the long term, and, from a technological point of view, new developments will be added using the mechanism of Enhancement Packages.

As an integration and composition platform, SAP NetWeaver is optimized for the integration of SAP applications and non-SAP solutions. Its technology is geared to current standards and innovations.

In the short term, the Composition Environment will be enhanced with Business Process Management techniques. Other technologies such as Business Intelligence, Master Data Management, and SAP NetWeaver Portal will also be with innovations at shorter intervals. The decisive factor in the provision of these innovations is their compatibility and interoperability with SAP solutions that have already been implemented.

This chapter introduces you to the SAP NetWeaver Developer Studio. First, you'll learn about the general design concepts and the specific integration platform enhancements, based on SAP's Java development and modeling environment. Followed by an overview of the perspectives and features, an extensive range of tools and utilities are detailed. Finally, the installation and update mechanism is presented.

2 Overview of the SAP NetWeaver Developer Studio

The SAP NetWeaver Developer Studio (also known as the Developer Studio) is SAP's own development environment for developing and modeling Java-based, multilayered business applications. The Developer Studio is based on Eclipse, an open source product whose architecture provides a suitable platform for integrating specific functions. Although Eclipse provides extensive built-in Integrated Development Environment (IDE) features, these features are mostly generic. The development of large-scale, server-based business applications involves specific requirements that can be met only by making far-reaching enhancements to the Eclipse platform.

Eclipse as a platform

For example, in the case of extensive Java projects that involve large teams of developers who are distributed across many geographical locations but working on the same components, you could provide a robust infrastructure, enable efficient collaboration, and cover the entire development cycle right up to transport management and production. In addition, the optimal way to support additional project types as well as logical views of the projects and their development objects (instead of the file and directory-based view, which is typical in Eclipse) is to enhance the infrastructure so it can implement new tools.

Eclipse, therefore, provides a platform that can seamlessly incorporate any number of additional functional enhancements according to a standardized mechanism. This also includes the integration of open source projects for the standard Java developments J2EE (Java 2 Platform, Enterprise Edition) and Java EE (Java Platform, Enterprise Edition). For example, standard tools from the Eclipse Web Tools Platform (WTP) are integrated in the Developer Studio and therefore contribute to consequent support of a uniform development paradigm within the scope of standard Java development.

2.1 User Interface

Before we examine the features, let's look at the Developer Studio's user interface and appearance.

Window
The basic modules of the user interface are based on the Eclipse user interface paradigm; the IDE user interface is comprised of perspectives, views, and editors. All of the components that are visible at any one time are represented by a *window*. A window, therefore, represents the Developer Studio's actual user interface and usually provides users with several perspectives, of which only one is visible at any one time. Figure 2.1 shows a window with a section of the Web Dynpro perspective.

Perspective
A perspective always has a toolbar and a set of views and editors that are combined according to task-specific aspects. Users can open different perspectives with a click of the mouse to perform additional tasks within the development environment. Each perspective initially provides a set and an array of views and editors, although users can easily combine them, thereby adapting them to their individual requirements. In addition to the basic perspectives already included in the standard Eclipse platform, the Developer Studio provides a series of additional perspectives for various application development requirements. Each of these additional perspectives is presented later in this chapter.

Editors
Editors are required to process development objects. They enable users to open, process, and save development objects. The changes made by users in an editor are not saved automatically, but follow the *open-save-close sequence* that is typical for files.

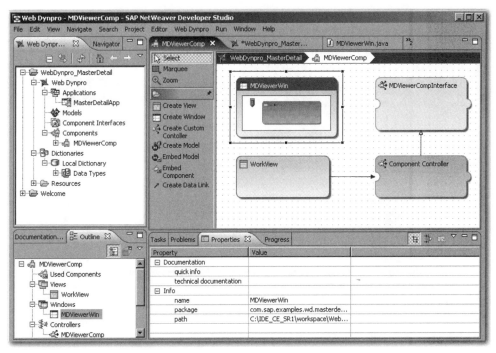

Figure 2.1 User Interface for the SAP NetWeaver Developer Studio with the Web Dynpro Perspective

In addition to the standard editors for texts and Java source texts, the Developer Studio provides additional editors for processing special development objects. Graphical editors play a significant role in the Developer Studio because they support application developers in optimizing organization of their tasks. For example, the data modeler in the Web Dynpro perspective in Figure 2.2 is connected to a Web Dynpro component. The Web Dynpro component represents a complex logical object, not a file, which, in addition to the controller, also combines the corresponding controller interface and other embedded visual components in a Web Dynpro project.

As a graphical editor, the Web Dynpro data modeler also provides a central entry point for working with Web Dynpro components. The graphical icons allow users to navigate directly to the individual elements of the Web Dynpro component. To create additional subcomponents, users can access tools that are available in an integrated palette. Furthermore, this editor also allows the visualization and definition of relationships for the individual subcomponents. The source code generation associated with all changes takes place in the background; developers do not need to follow this process in detail.

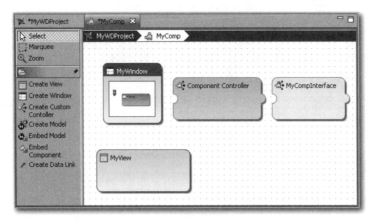

Figure 2.2 Subcomponents and the Representation of Their Relationships in the Data Modeler of the Web Dynpro Perspective

Views Typically, views are used to represent a tree of structured data and are therefore suitable for visually displaying projects or the internal structures of XML files. Figure 2.4 shows the Web Dynpro Explorer as an example of a view providing a logical view of a certain project structure. Views and editors are also often closely connected. Editors are usually started from a view to open an object for processing from the tree structure. In many cases, certain information is required about an object that is being processed. This is a typical area where the *property view* is used. This chapter, along with Chapter 3, *SAP NetWeaver Developer Studio — Step-by-Step to a Sample Application*, describes a number of additional views.

2.2 Workspace, Projects, and Development Objects

The Eclipse *workspace* is a central concept for managing all project resources locally. The workspace is not only the physical directory where project resources are saved locally, but it is also the place where metadata is stored for managing information about projects, and, alternatively, for managing information about user-specific IDE settings. This workspace concept, therefore, abstracts from the physical file storage location and allows local resources to be organized flexibly under the IDE's control.[1]

All development resources can be used as a workspace component in the Developer Studio. A workspace consists largely of one or more projects, where each project is mapped to the corresponding user-specific directory in the file system.

Workspaces combine a user's projects

This is displayed in Figure 2.3; in any given workspace, two projects can be linked to different directories, even on different disks. Each workspace has a default directory, where metadata is stored in a separate file. This means that the metadata can be stored in a different location than the one containing the actual project resources. A workspace directory such as this can also be used as physical storage for project resources. However, experience shows that it is best to differentiate between the workspace and the physical representation of the project data.

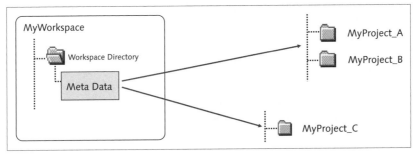

Figure 2.3 Mapping User-Specific Project Directories Using the Workspace Metadata

As with many other development environments, the Developer Studio groups related resources. In principle, a project can contain any number of files and directories. A special feature of projects is that they cannot contain additional projects. In this way, resources can be encapsulated optimally in a project. The group of development resources within a

Projects as containers for development objects

---

1 This workspace concept is fundamentally important for organizing any resources controlled by the local IDE. It should not be confused with the DTR workspace, which will be discussed in Chapter 10, *SAP NetWeaver Development Infrastructure and the Component Model — Concepts*.

project is oriented according to clearly defined task areas. For example, Enterprise JavaBeans (EJB) cannot be created in the Web module project; conversely, EJB module projects do not allow developers to include Web resources, such as servlets or Java Server Pages (JSP).

In summary, projects are containers in which the related development objects are managed at the time of design by the development environment. A workspace can contain any number of projects, which are all displayed in the *navigator view*. The resources for the individual projects are shown as files that are also displayed hierarchically in the form of a tree structure.

Logical views of development objects
Unlike a file and directory-based arrangement, all SAP-specific projects offer a logical view of the resources that are also displayed as a tree structure. Starting with the project structure, developers can start different context-specific actions, such as creating a new object, opening the editor, and so on.

By default, several views of a project type are available, each of which emphasizes different aspects of a project. Figure 2.4 shows the structure of a Web Dynpro project in the Web Dynpro Explorer. In contrast to the file and directory-based arrangement in the navigator view, the tree structure is sorted into logical units on a project-specific basis.

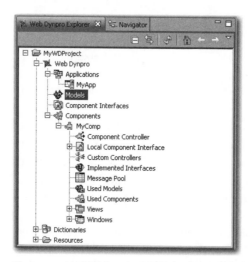

Figure 2.4 Logical View in the Web Dynpro Explorer of the Development Objects in a Web Dynpro Project

2.3   Open Source Initiative

The SAP NetWeaver Developer Studio is based on the Eclipse platform, which is available as an open source platform for a wide developer community from the Eclipse Foundation. The Eclipse platform represents the result of a worldwide movement to create a large and active environment in which leading technology providers and start-ups together with research institutes, universities, and many individuals can continually enhance and extend a platform to reflect current trends in technology. The efforts of this open source initiative are focused principally on making an open and innovative development platform available, comprising extendible frameworks, tools, and runtime environments for development, distribution, and management of software products through all phases of the software lifecycle.

Eclipse defines a fundamentally open architecture that enables the integration of tools and frameworks to cover almost any requirements posed by application development. Eclipse's design, therefore, places it more as a platform for IDE extensions rather than as a predefined set of end-user tools. However, this corresponds exactly to the objective of the open source initiative, which consists of providing a robust and universal infrastructure whenever possible for developing tools with a high level of integration. The focus is on implementing tools and utilities for the actual requirements of application development. The objective is to be able to process almost any contents and types of data (Java, C, JSP, XML, HTML, etc.) and enable seamless integration of different tools, which can also originate from different manufacturers. Implementation of this kind of concept is possible due to well-defined Java-APIs, which are open to the tool manufacturers for their own IDE extensions.

SAP Java IDE open for coexistence with open source

Before we examine the specific functions of the individual tools and frameworks in more detail, let's look behind the scenes at the architecture on which the SAP NetWeaver Developer Studio is based. Figure 2.5 shows a simplified view of the architecture. We distinguish between the following three software levels in the Developer Studio from an implementation point of view:

Architecture

▶ Eclipse Software Development Kit (SDK) as an integration platform

▶ APIs and tools from the Web Tools Platform (WTP) open source project

▶ Various SAP toolsets for developing applications and integrating the SAP infrastructure

▶ Generic framework plug-ins for embedding the tools and infrastructure

▶ Extensions from third-party providers based on the IDE version delivered

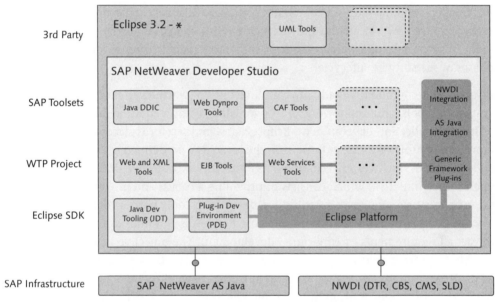

Figure 2.5 Tool and Infrastructure Connectivity in the SAP NetWeaver Developer Studio

2.3.1 Eclipse Software Development Kit

The Eclipse SDK is the core of the IDE architecture. The SDK comes with a powerful concept for extending it based on plug-in technology. As shown in Figure 2.5, the Eclipse SDK is comprised of the actual Eclipse platform and two extensive toolsets. The Java Development Tooling (JDT) provides the required tools for standard Java development. Accordingly, JDT represents a pure Java development environment and includes the precise functions that allow the user to edit Java code and validate it at design time, as well as compile, test, and debug it. One of the fundamental components of the Eclipse SDK is the plug-in development environment (PDE), which provides a powerful environment especially for developing plug-ins and making platform extensions available.

The Eclipse platform consists of a platform runtime and several subsystems, which in turn are implemented using one or more plug-ins. This basic platform delivers only the IDE core functions without supporting a specific programming language. The majority of the functions of this basic development environment are rather generic in nature. The tools in this basic platform allow developers to create only generic projects and use only generic text editors to edit the associated files. Nevertheless, the Eclipse platform establishes the basis for the behavior of its extensions. For example, the UI model for all other tools is defined here, as is the way to connect a project resource management system or the Eclipse Workbench.

From a technical perspective, the Eclipse extension concept is based on plug-ins and extension points. For example, new features, in the form of new tools, are implemented using *plug-ins* and made available by means of defined platform extensions. A plug-in is the smallest unit with which a function can be developed separately and made available for the platform. A small tool can be implemented using a single plug-in, although more complex tools may have to be distributed using several plug-ins.

Plug-ins as technical modules for IDE extensions

Eclipse uses the concept of *extension points* for its extensions. Extension points are a set of well-defined entry points in the platform, with which new plug-ins can use existing platform functions. In this way, extension points define the places where the platform functions can be extended. In addition, new plug-ins can define their own extension points for a possible connection and therefore present themselves as service providers. Other plug-ins can then use these entry points to contribute their functions to the platform.

The three components that the Eclipse SDK is comprised of include the Eclipse platform, the JDT, and the PDE, provide a complete Java development environment, including all APIs and tools for platform extensions.

2.3.2   Integration of the Web Tools Platform

The integration of the Eclipse project Web Tools Platform[2] (WTP) in the Developer Studio represents a significant step toward uniform project support that is generally accepted in the open source community for standard development in Java.

Standard development with WTP tools

The objective of standardization at tool level, which is linked with the WTP project, is to use proven solutions for standard development in Java. This step is linked with investment security for everyone involved, above all with regard to long-term use.

In accordance with this objective, this open source project provides a range of APIs and tool support for developing Web-based applications based on the J2EE and Java EE programming standards. The scope of the WTP tools contains both source code editors and graphical editors, plus numerous wizards, generators, validation functions, and other tools for efficient support of application developers during the construction of EJBs and Web resources (Java Server Faces, JSPs, Servlets, XML, HTML), as well as during the provision and use of Web services.

In addition, developers have the necessary tools and APIs to deploy, execute, and test new Web applications and services in an integrated server environment. The end-user WTP tools are embedded in the Developer Studio using the J2EE perspective; in addition, developers can access them in the same way, regardless of whether the tools are used to create projects or for server administration.

Figure 2.6 demonstrates the use of the Servers view during deployment of a Java EE standard application on the SAP application server. In addition to the **Publish** operation, this WTP tool also allows developers to use other basic administration functions for servers from various manufacturers.

---

2 The version of the Developer Studio installed with the DVD accompanying this book is based on WTP 1.5. In contrast, the complete integration of WTP 2.0 is planned for the subsequent releases that are part of the installation of SAP NetWeaver Composition Environment 7.1. WTP 2.0 contains distinct enhancements compared to WTP 1.5 and is provided as part of an ambitious project that the Eclipse consortium presented to the open source community with the annual release under the codename "Europa." WTP 2.0 is only one of a total of 21 projects that the Europa release contains.

Figure 2.6 Figue 2.6 Deployment of a Java EE Application on the SAP NetWeaver Application Server Java

WTP makes not only a range of end-user tools available but also a set of APIs and extension points that allow the tool developer to create extensions. For example, they are used for the Developer Studio, if the connection to the SAP NetWeaver Development Infrastructure has to be implemented for all types of projects in the J2EE perspective.

2.3.3 SAP-Specific Extensions (Tools and Infrastructure)

The Developer Studio assumes the presence of all standard components and features of the Eclipse Workbench, which is installed with the Eclipse SDK, and extends them with a range of tools and services, which are grouped in corresponding SAP-specific perspectives depending on the tasks involved.

Development on the Basis of SAP-Specific Projects

This is how the Developer Studio integrates the design time for the Composite Application Framework (CAF) and provides access to a comprehensive composition and development environment with its own abstraction layer and its own programming and meta model, as well as adequate tool support during the creation of composite applications.

Model-driven
approach

The strength of the CAF design time, the tools of which are grouped in the CAF perspective, lies in the consequent support for a model-driven approach during the creation of business objects and services, combined with the means to embed existing and external services in the composite application. Developers can use mostly declarative steps to create the component for a CAF application so that the programming effort is reduced to a minimum.

The Web Dynpro UI programming model follows a similar model-driven approach. The associated design time tools are integrated in the development environment through the Web Dynpro perspective. Generation of development objects in Web Dynpro projects is also based on a metadata model provided specifically for this purpose. The Java Dictionary is also a pure SAP-specific technology. The associated design time tools are integrated in the Developer Studio through the Dictionary perspective and allow developers to define tables independent of the database and to create global dictionary types and structures.

SAP Component Model

NWDI integration
at project level

The SAP-specific component model supports all project types that are relevant for application developers. As part of the SAP NetWeaver development infrastructure (NWDI), the component model is embedded firmly in the Developer Studio. The SAP component model helps to structure the software based on individual components, which define clear use relationships between each other and therefore form a prerequisite for modularization and reuse. In contrast to typical projects, the component-based projects are capable of consuming large amounts of metadata, which developers can use to determine interfaces for the external use of, dependencies on, or the visibility of development objects.

Integration of All Services in Software Lifecycle Management and Logistics

Comprehensive development projects and large-scale team development are dependent on optimum support from lifecycle management in distributed development landscapes. Seamless integration in the SAP

NetWeaver Development Infrastructure allows developers to store and manage all development objects created in a central Design Time Repository (DTR), to have them built in a central build process using the Central Build Service (CBS), to add them to the change management system, and then to distribute them using a defined software logistics process.

Integration of the SAP NetWeaver Application Server Java

Numerous integrated tools and utilities are provided to allow access to the SAP NetWeaver Application Server Java (AS Java) starting in the development phase. Beginning from the Developer Studio, developers have access to several basic functions to monitor and administrate the SAP application server and the corresponding server instances. In this way, developers can control both local and remote server processes without having to turn to additional tools outside of the development environment.

Server administration in the Developer Studio

SAP Security

With the provision of enterprise applications, developers are forced to also take into account security aspects. The SAP NetWeaver Composition Environment (CE) provides a range of different security and user management functions, which can be included in various types of projects and development components (Java EE, Web Dynpro, Web services, and CAF components). Even though the AS Java is delivered with a set of standard logon modules and the majority of authentication and SSO scenarios only need to be configured appropriately by the system administrator, application developers still have the option, for example, of designing a custom logon module to meet the specific requirements within a company.

SAP NetWeaver Scheduler for Java (Java Scheduler)

With the SAP NetWeaver Scheduler for Java, the AS Java contains a core service that allows the scheduling of jobs for automatic background processing, in conjunction with Java applications. Developers use the Java Scheduler API to link this type of background job with certain Java applications during the development process. In other words, they can

Core service

use this API to schedule jobs for background processing in their program. The implementation of the logic defined for background processing is done in the Developer Studio on the basis of EJB modules using message-driven beans.

SAP Logging API

Together with the services for integrating tools in the Developer Studio, special APIs, such as for archiving or logging and tracing are also integrated. For example, developers can use the SAP Logging API to connect any tool with minimal effort and in a standardized way to a tracing configuration.

In general, the SAP Logging API differentiates between two main types of messages:

▸ Conventional log messages with permanent recording and the status of a system or application

▸ Trace messages for detailed analysis of the source code by developers in the event of problems

Generic Services for Uniform Tool Integration

Service layer The SAP NetWeaver Developer Studio builds on the predefined Eclipse platform with a service layer intended specifically for tool integration. This service layer forms the actual basis for integrating tools in the Developer Studio. The reasons for this additional effort are as follows:

▸ First, a generic approach is required to create a link between the pure file- and directory-based view that prevails in Eclipse and the logical view of complex development projects in various types of projects.

▸ Second, we aim to make plug-in development more efficient throughout SAP and to standardize the tools. For example, all DC project types should be based on a specific metadata concept and, starting from a logical view, the same DTR operations (synchronizing, checking DTR activities in and out) should function in the same way in the different toolsets and types of projects. Moreover, the basic steps to create plug-in user interfaces were unified and simplified using a further abstraction layer in the UI programming model.

Services for tool integration generally contain two different layers, one for the model abstraction and a tool service layer.

▶ The model abstraction layer is a generic layer that is used as the basis for both the graphical connection and the presentation of design time objects at the logical level. Accordingly, this layer represents an abstraction of the physical file and directory nature of the objects and therefore also fulfills the requirement for a uniform navigation model.

▶ The tool service layer provides various services for consistent and uniform tool integration, which includes the SAP logging and tracing functions, for example.

2.3.4 Extensibility by Third-Party Providers

In spite of the variety of tools and frameworks delivered with the Developer Studio and despite immense activities on the part of the open source initiative regarding Eclipse projects, it is safe to assume that the trend toward extensive tool development by third-party providers will continue. The Developer Studio provides the option of extending the tool offering based on the delivered versions. Further development of the scope could be targeted at the specific requirements of SAP NetWeaver customers, which result in tailored solutions. Enhancements of this type could be made in numerous ways, for example, the addition of a graphic- and model-oriented tool offering, or in the area of specific adapter solutions, as well as enabling connection to any customer infrastructure, which could be the case for a predefined lifecycle management system, for example.

Extension of the offering

2.4 Integration Platform

The SAP NetWeaver Developer Studio provides full support when developing large-scale Java projects for standard technologies (J2SE, J2EE, Java EE, XML, Web services, etc.) and for SAP technologies (Web Dynpro, Java Dictionary, Composite Applications, etc.). The Developer Studio gives application developers a central point for developing presentation and business logic, including data retrieval and persistence.

2.4.1 Integrating the SAP NetWeaver Development Infrastructure

The special feature of the SAP NetWeaver Developer Studio is that — in addition to providing toolsets for different Java development requirements based on corresponding project types — it is integrated consistently into a robust SAP development infrastructure. The combination of both aspects makes the Developer Studio a highly productive and comprehensive development environment that spans the whole development cycle of Java projects, including integration of a source management system, plus configuration and transport management. This solution is particularly advantageous when you create extensive server-based business applications requiring large teams of developers.

Design Time Repository

The SAP NetWeaver Development Infrastructure (NWDI) includes a range of services, which can be seen in the context of the development process in Figure 2.7. The Design Time Repository (DTR) is a repository for saving and versioning Java source texts and other design time objects centrally. The DTR has mechanisms that efficiently coordinate comprehensive projects that can be distributed across geographical locations if there are multiple users. The DTR is integrated in the Developer Studio using the DTR client. The main developer activities, such as checking in and out, are already available in the Developer Studio for all project types. Furthermore, special tools are available to developers in the development configuration perspective or in the DTR perspective, depending on the focus of the task.

Component Build Service

An important part of the whole infrastructure is the central build on which the SAP component model is based. The CBS keeps the build results and the environment required for the build (for compiling required libraries, generators, and build scripts) ready in a central archive pool. Developers can download these archives from the Developer Studio to their local environment. For each configuration that is used, the CBS then keeps the appropriate versions of the archive ready.

Change Management System

Code lines are created, consolidated, validated, and deployed in central systems on the basis of a defined software logistics process. The Change Management System (CMS) manages the transportation of software changes within a Java development landscape. The CMS is represented in the Developer Studio by adequate transport tools. Developers use the *Transport View* to release the software changes for transport through the development and consolidation landscape.

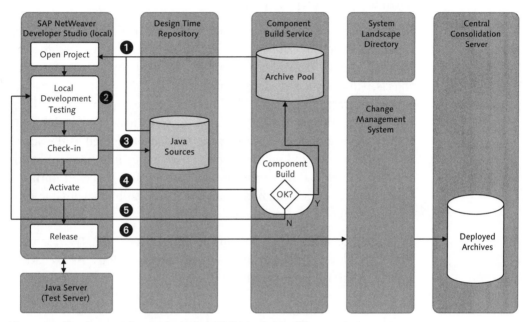

Figure 2.7 Development Process Including All Components of the SAP NetWeaver Development Infrastructure

Transporting software packages requires a description of the system landscape, for which the SAP System Landscape Directory (SLD) provides a solution. All descriptions of the system and transport landscape are saved centrally in the SLD. As a central check instance of names of development objects, the name service is also part of the SLD. To avoid naming conflicts, the name reservation service makes it possible to reserve unique names globally.

System Landscape Directory

In addition to the infrastructure services described previously, the SAP component model is a central component of the NWDI. This is based on the concept of the software and development components (SCs and DCs) and is used to structure the software on the basis of individual components that define clear use relationships between each other and therefore form a prerequisite for modularization and reuse. However, devel-

SAP component model

69

opers work with projects in the Developer Studio as before. In other words, a development component is identified with a project in the Developer Studio and is also used to group development objects as suited to a certain type of project.

Furthermore, the development component can consume quantities of metadata, which developers can use to determine interfaces for the external use of, dependencies on, or the visibility of development objects. This means that development components present an abstraction in contrast to the standard projects, as these appear in the Eclipse Workbench. Alongside their function as containers for development objects, development components can also be considered as the actual build units in a central build service. Unlike the Eclipse standard build, not only a compilation of the project resources is triggered during a development component build, but their compatibility with the SAP component model is also checked.

Depending on whether or not, and to what extent, the NWDI is used during the development process, we can derive various use scenarios, which are described in the following sections.

Developing in a Team Using the Full NWDI

Larger development projects necessitate distribution in a number of subprojects that have clearly defined dependencies on each other. The development tasks are then often distributed among several teams. Therefore, the development process must optimally support teamwork, for example, to synchronize resources that are used by many of the team members. The full scope of the NWDI, which includes all services both in the background and in the component model, is beneficial for this type of large-scale development.

Developing Locally Without the NWDI

On the other hand, the Developer Studio also supports a local development process, in which the SAP NetWeaver Development Infrastructure is not used at all. In this scenario, developers work on tasks of limited scope in their projects and usually only want to run the application on a

PC. In general, developers define no references outside the project either to make its functions available to other projects. Assuming that there is no central repository for the project resources, they are created solely on a local PC. Typical use cases for this type of local project include test and demo scenarios or sample applications. In this case, local projects are preferable during the familiarization or evaluation phase.

Developing Locally with the SAP Component Model

Another important variant in addition to those described previously is the one in which local development is combined with the SAP component model. In this case, the SAP component model is used only in the form of local development components to structure the software without making use of other NWDI services.

If we concentrate on the standard scenario, which assumes developers are using the full scope of the NWDI, the development process can be described as follows: The development environment has to be configured first so that it can use the SAP NetWeaver Development Infrastructure. Developers, therefore, must have the corresponding authorizations in order to log on as NWDI users. In addition to accessing the components of the infrastructure (DTR, CBS, or SLD server), developers also require a suitable view of the NWDI environment, which is why they have to import a predefined development configuration[3] from the SLD to the Developer Studio before. The development configuration then provides its local development environment with all the necessary information for addressing the infrastructure services. Even the components and libraries that are required for the development are identified in this configuration step. Each development configuration generally consists of a set of software components, which are in turn assigned to a set of development components.

---

3 A development configuration can best be compared with an R/3 development system in ABAP development. Here, too, developers have to log on to a system before they can create, edit, and change the status of their development objects within a defined package hierarchy.

Development Process When Using the Full NWDI

Aside from several preparation steps, the development process from the perspective of Developer Studio users is as outlined in Figure 2.7.

1. If the developer opens a corresponding project[4] in the Developer Studio, the required components and libraries, as well as the relevant Java source code, are available on the local PC.

Local build for test purposes
2. The developer can make the required changes to the project, perform a local build,[5] and then test these changes in the local environment. To access a test server, only the corresponding J2EE server from the LAN has to be entered in the Developer Studio settings.

3. When checking the objects back in, the developer saves the changed source code in the central repository, the DTR.

4. The Developer Studio enables the developer to activate the changed objects. The objects that were previously inactive now become active.

Central build
Activation always requires a successful central build process. The build request is passed to the CBS. The build service works in the background, checks all dependencies for the changed source texts and triggers the central build process.

The main benefit of this activation is that a build can take place promptly at the developer's request, resulting in less troubleshooting time compared with a *nightly build*. Only those components that the CBS could successfully build become active. In other words, the build service makes the relevant archive available to other developers in the team only if the build was successful. The team is therefore provided with error-free components and libraries. However, if an error occurred during the build operation, then a corresponding error message appears immediately. The developer can then either make the

---

4 Each development component is identified by exactly one project in the Developer Studio. DC-based projects are the prerequisite for developing the basis of the SAP component model.

5 Beginning with a project, the component build can be started locally to check the changes that were made at an early stage. Unlike the Eclipse standard build, the component build not only triggers the compilation of the project resources, but it checks their consistency with the component model as well. This build operation is the same as the one performed following central activation in the Component Build Service.

necessary changes to his or her local environment and test them straight away, or debug it first.

5. When all tests and the activation are successful, the changes can be released for transport. The developer can also control the transport release from the Developer Studio; only then is the CMS responsible for controlling the transport using a defined transport landscape.

Release for transport

The CBS processes the release request and then incorporates the changes in the assigned consolidation system's import queue. The changes from the queue are imported into the consolidation system at established intervals. When the import into the consolidation system is successful, the archives that are created by the build server are summarized as a new version and deployed on a J2EE server. Consequently, the new archive is forwarded to a central consolidation server.

When the test run has been successful as part of quality management measures, the QM team releases the new software version for productive use.

2.4.2 Integrating the SAP NetWeaver Application Server Java

For the development process to be supported efficiently, it must be easy to access a deployment and server environment. The current status of a project can be deployed on an application server in the LAN with minimal administrative effort and the application can be executed on this server for test purposes. Another important requirement is that debugging can be initiated from the development environment and controlled centrally in all steps. The Developer Studio provides an optimum infrastructure for doing this as well as the relevant tool support.

Transparency of the Cluster Architecture

The tight server integration makes the cluster architecture of the SAP NetWeaver Application Server Java transparent for the Developer Studio and allows it to appear as a single server unit with all available Java instances and the associated server processes. Figure 2.8 shows the main components of the SAP application server grouped as you will find them in the Developer Studio using various displayed modes.

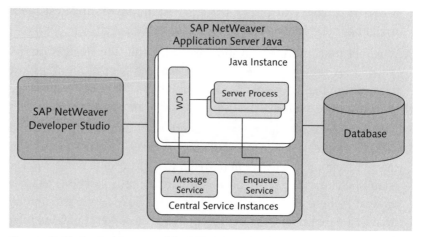

Figure 2.8 Cluster Architecture of the SAP NetWeaver Application Server Java

SAP Application
Server Java

An AS Java cluster consists of various types of instances, which can all be started and stopped separately, as well as monitored and controlled using suitable monitoring tools. We differentiate between the following instances:

▶ The actual Java instances

▶ The central service instances

▶ One or more database instances

Each Java instance in an AS Java cluster can be perceived as a unit, which is identified by an instance number and in turn consists of a component known as the Internet Communication Manager (ICM) and usually several server processes. The ICM is a kind of entry point for each Java instance and mainly has the task of receiving the inbound requests and distributing them to the available processes. The server processes are used to execute the actual Java applications and pick out precisely those requests that the ICM assigns to them. Furthermore, each installation of an AS Java contains central service instances. These form the basis for communication and synchronization within an AS cluster and comprise mainly the message service and the enqueue service. While the message service is responsible for the exchange of information and load balancing in the cluster and therefore provides the ICM with information about the availability of individual server processes, for example, the enqueue service has the task of managing lock objects and thus ensuring internal synchronization within a cluster.

Depending on the use scenario and the scope of the SAP NetWeaver Application Server Java components to be installed, we distinguish between the following configurations for server operation:

▶ A minimal setup for the server operation consists of only one Java instance, which always includes an ICM and at least one server process. This installation also includes two central service instances, the message service, the enqueue service, and a database.

Minimal AS Java installation

▶ In contrast, a typical cluster installation has more than one Java instance, the central service instances, and additionally one or more databases. In this case, various instances can be distributed among different machines in the network. On the other hand, the message service and the enqueue service are installed on a central host that serves all participating instances.

AS Java cluster installation

Server Operation Support in Run and Debug Mode

In the simplest scenario for the minimal AS Java installation, the application server is installed on the same local developer PC as the Developer Studio. This simple stand-alone version is generally based on a single-server configuration. In this case, the application server consists of only one instance (shown in Figure 2.9 as *00*), which in turn includes the ICM and the actual server process (shown in Figure 2.9 as *Server0*) as further processes. With the server process node, you can toggle between the run mode and the debug mode for the server process nodes. If debugging has been activated once, the server is stopped and the connection to the server is reserved completely for the debug session.

In general, developers access an application server from the Developer Studio, which is installed on any computer in the LAN. The Developer Studio and the server (including the database) can be distributed to different servers. Nevertheless, a single-server configuration should be the exception rather than the rule in developer teams; instead, you will usually find a cluster configuration in these circumstances.

LAN scenario

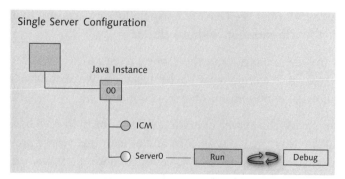

Figure 2.9 Nodes for the Single-Server Configuration

A typical AS Java cluster configuration groups together several Java instances (shown in Figure 2.10 as *00*, *03*, and *07*). Each of these instances consists of an ICM and one node or several nodes that represent the actual server processes (*Server0*, *Server1*, ..., *ServerN*). In such a cluster configuration, one or possibly even several server nodes can be reserved for debugging.

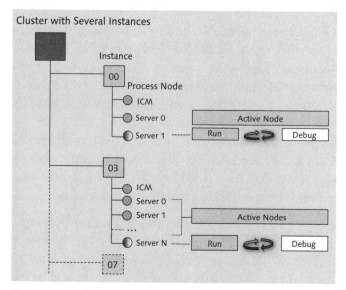

Figure 2.10 Nodes in a Cluster Configuration with More Than One Java Instance

When debugging has been activated, the reserved server is removed from the cluster configuration by the message service and it is then reserved solely for debugging. For that reason, incoming requests are no longer forwarded to the reserved nodes. A debug session can take place using the debug port of the reserved debug node without influencing the remaining server nodes in the cluster.

In a production system, most nodes are reserved for operating the application server and therefore have a *productive* status. Such productive server nodes cannot be used for debugging.

In the WAN scenario, the application server runs outside of the firewall. An important example of the use of this scenario is remote debugging in a customer system. SAP provides special services for accessing applications on the customer side using HTTP and debugging the corresponding projects. The server connection is made using the SAP router technology through firewalls.

WAN scenario

Tool Support

The appropriate server integration information and settings are entered in the Developer Studio on the **Preferences** page. As shown in Figure 2.11, this page displays two different settings depending on the installation option. Depending on whether the assigned AS Java is installed on the local developer PC or on any address in the LAN, you must select the options appropriate for the remote installation or the local installation.

Registering the AS Java using the Preferences page

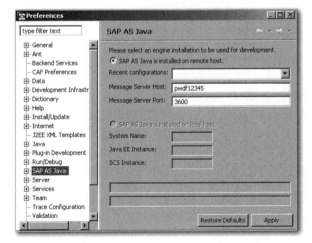

Figure 2.11 Information About the SAP Application Server on the Preferences Page

Simplified view
of AS Java

The **AS Java Cluster Overview** provides a simple tool for developers to not only display information about the status of the assigned server at any time, but also allows them to control individual process nodes. The view is divided into two windows (Figure 2.12):

▶ The left part of the window in this view contains a tree display of the individual instances and process nodes. Figure 2.12 displays a single-server configuration, to which the process nodes for the ICM and a server process belong. You can use the context menu for the individual tree nodes to perform operations such as starting or stopping a process, or switching to debug mode.

▶ The right part of the window displays the status information for the selected node; for example, whether it is a productive node, the current status of that node, or whether the user is in debug mode.

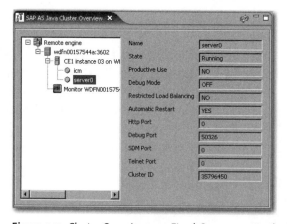

Figure 2.12 Cluster Overview as a Fixed Component in the Developer Studio

Extended view of
the AS Java in the
administration
perspective

The simple cluster display provides a rather limited view of the AS Java and allows developers to perform only certain standard activities on the individual server process nodes. A significantly extended view of the AS Java is available in the Developer Studio with the various application server tools and utilities in the SAP Management Console perspective.

Beginning from the Developer Studio, developers now have access to certain basic functions for monitoring and managing the SAP application server and the associated server instances. In this way, they can control local and remote server processes without reverting to additional tools outside of the development environment. In contrast to the standard tools for AS Java system administration, the scope is limited here to a set of basic functions and is tailored more to the requirements of application developers.

Figure 2.13 shows the representation of a server instance with the assigned nodes and some basic functions in the **SAP Management Console (Tree)** view.

Figure 2.13 Using the SAP Management Console to Administrate the AS Java in the Developer Studio

General Debugging Process

The integration of the AS Java in the Developer Studio results in the following steps for the general debugging process:

1. **Check the general requirements for debugging:**
   Only server process nodes that are not defined for productive use can be switched to debug mode. In a cluster configuration, the relevant node also must have the status **Restricted Load Balancing**. Only such server processes can be isolated from a cluster.

2. **Register the server connection:**
   To start the application on the server from within the IDE, you must enter the connection data for the AS Java on the Preferences page in the Developer Studio.

3. **Activate debugging:**
Note that in a cluster configuration, a debug mode remains integrated in the cluster until a debug session is activated for it. Accordingly, choosing **Activate Remote Debugging** means that the relevant debug node is isolated from the cluster. The message service then removes the node from the list of its destinations so that inbound requests can no longer reach the debug node. From the time of the activation, the debug node is no longer involved in the cluster communication and will have to be restarted after the debug session.

In a single-server configuration, the server is stopped when debugging is activated and it is reserved only for the debug session.

4. **Set the breakpoints:**
To better narrow down error situations, you require breakpoints at suitable points in the Java source code.

5. **Start debugging:**
Based on a debug configuration, you can start the debug session from within the Developer Studio.

General Deployment Process

The process for deploying archives is not the same for all types of projects using the means provided in the Developer Studio. There are different approaches depending on whether the project in question is an SAP-specific or a standard Java project.

Provided that the current instance of the AS Java is active, the following steps can be distinguished:

1. Register the server connection under Windows Preferences in the Developer Studio.
2. Update the project data within the Developer Studio.
3. Generate a transportable archive (EAR, WAR, JAR, RAR, or SDA).
4. Deploy the archive.

Developers can start the actual deployment of the archives in various places. For example, they can deploy SAP-specific components, such as Web Dynpro archives or Dictionary archives, directly from the project view. For standard applications based on Java EE 5 or J2EE 1.4, they generally use the **Servers View** to launch the Publish function. Furthermore, the Developer Studio contains a **Deploy View** that allows developers to deploy both SAP-specific components and Java EE and J2EE archives in the same way.

As shown in Figure 2.14, this tool contains a variety of options and allows developers, for example, to define in advance conditions for possible updates of the archives or behavior in error situations.

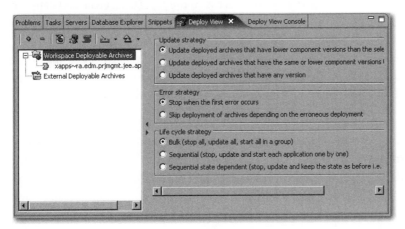

Figure 2.14 Options for Deploying Archives Using the Deploy View

2.5 Tools and Perspectives

The SAP NetWeaver Developer Studio provides a range of tools for various aspects and tasks in developing applications. Connected tools are summarized according to task-specific requirements in perspectives. The following section is an overview of the functions of the most common developer perspectives and toolsets.

2.5.1 Development Infrastructure Perspective

The development infrastructure perspective is used frequently as a starting point for working with the SAP NetWeaver Development Infrastructure and also for developing projects on an SAP component basis. This perspective can be used in both online and offline mode.

Starting point for working in the NWDI

Whenever developers open the perspective in online mode and want to use central services, their first step is to log on to the NWDI. To configure the Developer Studio for the NWDI connection, developers need a corresponding development configuration. Importing a development configuration automatically sets up the access paths for the services that are used in the development environment, such as the URI belonging to the DTR that is used, the CBS that is assigned, and the name service.

In online mode, users have full access to the NWDI services and can, for example, check out sources from the DTR, release DTR activities, or trigger a build process in the central CBS. In offline mode, no NWDI services are available, so this mode is better suited to accessing local resources. In particular, it is then possible to develop locally in conjunction with the SAP component model (local development components).

To launch the development infrastructure perspective in the Developer Studio, choose **Window · Open Perspective** and then select **Development Infrastructure**. The main components of the development infrastructure perspective include tools for browsing repository contents, wizards for creating software and development components, editors for comfortable entry of component properties, and lists of open DTR activities.

View of the repository
As a central tool, the component browser displays the components in a hierarchy at a logical level. Each development configuration defines a corresponding section of the contents to be displayed, thereby defining the repository view for the respective user. By default, a development configuration has several software components, and a set of development components is assigned to each of these. In addition, the corresponding tree structure can be modified flexibly using a filter and, for example, display only local development components, all development components that have already been activated, or all development components that are still inactive.

All DC metadata at a glance
All declarative component properties can be entered centrally using the **Component Properties** editor. Regardless of whether the information to be entered concerns dependencies on other components, external use by public parts, or other DC metadata, developers do this in identical

ways. This editor also provides users with current status information about their components and their parts.

When changes have been made to project resources, access to all underlying DTR operations makes a view that lists all of a user's current activities available. The DTR activities contain all changes to the project resources. The **Open Activities** view lists the user's open activities with each individual change.

List of the
DTR activities

The **Activation View** allows developers to activate changes, and therefore transfer the relevant DCs from an inactive to an active state.

Activation view

Figure 2.15 shows a section of the development infrastructure perspective. The **Component Browser** in the left part of the window lists the contents of the local repository. This predefined logical view of the repository content is provided by a development configuration called Local Development. In this section, the user sees only all available software components that are stored in the local file system. In the right part of the window, a property overview displays the **Component Properties** for the selected object in the editor. The **Infrastructure Console** displays important status information and allows access to the log of operations performed during the session.

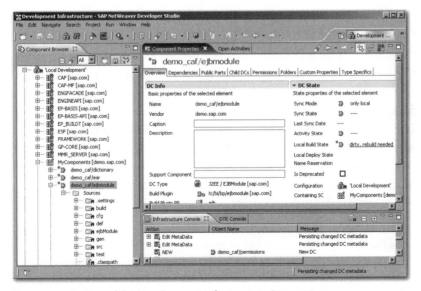

Figure 2.15 Section of the Development Infrastructure Perspective

The most important functions in the development infrastructure perspective can be summarized as follows:

- Import or create new development configurations
- Create new software components
- Browse component contents in the central repository and in the local file system if necessary
- Check out entire DC projects or individual project resources
- Create new DC-based projects for various types of projects (Web Dynpro DC project, Dictionary DC project, etc.)
- Declare component metadata
- Integrate all basic DTR operations, such as creating new activities, assigning changes to activities, displaying changes, checking into the repository, or undoing changes
- Integrate the build and deploy functions
- Activate development components
- Display the properties of any entities (development configuration, software component, development component, development object, activity)

2.5.2 Dictionary Perspective

Java Dictionary design time tools

Developing portable and high-performance database applications requires not only a powerful persistence framework but also tool support that allows platform-independent definition of database objects at design time. For this purpose, all tables in a central Java Dictionary[6] are defined for multiple platforms. The Developer Studio provides the necessary design time tools in the dictionary perspective. The dictionary perspective contains various tools for defining database objects such as tables, indexes, and database views independently of the platform, as well as defining global data types including simple types and structures.

---

6 With the Java Dictionary, the AS Java provides a framework for the platform-independent definition and the central storage and management of database objects and global data types. The objects in the Java Dictionary are used for multiple applications in the field of Java-based projects. The dictionary perspective provides the Java Dictionary's most important design time tools.

With the Dictionary Explorer, the perspective shows the logical structure of the dictionary projects. This view is used as the starting point for the relevant development activities, such as creating or processing dictionary data types, tables, and views. The procedure here is the same as it is for many other types of projects: To create a new development object starting with an initial project frame, developers select the required category from the context menu at the required node and start the corresponding creation wizard. In this way, global data type definitions (simple types and structures), as well as tables and indexes, can be create a database of objects based on XML metadata descriptions.

Dictionary Explorer

User-defined, global data types are specified in a designated editor. This helps developers define *simple types* and structured types, which in turn consist of several elements. When defining data types, you can record semantic information about a type. You can also link UI text information to a data type, and centrally store texts to be used as input help, field labels, column headers, or quick info. You can display these texts when you use the data type in the layout of Web Dynpro applications, for example. The value ranges of the new data types are derived from the predefined (built-in) types[7] that are automatically mapped to the standard JDBC data types.

Editor for global data types

The table editor from the dictionary perspective allows database-independent definition of tables. A table definition is mainly specified by table fields (table columns) and key fields. Furthermore, table indexes can be defined for selected fields and the technical settings can be used to buffer the table and determine the type of buffering. A table definition that is saved in the Java Dictionary in this way is created as a physical table definition in the database when the table is deployed, and is translated into a representation of the respective database.

Editor for tables and indexes

Developers can use previously defined tables to create database views in the dictionary perspective. A view represents a virtual table, the data records of which are taken from one or more database tables. The view

Editor for database views

---

7 The Java Dictionary provides a set of predefined data types (built-in types), which are either used directly or when creating user-defined data types. Examples of predefined types are: `string`, `short`, `time`, `timestamp`. Both the predefined and the derived simple types are portable data types that are converted to standard JDBC types without any additional effort and can therefore run on all DBMS platforms that are supported.

editor allows developers to specify how data records from the original tables flow into a new composition of the view. When doing this, the required view columns from the underlying tables can be assembled using graphical tools and join conditions and where clauses can be added. A direct edition of the SQL statements is also available as an option.

Figure 2.16 shows an example of a dictionary project with the project structure displayed in the **Dictionary Explorer** (top left). To the right of this, you can see the graphical **View Editor**, in which developers can specify a database view. A compressed XML description of the table that is currently selected is shown in the **Outline View**.

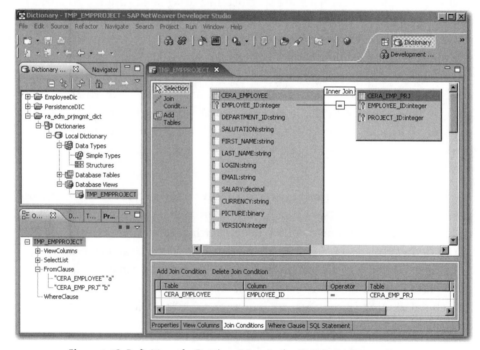

Figure 2.16 Definition of a Database View in the Dictionary Perspective

The dictionary perspective's scope includes the following tasks:

▸ Generate a project framework for dictionary projects, both for local projects and projects based on the SAP component model

▸ Create platform-independent database tables and table indexes as part of the Java Dictionary

▶ Create database views as part of the Java Dictionary

▶ Create user-defined, global data types (simple types and structures) as part of the Java Dictionary

▶ Automatically map predefined dictionary types and simple types to appropriate JDBC data types

▶ Generate transportable archives

▶ Deploy archives

▶ Rename tables and table fields

▶ Delete tables and views

2.5.3 J2EE Perspective

The J2EE perspective provides a range of tools and other utilities for standard-based development of components within the scope of the two programming standards Java EE 5 and J2EE 1.4. Moreover, developers have the necessary tools and APIs for deploying and testing applications in an integrated server environment.

Java EE and J2EE development based on WTP tools

Various types of projects are available in the Developer Studio for distributing application resources:

▶ EJB projects define a project scope for developing Enterprise Java-Beans. All EJB components (entity beans, session beans, message-driven beans, and Web services) can be created and implemented using wizards — as required by the underlying specification. If it is necessary to configure the EJBs, developers can pull in the associated deployment descriptors. All these project resources, including all of the configuration files, are combined into a Java archive (JAR). Depending on which program model the component development is based on, we distinguish between two types of projects. While the EJB project is intended for developing components based on J2EE 1.4 (and < 1.4), the EJB project 3.0 supports the new Java EE 5 programming model and therefore the specification for EJB 3.0.

▶ Web components for a standard application based on the programming models previously named are managed in a separate Web project. Two different flavors of Web projects are available: dynamic projects and static projects. Within a dynamic Web project, developers can create dynamic resources, such as servlets, JSP, JSF, and filters, and also static resources, such as graphics and HTML pages, and use embedded tools to edit these, whereas the static Web project can contain only static resources. All the resources in a project of this type are combined together with the associated deployment descriptors into a Web archive (WAR).

▶ An enterprise application project combines all J2EE or Java EE resources that are relevant for deployment into a kind of overall application. Basically, such a project contains a set of references to other J2EE and Java EE modules and also to other Java projects that are combined into an enterprise application archive (EAR), if necessary. The referenceable projects include Web modules, EJB modules, application client modules, connector modules, and Java projects that can contain any number of helper and utility classes.

Consequently, enterprise application projects are used to group together various components to create a deployable overall application, which contains references to the associated modules as well as the deployment descriptors for configuring the application. The resulting archive, the EAR, therefore represents a unit of a J2EE or Java EE applications that can be transported. Depending on the programming model that the referenced modules refer to, we distinguish between the Enterprise Application Project (based on J2EE) and the Enterprise Application Project 5 (based on Java EE 5).

▶ The connector projects are required when developing connector components based on the J2EE resource adapter architecture. In this context, a connector provides a standard mechanism for enhancing J2EE containers, which allow developers to implement the connection to and communication with a non-J2EE system and vice versa. Consequently, connector projects help to manage the connector module resources as well as the appropriate deployment descriptors.

▶ Application client projects contain application client resources. Application clients are standard J2EE or Java EE components and, like the other components (EJBs), they can make use of all the services of the application server. However, in contrast to the other standard components, an application client runs on a separate Java Virtual Machine (JVM).

The **Project Explorer** view displays all types of projects in the J2EE perspective in the form of a tree structure. It conveys a logical view for navigation in the respective project structure and also acts as a starting point for developer activities, such as creating or editing development objects as well as configuring the respective project components.

Starting with a given project structure, developers always create new development objects according to the same pattern: They choose the corresponding node within the project hierarchy and use the Create operation to launch the first page of a wizard. This processes the individual dialog steps that are required to specify the new object. The sequence of the individual steps is fixed in the wizard; in the final step, developers trigger the generation of corresponding resources. After completing the wizard, the resulting object is added to the project view. Wizards significantly accelerate the development process and ensure the integrity of the generated source code. These declarative steps result in a type of default version of the generated objects.

The **Servers View** allows developers to perform basic operations for managing servers from various manufacturers. For example, this easy-to-use tool lets developers select the projects they want to deploy and then lets them deploy the archive in question on the server. In addition to the Deploy operation, the servers view allows access to the operations for starting and stopping server instances, without having to leave the Developer Studio.

To open the J2EE perspective in the Developer Studio, choose **Window • Open Perspective** and then select **J2EE**. Figure 2.17 shows a section of the J2EE perspective with the **Project Explorer** (left), the **Java Editor** containing the source code of an entity (right), and the **Servers View** (bottom).

In accordance with the fact that the J2EE perspective supports the development process on the basis of the J2EE 1.4 and Java EE 5 specifications, the scope of the tool can be summarized as follows:

▶ Create J2EE and Java EE projects based on the tools of the WTP open source project

▶ Optional use of projects based on the SAP component model

Project explorer

Wizards, generators, and validation functions

Servers view

- ▶ Automatic validation of the generated source code in accordance with the rules of the respective specification
- ▶ Wizard support for creating and defining Enterprise JavaBeans (session beans, entity beans, and message-driven beans)
- ▶ Wizard support for creating and defining Web resources (HTML pages, JSPs, servlets, filters, and listeners)
- ▶ Wizard support for creating connector components
- ▶ Wizard support for creating and editing application client components
- ▶ Create and configure overall enterprise applications
- ▶ Export and import function for enterprise archives (JAR, WAR, and EAR)
- ▶ Deploy archives
- ▶ Access basic operations for server administration

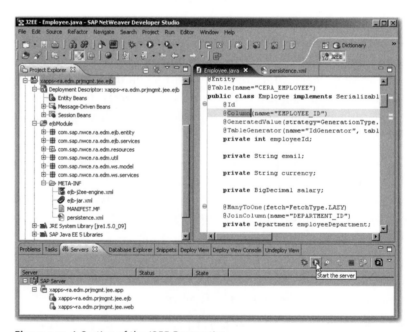

Figure 2.17 A Section of the J2EE Perspective

2.5.4　Perspective for Composite Applications

With the SAP NetWeaver Composition Environment, a new generation of business applications comes into play: known as composite applications, they comply with the principles of a service-oriented architecture (SOA) and feature a high level of reuse of existing business data and functions, which developers can integrate in new business processes by means of services. New functions that are to be developed based on this architecture are independent of any predefined system landscape and can be made available on a cross-application and intercompany basis.

Composite Application Framework

The Composite Application Framework (CAF) provides a suitable platform for standardized development of composite applications. This approach already includes the integration of components from all SAP NetWeaver solutions (Portal, Knowledge Management, etc.).

The development of new components within the CAF clearly makes a model-driven approach the priority and is based on a separate abstraction layer that works without low-level APIs to a large extent. The integration of the CAF design time in the Developer Studio provides developers with tools for modeling business objects and for implementing the business logic as part of composite applications. In contrast to the traditional development approach, developers model the required components on the basis of CAF metadata using tools within the CAF perspective. On the basis of this metadata, the framework handles the generation of Java source code based on low-level APIs. This allows generation of the persistence layer of the business objects, based on the Java Persistence API, and the service calls, based on the EJB 3.0 specification for session beans, without forcing developers to familiarize themselves with the underlying APIs.

The main components of the CAF include the following:

▸ **Business objects**
Business objects are the smallest uniquely identifiable logical units in a business process. Developers use the CAF Design Time to create business objects as semantic entities within a project, to store attributes and their data types there as well as to generate the associated database table definitions. All new business objects are already equipped with a set of predefined attributes and can be declaratively

extended. In the course of modeling business objects, persistence options, authorization behavior, and relationships between objects can be defined and the implementation of fundamental operations (read, write, update, delete, and query functions for searching for data records) can be generated.

▶ **Application services**
Application services are used to provide additional business logic required based on the business objects and other services contained in the project and by including external services. Starting with the existing objects and services, developers can model additional methods that can formulate very specific requests to the business logic. During the definition of such service methods, developers can easily assign input and output parameters, and specify access restrictions, transactional behavior, and exception handling.

▶ **External services**
External services are required for communication with external back-end systems and applications. The integration of external services is a means to reuse the existing functions in these systems and applications in CAF projects independent of the respective technology and platform. Within CAF projects, this integration is done with two different import functions, one for remote function calls (RFCs) and the other for Web services.

Composite
Application
Explorer

To open the CAF perspective in the Developer Studio, choose **Window •
Open Perspective** and then select **Composite Application**. Figure 2.18 shows a section of the CAF perspective with the **Composite Application Explorer** (left) and the editor for modeling the application services (right).

Some of the functions of the CAF tools include:

▶ **Provide a project scope for developing new composite applications**

   ▶ Create a project scope with a connection to the SAP component model

▸ Provide access to CAF basis components with a set of predefined object, data types, and services

▸ Integrate isolated toolsets, including the Java Dictionary for table definitions and the EJB modules for entities and session beans

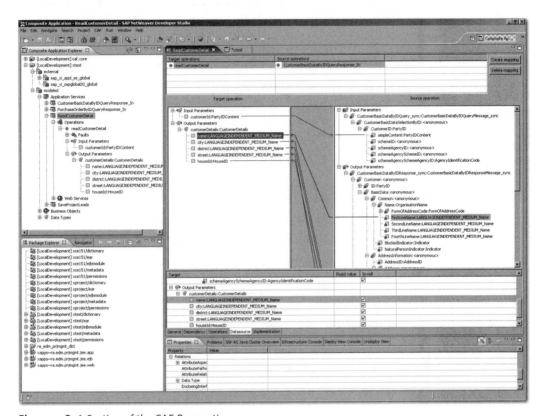

Figure 2.18 A Section of the CAF Perspective

▸ **Model business objects and generate the persistence layer**

▸ Create a data structure for new business objects with a set of predefined attributes and basic operations (lifecycle methods)

▸ Create additional attributes for business objects

▸ Create and edit additional data types required based on the Java Dictionary

- Define specific operations (methods) for business objects
- Specify associations between business objects
- Define the persistence options[8] (local and remote persistence)
- Define the access restrictions (authorization) at the level of individual operations
- Generate a Web service starting with the business object

▶ **Provide the business logic in the form of application services**

- Create new application services
- Define service dependencies on other services or business objects
- Model service operations with inclusion of transactional behavior
- Define the access restrictions (authorization) at the level of individual operations
- Embed filter operations for query methods
- Create a Web service starting with the application service

▶ **Embed external services (Web services, BAPIs, RFCs)**

- Import RFC module metadata for access to ABAP-based functions in SAP systems
- Import Web service definitions either from a service registry or using a URL that points to the respective WSDL file

▶ **Availability of general functions**

- Validate all components in the project
- Deploy new business objects and services
- Integrate the project in a test environment

---

8 Regarding the persistence, two options are available for the generation of CAF business objects: Local and remote persistence. With local persistence, the CAF generates a data model in the system database of the AS Java on the basis of the Java Persistence API (JPA) as well as session beans in accordance with EJB 3.0 and is therefore compatible with the new Java EE 5 programming standard. In contrast, the option for remote persistence is used to specify that the data is persisted in an external backend system. The communication with remote systems takes place either using remote function calls (RFCs) or using Web services. Unlike local persistence, the use of remote persistence necessitates the mapping of methods and attributes of CAF business objects to the corresponding external service methods and parameters.

2.5.5 Web Dynpro Perspective

Web Dynpro has initiated a new generation for creating professional user interfaces for browser-based business applications as part of SAP NetWeaver. The Web Dynpro technology provides not only the necessary runtime services and the metadata model, but also a range of design time tools.

From modeling to deployment

The tools that are relevant to Java developers are included as part of the Developer Studio in the Web Dynpro perspective. They support developers during the entire development cycle of Web Dynpro applications, starting with generating project components and implementing controllers to deploying and testing the finished application. Most of a Web Dynpro application is usually generated declaratively. The objects in a Web Dynpro application are usually created using wizards or graphical tools, thereby keeping the work based on manual programming to a minimum.

The most common tools in the Web Dynpro perspective are described below:

Tools

▶ **Web Dynpro Explorer**
The Web Dynpro Explorer is a central component of the Web Dynpro perspective. It provides a logical view of local- and DC-based Web Dynpro projects within the SAP component model. Developers can use the project structure shown in the Web Dynpro Explorer to access all Web Dynpro entities and source texts. Furthermore, each Web Dynpro project provides a local Java Dictionary that can be used to create user-defined dictionary types.

▶ **Component Modeler**
The Component Modeler is suitable as a central entry point for creating and modeling the main components of Web Dynpro projects. For example, developers can create new Web Dynpro components as well as model and application objects to define their relationships to each other.

▶ **Data Modeler**
The Data Modeler allows the modeling of all entities within a Web Dynpro component. In particular, it gives developers the means to use graphical tools to create and arrange the visual components (win-

dows and views) as well as to map the flow of data through a component.

▶ **Navigation Modeler**
The Navigation Modeler is another graphical tool that can be used to create individual modules of user interfaces, the views, determine their arrangement within the view set, and model the application's navigation structure.

▶ **View Designer**
To design the layout of the individual views, the developer starts the View Designer, which provides several predefined view elements (controls). View elements can then easily be added to the layout panel using drag & drop.

▶ **Context Editor**
Developers can use the Context Editor to specify the context assignment to a view controller, and map the view data fields to the model data, to dictionary types, or even to the context of a different view controller.

▶ **Model Tools**
Web Dynpro tools also ensure that the backend logic is integrated seamlessly. According to the model view controller paradigm (MVC), persistent data is provided in Web Dynpro by a model layer of the entire application.

There are appropriate model types for the various backend scenarios. For example, this is how the business functions that are encapsulated with BAPIs are accessed using the adaptive RFC model. A model is provided declaratively within the Web Dynpro project. Powerful wizards and generation tools are available to assist developers.

▶ **Local Dictionary**
User-defined data types and UI service information (text and value services) can be created using a local Java Dictionary.

Figure 2.19 shows a section of the Web Dynpro perspective with the **Web Dynpro Explorer** (left) and the **View Designer** (right).

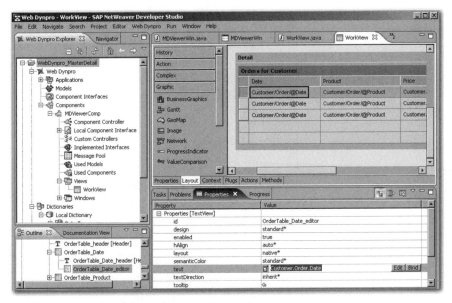

Figure 2.19 A Section of the Web Dynpro Perspective

Some of the functions include:

▸ Generate a Web Dynpro project framework with and without a connection to the SAP component model

▸ Create Web Dynpro components as reusable and structuring units in the application

▸ Model subcomponents in the Web Dynpro application with graphical tool support

  ▸ Define relationships and dependencies between components of a Web Dynpro project

  ▸ Create views

  ▸ Define the view sequence using navigation links

▸ Design the view layout with the graphical view designer

▸ Define view contexts to store local view controller data and its references (to model data, to dictionary types, or to other view contexts)

▸ Integrate a project-related Java Dictionary in which user-defined data types (simple types and structures) as well as UI information can be entered and managed

▶ Import model descriptions for various backend systems to achieve backend connection

  ▶ Using the adaptive RFC model for ABAP systems

  ▶ Using the adaptive Web service model for Web services

  ▶ Using the bean model for EJBs

2.5.6 Administration Perspective

SAP system administration using the tools in the Developer Studio

The administration perspective provides a set of basic functions, to monitor and control the SAP NetWeaver Application Server Java from within the Developer Studio. In this way, developers can manage local and remote SAP systems without having to turn to additional tools outside the development environment. The system administration is reduced to a set of common basic functions and tailored to the requirements of application developers. This is of particular benefit when developers also perform the tasks of the system administrator. However, the prerequisite for doing this is that developers have the necessary administration permissions. This is often the case when teams of developers have to set up and monitor their own SAP systems to test their applications.

To open the administration perspective in the Developer Studio, choose **Window • Open Perspective** and then select **SAP Management Console**. By default, the navigation tree then displays all instances that are installed on the host that you are currently connected to. Figure 2.20 illustrates the simple arrangement of the tools within the administration perspective: The left window displays the available information in the form of a tree hierarchy and is used above all for navigation purposes. The nodes for Java instances, their processes, and alerts can be expanded to display an extended set of entries. If developers choose a tree node from the **SAP Management Console (Tree)** view, they can see the available details in the results view of the **SAP Management Console (Results)** — these are usually displayed as a table. System icons and nodes for instances and processes are highlighted in different colors and therefore also contain status information. Tracing and log files can be made accessible for the context in question and are displayed in an additional output view.

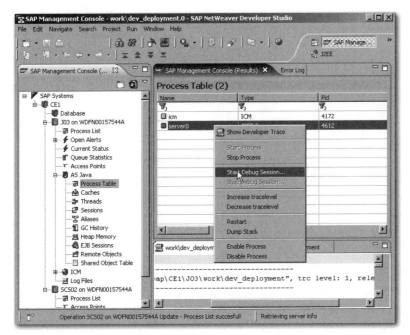

Figure 2.20 A Section of the Administration Perspective with the Navigation and Results View

The list below contains a summary of the features of the administration perspective for the AS Java:

▶ Start, stop, and restart the SAP application server and the associated server instances

▶ Toggle the server processes between the debug mode and the run mode

▶ Start applications that have already been deployed

▶ Display and, if necessary, change the preconfigured communication ports (access points) for the internal and external communication of the SAP application server

▶ Provide access to important information on system operations using logging and tracing functions

▶ Display the start profiles, instance parameters, and other system environment parameters

▶ Monitor system alerts

- Display details and statistics regarding server threads, sessions, memory consumption, and EJB sessions

- Provide access to external administration tools (such as Telnet) to use extended functions for administrating and configuring the SAP application server

2.5.7 DTR Perspective

Tools for the
DTR experts

With the DTR perspective, the Developer Studio provides expert tools that are used in special cases such as solving version conflicts or during repository administration. The DTR perspective is available only in online mode; consequently, the user must be logged on to the DTR server at all times. Unlike the development configuration perspective, the Repository Browser offers a pure file- and directory-based view of the DTR contents. The logical view, with a predefined structure for the DCs and their development objects as provided in the development configuration perspective, is missing here. For that reason, the Repository Browser is used only by those users who are most familiar with the repository's directory structure.

In summary, we should add that this perspective is reserved for DTR specialists who can perform more complex operations on the DTR server to solve special conflicting cases or to carry out certain DTR administration tasks.

The DTR perspective groups several views:

- The **Repository Browser** provides a file- and directory-based view of DTR contents.

- **Open Activities** displays a list of all activities that are still open.

- **Closed Activities** displays a list of all activities that are already closed.

- **Version Graph** displays the version graphs for the required resource.

- **Integration Conflicts** displays the version conflicts that occurred during integration.

- **Command Output** is used to output commands for the operations that were performed by users. The errors and failures that occurred during DTR operations are output here in particular.

Figure 2.21 shows a section of the DTR perspective with the Repository Browser (top left in the window) and two views for the DTR activities and the command output (at the bottom of the screen).

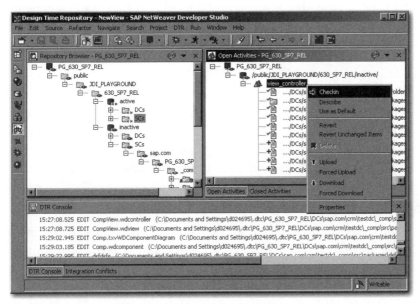

Figure 2.21 A Section of the DTR Perspective

The range of functions in the DTR perspective includes all underlying DTR operations (such as adding changes to activities, creating new activities, viewing changes, checking into the repository, etc.) and extended operations for solving version conflicts. Lastly, this perspective also enables you to access different administration tasks, such as managing files within DTR workspaces or configuring the DTR server.

2.6 Installation and Update — Outlook

As a result of the fundamental significance of this subject for developers' daily work, we will take a look into the future here and outline the procedure of installing and updating the SAP NetWeaver Developer Studio as it is planned for the upcoming deliveries of the SAP NetWeaver Composition Environment.

2.6.1   Installation and Update Framework

The SAP NetWeaver Developer Studio uses the standardized Eclipse framework to ensure the installation of the developer tools and their continual update. Therefore, we will briefly go into the components involved and by doing this explain the underlying concepts and the functioning of the installation and update framework.

Products and Features

Features as installable units
Autonomously executable applications that are based on the Eclipse platform are managed as products, in accordance with the Eclipse notation. A product is comprised of one or more features, which in turn each bundle a set of plug-ins to units that can be installed together. In other words: Eclipse features represent a means to technically classify an Eclipse product as a unit and to describe its functions.

Features are used to group together plug-ins that provide the actual functions of a product. However, features do not contain executable code, but only a metadata description. In essence, this metadata delivers a compilation of plug-ins, which together define the functions in a specific feature. Furthermore, it contains information about how to install or update this metadata for a newer version. As a result, a feature defines the smallest unit of downloadable and installable functions in an Eclipse product. The modular structure of Eclipse products therefore allows subsequent installation of additional features and plug-ins or update of the existing product features and plug-ins.

Update manager
Generally, this can happen using a conventional installation, completely independent of Eclipse, or using the update manager, which is part of the Eclipse platform. The update manager is a basic component of the standardized installation and update framework of the Eclipse platform. The tasks of the update manager include locating, downloading, and installing the features and plug-ins to be updated, starting from an update site specifically configured for this purpose by the administrator within the system landscape.

Update site and update policy
However, the prerequisite for referencing this local update site is a redirection mechanism. An update site URL in the form of a symbolic name is assigned to each feature when it is created. The update manager uses

this URL when a feature update is requested and is redirected to the local update site by means of an update policy. The update policy is stored in the form of an XML file and contains the entry for the update site URL that is configured locally. In turn, the policy is referenced using an entry on the corresponding Preferences page in the Developer Studio.

The basic framework schema can be identified easily in Figure 2.22:

❶ The first step in the installation process sets up the NWDS platform, a basic feature of the IDE, on the developer's local PC using a specific installer for this purpose. As a result of this installation, the update manager is then available as part of the NWDS platform.

❷ As soon as the NWDS platform has been installed on the local PC, the Developer Studio starts automatically and launches the update manager; subsequently, the other features can be requested for local download.

❸ The installation of the selected features comes from the configured update site, which retains a list of all installable features. This list bundles the features in question into installable units that are called main features later in this chapter. All features of this type are based on the NWDS platform. Moreover, the dependency of features on each other is taken into account during the installation process so that all dependent features are automatically installed as well.

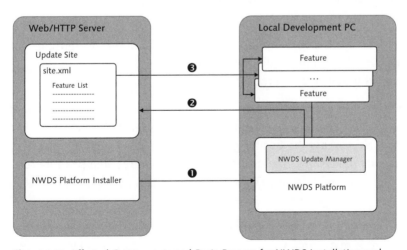

Figure 2.22 Affected Components and Basic Process for NWDS Installation and Update

The SAP NetWeaver Developer Studio uses precisely this standardized Eclipse framework to ensure the installation of tools and their continual update. The update site for the Developer Studio can be in various locations: On the one hand, it can be a local copy of the installation DVD (offline installation) or a global SAP update site that can reached through SAP Service Marketplace (*http://service.sap.com*) or through SAP Developer Network (*http://sdn.sap.com*, online installation). Another option available is the NWDS update site, which can also be installed locally as part of a reference J2EE system within the customer landscape.

The basic update procedure can be described as follows: Each installed feature and each plug-in contained in a feature is stored, usually as a JAR file, below the IDE installation directory in a subdirectory with a name that contains a version ID. With each new update, the system automatically creates a new subdirectory containing the associated JAR file. As a consequence, different versions of a feature or plug-in lie in separate directories. This ensures that there can be more than one version of one and the same feature or plug-in on the local hard disk.

This means that each feature update also entails the local storage of additional files because the files to be updated are neither deleted nor overwritten. As soon as all associated files are available in a new version in the installation directory on the hard disk, a new feature configuration is compiled. The crucial, new features and plug-ins are activated and the previous versions are deactivated.

Feature configurations
As a result, the IDE supports several configurations at the same time, although only one configuration can be active. Configurations can be explicitly saved to revert to if the need should arise.

Very comprehensive products, such as the SAP NetWeaver Developer Studio, organize the features to be installed in tree hierarchies. The root node represents the overall product and includes smaller units, which include the NWDS platform, certain main features, and possibly certain other optional features. The last features in this list are often called add-ons.

Version labeling for features
In the SAP NetWeaver Composition Environment, the Developer Studio could display a tree structure such as the one shown in Figure 2.23. As you can see in this figure, the product is characterized by a set of fea-

tures: The associated version label (CE 7.1) follows the name (in the figure: SAP NetWeaver Developer Studio), the version ID is followed by the version number of the service package (SP03), and finally the number of the patch level (PAT0000). The installable main features are identified by their names and the feature version.

Figure 2.23 Possible Selection During Feature Installation of the Developer Studio for the Composition Environment

NWDS Platform

The NWDS platform is a basic unit of the Developer Studio, which is the very first feature installed. The NWDS platform is not installed using the update manager, but using a special platform installer.

When the NWDS platform has been installed on the local PC, developers can start the Developer Studio to download the other features using the update manager.

Platform installer

The NWDS platform contains the Eclipse platform, which also includes the Eclipse update manager, and an NWDS branding plug-in with all remaining components that are responsible for the update process. The platform installer also configures the update policy (*policy.xml*) and therefore defines the URL for the location of the update site.

Main Features

Each main feature is a clearly defined set of plug-ins that are always installed and updated together. However, they form not only a technical unit, but also a semantic one, which is usually orientated to a standalone use case. For example, the following main features are potential candidates:

Main features as installable units

▶ **Java EE**

This selection provides all standard tools for both Java-based development without an application server and server-side development on the basis of the Java EE development scenario, including all client-side tools for server administration.

▶ **Development Infrastructure Client**

All perspectives and tools that enable integration of the SAP development infrastructure in the Developer Studio are combined in a separate feature. The NWDI client is also required for development on the basis of the SAP component model.

▶ **Web Dynpro User Interfaces**

All tools necessary for Web Dynpro development can also be installed separately.

▶ **Composition Tools**

The design time tools to support the SAP composition scenario in the Developer Studio group the majority of the tools into one installable main feature.

2.6.2 Installing and Updating Features

By default, developers can choose **Help · Software Updates · Find and Install...** in the Developer Studio to launch the installation and update procedure. The wizard that is launched provides a choice of two options as shown in Figure 2.24:

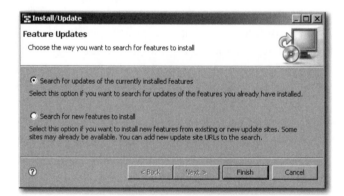

Figure 2.24 Wizard Integrated in the Developer Studio for Updating and Installing Features Using the Update Manager

▶ The **Search for updates of the currently installed features** option allows developers to update features that are already installed.

▶ The **Search for new features to install** option searches through all update sites listed for new features, puts together a list of new features in the update manager, and allows developers to install them.

2.6.3 Deinstalling Inactive Feature Versions and Plug-In Versions

Although using the update manager to update features has significant benefits for users, updating features and plug-ins several times can lead to an undesired effect. As previously mentioned, each feature update results in the creation of a new subdirectory to store the associated files on the local developer PC. This happens for each new version of a feature or plug-in. The update manager does not delete or overwrite the files to be updated. Therefore, an increased amount of memory space is required. Moreover, each updated version reduces the necessity of retaining older versions.

For exactly this reason, the Developer Studio introduced an option that allows developers to uninstall all features that have been deactivated and the associated plug-in versions. As a result of such a cleanup procedure, only the version that is currently activated is retained. However, all features and plug-ins that were not installed using the update manager are excluded from this process.

Deleting older feature versions

As Figure 2.25 shows, this deinstallation procedure is launched by default in the Developer Studio by choosing **Help · Software Updates · Uninstall disabled Features**.

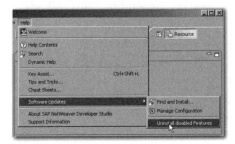

Figure 2.25 Deinstallation of All Inactive Features in the Developer Studio

2.6.4 Installation Scenarios

By default, the SAP NetWeaver Developer Studio is not delivered on its own, but as part of a larger product and, therefore, together with the associated runtime components, the JEE system.[9] In the context of the installation of the SAP NetWeaver Composition Environment, we can assume there are various scenarios, with the main difference between each one being the scope of the components to be installed. The other installation attributes result from the location of the installer and the update site:

Online and offline installation

While, in the case of an online installation, you have to connect to a global SAP update site through SAP Service Marketplace (SMP) or SAP Developer Network (SDN); in the case of an offline installation, a local copy of the installer and the update site is available in the form of an installation DVD.

Another special feature of the Developer Studio is the combination of installations and updates. This is a clear move away from the practice of a monolithic installation, which installs the entire product in a single step, and an update involving a deinstallation and a complete new installation. An installation now starts with an initial installation and, as such, sets the scope for the subsequent update process, which also includes the installation of new features that have become available.

Depending on the scope of the components to be installed, we distinguish between various installation scenarios.

Local PC Installation

Installation of the Developer Studio with runtime components

This scenario incorporates a shared installation of a J2EE system and the Developer Studio on a single developer PC. Depending on whether the installation is done from a DVD or downloaded from the Internet, other variants of this installation are also possible. Accordingly, the respective update site is available either locally on the DVD or globally on SDN or through SAP Service Marketplace.

---

9 In this context, the JEE system can be understood as an overall system that is comprised of several components that are installed together. These components include the SAP VM, the database, the SAP NetWeaver Application Server Java, and the corresponding administration tools.

This simple installation scenario has a limited focus and targets an individual developer workplace. On the basis of the Composition Environment, developers use the Developer Studio tools to create applications, and then deploy and test them on the local application server. An installation of this type could be used primarily to evaluate the Composition Environment and for developments on a small scale.

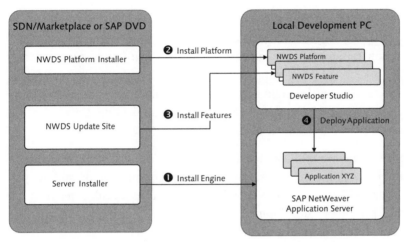

Figure 2.26 Overview of a Local PC Installation of the Composition Environment

The most important components and the main installation steps are shown in Figure 2.26:

❶ Depending on whether the installation in question is online or offline, the CE engine installer is launched from the SDN download page or a DVD. Developers can choose different options for the server installation. The server installer installs the entire JEE system, including the SAP NetWeaver Application Server, on the local developer PC.

❷ During the next step, the developer starts the NWDS platform installer, which configures and installs the NWDS platform. This step provides the Developer Studio locally on the developer PC in a basic configuration.

❸ The Developer Studio now starts automatically and requests the installation of other features. The update manager installs these features by referring to the configured NWDS update site. Depending on whether it is an online or offline installation, all installable features are available either on the SDN or SAP Service Marketplace update site, or on a DVD.

❹ With this step, the initial installation is complete and developers can now start developing their own applications in the Developer Studio and run them on the local AS Java installation.

Multi-User Installation

For real development projects on the basis of the SAP NetWeaver Composition Environment, a suitably dimensioned infrastructure is necessary, which optimally supports distribution among a number of subprojects. The development tasks can then be distributed between several teams, which each requires its own set of features in the Developer Studio and possibly the associated test systems.

For this kind of multi-user installation of the Composition Environment, a reference JEE system is set up in the development landscape. As you can see in Figure 2.27, this type of system acts as a bridge between the actual productive development infrastructure on one side and the pure installation components on the other side.

Continual update process

Therefore, this type of architecture is suitable for supporting a continual update process, regarding both the design time components and the runtime components, as well as the synchronization of both design time and runtime. As a result, the reference JEE system is comprised of both an NWDS update site for installing and continuously updating features for various configurations of the Developer Studio and the live update function, which supports continual updates of the JEE systems in the development landscape.

The installation procedure and the interaction of the most important components involved can be summarized as shown in Figure 2.27:

❶ In a development landscape, the administrator sets up a reference JEE system. This system is installed from the CE installer, which is obtained from either SAP Service Marketplace or a DVD.

❷ The CE installer loads the entire content of the NWDS update site from SAP Service Marketplace or the DVD to the local update site in the reference JEE system.

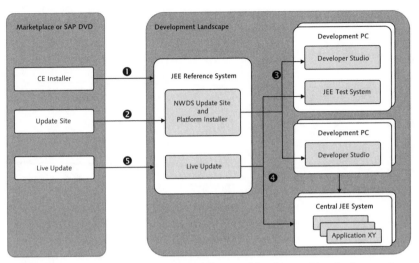

Figure 2.27 Overview of a Multi-User Installation of the Composition Environment

❸ Individual developers trigger the installation of their own development environment. As usual, they first configure and install the NWDS platform on the developer PC. Subsequently, they use the local update manager to select and install the individual features. The features can be selected specifically for the individual developer workplace.

❹ Starting from the JEE system installer in the reference system, the individual JEE systems can be distributed within the development landscape so that they are available as either local test systems or central production systems.

❺ In addition, the JEE systems and the NWDS versions can be continuously updated using a live update process. However, a mirror process does not take place automatically, but must be specifically triggered by the administrator. When new updates are available, the administrator has the option of updating the reference JEE system.

As a result of a mirror process of this type, a new version of the JEE system and the NWDS update site is available in the development landscape. Consequently, developers can update their NWDS themselves. The individual distributed JEE systems are updated either by the administrator or by individual developers.

Using a concrete example, this chapter will introduce you to the practical side of working with the SAP NetWeaver Developer Studio. On this guided tour, you will set up — step-by-step — a simple employee application using the Java EE 5 standard. The ultimate aim is to then deploy and execute the application on the SAP NetWeaver Application Server. You will have the opportunity of getting to know the close interaction between different tools of the development environment.

3 SAP NetWeaver Developer Studio — Step-by-Step to a Sample Application

You will get optimum use out of this chapter if you are very familiar with the Java programming language and, in addition, already have experience with using the Java EE 5 programming model. To be able to reconstruct the steps in a practical way, you need the SAP NetWeaver Developer Studio and access to the SAP NetWeaver Application Server Java. The SAP NetWeaver Composition Environment 7.1, on the DVD of this book, is suitable for this purpose. It is best if you install this version before you start with the hands-on exercises.

Prerequisites

The tutorial application, which you will develop step-by-step, is focused more on didactic aspects than on any endeavor to implement a realistic application scenario. Therefore, you need neither a bank application nor a complex warehouse scenario. Rather, it is our intention to introduce to you, with the help of a straightforward example, the options that the Developer Studio provides as a development environment for enterprise applications on the basis of established Java standards. In the foreground, therefore, you have the interaction between different toolsets, and the linking up of services that efficiently support the development process and the daily work of the developer.

Goals

You can view this chapter as an introduction to working with the Developer Studio. After processing all the steps of this chapter, you will be able to organize the basic processes and development steps (UI and EJB development, layout of the data model, etc.) within the framework of the Java EE standard development using suitable tools. You will also be able to map the tasks to the appropriate project types and corresponding development objects.

Local development process
All the steps are described solely from the viewpoint of a local development process. The project resources are created and managed exclusively on the local hard drive. The SAP component model is not used in the tutorial application. The projects concerned are not development components, unlike the scenario based on the use of the SAP NetWeaver Development Infrastructure. However, in Chapter 9, *Developing Composite Applications*, you will learn how to migrate this tutorial application in the NWDI context onto the SAP component model and also migrate it using the corresponding services.

3.1 Employee Tutorial Application

The tutorial application uses a simplified employee data model and should enable the user to create new employee data records and to print data on existing employees. In the application architecture, we make a distinction between clearly defined layers — for example, the presentation layer, the business logic layer, the data retrieval layer, and the persistence layer. Actually, this would not be as absolutely necessary for such a simple case as the one here. Nonetheless, you should familiarize yourself from the beginning with the typical architecture of business applications. In particular, you will get a first impression of how this architecture is mirrored in the development process and how the developer is supported with the organization of his projects through the Developer Studio.

Architecture of the Tutorial Application

While developing the user interface, you access the UI technology called JavaServer Pages (JSP), which has established itself within the standard

Web applications. With the help of a simple example, you will see how you can set up a simple interface and also access the server components underneath it.

The business logic is based on Enterprise JavaBeans 3.0 and is limited to one single, stateless session bean. With the session bean, we can formally distinguish between the business interface and session bean implementation. All the business methods of the session bean are linked to a corresponding business interface so that JavaServer Pages can access the session bean with the help of this interface. In addition, the session bean encapsulates the respective accesses to the persistence layer API.

You model the business data using a single entity that is used both in the business logic and the presentation layer. Because entities are regular Java objects, they can also be used for the data transport to the presentation layer. Corresponding data transfer objects are thus not required. In this connection, the entity is detached from the current transaction context. This is clearly shown in Figure 3.1 by the dotted border.

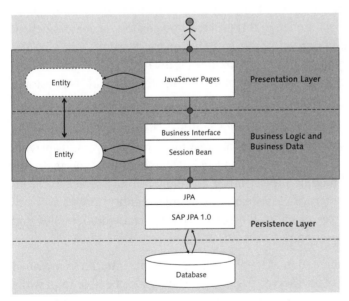

Figure 3.1 Typical Architecture of a Java EE 5 Business Application

Business applications generally cannot do without keeping data persistent in a database. With Java EE 5, a new object-relational persistent framework — the Java Persistence API (JPA) — has been introduced as part of the Java EE standard. This type of framework has, essentially, the following tasks: ensuring mapping of Java objects onto the relational database; translating various queries as well as changes to Java objects into suitable SQL statements; and, finally, taking care of the entire communication with the database.

As shown in Figure 3.1, the current SAP NetWeaver Application Server contains the actual JPA implementation with the name SAP JPA 1.0. The JPA, however, does not supply the required database tables or table definitions onto which the respective entities are mapped. Instead, it assumes that these tables already exist. You will provide the required tables with the help of the Java Dictionary. Using Open JDBC, you can create the actual database objects in the assigned database schema using the table definitions.

Project View of Tutorial Application

You will begin the development of the tutorial application by first creating the basic data model. In this process, you create a database-independent table definition using the Java Dictionary. Starting from a Dictionary project, you create an SDA archive (Software Delivery Archive) and deploy it on the application server. After this step, the table is physically available on the database.

For access to data records, use JPA entities. The implementation of the business logic for the application (creating new employees, displaying employee data) is taken over by an EJB 3.0 Stateless Session Bean. In this case, the EJB module project in the Developer Studio serves as a container for all enterprise JavaBeans, including the entity, as well as for all further resources, such as the corresponding configuration files and deployment descriptors.

For the implementation of the Web client, a simple interface is provided with the help of JavaServer pages. This should also be able to pass the data to the session bean. All Web resources are managed in a separate project — the Web module project — together with the appropriate configuration files.

In an enterprise application project, you then bring all the resources together to a type of Java EE 5 overall application. You need to deploy the resulting archive (EAR) first before you can call the employee application for the first time. Figure 3.2 groups the basic activities together and depicts the organization of the most important development projects in the respective project types of the Developer Studio.

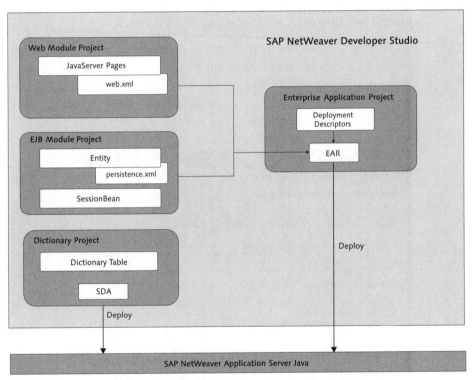

Figure 3.2 Organization of the Development Objects of the Employee Application in the Developer Studio

3.2 First Steps

To start the Developer Studio, the activated platform runtime requires, in addition to access to a Java Virtual Machine (VM), a path specification for storing all the metadata for project information and user-specific settings. A standard Java VM is normally assigned during installation of the Developer Studios and entered as the start parameter.

Start parameters

When you start[1] the Developer Studio for the first time after installation has been completed, you must generally specify the default workspace. The start process will then be interrupted and the system displays a dialog box for selecting the workspace directory. You will then either accept the default value or choose a different directory for the default workspace in order to continue the startup process. When you start the Developer Studio again, the assigned workspace will be used. The start process will then be performed without interruption.

When called up for the first time, the development environment displays a greeting page that looks similar to the one in Figure 3.3. You can consider this page as the starting point for your development activities that will supply you with tutorials, example and reference applications, and selected links to documentation and other information material.

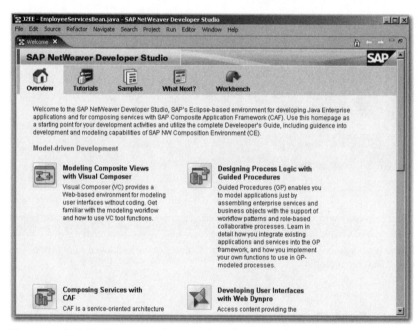

Figure 3.3 SAP NetWeaver Developer Studio After First Call — Greeting Page

---

1 In general, you start the Developer Studio using the desktop shortcut or from the Microsoft® Windows® Start menu. One alternative and very flexible option is if you use batch files. Even several batch files can be used as configuration files to start the Developer Studio, depending on requirements, using different parameters.

At this point we recommend that you familiarize yourself with the standard settings of the Developer Studio and that you add more entries, where required. You can reach the preferences page through the menu path **Windows • Preferences**. When you are working through the steps in this chapter, you will need the link to the Java application server. Therefore, you should have a corresponding entry set under **SAP AS Java**. We will look at other settings that you require for being able to use the Java development infrastructure in Chapter 11, *SAP NetWeaver Development Infrastructure — Configuration and Administration*.

Settings under Windows Preferences

3.3 Defining the Data Model

Before you develop the employee application, you must first define a suitable data model that will serve as the basis for this application. For didactic reasons, however, no great emphasis is placed on a sophisticated data model with a large number of complex tables and relationships to one another. Instead, the data model should be kept relatively simple so that you can manage with a single table that takes on the management of persistent employee data.

In this first practical step, you will create a new table in the Java Dictionary and add the required columns in the corresponding editor. Afterward, you will create an appropriate archive for this table definition. From the Developer Studio, you are then in the position to deploy this archive on the application server. This way you ensure that the table definition, which is initially available only on a local basis, is converted into physical representation on the database instance.

3.3.1 Creating a Dictionary Project

To create tables, you first need a suitable project in the Developer Studio. Dictionary projects are intended precisely for this purpose. These are projects that serve, at design time, as containers both for Dictionary data types and structures as well as for tables or views in tables. You can create an initial project framework for the new Dictionary project using a wizard.

New project wizard
1. You start the creation wizard through the menu path **File • New • Project**. In the Wizard window you now see, select the category **Dictionary** and then the entry **Dictionary Project** (Figure 3.4). To get to the next dialog step, choose **Next**.

Figure 3.4 Selection of Dictionary Project in New Project Wizard

2. In the displayed wizard window, you will be prompted to assign general project properties. For this purpose, enter the name "EmployeeDic" for the Dictionary project in the corresponding input field, but leave the standard settings for **Project contents** and **Project language** unchanged (Figure 3.5).

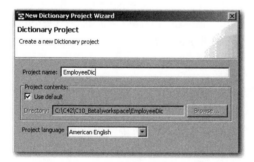

Figure 3.5 General Specifications for Dictionary Project

3. Now you only need to choose **Finish** and leave the rest of the work to the creation wizard. This generates a standard structure for the new

Dictionary project and creates the project folder with the name *EmployeeDic* in the assigned workspace directory. If you now open the Dictionary perspective, a project node with the same name can be seen in the Dictionary Explorer.

In the same manner, it is possible to create, in the Developer Studio, other project types such as Web Dynpro projects, for example, or the different Java EE project types using a suitable wizard.

3.3.2 Defining an Employee Table

In the next step, you create a table for the employee table as part of the project you have just created and then enter the required table fields as columns.

1. To create a table, it is best if you display the project **EmployeeDic** in the Dictionary Explorer. There you can expand the project structure and open the context menu for the node **Database Tables**.

2. To start the creation wizard, simply choose the menu path **Create Table** from the context menu (Figure 3.6). In the displayed dialog box, you will be prompted to assign a name for the table.

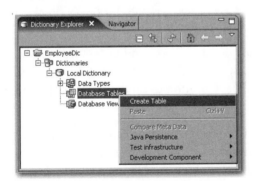

Figure 3.6 Creating a Table in the Dictionary Project

Keep in mind that, as a rule, a standard prefix is already provided for the table name in the input field. As you can see, this prefix is derived from the default setting that is entered for the Dictionary objects under **Windows • Preferences • Dictionary • Name Server Prefix**. This name prefix is based on the naming convention for database tables

Name conventions for database objects

and enables you to uniquely separate development objects that are created at customer sites, partner sites, and at SAP — with the aim of avoiding name conflicts.[2] The two namespaces TMP_* and TEST_* are of special importance here. These can be used for test objects and prototypes.

3. In this current example, therefore, it will suffice if you use the name prefix "TMP". For the suffix itself, enter the name "EMPLOYEES" and choose **Finish**.

4. As a result, there is a corresponding entry for the new table in the project structure under the node **Database Tables**. By double-clicking the table name, you start the table editor and can now add the individual table fields.

Table fields

5. The first field should have the name "ID". Enter it under **Column Name** in the first line of the table matrix. Because this table field is the primary key of the table, check the field **Key**. Under **Built-In Type**, choose the data type long and enter a short description "Employees ID" under **Description**. In the standard version, the property **Not Null** is set for each new field and you use the option of defining initial values for each field of the database table.

6. The second table field contains the name "LAST_NAME". In addition, a **String** of length **30** is assigned as data type[3] to this field as well as the short text "Employees last name".

7. Additional table fields include FIRST_NAME and DEPARTMENT and VERSION. You can see how these are defined in Figure 3.7. Finally, save the current status of the table definition using the appropriate icon in the toolbar.

Now the basic properties of the employee table are set. However, we would like to point out an important general aspect here: You will learn how to set up an index for a table column and how you can activate the table buffering in the table editor. It is a good idea to follow the basic principle: Make as many decisions as possible already at design time!

---

2 Under *http://service.sap.com/namespaces*, customers and partners of SAP can reserve a name prefix for database objects.

3 From the specifications for the **Built-in Type** and **Length**, you get the assignment to the JDBC Type. This is automatically converted by the wizard.

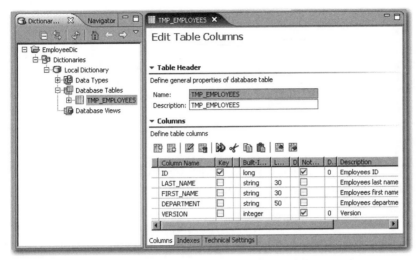

Figure 3.7 Definition of Columns for Table TMP_EMPLOYEES in the Table Editor

Generally speaking, there is a distinction between the primary index and the secondary index for tables — and you will use a secondary index. The primary index is sorted by the key fields of the table and automatically created together with the physical table on the database. Normally, data records are sorted by the value in the primary key. However, if you expect to have frequent access in the application to another field in data records, we recommend that you set up a secondary index for this field.

Secondary index

1. To create, for example, an index to the field LASTNAME, simply click the tab **Indexes** in the table editor and then choose the plus character icon on the left in the toolbar.

2. In the displayed wizard, enter "EMPLOYEES_I1" as a suffix for the index name[4] and complete this step with **Finish**. Afterward, expand the tree structure you have just created for the new index and choose the option **Add/Edit Index Fields** from the context menu of the **Fields** node.

3. You now get a list of the table fields and you can choose the field you require (Figure 3.8).

---

4 Similar to the table name, the standard prefix flows into the index name. Just like table names, index names are limited to 18 characters.

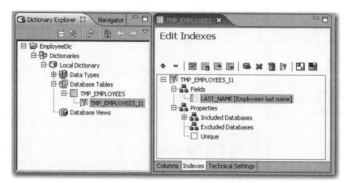

Figure 3.8 Definition of an Index in the Table Editor

Technical settings 4. To activate a table buffer, too, you only require a couple of mouse clicks. Simply choose the tab **Technical Settings** in the table editor, select the respective checkbox, and assign the buffer granularity,[5] as displayed in Figure 3.9.

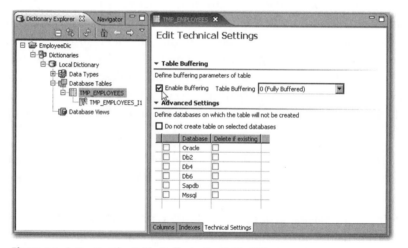

Figure 3.9 Activating the Table Buffer in the Table Editor

5. In the course of the previous procedure, certain table definition data was generated for this project. To save the entire result of your efforts so far, choose the appropriate icon in the toolbar.

---

5 With the granularity function, you can define whether the table is to be loaded with all data records (fully buffered) or only partially loaded into the buffer as soon as the first data record is accessed.

In this way, the table is completely defined and exists as a local project resource in the form of an XML file. A further result is that the table is now part of the Java Dictionary and has a database-independent definition.

3.4   Implementing Access to Table Data

At this point, you need to decide how you wish to perform access to table data records in a Java application. Generally speaking, there are several options for data persistence within the framework of Java development and all have their special aspects and strengths. Because the SAP NetWeaver Application Server Java already supports the newer version Java EE 5-Standard, you will use the Java persistence API (JPA) in the current tutorial application. A discussion of the various persistence records in the AS Java context is provided in Chapter 4, *Java Persistence*. This chapter is concerned solely with the topic of persistence.

Java persistence API

The JPA is the new object-relational persistence API for Java EE 5 and implemented as an integral part of the Java EE standard. With this technical solution that is extremely easy for the programmer to use, the "lightweight" Java objects, also called entities, are mapped onto relational database tables. Entities are based on regular Java objects, often called POJOs (Plain Old Java Object), and do not have to implement special interfaces or enhance special classes. In addition to the typical class implementation, however, you will also have to provide mapping to suitable database tables as well as mapping of persistent attributes to the respective table fields.[6] For specifying this type of metadata, the JPA provides the comfortable use of annotations that can be added — either manually or using OR mapping tools — to the source code of the entity class.

---

6 Within the framework of the pending delivery of the SAP NetWeaver Composition Environment, you can find very easy-to-use solutions based on close integration between the individual tools and frameworks. Accordingly, it should be possible, using the table definitions from the Dictionary project, to generate entities for the EJB module, and vice versa.

3.4.1 EJB-Creating a Module Project

To create entities, you first need a new EJB module project.

1. For this purpose, once again start the **New Project Wizard** through the menu path **File • New • Project**. As seen in Figure 3.10, select the category **EJB • EJB 3.0** and then **EJB Project 3.0** in the displayed wizard window.

Figure 3.10 Selection of EJB Module Project in the New Project Wizard

2. By clicking **Next**, you proceed to the next wizard window. There you enter "EmployeeEjb" as the name for the new project. In addition, you accept the default settings and complete this procedure with **Finish**.

3. The creation wizard generates an initial project framework for the new EJB project and creates a project folder in the directory.

4. Now start the J2EE perspective, if you have not done so already, and display the project structure in the **Project Explorer**. This view will now serve as your central starting point for all future activities concerning the EJB 3.0 development.

In the next step, add an entity named Employee to this project.

3.4.2 Defining an Employee Entity

As already mentioned, the data model should be kept as simple as possible in this introductory example. Therefore, you should define only one single entity named Employee, to correspond with the already existing table called TMP_EMPLOYEES.

General Properties of the Entity Class

In the next step you create a new, serializable Java class. This will be a class that, for the most part, declares the appropriate attributes and provides the corresponding set and get methods.

1. To create such a class for the EJB module project, open the context menu for the project node and choose the option **New · Class**.

   New class wizard

2. Enter "Employee" as the name for the new class and assign the package com.sap.demo.entity. In addition, activate the option **Constructors from Superclass** and add the interface **Serializable** to your selection.

3. Then accept the standard default settings and create the class by pressing **Finish**.

4. When you have completed the creation procedure, start the Java editor and add some field definitions to the actual class body[7]:

```
private long employeeId;
private String lastName;
private String firstName;
private String department;
private int version;
```

In this way, you equip the entity class with the exact fields that you created in the corresponding employee table as table fields.

---

7 In accordance with the specification, we recommend creating a version field (version) for the entity. This field is used by the JPA container at runtime in order to implement optimum verification and thus ensure that no competing accesses are implemented for one and the same data source. As soon as the container registers accesses of this type, an exception is thrown for the transaction. The most recent data state is then retained and a rollback is set for the current transaction. With these simple means, you help to maintain data consistency.

5. Then, in the editor, select all the rows with the fields you have just created and choose **Source · Generate Getters and Setters...** from the context menu. In the displayed window, click the key **Select All**. In this way, the corresponding getter and setter methods are generated for all fields, in accordance with Listing 3.1.

```
public class Employee implements Serializable {
    private static final long serialVersionUID = 111L;
    private long employeeId;
    private String lastName;
    private String firstName;
    private String department;
    private int version;
    // non-arg constructor
    public Employee() {
    }
    public String getDepartment() {
    return department;
    }
    public void setDepartment(String department) {
    this.department = department;
    }
    public long getEmployeeId() {
    return employeeId;
    }
    public void setEmployeeId(long employeeId) {
    this.employeeId = employeeId;
    }
    [...]
}
```

Listing 3.1 Implementation of a Regular Java Class Named Employee

6. Finally, save the current editor content using the appropriate icon in the toolbar.

The implementation of the class Employee has thus far shown no anomalies. It defines five fields: employeeId, lastName, firstName, department, and version, and places the getter and setter methods at your disposal in accordance with the name convention for JavaBeans. It should be mentioned, however, that the JPA demands a parameter-free constructor for an entity. But further constructors can be added.

Because this is not an abstract class that also avails of a `public` constructor, you have thus far been dealing with a POJO that can already be instantiated. Moreover, the class implements the interface `java.io.Serializable` so that entity objects can be serialized through remote calls or in Web service calls, respectively.

In this connection, follow the general recommendation and explicitly declare a version number[8] named `serialVersionUID` for the serializable class. For this reason, a same-name field that is `static`, `final`, and of the type `long` was added subsequently in the declaration part.

Object-Relational Mapping

Strictly speaking, we do not yet have an entity here, but only a simple JavaBean object. What is missing is a type of meta information[9] that describes the mapping of the Java object onto the relational database. Using the JPA, this is easily achieved, simply by adding the annotations to the source code of the Java class.

With the simple addition `@Entity` to the class definition, you identify the class `Employee` as an EJB 3.0 Entity. With this step, you set the command that the entity is suitably mapped to a database table. In addition, the persistence framework requires information as to how the entity is mapped to the relational database table.

It should be remembered that the JPA provides the application developer with a very comfortable path to realize this kind of object-relational mapping, based on a record of plausible default rules. If no explicit specifications are made — for example, for the name of the table or the individual table fields — the JPA assumes certain plausible assumptions.

---

8 The version number `serialVersionUID` is required by the serialization runtime for each serializable class for verification purposes. If a serializable class does not explicitly declare a `serialVersionUID`, a default value is calculated by the runtime for this version number. This default value can, however, depend on the compiler implementation. To guarantee a consistent version number for all compilers, we recommend that you explicitly declare a `serialVersionUID` for the class.

9 With the JPA, meta information can be stored for the entity class in the form of a separate XML file, as before, using deployment descriptors. The use of annotations, however, is to be preferred — in particular, because this is normal practice in the standard Java SE 5.0.

In this example, an entity with the name Employee would be mapped onto a database table with the name EMPLOYEE in accordance with these rules. However, because the names in this case are to be different, you have the option of overwriting them using the annotation @Table. You proceed in a similar fashion when mapping the persistent fields of the entity to the corresponding table fields. If a persistent field deviates from the name of the table field onto which it is to be mapped, the annotation @Column is added with the specification of the corresponding field name. This situation applies, for example, to the field EmployeeId, which is mapped onto the table field with the name ID. The situation is different, however, with the persistent field department, which is mapped onto a table field with the same name.[10] Here you do not have to make any explicit specification. To identify the version field as such, it is necessary for you to add the corresponding annotation @Version to the field version.

1. Now add the required annotations to the Java source code of the class Employee, as displayed in Listing 3.2.

```
@Entity
@Table(name="TMP_EMPLOYEES")
public class Employee implements Serializable {
    @Column(name="ID")
    private long employeeId;
    @Column(name="LAST_NAME")
    private String lastName;
    @Column(name="FIRST_NAME")
    private String firstName;
    private String department;
    @Version
    private int version;
    [...]
}
```

Listing 3.2 Annotations in the Source Code of the Employee Class

10 The JPA specification supplies no guidelines on adherence to uppercase or lowercase lettering for tables and field names. For the implementation of SAP JPA 1.0, the following rule therefore applies: If the name of the table or table field is listed explicitly using the annotation, uppercase and lowercase lettering is taken into consideration. If, on the other hand, the table name or table field is generated in accordance with the default rule, uppercase lettering is used.

2. If you have not already done so, finally create the missing imports for the employee class. For this purpose, click on an arbitrary position in the Java editor and choose **Source • Organize Imports** from the context menu.

3. The missing import lines are then added, as shown in Listing 3.3. Now, no more errors should be displayed in the source code of the Bean class.

```
import javax.persistence.Column;
import javax.persistence.Entity;
import javax.persistence.Table;
import javax.persistence.Version;
```

Listing 3.3 Supplementing Certain Import Lines for the Class Employee

Generating the Primary Key

So that each instance of an entity can be uniquely identified, the entity class must have an identifier that can simultaneously serve in the assigned table as a primary key. For this reason, a field of the name `EmployeeId` is already created and you will use it as an identifier for the employee entity. The specification of the identifier field is done easily with the annotation `@Id`, which you place in front of the field. In this case, this field with the primary key of the corresponding database field is identified through the mapping onto the table field `ID`.

Now you are faced with the question as to which generation method is to be used to generate the primary key. Admittedly, there are many solutions and strategies, but it would go beyond the scope of these explanations. But this much should be said: Generally speaking, key fields can be provided using the database or using the server container, or even through the application itself. The JPA specification is again of help to the developer and provides various strategies for automatic ID generation. The developer does not need to implement any ID generation logic, but instead can initiate automatic primary key generation using the annotation `@GeneratedValue` and can also use the various generation strategies.

In the following section, you will see how the table strategy is implemented. Here a special table for the generation of the ID value is used.

Table for ID generation

131

First, however, you must create a corresponding table because it is not automatically provided by the framework as a type of system table. This work step is very simple.

1. Again start the Dictionary perspective and add a further table definition named TMP_ID_GEN to the already existing project **EmployeeDic**.

2. The new table should be defined exactly as shown in Figure 3.11 and contain the two fields GEN_KEY and GEN_VALUE.[11] The field GEN_KEY defines the table key and will contain the fully qualified class name at runtime. The field GEN_VALUE is provided for storing the last generated ID value.

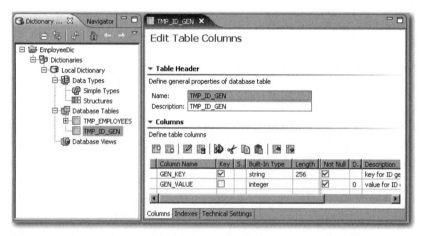

Figure 3.11 Creating Another Table Definition for ID Generation in the Dictionary Project EmployeeDic

Annotation for the
ID generator

3. As displayed in Listing 3.4, it is possible to generate a suitable ID generator with the help of this new table. In the source code of the employee class, therefore, add the appropriate annotation @TableGenerator by putting the class name in the front. The element table references the table you have just created for ID generation while the element name is used to identify the generator. The name of the generator, in turn, is specified through the element generator using

---

11 The two table columns GEN_KEY and GEN_VALUE identify the standard names of the SAP JPA implementation for tables for ID generation. Alternatively, you can define other column names for the ID table, but in this case you must ensure corresponding mapping in the annotation for the table generator (@TableGenerator).

the annotation @GeneratedValue. As shown in Listing 3.4, add this annotation to the class attribute employeeId. Through the other element strategy, you instruct the container to use the generation method with the strategy of the type TABLE at runtime.

```
@TableGenerator(name="idGenerator", table="TMP_ID_GEN",
pkColumnName="GEN_KEY", valueColumnName="GEN_VALUE")
public class Employee implements Serializable {
@Id
@GeneratedValue (strategy=GenerationType.TABLE,
                 generator="idGenerator")
@Column(name="ID")
private long employeeId;
[...]
```

Listing 3.4 Definition of a Primary Key for the Employee Entity

Formulating the Query Using an EJB QL Statement

Search queries are often used during access to database data. The specification for EJB 3.0 provides multiple options on how you can implement queries. The named parameters are an important element here; they are used both in static and dynamic queries.

Search queries in finder methods

You may remember how for the earlier EJB versions' static queries were defined in the EJB deployment descriptor and then, in an additional step, how the behavior of the finder methods were to be specified using the EJB QL statements. EJB version 3.0 continues this approach and provides for this purpose a simplified execution method. It allows the programmer to add static queries using the annotation @NamedQuery within the Java source code. This is a predefined query that is identified by its name. As is standard with finder methods, the method behavior is not specified using Java source code but through EJB QL statements. You can use these to formulate suitable search queries.

This is precisely what you will do at this point by formulating the required EJB QL statement for a query named Employee.findAll.

1. Create the annotation @NamedQuery in the Java Editor, before the definition of the class Employee.

2. The element `name` serves to identify the query using a string value. The element `query` adopts the EJB QL statement `SELECT e FROM Employee e` (Listing 3.5).

```
@NamedQuery(name="Employee.findAll",
            query="SELECT e FROM Employee e")
@Entity
@Table(name="TMP_EMPLOYEES")
public class Employee implements Serializable {

[...]
```

Listing 3.5 Definition of a Query for Displaying All the Employee Objects

3.4.3 Configuring the Application for Database Accesses

So that the EJB container can handle the database accesses in the first place, it must know certain global settings for persistence, such as the name of the data source, which is required for the link to the database. As a rule, configuration tasks are taken on by the server, but there are some exceptions. Therefore, we will describe how these few configuration tasks are to be executed once by the developer for the EJB project. This manual configuration of the Java persistence takes place in a special persistence descriptor with the name *persistence.xml*.

Defining the Persistence Unit

In a typical EJB application, the data model consists mostly of several entities that reference each other and are to be mapped onto one and the same database schema. You must now ensure that all entity classes that belong together also build a logical unit for the EJB container at runtime, are managed by the entity manager as such, and fall back on one and the same data source. This kind of logical unit is described as a persistence unit.

Persistence unit combines entities

The persistence unit is comprised of entities of an application that are addressed at runtime through the Entity Manager. Remember that a persistence unit must be set explicitly — even when, as in this case, only a single entity is involved.

All entities that belong together and form a persistence unit can be listed explicitly in the configuration file. This, however, is not absolutely necessary because the persistence framework otherwise searches through the application for entities and automatically finds them. In this tutorial application, only the name and a short description should be specified for the persistence unit. The basic principle is to perform configuration only in an exceptional case. In addition, two further specifications are required — one for the JTA data source and one for the version generator.

Because this kind of configuration file is not yet contained in the current EJB project, create the file *persistence.xml* using the appropriate XML schema.

Configuration in persistence.xml

1. To do this, select the EJB project in the **Project Explorer** and navigate to the folder **META-INF**.

2. From the context menu for this folder, choose the menu path **New · Other · XML · XML** and navigate with **Next** to the next step.

3. On the displayed wizard page, select the option **Create XML file from an XML schema file** and again press the **Next button**.

4. On the following wizard page, enter "persistence.xml" as the file name and choose **Next**.

5. As shown in Figure 3.12, now decide on the option **Select XML Catalog entry** and then **persistence_1_0.xsd** from the displayed XML catalog.

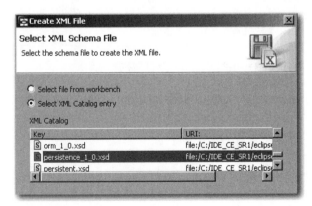

Figure 3.12 Selection of XML Schemas when Creating persistence.xml for the EJB Project

6. On the next wizard page, confirm your selection by pressing **Finish**.

7. To complete the content for the persistence descriptor, use the design view (Figure 3.13) and, using the context menu for the last entry, create a few additional tags. You will find the required configuration specifications in Table 3.1.

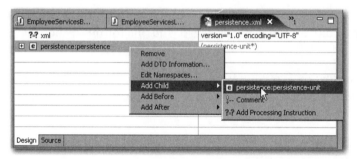

Figure 3.13 Creating More Tags in the Design View of persistence.xml

XML Tag	Assigned Value
persistence-unit | name	EmployeePU
persistence: description	**Sample Application Persistence Unit**
persistence: jta-data-source	TMP_EMPLOYEES_DATA
persistence: properties	
property | name	com.sap.engine.services.orpersis-tence.generator.versiontablename
property | value	TMP_ID_GEN

Table 3.1 Specifications for Persistence Unit in persistence.xml

8. The name of the persistence unit is generally optional and is added to the XML source within the element `<persistence-unit>`. We will refer to the persistence unit again when the instance of the unit is to be accessed in the session bean using the Entity Manager.

9. Within the element `<persistence-unit>`, use the tag `<jta-data-source>` to enter the data source alias. We will also deal with this in more detail at a later point.

10. Finally, enter a ⟨property⟩ to enable versioning of the data source. This specification is necessary for the following reason:

So that versioning of the data source is at all useful, the JPA specification requires that the data source uses the isolation level READ_COMMITTED. However, to cater to the difference between this requirement and the actual isolation level READ_UNCOMMITTED, you will need a suitable version generator. You address this kind of generator in the *persistence.xml* through a certain property of the persistence unit. You specify this property using the name element from Table 3.1.

In addition, a version generator requires a suitable database table. Any arbitrary generator table that has the field names GEN_KEY and GEN_VALUE is suitable for this. By all means, the table TMP_ID_GEN previously created is suitable for this purpose. Therefore, assign it as the property value.

11. The generated XML source then corresponds to the lines in Listing 3.6:

```
<?xml version="1.0" encoding="UTF-8"?>
<persistence xmlns=
 "http://java.sun.com/xml/ns/persistence" [...]>
<persistence-unit name="EmployeePU">
  <description>
    Sample Application Persistence Unit
  </description>
  <jta-data-source>TMP_EMPLOYEES_DATA</jta-data-source>
  <properties>
    <property name = "com.sap.engine.services.
                      orpersistence.generator.
                      versiontablename"
                      value= "TMP_ID_GEN">
    </property>
  </properties>
</persistence-unit>
</persistence>
```

Listing 3.6 Resulting XML Source of persistence.xml

3.5   Defining the Business Logic

After you have completed the data accesses in Section 3.4, *Implementing Access to Table Data*, using a JPA entity, now turn to the business logic. Because you are using EJBs, session beans[12] are usually the best way of encapsulating the business logic.

Stateless session bean
For this purpose, you will now create a stateless session bean named `EmployeeServices`, and then add and implement the required business methods. Using the business methods, arbitrary clients should be in a position to adopt the employee registration data entered by the user and finally pass them for storage to the entity `Employee`. Also, it should be possible for all existing data records on all existing employees to be passed to clients for display purposes.

3.5.1   Creating a Session Bean

To create a session bean named `Employee Services`, start the appropriate creation wizard.

1. Start the context menu on the project node **EmployeeEjb** in the Project Explorer, and choose the menu option **New • EJB • EJB 3.0 • EJB Session Bean 3.0**.

2. In the displayed dialog box, assign certain elementary properties in accordance with the list in Table 3.2.

3. Because no further options are required for the session bean you want to create, choose **Finish**. By doing this, you start the generation procedure.

---

12 In distributed applications, session beans implement the application-relevant processes and tasks, take care of the transaction management, and arrange access to low-level components, such as entities or other data access components as well as auxiliary classes. This use of session beans matches the session façade design pattern and serves to define a clear separation between the different levels (data accesses and business logic) with the aim of increasing performance at runtime.

Field Name	Assigned Value
EJB Class Name	`EmployeeServices`
EJB Project	`EmployeeEjb`
Default EJB Package	`com.sap.demo.session`
Session Type	Stateless
Transaction Type	Container
Create Business Interface	Checkbox **Local** activated

Table 3.2 General Properties when Creating the Session Bean EmployeeServices

4. As shown in Figure 3.14, the wizard creates a bean class `EmployeeServicesBean` and the respective business interface `EmployeeServicesLocal`.

Figure 3.14 Session Bean EmployeeServices in the Project Explorer

When you created the session bean, you assigned the type `Stateless`. Therefore, this meta information is stored in the generated bean class by placing the respective annotation `@Stateless` in front of the class name. In contrast to stateful session beans, this session bean is not able to store its state in its instance variable. The application does not provide for storing user-specific information. As a result, the methods of the session bean will behave as stateless.

The declaration of the business interface as a local interface in turn means that the annotation `@Local` is generated for the interface name. As already mentioned, business methods of the session bean are exposed at this business interface so that a client can access the session bean with the help of this precise interface. In the case of a local interface, one can assume that the EJB and the client are on the same server.

3.5.2 Implementing the Session Bean Class

Business methods So far, the procedure has been mostly declarative in nature. Now the implementation of the specific service functions for the tutorial application will follow. Using the business methods, you will implement the functions that are also available to the client application. In the case of business methods, you are dealing with special methods of the session bean that implement their specific service functions that are available on an external basis.

Generally speaking, business methods are declared as regular Java methods in local, remote, or, if necessary, in both business interfaces, and are implemented in the respective session bean class. Depending on the business interface that provides the appropriate business method, this method is available either for local or remote clients, or for both.

In the following explanations, you will see that you only need to supply local clients with data and implement certain business methods that already show, in the examples, how some of the basic operations on persistent objects are to be performed. In this way, you will learn — with the help of the method `createEmployee()` — how a new data record is created and how it is stored permanently in the database. You will also learn how to implement the search for a data record with the primary key using the method `getEmployeeById()`. A further read access is connected with a query execution and defines the third business method `getAllEmployees()` for the tutorial application.

Keeping the Instance of the Entity Manager

Entity Manager as interface to database Business methods should be able to create new data records, manipulate existing ones, and finally synchronize the changes with the database. For this reason, you require a kind of local interface for interaction with the database. The JPA provides the application developer with such an interface to the Entity Manager. The purpose of the Entity Manger is to control the lifecycle of entity objects and to change their status. Using the Entity Manger, you can perform all database operations on entities and thus create, change, read, search for, or even delete objects on the database. Listing 3.7 shows you how you access the persistence unit, starting from the session bean, and how you define the Entity Manager for the persistence unit.

```
@Stateless
public class EmployeeServicesBean implements
EmployeeServicesLocal {
    @PersistenceContext (unitName = "EmployeePU")
    private EntityManager eManager;
[...]
}
```

Listing 3.7 Access to the Entity Manager Within the Session Bean

As you can see from Listing 3.7, the session bean declares a variable of the type EntityManager, without having a certain value assigned to it. Two aspects are of interest here: First, the source code is part of the session bean and is executed on the application server. On the other hand, the variable is provided with the annotation @PersistenceContext. In addition, this annotation contains the element unitName. Using this parameter, you enter the name of the persistence unit on which the Entity Manager operates. You will surely remember that the entered value corresponds exactly to the name you have already entered in the configuration file *persistence.xml*.

This is of interest here because the session bean uses a technique called resource injection. Due to the annotation, it is left up to the server to supply the variable (here: eManager) with an EntityManager instance. In this way, you ensure that this variable is always correctly initialized when a business method is called for the first time.

Creating a New Employee Data Record on the Database

After you have seen how you can access the Entity Manager in the bean class, you will now see — on the basis of the business method createEmployee() — how easily a new data record can be created on the database. First, an instance of the entity Employee is created using a constructor. The data required for specifying an employee is passed in the form of a method parameter. Access to the persistent fields is performed using the setter methods. The fully specified object employee is finally passed using the method persist() to the Entity Manager that triggers permanent storage on the database. As a result, the business method returns an ID of the type long.

The complete implementation of this method can be seen in Listing 3.8.

```
public long createEmployee(String lastName, String
firstName, String department) {
     long result = 0;
     Employee employee = new Employee();
     employee.setFirstName(firstName);
     employee.setLastName(lastName);
     employee.setDepartment(department);
     eManager.persist(employee);
     result = employee.getEmployeeId();
     return result;
}
```

Listing 3.8 Source Code for the Business Method createEmployee()

Searching for a Data Record Using an ID

Frequently, an application must be in the position to first identify a certain data record on the database before it can perform a new operation on this data. The search for a certain employee data record using the ID (that is, the primary key) is shown as an example in Listing 3.9.

```
public Employee getEmployeeById(long empId) {
     Employee employee =
     eManager.find(Employee.class, Long.valueOf(empId));
     return employee;
}
```

Listing 3.9 Source Code for the Business Method getEmployeeById()

In this case, the call takes place using the find() method of the Entity Manager. This method contains two arguments: The first argument is the entity class of the object to be searched for, while the second argument is the object representation of the entity identifier, that is, the key field. The `find()` method returns the found entity instance or `null` if no such entity was found in the database. Because the `find()` method was implemented generically, a casting of the resulting value is not required in this case. In other words, the `find()` method is parameterized in such a way that the type of the returned result matches the type of the first argument of the method call. Whatever the case, an instance of the type `Employee` is returned.

Executing a Query

Another business method `getAllEmployees()` will now solely be used to demonstrate how a query can be used to read a resulting set. You will remember how you formulated a named query in Section 3.4.2, *Defining an Employee Entity*, using a select clause. In that case, a search query was stored with the symbolic name `Employee.findAll` in the source code of the `Employee` entity. Now you should use these queries to read the database records. It should be possible to return a list of all existing employees for a particular client.[13]

As you can see from the implementation of this finder method in Listing 3.10, query objects can be created through the Entity Manager. This is done by calling the method `createNamedQuery()`. As a parameter, a place holder that contains only the name of the defining query is passed. The execution of the query in the database and the reading of the resulting set is performed using the query method `getResultList()`.

```
@SuppressWarnings("unchecked")
public List<Employee> getAllEmployees() {
      Query query =
        eManager.createNamedQuery("Employee.findAll");
      List<Employee> result =
      (List<Employee>) query.getResultList();
      return result;
}
```

Listing 3.10 Source Code of the Business Method getAllEmployees()

---

13 The clients can be Java Server Faces, JSPs, servlets, Java classes, a different EJB, or a Web service client. Clients, particularly in large applications, have the advantage that they themselves do not have to define any search queries. Changes and adjustments to the query form can be done centrally, without any effect on the client.

To minimize the number of warnings at compiler time, add the appropriate annotation to the source code. @SuppressWarnings is used solely to suppress certain compiler warnings in connection with this method.

Defining the Transaction Behavior of the Business Methods

So far you have not made specifications at any time regarding the transaction behavior of the business methods. Only when you created the session bean did you determine the transaction type with the attribute **Container**. This means that, in such a case, the EJB container takes over control of the transaction. In relation to the Entity Manager, you have already seen that the EJB container takes over important standard tasks from the programmer.

With this transaction type, you do not have to set the commit or rollback methods. You can leave this task entirely up to the EJB container. As a rule, there is the option with EJBs of implementing the transaction logic on a program-controlled basis in the bean class itself. However, the decision in favor of transaction behavior based on the container-supported approach when a session bean is created has already been made.

Transaction attributes
You determine the desired transaction behavior for the individual business methods of the application using transaction attributes. As a result, all operations that go beyond read access to data records must take place within a transaction. Because transaction attributes are metadata, we use, as usual, predefined annotations. The required additions in the source code are shown in Listing 3.11.

```
@Stateless
@TransactionManagement
  (value=TransactionManagementType.CONTAINER)
public class EmployeeServicesBean
              implements EmployeeServicesLocal {
[...]
   public long createEmployee(String lastName, String
   firstName, String department) {
   [...]
   }
   @TransactionAttribute(TransactionAttributeType.SUPPORTS)
   public Employee getEmployeeById(long empId) {
```

```
[...]
}
@TransactionAttribute(TransactionAttributeType.SUPPORTS)
public List<Employee> getAllEmployees() {
[...]
}
[...]
}
```

Listing 3.11 Transaction Attributes of the Business Methods of the Session Bean
EmployeeServices

First, the annotation `@TransactionManagement` defines that transaction control for the entire session bean is delegated to the container. Another annotation, `@Transaction Attribute`, enables you to adapt the transaction context individually to each single method. Remember that no annotation was added to the method `createEmployee()`. The reason for this is solely that the default behavior is to be applied to the basic operation. The corresponding transaction attribute is called `REQUIRED` and requires that a new transaction is always started whenever this is necessary. If, for example, at the time of the method call no transaction is active, the application server automatically starts a new transaction, executes the business method, and sets a transaction commit immediately thereafter. On the other hand, if a transaction is already available, this one is used. This way you can see that creating a new employee data record definitely requires a transaction, albeit one that is not necessarily exclusive. For this purpose, the transaction attribute `REQUIRED` is ideal.

The methods `getEmployeeById()` and `getAllEmployees()` are quite different. Both methods implement solely reading accesses. Because no changes to data records result, a transaction is actually not required. If, however, a transaction is active at the time of the method call, this one is used. A new transaction, on the other hand, is not started. On the basis of this tolerance toward the transactions, the default behavior can be overwritten with the transaction attribute `SUPPORTS`. In this way, the source code of the bean class is complete. If you have not done so already, add the missing imports to the bean class. Then click on an arbitrary position in the Java editor and select **Source • Organize Imports** from the context menu. The missing import lines are then added. Now no further errors should be displayed in the source code of the bean class. Finally, adapt the formatting of the new lines by choosing **Source** · **Format** from the editor context menu and then save the editor content using the corresponding icon in the toolbar.

3.5.3 Adding Business Methods to the Business Interface

Because the business methods already defined in the bean class are not automatically added to the appropriate business interface, you must perform this step manually.

1. To propagate individual business methods from the bean class to the business interface, select the bean class in the project explorer by double-clicking it. If no outline view is displayed in the current view, open this one first.

2. As shown in Figure 3.15, select all the business methods within the outline view, open the context menu, and then choose the option **EJB Methods · Add to Local Interfaces**.

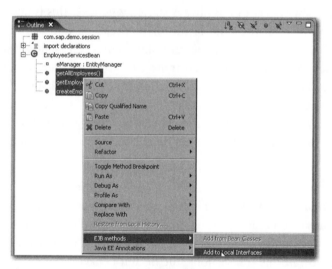

Figure 3.15 Propagating the Business Methods to the Business Interface, Starting from the Outline View

3. Listing 3.12 shows the resulting source code of the business interface.

```
import javax.ejb.Local;
import java.util.List;
```

```
import com.sap.demo.entity.Employee;

@Local
public interface EmployeeServicesLocal {
      public List<Employee> getAllEmployees ();
      public Employee getEmployeeById (long empId);
      public long createEmployee (String lastName, String
                  firstName, String department);
}
```

Listing 3.12 Business Methods in the Business Interface EmployeeServicesLocal

3.6 Creating a JSP-Based Web Application

The Developer Studio provides a special project structure for managing Web resources such as JavaServer pages, JavaServer faces, servlets, static HTML pages, and custom-tag libraries, as well as screen and graphic files. To prepare the initial project frame, you will create a corresponding project — that is, a Web module project — at the very outset.

To keep the Web application as simple as possible, add a JSP to the project as the only resource and implement with it the user interface of the Web client. In addition to the actual presentation editing, the accesses to the business methods of the session bean EmployeeServices should be implemented. As an example, use some information on the configuration of the Web application in the corresponding deployment descriptor.

3.6.1 Creating a Web Module Project

To create a Web module project, perform the following steps:

Container for Web resources

1. Start the **New Project Wizard** through the menu option **File · New Project**.

2. In the displayed wizard window, select the category **Web · Web 2.5** and then **Dynamic Web Project 2.5**.

3. With **Next**, you proceed to the next wizard window. There you enter "EmployeeWeb" as the project name. Otherwise, take the default settings and close the procedure by pressing **Finish**.

4. The best way of looking at the project frame is in the Project Explorer. In the JSP, you want to access resources from the Ejb module project. Therefore, you must also take this project dependency into account. For this purpose, click the project name **EmployeeWeb** and select the menu option **Properties** from the context menu.

5. In accordance with the specifications in Figure 3.16, select the property **Java Build Path**, click the tab **Projects**, and assign the desired project.

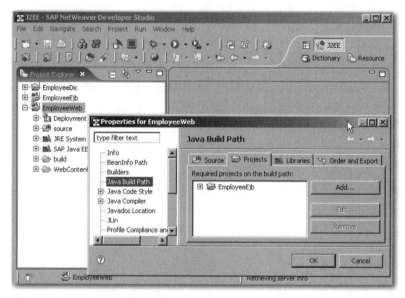

Figure 3.16 Assigning Java Build Path to the Project EmployeeWeb

3.6.2 Implementing the User Interface with JSP

Now you can begin with the implementation of the user interface in the JSP editor.

1. To add a JSP to the new project, click on the entry **WebContent** in the Project Explorer and choose the menu option **New • JSP....**

2. You now see a wizard in which you can enter the name "index.jsp".

3. Further specifications are not required. Close the procedure by pressing **Finish**.

Generally speaking, there are two sections in the source code of the JSP:

▶ A HTML basic structure that, for the most part, defines a static input form for the Web application

▶ A dynamic Java-based section with which you can implement accesses to the business logic

HTML Basic Structure

The form for registering new employees could hardly be easier. It contains, in addition to the two input fields for the names, a selection list with the corresponding departments and a pushbutton with which the user can trigger registration. All these interface elements are listed within a HTML table. The complete structure is displayed in Listing 3.13.

```
<%@ page language="java" [...] %>
<!DOCTYPE html PUBLIC  [...] >
<html>
[...]
<!-- Import statements   -->

<!-- Reference to Session Bean  -->
<body style= "font-family:Arial;"  bgcolor="D2D8E1">
<h2>
Register New Employee
</h2>
<form method="GET">
<table border=0 align=center>
<tr>
<td width="150" >First name: <td>
<input type="text" name="firstname" value = "" size="20">
<tr>
<td width="150" >Last name: <td>
<input type="text" name="lastname" value = "" size="20">
<tr>
<td width="150" >Department: <td>
   <select name="department" >
    <option value="DEVELOPMENT">Development</option>
    <option value="TRAINING"> Training</option>
    <option value="MANAGEMENT"> Management</option>
    <option value="ARCHITECTURE"> Architecture</option>
```

```
   </select>
<tr>
<td><td><br>
<input type="submit" value="Create" name="create">
</table>
<br>
</form>
<!- Invoke business method -->
</body>
</html>
```

Listing 3.13 HTML Basic Structure for the JSP

Access to the Session Bean

In accordance with Listing 3.14, first supplement the JSP source code with some page directives whose import attributes contain the required package for JNDI Lookup as well as the business interface.

So that the reference to the session beam is retained, a JNDI Lookup is performed on the context variable context. Remember that with EmployeeRegister in Listing 3.14 you use a symbolic name for the session bean. This name must also be specified as the reference name in the deployment descriptor of the Web application. The result of the lookup is assigned to the local employee object employeeService after the business method casting is completed.

```
<%
<!-- Import statements   -->
<%@ page import="javax.naming.*" %>
<%@ page import=
        "com.sap.demo.session.EmployeeServicesLocal" %>

<!-- Reference to Session Bean   -->
<%!
private EmployeeServicesLocal employeeService;
private void lookup() {
   try {
      InitialContext context = new InitialContext();
      employeeService = (EmployeeServicesLocal)
      context.lookup("java:comp/env/EmployeeRegister");
   } catch (Exception ex) {
```

```
        System.out.println("Couldn't find bean"+
                            ex.getMessage());
    }
}

public void jspDestroy() {
    employeeService = null;
}
%>
```

Listing 3.14 Dynamic Section of the JSP — Access to the Session Bean

Calling the Business Method

In the following section, not all business methods will be called within this simple Web application. We merely wish to show an example of how, starting from a JSP, the business method createEmployee() can be called in order to create a new data record on the database. This, too, is an intended simplification because, normally, a JSP-based Web application consists of a combination of JSPs and servlets, and possibly also further JavaBeans as auxiliary classes in order to achieve strict separation between the actual presentation layer and the controller layer. While JSPs are preferred for presentation editing and thus also preferred as a view component, servlets or JavaBeans usually act as a controller and implement the application logic.

To save some of the typing work, the call for the method createEmployee() is embedded in the JSP source. However, it could be transferred easily to a servlet or to a JavaBean in the role of a controller. As you can see from Listing 3.15, a JNDI lookup precedes the actual call of the session bean method. This lookup was previously encapsulated in a separate method lookup(). Therefore, the local session bean object employeeService calls the business method createEmployee(). The local variables lName, fName and eDepartment are passed as parameters. They were defined in the first lines of the source code excerpt and adopt the currently entered user values. Whenever the business method is successfully executed in the EJB container, it returns a valid EmployeeID. Otherwise an exception is thrown and a corresponding text is displayed on the user interface.

```
<%
  lookup();
  if(this.employeeService == null) {
    throw new IllegalStateException("Bean not available!");
  }

  String fName = request.getParameter("firstname");
  String lName = request.getParameter("lastname");

  String eDepartment = request.getParameter("department");
  if(lName == null || fName == null
    || lName.length() == 0 || fName.length() == 0) return;
  long empID = employeeService.createEmployee(lName, fName,
              eDepartment);
  if(empID == 0)
      out.println("<H3> Failed!  </H3>");
      else
      out.println("<H3> Success! </H3>");
%>
```

Listing 3.15 Dynamic Section of the JSP — Business Method Call

3.6.3 Descriptions in the Deployment Descriptor web.xml

You can get information on the configuration of the Web application from the deployment descriptor *web.xml*. The entries contained there are evaluated at deployment time by the Web container. On one hand, the Web container receives all information as to how the individual resources of the project fit with each other. On the other hand, the assignment of security roles is contained in *web.xml*. These are the security roles through which the access authorization for the Web application can be controlled at runtime.

However, only certain mapping information is stored in the descriptor. In the following step, you will define, as an example, a reference to the required session bean using a symbolic name, but you will not make any further specifications on the configuration of the Web application.

Symbolic Name for the Session Bean

Reference to session bean For access to the session bean, we have used a symbolic name, not the real bean name, in the JSP source code (see Listing 3.14). So that the

Web container can assign such a name at runtime as well, a corresponding mapping regulation must be stored in the deployment descriptor.

1. To define a symbolic name for a reference to the session bean, open the deployment descriptor *web.xml*. Click on the tab **Design** and add a further tag for the EJB reference.

2. Similar to the specifications in Figure 3.17, set the EJB name "EmployeeRegister" so that it matches the entry in the JNDI lookup in the JSP source code from Listing 3.14.

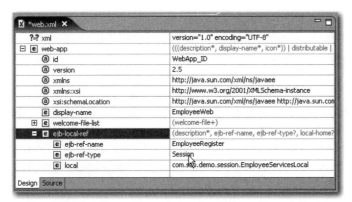

Figure 3.17 Setting the EJB Reference to the Session Bean in web.xml

3. The new entries are automatically added to the XML source at a suitable position. You can ensure this is the case by clicking on the tab **Source** and then navigating in the displayed XML source to the element `<ejb-local-ref>` (Listing 3.16).

```
<?xml version="1.0" encoding="UTF-8"?>
<web-app id="WebApp_ID" version="2.5" [...]">
  <display-name> EmployeeWeb</display-name>
  <welcome-file-list>
     [...]
  </welcome-file-list>
  <ejb-local-ref>
    <ejb-ref-name>EmployeeRegister</ejb-ref-name>
    <ejb-ref-type>Session</ejb-ref-type>
    <local>
      com.sap.demo.session.EmployeeServicesLocal
    </local>
```

```
</ejb-local-ref>
</web-app>
```

Listing 3.16 Generated XML Source for the Reference to the Session Bean

4. With this entry, you have now defined a mapping between a freely selectable reference name (symbolic name) and the real bean name. Thus, the reference name assigned in the source code of the JSP for the session bean can be used, and it remains unchanged there, even if the bean name changes.

3.7 Defining and Deploying the Java EE Overall Application

While the business functions are provided with the EJB module, the suitable Web components have now been added with the Web module. At this point, only the components for a Java EE overall application need to be combined. The Developer Studio provides a special project type for this purpose. It is referred to as an enterprise application project.

To create the employee overall application, first create an enterprise application project named "EmployeeEar". Here you also set up a configuration file for the data source alias before you generate the appropriate EAR for the overall application and finally deploy this on the Java application server.

3.7.1 Creating the Enterprise Application Project

To create the project, proceed as follows:

1. Start the **New Project Wizard** through the menu option **File • New Project**.

2. In the displayed wizard window, select the category **J2EE • Java EE** and finally **Enterprise Application Project 5**.

3. By pressing **Next**, you proceed to the next wizard window. There you enter "EmployeeEar" as the project name. Accept the default settings and proceed to the next wizard window by pressing **Next**.

4. In accordance with the specifications in Figure 3.18, assign the EJB module *EmployeeEjb.jar* and the Web module *EmployeeWeb.war* to the EAR project before you complete the procedure by pressing **Finish**.

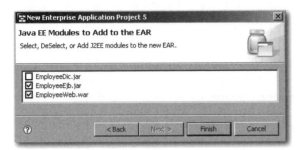

Figure 3.18 Creating the Modules Ejb and Web for the EAR Project

3.7.2   Creating the Data Source Alias

You will remember that you entered a name for the data source alias in the deployment descriptor *persistence.xml*. Such a data source alias has not been created anywhere so far. You will now perform this step. However, before continuing further, we would like to illustrate briefly the importance of the data source alias.

> **Excursion into Database Accesses and the Data Source Alias**
>
> The data source alias is required in order to enable communication to the database for table accesses from the application. A data source alias is a logical name for server-side access to a database resource (in this case, the table). The connection pool on the application server has knowledge of the path to the database table — that is, the actual data source that must already exist on the server.
>
> The default data source (also called system data source) plays a special role here. This data source is automatically created during the installation of the AS Java and is not associated with a specific application. The default data source is intended as a default connection pool for use by several applications.
>
> If you now create the data source alias in the Enterprise Application Project, you will associate it with the default data source. The use of an alias at this point has several advantages:
>
> ▶ The developer does not have to specify the physical path name for the database resource. Only the database system requires this information for managing its own resources.

Data source alias as link between application and database

> ▶ In addition, the alias is assigned in the Developer Studio and assigned to a specific project. Thus, the administrative task that the developer would be required to take on in a separate administration tool is dispensed with.
>
> ▶ Last, the use of a data source alias enables you to keep the entire application portable.

Because a corresponding configuration file for the data source alias is not yet contained in the current project, you will now create this first — starting from the appropriate XML schema.

1. In the **Project Explorer**, select the project and navigate to the folder **META-INF**.

2. From the context menu of this folder, select the menu path **New • Other • XML • XML** and press the button **Next**. On the displayed wizard page, choose the option **Create XML file from an XML schema file** and press **Next**.

3. On the following wizard page, enter "data-source-aliases.xml" as the file name and again choose **Next**.

4. As you can see in Figure 3.19, you decide on the option **Select XML Catalog entry** and then select **data-source-aliases.xsd** from the displayed XML catalog.

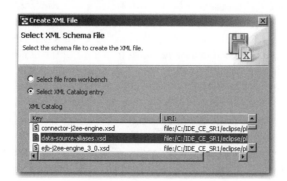

Figure 3.19 Creating a Data Source Alias for the EAR Project

5. On the following wizard page, select **data-source-aliases** for the **Root element** and confirm this by pressing **Finish**. With this step, the XML file named *data-source-aliases.xml* is created. It is then visible in the project structure.

6. Now open the XML editor and enter the system data source "${com.sap.datasource.default}" and the name "TMP_EMPLOYEES_DATA" for the alias.

The alias name is assigned to the system data source at deployment. You can easily follow this by looking at the generated XML source. It matches the lines shown in Listing 3.17.

```
<?xml version="1.0" encoding="UTF-8"?>
<data-source-aliases [...]>
  <aliases>
    <data-source-name>
      ${com.sap.datasource.default}
    </data-source-name>
    <alias>TMP_EMPLOYEES_DATA</alias>
  </aliases>
</data-source-aliases>
```

Listing 3.17 com.sap.datasource.default as Representation of the System Data Source on the AS Java

3.7.3 Deployment of the Employee Application

Before the deployment of the application starts, you should check that the server process was started and that the database is online. The prerequisite for this, however, is that the AS Java has been registered in the Developer Studio.

Preparations for deployment

As shown in Figure 3.20, two different options are provided on the **Preferences** page. Depending on whether the assigned AS Java was installed on the local host or under an arbitrary address in the LAN, you must distinguish between the option for the remote installation and the option for local installation. The required entries are contained in the system information, which you will find on the server welcome page.

Deploying the Dictionary Table Definitions

To be able to transfer the table definitions from the Dictionary project to a database instance, you need an archive file. This kind of Dictionary archive represents a transportable unit of the Dictionary project and combines all the Dictionary definitions of the project from the generated metadata. Only when the created archive is deployed on the application server is the physical representation of the corresponding table generated on the database instance on the assigned database using CRE- ATE TABLE.

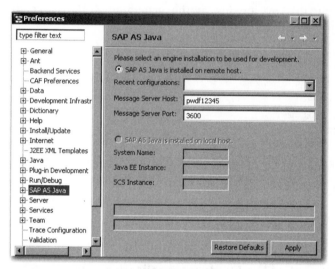

Figure 3.20 Registering the Application Server Java Under Preferences

1. To create the archive, choose the project node in the Dictionary Explorer, open the context menu, and select the option **Create Archive**.

2. Afterward, choose **Deploy** from the context menu of the project node (Figure 3.21).

Figure 3.21 Deploying the Table from the Dictionary Project

3. From the **Deploy View Console** (Figure 3.22), you immediately get a report as to whether or not the deployment activity was successful. From this view, you can also look at the corresponding log file.

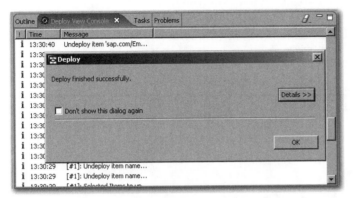

Figure 3.22 Displaying the Deploy Output View After Successful Deployment

4. If you are implementing the MaxDB as a database system and have installed the SQL studio, you can now easily check that both tables have been correctly created on the database instance. For this purpose, you need only to log on to the database server through the SQL Studio and to search for TMP_EMPLOYEES and TMP_ID_GEN in the list of all currently deployed tables on the server. If you have knowledge of SQL, you can also create some data records for the new employee table in the SQL Studio.

SQL Studio

Creating and Deploying the Enterprise Application Archives

The Enterprise Application Archive groups the JAR and WAR archives into one single archive with information from the corresponding deployment descriptors. The EAR contains, in addition to the business logic components, the presentation components. It can be easily created and deployed in one step from the Developer Studio using the Servers view.

1. Open the **Servers** view. The entry **SAP Server** should already be displayed here.

2. From the context menu, choose the option **Add and Remove Projects**. As shown in Figure 3.23, select the EAR project and confirm with **Fin-**

ish. Thus, in one single step you have added the deployable projects to the Servers view, generated the respective archives WAR, JAR, and EAR (and added them to the project view in the Project Explorer), and immediately triggered the deployment.

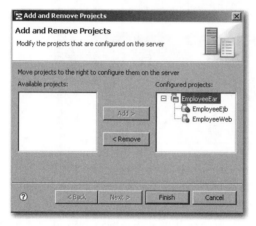

Figure 3.23 EAR Deployment Using the Servers View

3. If your deployment activity has been successful, you will receive the message "Deployment finished successfully".

3.7.4   Starting the Employee Application

Provided the server is called **localhost** and can be reached under the port **50100**, you can start the employee application with the URL *http://localhost:50100/EmployeeWeb/index.jsp* (Figure 3.24).

Figure 3.24 Starting the Employee Application in the Browser

With JDBC and JPA, Java developers have two standards available for persisting data and objects. This chapter focuses on their implementation and their interaction with the SAP persistence infrastructure in the SAP NetWeaver Composition Environment. However, this underlying infrastructure is first introduced.

4   Java Persistence

In Java, Java Database Connectivity (JDBC) is the standard for dynamic database queries on which object-relational persistence frameworks such as the Java Persistence API (JPA) are based. Strings are dynamically generated at runtime, are forwarded to the database by statements, interpreted there, and answered in the form of ResultSets. JDBC defines only the programming interface, not the content or the syntax of the SQL strings.

This can, of course, be used to utilize special properties of the underlying database system, but has the disadvantage that an application cannot be ported to another database without significant effort. For projects in which you know which database system is going to be used, this makes sense. However, developers often do not know the databases on which their application will later run. The partially-different SQL syntax of the database vendors also causes additional programming and testing effort.

4.1   Open JDBC for Java

As part of the SAP NetWeaver Composition Environment infrastructure, Open JDBC for Java allows developers to write database-independent code. The Open SQL grammar is available for this purpose. It is based on ISO Standard SQL-92 (ISO/IEC 9075, third revision) and contains extensions that allow the use of internal and external joins and the specifica-

Database-independent programming with Open JDBC

tion of dynamic parameters. Statements created with Open SQL can be executed by all supported databases, once they have been converted database-specifically by the Open SQL runtime.

The reduction to SQL that can be understood by all databases initially seems like a restriction. However, with the auxiliary class `com.sap.sql.NativeSQLAccess`, you can use any SQL in exceptional cases. However, a small downside remains: Open SQL for Java is not completely JDBC-compatible. The Java API is restricted to classes and methods that are supported by all databases.

Features In addition to the portability between different database systems, Open JDBC provides additional functions:

▶ Syntax checks of the SQL queries against the Open SQL grammar at runtime

▶ Type security of the SQL queries at runtime for tables that were defined using the Java Dictionary (see Chapter 2, *Overview of the SAP NetWeaver Developer Studio*)

▶ Table buffering

▶ SQL trace

▶ Statement pooling

The last four points will be detailed later in this chapter.

4.2 Persistence Infrastructure of the SAP NetWeaver Composition Environment at Runtime

The persistence infrastructure of Open JDBC consists of three layers one above the other. Each successive layer represents a higher abstraction from the underlying database (Figure 4.1). A general overview of the uppermost layer, Open JDBC, was given previously. We will now consider the layer below this, Vendor JDBC and Native JDBC, in more detail.

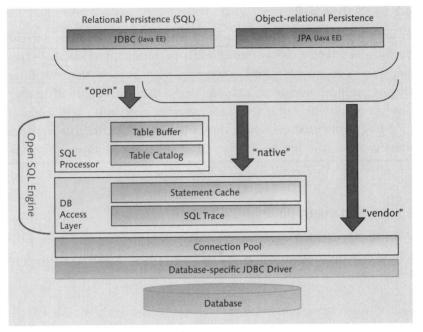

Figure 4.1 Three layers of Open JDBC for Java

4.2.1 Vendor JDBC

The lowest level is known as Vendor JDBC and contains the JDBC implementation of the database vendor. Only the database connections are encapsulated using the JDBC pool. This encapsulation is standard with all Java EE servers and is done primarily for two reasons: Databases can only keep a limited number of connections open, and creating a database connection costs time.

The JDBC drivers are extensively tested for the databases supported by the SAP NetWeaver Composition Environment, but in principle, any databases could be connected using their JDBC drivers. This can be necessary for applications that, for example, need to access data that already exists. These databases should only be accessed using the JDBC API, and not using object-relational mechanisms.

4.2.2 Native JDBC

As with Vendor JDBC, the SQL queries are forwarded unchanged to the database. Therefore, no syntax check is performed, and database-specific queries are possible. From a technical point of view, Native JDBC is simply an encapsulation of the database's JDBC driver, which passes through everything, but if necessary can write statement traces, and can hold frequently-used queries in the cache. Therefore, the same restrictions apply as for the underlying layer regarding connecting unsupported databases and using object-relational persistence.

4.2.3 Statement Pooling

Improving performance

With static database queries, prepared statements offer a way to improve performance. Listing 4.1 shows how this looks in the Java source code:

```
public void findEmployeeByName(Connection con, String name)
        throws SQLException
{
    String sql ="Select * from PER_EMPLOYEE where NAME = ?";
    PreparedStatement ps = con.prepareStatement(sql);
    ps.setString(1, name);
    ResultSet rs = ps.executeQuery();
    ...
    ps.close();
}
```

Listing 4.1 Prepared Statement

When the method prepareStatement(String sql) is called, the SQL query is forwarded to the database. It is analyzed there, and an optimal query execution plan is determined. This is usually a time-intensive operation. As long as the prepared statement is not closed, the method executeQuery() can be called any number of times without the database needing to analyze and plan again. With Native JDBC, the statement is not closed but rather passed to a pool. There is a pool of this type for each database connection. Because the connections are not released, the query can be used again later, reducing the load on the database. Because prepared statements are intensively used in the implementations of the JPA, significant performance improvements can be achieved in this way.

4.2.4 SQL Monitor

Because of the Native JDBC layer, the SQL trace can be activated if required. The trace is administered and analyzed through the browser, with the SAP NetWeaver Administrator (*http://<hostname>:<port>/nwa*), using the path **Problem Management** · **Database** · **Open SQL Monitors**, and this can only be done by a user with administrator authorizations. The application allows the activation and deactivation of the trace, and the deletion and analysis of existing files. For the analysis, you can set a filter on the database accesses to be displayed. This filter covers the session, the application, the user, and the date of the access. This allows you, for example, to filter out all SQL queries for the user **Guest** in the application *sap.com/PersistenceEAR* that took place on 11.07.2007 between 10:00 o'clock and 11:00 o'clock. You can view every query in detail, for example, also the parameters connected to a statement (Figure 4.2).

Browser-based analysis of the database queries

Record Details	
Time	11.07.2007 11:45:23,307
Duration in Microseconds	651
Method Name	com.sap.sql.jdbc.direct.DirectPreparedStatement.executeUpdate()
Statement	INSERT INTO "PER_PROJECT" ("ID", "DESCRIPTION", "CREATEDAT", "NAME") VALUES (?, ?, ?, ?)
SQL Statement Bind Parameters	Parameter 1 = 103 Parameter 2 = project3 Parameter 3 = 2007-07-11 11:45:24.297 Parameter 4 = project3
Result	1
Database Id	SAPCE1DB?SAPCE1DB
J2EE User	Guest
J2EE Session	306
Table Names	Table 1 = PER_PROJECT
Thread	HTTP Worker [2]
DB Session Id	2488@T38
Vendor SQL Connection Id	13297043
Vendor SQL Statement Id	30252983
DSR Transaction Id	728f63902f9311dcad65001558c33632
Unique Log Record Id	001558C33632001D000007CB000013F802356FFE5632517B

Figure 4.2 SQL trace details

The trace files can grow to a maximum size of 10 MB, and a maximum of five trace files can be created for each trace. This means that a trace can grow to up to 50 MB in size. If the fifth file reaches its maximum size, the first file is overwritten. You can change these settings in the **Log Configurator** of the server using the SAP NetWeaver Administrator (**Configuration Management · Infrastructure · Log Configuration**).

4.2.5   Table Buffering

Local cache for tables

The table buffer is a local cache that is created on every server node of the SAP NetWeaver Application Server. The data that is placed in this cache is defined at Design Time using the Java Dictionary. This can be entire tables, but also only parts of tables, which are defined using areas of the key fields.

Buffering is transparent for application programmers. The programmer's SQL query is analyzed in the Open SQL layer. If the table to which the query relates is contained in the buffer, no additional database communication is required. This only applies, however, for queries that relate to one table. Select queries that relate to multiple tables are always evaluated in the database.

Because buffering is active on all server nodes of a cluster, an invalidation mechanism ensures the consistency of the data. If buffered data changes, the data in the corresponding key areas on the other nodes is invalidated and, if necessary, reloaded from the database. This function should, therefore, only be used for tables for which write accesses are very rare.

4.2.6   Administration of Data Sources

You can administer data sources using SAP NetWeaver Administrator. To do so, choose **Configuration Management · Infrastructure · Application Resources** to display the overview of all existing resources (Figure 4.3).

To include a new database, you first need to add the associated JDBC driver to the list of all drivers. To create a new pool, you require a name, under which the pool is stored in the Java Naming and Directory Interface (JNDI), and the driver class, the connection parameters, the database user, and the password. If the data source supports distributed transactions, Java Database Connectivity Version 2.0 is used. In this case, the driver class expects parameters in the form of name/value pairs; you can maintain these on the **Additional Properties** tab page.

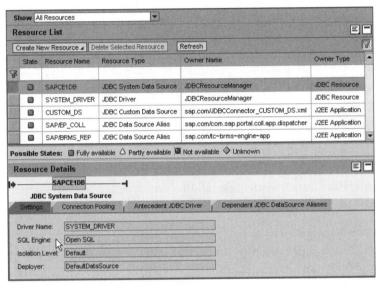

Figure 4.3 Administration of Database Connections in SAP NetWeaver Administrator

On the **Connection Pooling** tab page, you can, among other things, set the maximum number of connections that this data source provides. You can use the **Settings** tab page to determine which access layer is to be used, that is, Vendor JDBC, Native JDBC, or Open JDBC.

The SAP NetWeaver Composition Environment is installed with its own default database (system database), which holds the configuration data for the server. There is a default data source (system data source) for this database, for which the connection parameters cannot be changed. Open JDBC is, however, only possible for the default database. The reason for this restriction is that the Java Dictionary in the SAP NetWeaver Composition Environment can only be used for the system database and Open JDBC requires the metadata stored in the Java Dictionary. You can also create multiple aliases for a data source, with which it can be called in the JNDI. This compensates for a weakness of the Java EE 5 specifica-

System database and system data source

tion. According to the specification, the *lookup* path is specified in the deployment descriptor of the Web or Enterprise JavaBeans archive and must be adjusted before deployment. By defining an alias, the application can be deployed without changes to the descriptor.

4.3 Java Dictionary

The metadata for data types and tables that is used by Web Dynpro and the persistence layer at runtime is defined in the Java Dictionary, which was already described in Chapter 2, *Overview of the SAP NetWeaver Developer Studio*. The focus here is on the metadata that is relevant for persistence; that is, the table structures.

Benefits The first question that occurs in this context is about the benefits. Why should you make the effort to maintain metadata? The answers to this question are software logistics, portability, and type security at runtime and at design time.

- ▶ **Software logistics**
  An application does not run just on one database. During a development process, an application runs on developer databases, test databases, and finally on the productive database. Changes in the database schema must be transported through this landscape together with the software. This means that versioning must be possible for the metadata.

- ▶ **Portability**
  The description of database structures and data types in XML makes the maintenance of SQL scripts for each database type unnecessary. The deploy controller performs the creation, change, or deletion using the metadata.

- ▶ **Type security at runtime**
  Open JDBC for Java can map the JDBC data types to the corresponding types of the underlying database using the Java Dictionary table descriptions. A test of the data type compatibility is not possible for JDBC, because it is usually not possible to clearly locate the queries in the source code, and the queries must also not be static.

Only embedded or simple data types can be used to define database tables; the mapping of structured types is not supported in Developer Studio. Of the information that you can maintain for simple data types, only the database default value and the specification of whether null is permitted as a value are taken into account in the persistence layer. While the additional benefits of self-defined data types apply to Web Dynpro development, they are of less importance for persistence.

Definition of database tables in SAP NetWeaver Developer Studio

The Developer Studio has its own **Dictionary** perspective and the associated project type for the definition of database objects. The central view is the **Dictionary Explorer**, which maps the logical structure of the project (Figure 4.4). You can pack and deploy the metadata as XML files in an archive using the context menu for the project node. This means that the tables are created in the configuration database of the server, or tables that already exist are adjusted. The metadata is also stored in the database and is therefore available to the Open JDBC layer at runtime. The developer can also deploy individual tables using the context menu for the relevant table node, and can also create new tables, or delete tables.

Definition of database objects

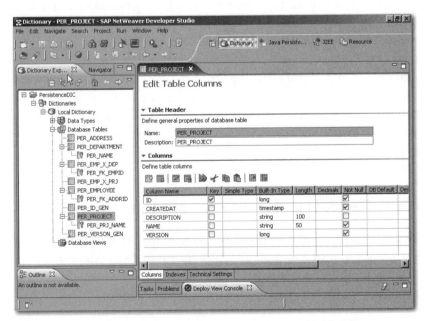

Figure 4.4 Dictionary Perspective with Dictionary Explorer and Table Editor

Metadata for a
table column
The metadata for the tables is maintained in the table editor. This has
three tab pages, one each for the definition of columns, indexes, and
buffer granularity (tab name: **Technical Settings**). The description of a
column consists of the following information:

- Name of the column

- Specification of whether the column is part of the primary key

- Data type; this can be a self-defined simple data type or one of the
  predefined types `binary`, `date`, `decimal`, `double`, `float`, `integer`, `long`,
  `short`, `string`, `time`, or `timestamp`

- Depending on the data type, the length of the number of decimal
  places

- Specification of whether `null` is permitted as a value

- Short description

- Default value for the database

If you activate table buffering for a table, you can also set the granularity
of the buffer. You can choose whether to cache the entire table, areas of
the table, or individual rows; that is, a row is only placed in buffer only
when it is read from the database. You can select table areas if the primary key is made up of more than one column. The granularity is specified by a number that is at least 1 and is smaller than the number of columns of the key. If you select the first n columns and read a data record
a `SELECT` statement reads all data records that are identical in the first n
primary key columns into the buffer. Complete buffering and single
buffering, therefore, only occur in the extreme cases $n = 0$ or $n = number$
$of key fields.$

4.4   Development of an Example Application

By getting to this point, and getting to know the theoretical side of the
persistence infrastructure of the SAP NetWeaver Composition Environment, you will now learn how to develop with the SAP NetWeaver
Developer Studio using an EJB 3.0 example application.

4.4.1 Project Management Scenario

The application is to represent a simple project management scenario. You consider employees who have an address, belong to a department, and can be involved in one or more projects, that is, you implement the four persistent classes `Employee`, `Department`, `Address`, and `Project` and the relations between them. Figure 4.5 shows the classes, their attributes, and the relations between them.

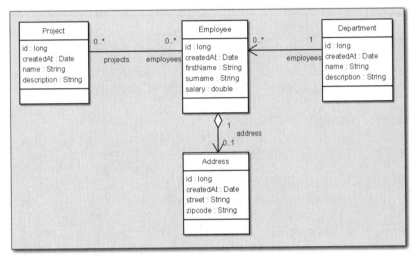

Figure 4.5 Persistent Classes of the Example Application

You implement the application logic as methods of a stateless session bean. This has the advantage that, with a few mouse clicks, you can expose the function as a Web service and test it with the Web Service Navigator. Because both the parameters and the return values must be serializable for a Web service, use Data Transfer Objects (DTO).[1]

To keep the example simple, do not correctly follow the pattern definition from the J2EE Pattern Catalog from the Sun Web page *http://java.sun.com/blueprints/corej2eepatterns/Patterns/TransferObject.html*, but rather forgo the interfaces and use the DTOs in the session bean interface.

---

1 If this surprises you in EJB 3.0 and JPA — when the keyword is "detached entity" — you can find out more about this at the end of section 4.5.4, *Programming the Application Logic*.

The methods of the session bean are to demonstrate the basic operations with persistent objects as an example. The business interface `Project-ManagementLocal` has the methods shown in Listing 4.2.

```
public long createEmployee(String firstName, String surname,
                           double salary,
                           String departmentName);
public long createDepartment(String name,
        String description);
public long createProject(String name,
        String description);
public void assignProjectToEmployee(long employeeId,
        String projectName);
public long assignAddressToEmployee(long employeeId,
        String street, String zipCode, String
        city);
public List<EmployeeDTO> findAllEmployeesInProject(
                        String projectName);
public List<ProjectDTO> findAllProjectsOfDepartment(
                        String departmentName);
public List <DepartmentDTO>
        findInvolvedDepartmentsOfProject(
        String projectName);
public List<EmployeeDTO> findEmployeesByLastName(
                        String lastName);
public double getOverallSalaryOfDepartment(
        String departmentName);
public DepartmentDTO findDepartmentByName(
                        String departmentName);

public ProjectDTO findProjectByName(String projectName);
public void increaseProjectMembersSalary(
        String projectName,
        int percent);
```

Listing 4.2 Business Interface ProjectManagementLocal

After defining the structure and functionality of the application, divide the rest of the procedure into four steps:

1. Definition and deployment of the required tables
2. Implementation of auxiliary classes; in this case, the data transfer objects

3. Implementation of the persistent objects and the session bean

4. Definition of the Web service and deployment of the application

Step 1 takes place in a separate Dictionary project, while steps 2 to 4 take place in a common EJB 3.0 project.

4.4.2 Implementing the Example Scenario in EJB 3.0 and JPA

Before the actual implementation of the example scenario, here a few thoughts about the aims: A realistic example scenario has been chosen, so that it is easy for you to understand the new possibilities offered by the object-relational persistence with JPA, and to use them in your own projects. The example also shows what you need to consider to avoid a design that is unfavorable for precisely these new possibilities.

Another key focus is on the interaction between JPA as a standard for object-relational mapping and Open JDBC as SAP's own implementation of the database connection and abstraction. Again, the possibilities that result, and points that may need to be considered are highlighted.

JPA and Open JDBC

Because SAP is taking a leading role in the support of open standards with the SAP NetWeaver Composition Environment, with the implementations of the current Java EE 5 runtime, it is obvious to underpin this standard with the use of the Web Tools Platform (WTP) in the Eclipse-based SAP NetWeaver Developer Studio; especially because with JPA there is no longer a need for proprietary object-relational mapping.

JPA is supported during design time in the SAP NetWeaver Developer Studio by the WTP subproject *Dali* Version 0.5, which in this version only partially allows forward mapping (scripts to create database tables are generated from the JPA entities by naming convention) and backward mapping (JPA entities are generated from table descriptions). Because tables are generated using the Java Dictionary in Open JDBC, and in more complex applications the table descriptions follow their own rules,[2] the tables should be created with the Java Dictionary here.

Dali and the Java Dictionary

---

2 They have, for example, their own name range that is not to be reflected in the class name.

This version of Dali is not yet able to work directly with the Java Dictionary. In a future version of SAP NetWeaver CE, a higher WTP and Dali version will also allow a direct connection to the Java Dictionary.

The following examples, therefore, show how you can nevertheless find an advantage by using Java Dictionary and Dali together.

Definition and Deployment of the Tables

You have already found out how to create a Dictionary project and tables, and how to deploy the project in the paragraph on *Definition of database tables in SAP NetWeaver Developer Studio* in Section 4.3. You now need to consider how the tables should look. You require a table for every persistent class, that is, you generate the tables PER_EMPLOYEE, PER_ADDRESS, PER_DEPARTMENT, and PER_PROJECT.

The mapping of the attributes in the data model is also simple. The table for the employees has, for example, the columns ID (built-in type long), CREATEDAT (timestamp), FIRSTNAME (string), SURNAME (string), SALARY (double), and VERSION (long),[3] where the first of these is the primary key. You represent the unique association of an address to an employee with the column FK_ADDRID (long) in the employee table, which is to hold the foreign key of the address. The m:n relation between employees and projects requires a two-column join table PER_EMP_X_PRJ, in which employees and projects are connected to each other using their keys. In this table, the two columns together form the primary key. You also model the unidirectional 1:n relationship between the department and its employees using a two-column join table, PER_EMP_DEP, which creates the assignment using the keys of employees and departments. In this case, too, the two columns together form the primary key. To express at table level that an employee can only be assigned to one department, on the **Indexes** tab page, add a unique index for the employees' keys for table PER_EMP_DEP.

The names of projects and departments should be unique. If you have looked closely at the session bean method, you will certainly have

---

3 The column VERSION was deliberately not mentioned when presenting the classes and attributes of the project management scenario. It will be discussed later, but to avoid another iteration of the Dictionary project, it is also created now.

noticed that some of the methods will otherwise not produce sensible results, such as findAllEmployeesInProject (String projectName). To ensure the uniqueness, it is sufficient to define a unique index for the respective table columns on the **Indexes** tab page.

You can, of course, also choose the name as a key. However, the renaming of a project, for example from "C42" to "CE," would then affect not only the data record in the project table, but also the foreign key in the join table.

Once you have declared the tables, deploy the archive of the Dictionary project. The precise background is explained in Section 4.5.2, *Preparing the EJB 3.0 Project.*

Implementing the Auxiliary Classes

Create an EJB 3.0 project for the four Data Transfer Objects, in which you will later also set up the session bean and the entities. Listing 4.3 shows the implementation of the class ProjectDTO:

```
package com.sap.examples.persistence.dto;

import java.io.Serializable;

public class ProjectDTO  implements Serializable{

    long id;
    String name;
    String description;

    public ProjectDTO(long id, String name,
                            String description) {
       this.id = id;
       this.name = name;
       this.description = description;
    }
     public ProjectDTO() {
     }
     // getter only:
     public long getId() {
         return id;
```

Implementing the
ProjectDTO class

```
    }

    public String getName() {
        return name;
    }

    public void setName(String name) {
        this.name = name;
    }

    // more getters and setters...
}
```
Listing 4.3 Implementing the ProjectDTO class

Caution with references in Data Transfer Objects The class does not have an attribute for the relation to the employees, but there is no reason not to include the list of employees in the object. However, you should consider a decision of this type carefully. If you can navigate from the projects to the employees and from the employees back to the projects in the DTOs, in unfavorable cases, all employees and projects could indirectly be attached to a project. An incomplete selection of possible strategies for this problem is listed below:

▸ A project can contain a list of the keys of employees.

▸ Different DTOs can be implemented, for example: `ProjectDTO` and `ProjectDTOWithEmployees`.

▸ The DTOs permit all navigation using references, but they are only actually created to a particular depth. This requires exhaustive documentation, and is only of limited suitability for published interfaces.

Implementing the Session Bean and Deploying the Application

You have already learned about working with Enterprise JavaBeans in the SAP NetWeaver Developer Studio in Chapter 3, *SAP NetWeaver Developer Studio — Step-by-Step to a Sample Application*. You, therefore, know how to create a stateless session bean and its business methods. For information about the definition of a Web service and the deployment of the application, refer to the other chapters. The implementation of the business methods themselves is described in the following sections.

4.5 Programming with Enterprise JavaBeans 3.0/Java Persistence API

The following presents the implementation of the application using EJB 3.0 and JPA, that is the description of persistent objects and working with them. To help you understand the JPA, we provide a short introduction to explain the basic principles of this programming model here.

If you want to obtain detailed knowledge about the JPA, we recommend, for example, the JPA specification (JSR 220) or the book *Pro EJB 3: Java Persistence API* by Mike Keith and Merrick Schincariol. More detailed descriptions of the SAP implementation of the JPA are available both at *http://sdn.sap.com/ce* and in the documentation for SAP NetWeaver Developer Studio or in the SAP Online Help at *http://help.sap.com*.

4.5.1 Basic Concepts

In short, the JPA provides a developer a transparent and simple way to work with persistent objects. In the simplest case, it is sufficient to write simple Java classes, and to annotate them as persistable[4] objects, known as entities.

JPA entities

If you have previously worked with container-managed persistence entity beans, this may seem a contentious assertion, and a developer familiar with Java Data Objects will also perceive this as a simplification, because no bytecode modifications are requested.

The entity manager is the central point of access to the entities. It creates persistent objects in the database from simple, persistable main memory objects, and enables the loading of persistent objects into main memory or the querying of them using the Java Persistence Query Language (JPQL).

Entity manager

An important property of the entity is that it has an identifier (ID) that makes it identifiable throughout its life cycle in main memory or indicates different main memory instances of the same persistent database object.

---

4 This does not necessarily mean that they are actually persisted.

If persistence is an issue, transactionality also comes into play, of course. Entities are normally generated, changed, or deleted within transactions, that is, their status is reconciled with the database. The law of gravity still applies to entities: They are and remain ordinary Java objects, which do not suddenly change their values due to database processes.

JPA annotations — Unlike EJB 2.1, the mapping of persistent objects, their attributes, and relations to database structures has now been standardized and is, as usual with Java EE 5, expressed using annotations. The principle of *configuration by exception* also applies here: If nothing is annotated, default values are used, which are sufficient for a quick start, meaning that the developer only needs to deal with the annotations when the default values no longer meet the increasing requirements and complexity of the application. As neat as this concept seems, its difficulty is also obvious. Unfortunately, the application developer does not *see* the default values, which does not release her or him from knowing them or the behavior achieved with them.

In this example application, the most important annotations (for relationships) are presented, partly to make them explicit for explanatory reasons, and also because the naming of the persistent objects and attributes should not be linked to the names of the database tables and their columns by naming convention.

4.5.2   Preparing the EJB 3.0 Project

Persistence unit — Before programming the entities of the project management scenario, you still need to define the persistence unit. The persistence unit defines the set of all entities that can be addressed using the entity manager at runtime in an application. It must also be mapped in the same database. All of this is stored in a file called *persistence.xml*. However, the file ultimately remains largely empty.

Declaration of the runtime data source — In addition to the name of the persistence unit, you declare the Java Transaction API (JTA) data source, which defines, among other things, the database schema in which the entities of the persistence unit are persisted. The set of all entities is declared here using configuration by exception, that is, all classes of this project annotated as entities are part of the persistence unit (as long as all the entities that are not listed in the file *persistence.xml* are not explicitly excluded).

You also need to enable the EJB 3.0 project to see the existing database tables, so that it can elegantly browse them when mapping the entities to the table structures at design time.

As explained in Section 4.4.2, *Implementing the Example Scenario in EJB 3.0 and JPA*, it will only be possible to use the table declarations stored in the Dictionary project in a future version of the SAP NetWeaver Composition Environment. However, you can easily bypass this weakness with a small trick. You have already deployed the archive of the Dictionary project, that is, physically created the tables. When deploying the Dictionary archive that contains the table declarations, Open JDBC uses the system data source of the server to physically create the described tables in its database schema. All table description metadata of the Java Dictionary is also stored in a separate table there. We will now exceptionally bypass the Open JDBC layer for read-only purposes and configure the EJB 3.0 project to work with the tables already created by Open JDBC:

Declaration of the design time database connection

1. Switch to the Java Persistence Perspective, and use the Database Explorer to create a new database connection. This is to point to the server's database schema (system database), in which you previously set up the tables created with the Java Dictionary through deployment (see *Definition and Deployment of the Tables* in Section 4.4.2).

> **Note**
>
> This database connection only exists in the development environment. This is not a data source that is available to the application at runtime.

2. In the **Database Explorer** view, choose **Connections,** right-click, and choose **New Connections....**
3. You can enter any name for the database connection. The database must be the system database of the server itself. Choose the JDBC driver class and its path and URL appropriate for your installation. You also need to enter the database user ID and its password. Figure 4.6 shows this dialog step.

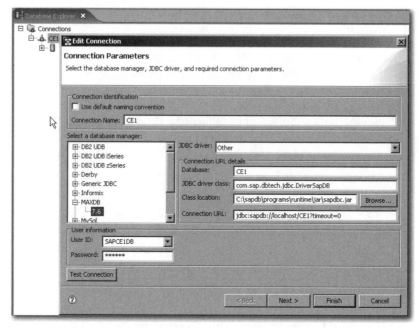

Figure 4.6 Including the Server Database Schema at Design Time

Table 4.1 shows the respective values for a default installation with the default instance name (CE1) and SAP MaxDB as the server's database. You do not need to define the filter offered in the second dialog step.

Connection Property	Value
Connection Name	CE1
Database Manager[5]	MAXDB 7.6
Database	CE1
JDBC Driver Class	com.sap.dbtech.jdbc.DriverSapDB
Class location	C:\sapdb\programs\runtime\jar\sapdbc.jar
Connection URL	jdbc:sapdb://localhost/CE1?timeout=0

Table 4.1 Parameters of the Design Time Database Connection

---

5 This parameter is important if tables are not created with the Java Dictionary, but with Dali using database-specific scripts to create the tables from the entities.

Connection Property	Value
User ID	**SAPCE1DB**
Password	**<your password>**

Table 4.1 Parameters of the Design Time Database Connection (cont.)

For EJB 3.0 projects, the declaration of the database connection that you have just created for mapping the entities at design time and the generation of *persistence.xml* with the persistence information for runtime are combined into a single step in the SAP NetWeaver Developer Studio:

1. In the EJB 3.0 project, right-click and choose **Java Persistence** • **Add Java Persistence....**
2. You now need to select the CE1 database connection and the **SAPCE1DB** schema, and to assign the name for the persistence unit (PersistenceSamplesPU) (Figure 4.7).

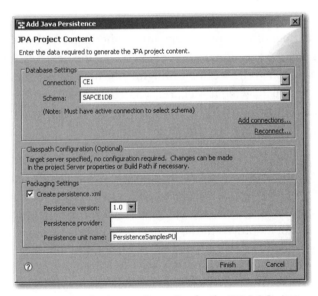

Figure 4.7 Java Persistence Properties for the EJB 3.0 Project

3. You can find the generated *persistence.xml* in the *META INF* directory of the EJB 3.0 project, and you need to add the declaration of the JTA data source (PROJECTMANAGEMENT_DS) used at runtime to it (Figure 4.8).

Figure 4.8 Persistence Unit

4.5.3 Implementing the Entities

If you recall the UML diagram of the project management scenario from Section 4.4.1, *Project Management Scenario*, you will notice that the modeled classes had a number of attributes in common. These are the ID (id) and the date of creation (createdAt). This property almost invites the use of the inheritance that is possible with JPA for persistent objects.

Inheritance

JPA provides a number of ways of implementing inheritance.[6] However, in this case, it is again a question of not only knowing the new possibilities, but also knowing *how* they can meaningfully be used. When implementing the project management scenario, you could have considered deriving the Manager entity from the Employee entity. In fact, you can find this example in the literature and on the Internet.

Unfortunately, inheritance is possibly an unsuitable approach for modeling these facts, unless the identity of the manager is definitively fixed. It is more realistic to make an existing employee into a manager, or possible to downgrade a manager to an employee. However, it is not possible simply to make an employee into a manager, rather a new object of the type manager needs to be instantiated, the values of the original employee object need to be copied, and finally the employee object needs to be deleted.

The problem becomes clear when you remember that the employee object has relationships with other objects. JPA entities behave like tra-

---

6 The optional TABLE_PER_CLASS strategy is not supported by the SAP JPA implementation in SAP NetWeaver Composition Environment 7.1.

ditional Java objects, that is, the relationships in which the Employee entity is involved must be suitably adjusted. This means, for example, that the Employee entity has to be removed from all of the projects in which it is involved, and the newly-generated Manager entity put in its place. No relationship can be neglected, to avoid an inconsistent database status. However, this is likely, unless the developer involved has internalized the entire domain model.

It is better to express this type of dynamic aspect of a domain model using attributes of the classes involved. In this case, a simple Boolean attribute isManager in the class Employee would be sufficient to express this fact. No other class would be affected by the changing of this attribute value.

> **Basic Rules when Using Inheritance**
>
> The following basic rules apply when using inheritance:
> ▸ Inheritance relationships apply only for *static* facts.
> ▸ *Dynamic* facts are expressed using class attributes.

Considered in more detail, an object that consists only of an ID and a creation date does not really qualify as an entity: Without the additional attributes, there would not really be any point in searching for an object of this type, or in instantiating it; in fact, it is difficult to think of a meaningful name for an object of this type, because it is actually only a set of attributes that are common to all entities in the domain. With transient objects, meta or status information of this type would normally be stored in an abstract superclass, from which concrete classes are then derived.

JPA analogously offers the mechanism of mapped superclasses, which allows precisely this property to be modeled for persistent objects. The attributes id and createdAt are declared, including getter methods, for a class annotated as a mapped superclass called BusinessEntity, and are also stored as database mapping.[7] A separate table does not yet exist for

Mapped superclass

---

7 To avoid overdoing the consideration of the mapped superclass and its properties, take the database mapping as specified. The procedure for database mapping is explained in Section 4.5.3, *Implementing the Entities*.

BusinessEntity; however, its attributes are mapped to the tables of the entities derived from it.

Create BusinessEntity as an abstract Java class in package com.sap.examples.persistence.entities of the EJB 3.0 project (see Listing 4.4).

▶ The attribute id is also identified as such for JPA with the annotation @Id.

▶ The attribute creationDate of type java.util.Date is initialized by processing the constructor with the current date. Because java.util.Date can be mapped to different database types, the @Temporal annotation specifies that Timestamp is a prerequisite at Open JDBC/database level.

```
@MappedSuperclass
public abstract class BusinessEntity {

    @Id
    @Column(name="ID")
    protected long id;

    @Temporal(TemporalType.TIMESTAMP)
    @Column(name="CREATEDAT")
    protected Date creationDate;

    public BusinessEntity() {
        creationDate = new Date();
    }

    public Date getCreationDate() {
        return creationDate;
    }

    public long getId() {
        return id;
    }
}
```

Listing 4.4 Mapped superclass BusinessEntity

The next two sections discuss additional aspects that were rolled out to BusinessEntity.

ID Generation

Instead generating an ID, you use the automatic ID generation function of JPA. The SAP JPA implementation in its current form supports only the TABLE strategy, that is, a separate table is used to generate the ID values. However, this is not created by default in the database schema of the server, and you therefore need to add it to the Dictionary project. Its name should be PER_ID_GEN, and it should have the two columns GEN_KEY and GEN_VALUE. GEN_KEY is the key field of type string and at runtime will receive the fully-qualified class name of the class for which the last-generated key, of type integer, is stored in the column GEN_VALUE (Figure 4.9).

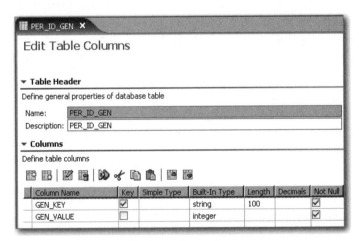

Figure 4.9 Dictionary Table for ID Generation

Once you have rebuilt and deployed the Dictionary project, you need to tell the JPA runtime to use the new table for ID generation. There are two ways to do this:

▶ **Declaration as default in persistence.xml**
  With this approach, you specify the table name as a Persistence Unit Property called com.sap.engine.services.orpersistence.generator.auto.tablename (Figure 4.10).

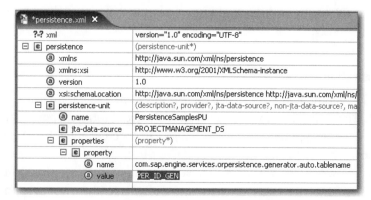

Figure 4.10 ID Generator Table Specification in persistence.xml

▶ **Annotation**

With this approach, a TableGenerator[8] (or potentially several) is declared with name and table (@TableGenerator). The id attribute is assigned the @GeneratedValue annotation, which specifies the respective strategy and the respective generator (Listing 4.5).

Annotation of the
ID generation

```
@MappedSuperclass
@TableGenerator(name="idGen", table="PER_ID_GEN")
public abstract class BusinessEntity {
    @Id
    @GeneratedValue (strategy=TABLE, generator="idGen")
    @Column(name="ID")
    protected long id;
    ...
}
```

Listing 4.5 ID Generation Annotations

Transactional Integrity/Competing Changes

The JPA specification requires the use of the isolation level Read Committed for database access, and does not make any statements about when within a transaction the changes are written to the database.

---

8 Stylistically, it would be more elegant to annotate @TableGenerator for the id attribute. A bug makes it necessary to do this at class level. This is corrected in subsequent versions.

To protect against competing changes in this type of scenario, the JPA specification implicitly requires the use of optimistic locks. When the changes are written to the database, the WHERE clause compares the value of a special column with its before image while the statement's UPDATE clause increments this value. This, therefore, checks whether the version has changed in the meantime, that is, whether a competing write process has changed the entity concerned.

You will now build this versioning mechanism into BusinessEntity. You have already created the VERSION column in the relevant tables of the derived entities in *Definition and Deployment of the Tables* in Section 4.4.2, meaning that you do not need to adjust the Dictionary project again. The VERSION column is also a canonical candidate for BusinessEntity, because it must be an annotated attribute of every entity. However, the version attribute should not be exposed and therefore does not receive any getter or setter methods (Listing 4.6).

Versioning

```
@Version
@Column(name="VERSION")
private long version;
```

Listing 4.6 Annotation of the Versioning

> **Note**
>
> Neither the version nor the id attribute should be changed. Read access is, of course, allowed, if the business logic requires it.

Object-Relational Mapping

With the implementation of BusinessEntity, you have already put in place good preliminary work for the implementation of the Employee, Department, Address, and Project entities. You learned in Chapter 3, *SAP NetWeaver Developer Studio — Step-by-Step to a Sample Application*, how entities without relations are created in the SAP NetWeaver Developer Studio. This chapter, therefore, places the focus on the mapping of the relationships between entities, and shows how to map the entities to tables using Dali.

1. In the J2EE perspective, first create the class `Department`, derived from `BusinessEntity`, in the package `com.sap.examples.persistence.entities` with the missing attributes `name`, `description`, and `employees` and their getter and setter methods. Then annotate this class as an entity.

2. Switch to the Java Persistence Perspective. Assume that the database connection CE1 that you created when preparing the EJB 3.0 project is active, that is, you are still connected to the database.

3. If you are no longer connected to the database, right-click the CE1 database connection in **Database Explorer** and choose **Reconnect...**, enter the **User ID** and **Password**, and choose the **OK** button (Figure 4.11).

Figure 4.11 Database Reconnect for the Java Persistence Perspective

4. Start with the `Department` entity. The **Persistence Outline** view recognizes the `Department` class annotated as an entity, and displays its persistent attributes without taking into account the inheritance hierarchy (Figure 4.12).

Figure 4.12 Persistence Outline of the Department Entity

Persistence properties view

5. In the **Persistence Outline** view, navigate to the `Department` entity. You can specify the associated table `PER_DEPARTMENT` in the **Persis-**

tence Properties here.[9] Dali makes the selection of tables available through the CE1 connection (Figure 4.13).

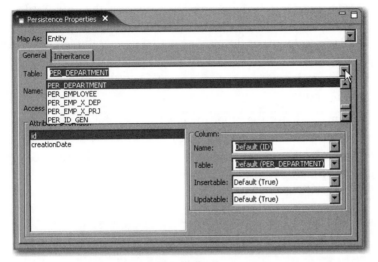

Figure 4.13 Selecting the Table as the Department Entity

The procedure for the persistent attributes and relations is just as elegant. In the **Persistence Outline** view, navigate to the name or description attribute, and follow the same procedure for column selection (NAME, DESCRIPTION) as you did for table selection.

Simple attributes

The **Persistence Properties** view proves to be particularly helpful when specifying the mapping of the relations, because it restricts the selection to the appropriate annotations for the respective cardinalities.

Relations

For example, JPA requires, the use of a join table for the mapping the foreign key relationship of a *unidirectional* 1:n relationship (**Map as: One to Many** in the **Persistence Properties** view),[10] although from experience a simple foreign key column would be expected. In this case, the **Persistence Properties** view only provides the mapping of the foreign key relationship using a join table.

---

9 Because the database schema of the server contains a large number of tables, type a "p" when selecting the table to quickly get to the tables with the prefix "PER."

10 A bidirectional 1:n relation is directly mapped using a foreign key column and does not require a join table.

Join table

1. In the **Persistence Outline** view, navigate to the `employees` attribute.

2. In the **Persistence Properties** view, choose **Map as: One to Many**.

3. After selecting the join table `PER_EMP_X_DEP` on the **Join Table** tab page, choose the **Edit...** button to create the foreign key relationship with the **join column** for the owning `Department` entity.[11] The foreign key column (**Join Column**) is `FK_DEPID`. The column referenced by it (**Referenced Column**) is the `ID` column (table `PER_DEP`) of the owning `Department` entity.

4. In the same way, for the other (inverse) side of the relation, the column `FK_EMPID` of the join table `PER_EMP_X_DEP` is selected as the inverse foreign key column (**Inverse Join Column**) for the `ID` column of the entity table `PER_EMPLOYEE`. The `PER_EMPLOYEE` table is implied by the referenced `Employee` entity (Figure 4.14).

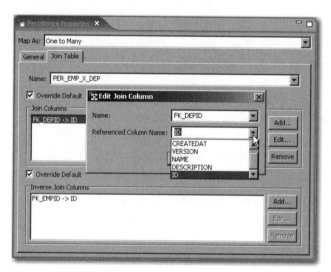

Figure 4.14 Unidirectional 1:n Relation

5. Listing 4.7 shows the annotations of the `employee` attribute of the department that this generates.

---

11 The entity that owns the relation is the one with the table that contains the join column, i.e. the one that determines the updates to the relationship in the database.

```
@OneToMany
@JoinTable(
joinColumns = @JoinColumn(name = "FK_DEPID",
                referencedColumnName = "ID"),
inverseJoinColumns = @JoinColumn(name = "FK_EMPID",
                    referencedColumnName = "ID"),
name = "PER_EMP_X_DEP")
protected List<Employee> employees =
                    new ArrayList<Employee>();
```

Listing 4.7 Annotations of the Employee Attribute

The bidirectional m:n relationship (**Map as: Many to Many** in the **Persistence Properties** view) between Employee and Project requires an annotation on both sides, where the mapping is, of course, performed using a join table.

For the members relation of the Project entity, choose PER_EMPX_PRJ with its columns FK_PRJID and FK_EMPID, and the associated ID columns of the Project and Employee entities (PER_PROJECT and PER_EMPLOYEE tables) to build the join column or the inverse join column (Figure 4.15).

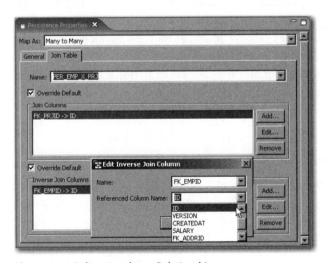

Figure 4.15 Bidirectional m:n Relationship

You do not need to specify the PER_PROJECT or PER_EMPLOYEE table, because it is uniquely determined by the referenced Project or Employee entity (Listing 4.8).

191

```
@ManyToMany
@JoinTable(name="PER_EMP_X_PRJ",
joinColumns = @JoinColumn(name = "FK_PRJID",
                referencedColumnName = "ID"),
inverseJoinColumns = @JoinColumn(name = "FK_EMPID",
                    referencedColumnName = "ID"))
protected List<Employee> members;
```

Listing 4.8 Annotations of the Members Attribute

The Employee entity is inversely annotated in the same way (Listing 4.9).

```
@ManyToMany
@JoinTable(name="PER_EMP_X_PRJ",
joinColumns = @JoinColumn(name = "FK_EMPID",
                referencedColumnName = "ID"),
inverseJoinColumns = @JoinColumn(name = "FK_PRJID",
                    referencedColumnName = "ID"))
protected List<Project> projects;
```

Listing 4.9 Annotations of the Project Attribute

Foreign key column

The unidirectional 1:1 relationship (**Map as: One to One**) between the Employee entity and the Address entity is mapped using a foreign key relationship. Although it is theoretically unimportant which table of the two entities involved contains the foreign key column, the JPA specifies here that you must create it on the side of the relationship on which the unidirectional relation is annotated. In this case, this is the Employee entity, address attribute (Figure 4.16).

1. In the **Package Explorer** view, choose the Employee class.

2. In the **Persistence Outline** view, navigate to the address attribute.

3. In the **Persistence Properties** view, choose **Map as: One to One**.

4. FK_ADDRID (table PER_EMPLOYEE) is the foreign key column (**Join Column**). The column referenced by it (**Referenced Column**), ID, belongs to the table of the Address entity.

5. Listing 4.10 shows the annotation of the address attribute of the Employee entity generated with the **Persistence Properties** view.

```
@OneToOne
@JoinColumn(name="FK_ADDRID", referencedColumnName = "ID")
protected Address address;
```

Listing 4.10 Annotations of the Address Attribute

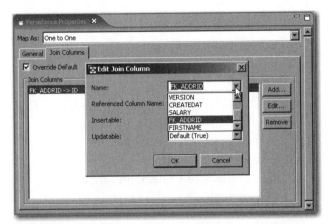

Figure 4.16 Unidirectional 1:1 Relationship

While this section has looked at the detail of the annotation of the relations and the special features to be taken into account in this context, the next section is oriented toward working with the entities, and therefore programming the application logic in the session façade.

4.5.4 Programming the Application Logic

You learned the methods of the stateless session beans in Section 4.4.2, *Implementing the Example Scenario in EJB 3.0 and JPA*. It is best to use the wizard to create the ProjectManagementBean as you learned in Chapter 3, and declare the methods in a separate business interface (Project-ManagementBeanLocal), which is a purely Java interface in EJB 3.0. Because the methods are later exposed through Web services, a local business interface is sufficient (Listing 4.11).

```
@Local
public interface ProjectManagementLocal {
    ...
}
```

Listing 4.11 Local Business Interface

The stateless session bean then simply implements this interface. A home interface is no longer required in EJB 3.0 (Listing 4.12).

```
@Stateless
public class ProjectManagementBean implements
                ProjectManagementLocal {
    ...
}
```

Listing 4.12 Implementation of the Local Business Interface

Entity manager, persistence context, and transactions

The entity manager is the central class for working with entities of the persistence unit. The persistence context contains all entities that the entity manager is currently managing, for which it synchronizes the statuses with the database. The excursus below outlines the connections between the entity manager, persistence context, and transactions, but you do not need to know this to understand the example scenario.

Excursus: Entity Managers, Persistence Contexts, and Transactions

There is a distinction between a container-managed entity manager, which is either injected or looked-up in the JNDI, and an application-managed entity manager, which is generated using the entity manager factory.

There are also two kinds of persistence context. A transaction-scoped persistence context ends when the transaction is completed with which it is associated. However, there is also an extended persistence context, for which the life cycle is not connected to the end of the transaction.

The possible combinations of entity manager and persistence context are linked to the type of transactions used (JTA server transaction or resource-local transaction of the entity manager). Table 4.2 shows all of the possibilities.

	Container-Managed Entity Manager	Application-Managed Entity Manager
Extended Persistence Context	JTA (stateful session bean only)	JTA/resource-local
Transaction-scoped Persistence Context	JTA	Combination not possible

---

Table 4.2 Entity Managers, Persistence Contexts, and Transactions

This example application is supposed to simplify the work for you. Therefore, leave the management of the entity manager life cycle to the container by injecting the entity manager. Leave the administration of the JTA transactions to the server, too. You do not require any additional annotations for this. This corresponds to the situation in Table 4.2 of a container-managed entity manager for a persistence context linked to the JTA transaction (transaction-scoped persistence context). This is the typical EJB 3.0/JPA configuration, with which the requirements of most applications can be covered.

If your application requires more precise resource management, consult the JPA specification, which addresses in detail the cases dealt with here in a very compressed form. Because the presentation there and in all other known publications is somewhat unclear, we hope that this compact table has made it easier to understand this complex material.

Annotate the entity manager as an attribute of the `Project-Management-Bean` and leave everything else to the container:

```
@PersistenceContext
EntityManager em;
```

Injecting an entity manager

For reasons of clarity, the error handling is left out of the following presentation of the session bean. The source code on this book's DVD also does not show any additional error handling. Because the transaction management for all methods of the bean is, by default, `required`, you do not need to make any additional annotations; the server will perform the `Begin`, `Commit`, and `Rollback` for the transactions.

Using the entity manager, you can now write the first object to the database, for example, to create a department (Listing 4.13):

```
public long createDepartment(String name,
  String description) {
  Department department = new Department();
  department.setName(name);
  department.setDescription(description);
  em.persist(department);
  return department.getId();
}
```

Creating a department

Listing 4.13 Persisting a Department Entity Using the Entity Manager

To generate a new department, call the `Department` entity constructor and set the attributes using the setter methods. The call `em.persist(department)` places the previously transient department object under the control of the entity manager, which assigns it to the persistence context allocated to the current transaction. The server's transaction manager takes over the entire transaction handling and ensures that the department object is written to the database during the next commit.

Searching for a department

You now want to find the department again using its name. The table definition ensures a unique name for departments. You use the Java Persistence Query Language (JPQL) for the first time here.

This search is implemented in the `ProjectmanagementBean` as shown in Listing 4.14.

```
public DepartmentDTO findDepartmentByName(String
                    departmentName) {
    Query q = em.createNamedQuery("findDepartmentByName");
    q.setParameter("depName", departmentName);
    Department dep = (Department) q.getSingleResult();
    DepartmentDTO depDTO = new DepartmentDTO(dep.getId(),
        dep.getName(), dep.getDescription());
    return depDTO;
}
```

Listing 4.14 Searching Using Query Interface

1. Use the entity manager's API to generate a named query object, transfer the name of the sought department as a query parameter, and have the result of the query returned, from which you know whether or not there is a department with this name.

2. Then copy the values relevant for the Department Data Access Object. The `DepartmentDTO` object is the return value of the session bean method `findDepartmentByName(String departmentName)`.

Static versus dynamic queries

Advantages of Static Queries

The container can analyze named queries once when the application is started and generate the corresponding SQL. A distinction is therefore made between *static* queries in contrast to *dynamic queries*, which are created and analyzed at runtime, and therefore also have worse runtime behavior.

You should only use these if the query really can only be determined at run-time, for example, due to user input or the application logic.

Because named queries need to be known at an early stage, they are annotated at entity level in the persistence unit and, as can be seen from the example, referenced by name at runtime. It is helpful to annotate named queries for those entities that occur in the result of the query. In accordance with this convention, the named query called findDepartmentByName is annotated in the Department entity (Listing 4.15).

```
@NamedQuery(
        name = "findDepartmentByName",
        query = "SELECT d FROM Department d
                 WHERE d.name LIKE :depName")
```

Listing 4.15 Declaration of the Named Query by Annotation

You require additional methods of this type for the application, such as searching for employees by their last name, creating projects, and searching for projects using their names. These methods are programmed in the same way as the previous method.

You also use the finder query findDepartmentByName when creating an employee (Listing 4.16).

```
public long createEmployee(String firstName,
            String surname, double salary,
            String departmentName) {
  Employee employee = new Employee();
  employee.setFirstName(firstName);
  employee.setSurname(surname);
  employee.setSalary(salary);

  Query q = em.createNamedQuery("findDepartmentByName");
  q.setParameter("depName", departmentName);
  Department dep = (Department) q.getSingleResult();
  dep.setEmployee(employee);
  em.persist(employee);
  return employee.getId();
}
```

Creating an employee

Listing 4.16 Creating an Employee with Department Assignment

A relation is used here for the first time: The newly-generated employee is assigned to the already-persisted department. Through this assignment, the entity manager automatically recognizes that it also needs to store the transient Employee entity. The command em.persist(employee) is therefore actually superfluous. However, you require it for another reason: As you already know, this command places the Employee entity under the control of the entity manager, that is, it is handled as a persistent object. This means that it also receives a unique ID that is automatically generated to be able to make it available as a return parameter of the method.

Creating an address

The assignment of an address to an employee again shows something new. The JPA runtime does not take over the management of the relations. If a new address is created and assigned to the employee, the old address is retained, but is not assigned to an employee any longer. Therefore, check first if the employee already has an address. If so, change the employee's attributes to the new values, otherwise generate a new address and assign it to the employee. JPA entities thus behave like normal Java objects, for which you also need to ensure the consistency of relationships.

Searching for an employee

When searching for a department using its name, you used a query. The search for an object using its key works in a considerably simpler way. If the desired result type and ID of the sought employee are specified, the find method of the entity manager returns the desired employee (Listing 4.17).

```
public long assignAddressToEmployee(long employeeId,
        String street, String zipCode, String city) {
    Employee employee = em.find(Employee.class, employeeId);
    Address address = null;
    if (employee.getAddress() != null) {
        address = employee.getAddress();
    } else {
        address = new Address();
    }
    address.setStreet(street);
    address.setZipcode(zipCode);
    address.setCity(city);
    employee.setAddress(address);
```

```
    em.persist(address);
    return address.getId();
}
```

Listing 4.17 Creating an Address

A bidirectional n:m relationship was defined between employees and projects. You make the assignment of an employee to a project by assigning an additional project to the list of all of the employee's projects (java.util.List).

Maintaining relations

Because you are working on an object-oriented basis, and the relationship is bidirectional, you also need to specify the inversion programmatically, that is, also add the new employee to the list of employees for a project, to keep the object model consistent. Otherwise the JPA does not guarantee the consistency of the object model in main memory with its representation in the database. In the source code, this is expressed as shown in Listing 4.18.

```
public void assignProjectToEmployee(long employeeId,
            String projectName) {
    Employee employee = em.find(Employee.class, employeeId);
    Query nq = em.createNamedQuery("findProjectByName");
    nq.setParameter("projectName", projectName);
    Project project = (Project) nq.getSingleResult();

    List<Project> projects = employee.getProjects();
    List<Employee> members = project.getMembers();
    projects.add(project);
    members.add(employee);
}
```

Assigning an employee to a project

Listing 4.18 Consistent Assignment of Employees and Projects

To remove the relation between project and employee, the last two program lines are replaced by the following dissociation:

```
members.remove(employee);
projects.remove(project);
```

You now perform a query that does not just involve a single object type, but rather stretches across a number of object types — this is known as a *join operation.*

Determining departments

You want to find out all of the departments involved in a particular project. However, this time, the results list is not to be the list of departments but a list of *projections*. This means that the contained data represents only a subset of the attributes of the Department entity. The DepartmentDTO contains, for example, only a subset of all department attributes. If the results list directly contains the DTOs, the subsequent copying of the values from the Department entity to the DepartmentDTO is omitted (Listing 4.19).

```
public List <DepartmentDTO>
findInvolvedDepartmentsOfProject(String projectName) {
    Query nq =
    em.createNamedQuery("findInvolvedDepartmentsOfProject");
    nq.setParameter("projectName", projectName);
    List<DepartmentDTO> departments =
     (List<DepartmentDTO>)nq.getResultList();
    return departments;
}
```

Listing 4.19 Projections as Query Results

With getResultList(), you receive a result set that could contain no objects or potentially more than one object.

The named query used here is shown in Listing 4.20:

▶ The keyword DISTINCT means that projects that are involved in different projects are still included only once.

▶ The NEW operator triggers the constructor expression for instantiating the class DepartmentDTO, which is to receive the results of the SQL ResultSet.

▶ The JOIN operator allows navigation along the object graph of the entities involved and their relations.

```
@NamedQuery(name = "findInvolvedDepartmentsOfProject",
query = "SELECT DISTINCT NEW
com.sap.examples.persistence.dto.DepartmentDTO(d.id,
d.name, d.description)
FROM Department d JOIN d.employees e JOIN e.projects p
WHERE p.name LIKE :projectName")
```

Listing 4.20 Declaration of a Projection

Proceed in the same way for the method findAllProjectsOfDepart-
ment(String departmentName) of the session bean ProjectManagement-
Bean. This is even somewhat simpler, because only the department and
the project are used for navigation in the query.

It would also be interesting to know the total salary of all employees of
a particular department. The ProjectManagementBean contains the query
call (Listing 4.21).

**Determining the
salary of the
department**

```
public double getOverallSalaryOfDepartment(
                String departmentName) {
    Query nq = em.createNamedQuery(
                "getOverallSalaryOfDepartment");
    nq.setParameter("departmentName", departmentName);
    double sum = (Double) nq.getSingleResult();
    return sum;
}
```

Listing 4.21 Determining the Total Salary for a Department

The associated named query getOverallSalaryOfDepartment uses a join
to select all employees of the department to whom the condition of the
WHERE clause, of having a particular department name, applies, and totals
the numerical salary attribute for these employees (Listing 4.22).

```
@NamedQuery(name = "getOverallSalaryOfDepartment",
query = "SELECT SUM(e.salary)
           FROM Department d JOIN d.employees e
           WHERE d.name LIKE :departmentName")
```

Listing 4.22 Aggregation: Example of the Salary for a Department

Query operations, such as totaling, are known as aggregation. The
remaining methods of the session beans are shown later. The functionality implemented until now is sufficient to test the project management
scenario. To do this, you expose the methods of the ProjectManagement-
Bean as a Web service.

At this point, we still need to clarify why Data Transfer Objects are used
when using Web services, instead of accessing the JPA entities directly.

Serialization of
entities
Because the parameters of a Web service call are serialized, an entity serialized here is no longer in the persistence context, that is, it is no longer under the control of the entity manager. An entity in this status is described as *detached*. For example, the loading of the set of employees of a department takes place only when this relation of the department is accessed, and not immediately when the department is loaded. If you have not yet accessed this relation while the department is under the control of the entity manager, the behavior after serialization is not defined, and the loading of the relation fails with an exception.

Using Data Transfer Objects, as they were introduced in *Implementing the Auxiliary Classes* in Section 4.4.2, avoids these difficulties, and therefore you do not need to give further consideration to the rules for working with detached entities.[12] However, there are still a few steps to be performed before deployment.

Creating an Open
SQL data source
Specifically, you still need to create the Open SQL data source with the isolation level **Read Committed** that is a prerequisite in the JPA specification (see Section 4.5.3, *Implementing the Entities*), and to create and deploy an Enterprise Application Archive (EAR) project for the application. You should not use the system data source of the server for two reasons:

▶ It uses the ISO level **Read Uncommitted**.

▶ The server accesses its database schema using database connections of this data source, which leads to situations where the server and applications are competing.

To be protected against competing changes with the ISO level **Read Uncommitted** using versioning, you need to deploy an additional table and direct the JPA runtime to use it to generate a value for the VERSION column of the entities. This table is then addressed using a separate transaction. However, this only solves the problem of protection against competing changes. If you use the system data source, you always need to anticipate Read Uncommitted phenomena. The necessary steps for using JPA with data sources that use the ISO level **Read Uncommitted**

---

12 For example, precautionary navigation using required relations before serialization.

are explained in the documentation for the SAP NetWeaver Developer Studio.

The Read Committed Open SQL data source to be created is to be called CUSTOM_DS with the values shown in Table 4.3 (see also Figure 4.17).

DataSource Property	Value
Driver Name	SYSTEM_DRIVER
SQL Engine	Open SQL
Isolation Level	Transaction Read Committed
Driver Class Name	com.sap.dbtech.jdbc.DriverSapDB
Database URL	jdbc:sapdb://localhost/CE1?timeout=0
User Name	**SAPCE1DB**
Password	**<your password>**

Table 4.3 Parameters of the Data Source CUSTOM_DS

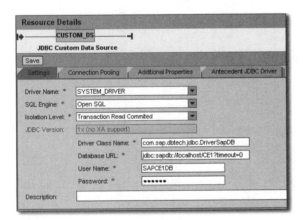

Figure 4.17 Alias for Data Source CUSTOM_DS

Although you are not using the system data source, you are using the database schema of the server, as you can tell from the database URL and the user name. It contains the tables and their metadata that Open JDBC implicitly created during deployment of the Dictionary project (see Section 4.5.2, *Preparing the EJB 3.0 Project*). For this reason, you can only use Open SQL data sources for the database schema of the server.

Section 4.2.6, *Administration of Data Sources*, introduced the term of an alias for a data source. It allows you to switch the data source used without making changes to the application. With this placeholder, the PROJECT MANAGEMENT_DS data source (alias) specified at design time in *persistence.xml* is to be mapped to the CUSTOM_DS data source that has just been created. The alias is deployed directly as part of the application and is specified as an additional descriptor in the EAR project.

You have not yet created the EAR project. Do so now by creating an **Enterprise Application Project 5**, adding the EJB project, and activating the additional Eclipse project facet for creating an alias.

The PROJECTMANAGEMENT_DS alias entry in the *data-source-aliases.xml* of the META-INF directory in the EAR project looks like the one shown in Figure 4.18.

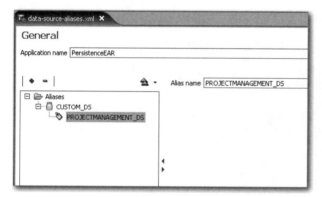

Figure 4.18 Alias for Data Source CUSTOM_DS

Once you have deployed the EAR project, test the application using the Web service interfaces in the Web Service Navigator.

4.5.5 Influence of Open SQL on the JPA Query Language

Because you are already using a method with which you can determine the entire salary of all employees of a department, it would be interesting to be able to affect this value. You can, for example, grant all members of project x a salary increase of y percent.

JPQL provides an expression option that allows the performing of mass changes without loading the employees individually into main memory or needing to leave the object-oriented JPA world.

Mass changes

Implement a method of the type shown in Listing 4.23 in the `Project-ManagementBean`. The familiar instantiation and parameterization of a named query is followed by the calling of the method `executeUpdate()`, with which the write query is performed.

```
public void increaseProjectMembersSalary(String projectName,
  int percent) {
    Query nq =
      em.createNamedQuery("increaseProjectMembersSalary");
    nq.setParameter("percent", percent);
    nq.setParameter("projectName", projectName);
    nq.executeUpdate();
}
```

Listing 4.23 Salary Increase for All Project Participants

However, the implementation of the named query is much more interesting (Listing 4.24).

```
@NamedQuery(name = "increaseProjectMembersSalary",
query = "UPDATE Employee e
SET e.salary = e.salary*(1+(:percent/100))
WHERE EXISTS (SELECT p FROM e.projects p
              WHERE p.name LIKE :projectName)")
```

Listing 4.24 Declaration of a Mass Change

It changes the salary of every employee that fulfills an *existence condition* by `percent` percent. This is, in turn, declared as a subquery. It specifies that the employee must be involved in a project called `projectName`.

If you test this new method, you will, however, determine that Open JDBC steadfastly refuses to execute this query. You have hit a limitation of the Open SQL grammar without noticing it, because you have abstracted away from Open SQL using JPQL: Open SQL forbids the use of parameters in arithmetic expressions.

The excursus below lists all restrictions when using JPQL in connection with Open SQL.

Excursus: JPQL Restrictions in Connection with Open SQL

The following JPQL restrictions apply in connection with Open SQL:

▶ The functions CONCAT, SUBSTRING, TRIM, LOWER, UPPER, LENGTH, and LOCATE are not supported.

▶ The date and time functions CURRENT_DATE, CURRENT_TIME, and CURRENT_TIMESTAMP are not supported.

▶ The arithmetic functions ABS, SQRT, and MOD are not supported.

▶ Input parameters in arithmetic expressions are not supported.

▶ The aggregation function COUNT can only be used together with DISTINCT.

▶ The result of a subquery can only consist of a single persistent field if the subquery is used for IN, ANY, SOME, and ALL.

Switching a data source to Native SQL

Because you certainly do not want to do without the salary increase, disregard the database portability of Open SQL and convert the CUSTOM_DS data source used from Open SQL to **Native SQL** (Figure 4.19), which deactivates the syntax check.[13]

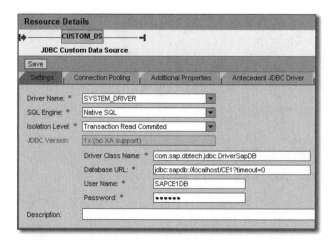

Figure 4.19 Converting the Data Source to Native SQL

---

13 A type of Open JPQL grammar that generated only SQL statements that conform to Open SQL or refused statements that cannot be mapped to Open SQL would be desirable. This would mean that there was a JPA implementation available that was portable across all of the databases supported by SAP.

However, you should not assume that converting the data source to Native SQL removes the influence of the relational world on the object-oriented JPA world. The next section examines this in more detail.

4.5.6 Influence of the Database on the JPA Query Language

This section investigates what it would mean to increase the salaries of all employees of a department x by y percent. The implementation of the session bean method is not repeated here.

At first glance, there do not seem to be any surprises when creating the named query; the task is largely identical to the previous one: The parameter in the arithmetic expression requires the use of Native SQL, two entities are involved in the query again, and so on.

The only difference is that you need to take account of a *unidirectional* 1:n relationship instead of a *bidirectional* m:n relationship.[14] As a result, you *cannot* use the department attribute of the Employee in the EXIST clause to specify that you are searching for an employee whose department has the name x.

Therefore, use two identification variables in the SELECT clause, for the employee and the department, to express that the employee for which you are searching must be contained in the set of employees of the department (Listing 4.25).

```
@NamedQuery(name = "increaseDepartmentMembersSalary",
query = "UPDATE Employee e
SET e.salary = e.salary*(1+(:percent/100))
WHERE EXISTS (SELECT e FROM Employee e, Department d
            WHERE e MEMBER d.employees
            AND d.name LIKE :departmentName)");
```

Listing 4.25 Salary Increase for All Department Members

A test of this named query ends with the following error message:

com.sap.dbtech.jdbc.exceptions.DatabaseException: [-7008]: Updates of this table not allowed.

---

14 Both are mapped using a join table.

This error message points to a problem at the SAP MaxDB level. You can also use the SQL trace with Native SQL to find the SQL statement in question (Listing 4.26).

```
UPDATE "PER_EMPLOYEE" SET "SALARY" =
  1005 WHERE EXISTS (SELECT "E"."ID" FROM "PER_EMPLOYEE"
  "E", "PER_DEPARTMENT" "D" WHERE ("E"."ID") IN (SELECT
  "ALIAS_1"."ID" FROM "PER_EMPLOYEE" "ALIAS_1",
  "PER_EMP_X_DEP" "ALIAS_2" WHERE "ALIAS_1"."ID" =
  "ALIAS_2"."FK_EMPID" AND "D"."ID" = "ALIAS_2".
  "FK_DEPID") AND "D"."NAME" LIKE 'Department1')
```

Listing 4.26 SQL Trace of the Failed JPA Query increaseDepartmentMembersSalary

You do not need to understand the statement in detail. It is sufficient to know that a selection was performed on the table to be changed within the UPDATE operation. This construct is not supported on a number of database platforms, including SAP MaxDB. Although the original JPQL statement is correct, the generated SQL cannot be executed on the database.

Why was another, simpler SQL statement not generated that manages without a selection on the table changed in the UPDATE clause?

The named query increaseProjectMembersSalary has already shown that an SQL statement of this type is possible, and its generated SQL statement would be in the form shown in Listing 4.27.

```
UPDATE "PER_EMPLOYEE" SET "SALARY" = 1010
WHERE EXISTS (SELECT "P"."ID" FROM "PER_PROJECT" "P",
"PER_EMP_X_PRJ" "ALIAS_1" WHERE "PER_EMPLOYEE"."ID" =
"ALIAS_1"."FK_EMPID" AND "P"."ID" = "ALIAS_1".
"FK_PRJID" AND "P"."NAME" = 'Project1')
```

Listing 4.27 SQL Trace of the Executable Query increaseProjcectMembersSalary

The solution to the puzzle is that JPA does not know anything about the possibility of a direct navigation of this kind; that is, it is not expressed in the object model: Although the relationship exists at the database level, the Employee entity does not have an annotated attribute that expresses its relationship to the Department entity.

There are therefore three options for implementing the task that was set:

▶ **Adjust the object model**
This option would be the most elegant solution, because JPQL would help with the generation of "correct" SQL and the relational aspects would not appear in the object-oriented JPA world, although it cannot be denied that a relational aspect would determine the object-oriented modeling. You would, of course, also have to adjust the annotations for a bidirectional 1:n relationship.

Adjusting the object model

▶ **Execute the SQL query using JDBC**
You could implement this approach by using a separate data source (isolation level **Read Committed**) and the execution of the SQL query using a database connection drawn from the data source within a JTA transaction.

JDBC SQL Query

▶ **Executing the SQL Query using the JPA Query Interface**
With this option, the SQL query would be passed to the JPA Query API for processing. With this procedure, the JPA runtime would take over the database connection and transaction management. You would only be responsible for formulating the SQL statement (Listing 4.28).

SQL Query using the JPA Query Interface

```
public void increaseDepartmentMembersSalary(String
            departmentName, int percent) {
  String SQL_QUERY  = "UPDATE PER_EMPLOYEE
  SET SALARY = SALARY*(1+(?/100))
  WHERE EXISTS (
  SELECT D.ID FROM PER_DEPARTMENT D, PER_EMP_X_DEP ALIAS_1
  WHERE PER_EMPLOYEE.ID = ALIAS_1.FK_EMPID
  AND D.ID = ALIAS_1.FK_DEPID AND D.NAME = ?)";
  Query q = em.createNativeQuery(SQL_QUERY);
  q.setParameter(1, percent);
  q.setParameter(2, departmentName);
  q.executeUpdate();
}
```

Listing 4.28 SQL Query Using the JPQL Native Query Interface

Note that, for reasons of simplicity, the consideration of versioning for mass changes was not taken into account. For more information about this, refer to the JPA specification.

Mass changes and versioning

4.6 Outlook

You have seen how a concrete persistence scenario would be implemented for the SAP NetWeaver Composition Environment 7.1 using JPA in the SAP NetWeaver Developer Studio. You should now be able to use and build on the knowledge gained in your own development projects.

It was not possible to handle all facets of the Java Persistence API or of Open JDBC. The topic of transaction management was only touched upon, because many aspects of this are defined in the Java EE standard. Explicit locking, the cascading of operations along the object graph, and the reintegration of detached entities in the persistence context were not addressed at all. Consideration of optimization strategies and the detailed behavior of the infrastructure, for example, which statements are written to the database when, was certainly beyond the scope of this chapter.

An excellent reference for these questions, in addition to the literature mentioned in Section 4.5, *Programming with Enterprise JavaBeans 3.0/ Java Persistence API*, is the SAP NetWeaver Developer Studio documentation or the SAP online help at *http://help.sap.com*.

Enterprise Services form the technological and semantic basis for enterprise SOA. The SAP NetWeaver Composition Environment supports the provision of Enterprise Services, in particular the use of these services in UI scenarios or composite applications. This chapter explains the Enterprise Services paradigm to you and also conveys how a consumer scenario is accomplished using an enterprise service already delivered by SAP.

5   Web Services and Enterprise Services in the SAP NetWeaver Composition Environment

The communication between business-to-business and application-to-application applications is largely based on manually defined, proprietary interfaces and message formats. Web services can help here to simplify the processes. They work with Web-based interfaces that can be integrated into the business scenarios of a company and are based on open, generally accepted standards. In this way, communication across system limits and even company limits is made easier to a measurable degree. To implement such scenarios, a Web service must meet certain requirements:

A Web service is a modularized, executable unit that can be called in heterogenous system landscapes, even beyond host limits. The communication is based on open Internet standards, such as Web Services Description Language (WSDL), SOAP, and Universal Description Discovery Integration (UDDI). Based on passed input parameters, the output is automatically determined and is then passed to the caller.

Web service definition

Web services are initially based on the technological option of standard-based provision of functions. The concept developed by SAP for Enterprise Service-Oriented Architecture (enterprise SOA) complements the

Enterprise Service-Oriented Architecture

technical side of Web services through a semantic and architectural component. Enterprise SOA is the blueprint developed by SAP for designing and implementing entire business processes on the basis of enterprise services. An enterprise service refers to a type of Web service that must meet certain criteria: The design of the service follows the methodology prescribed by SAP. It is embedded in the overall contest of an SAP solution and its metadata is stored in a central repository.

Concept of the
enterprise service The concept of the semantic, content-loaded enterprise service that both structures and bundles functions enables the user to change the paradigm in the relationship of business and IT. In many companies, it is the IT infrastructure that prescribes what is and is not possible in business processes. The concept of the modeled enterprise service that now just accesses the Web service technology merely as a basis makes, for the first time, the technology subordinate to the business processes, thus allowing optimization of business processes and also rendering them flexible. The option to enhance or modify the SAP-delivered services, or use them in composite applications, increases this flexibility. Not even the expansion and enhancement of the Enterprise Services, delivered by SAP, into customer-specific composite applications guarantees this flexibility that is necessary and demanded by so many customers.

The SAP NetWeaver Composition Environment is particularly suited for consumption of enterprise services — be it in composite applications or in user interface scenarios. The provision of services is currently possible, based on the Java EE 5 standard. How to consume an enterprise service on the basis of a typical scenario example will be explained in the following description.

The next Support Package of the Composition Environment will — as an optional deployment — also contain an Enterprise Services Repository. It will thus provide the entire range of functions of the enterprise services in accordance with SAP methodology. A short overview at the end of this chapter will shed more light on this aspect.

In this introductory section, the provider-consumer paradigm for Web services and define enterprise services will be explained. Because the Services Registry plays a central role in the composition and consumption of services, this will be explained in more detail. Finally, in the last part of this chapter, consuming a service on the basis of a real enterprise service will be detailed. At the end of the chapter, a short view of the Enterprise Services Repository will be presented.

5.1 Enterprise Services Paradigm

The SAP NetWeaver Composition Environment can act both as a *server* for Web services as well as a *consumer*. It implements the basic standards for Web services: Extensible Markup Language (XML), SOAP, WSDL, and UDDI) — that is, the core components of the Web service approach.

Provider and consumer as central parts of the service paradigm

SOAP provides a general, application-independent format for XML messages, which can then be exchanged between the communication partners using various transport protocols. WSDL provides the application-related component: With this language, the interface is described by actual Web services that consist of names of operations — such as methods, as well as input and output messages. These messages are packed into SOAP messages and transmitted at runtime. The UDDI-based Services Registry also provides the option of publishing and searching for Web services in a standard format. Figure 5.1 shows the basic architecture of the Web service paradigm.

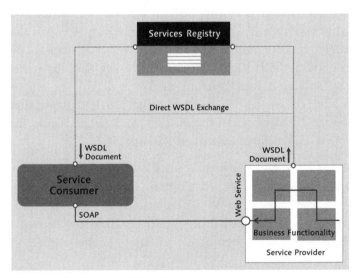

Figure 5.1 Architecture of Web Service Paradigm

Service provider

If the Composition Environment serves as a service provider, a Web service interface is created for the implemented function. This interface represents the Web service for the user. The functions used for providing services do not yet take a prominent position in the Composition Environment and, therefore, no complete chapter is dedicated to this topic.

Services Registry

Released Web services can be stored in a UDDI Registry, searched for in all registries, and also published in all registries that meet the required standard. SAP's Services Registry is closely integrated with the development environment so that WSDL files for service consumption can be imported directly from the registry into the Developer Studio (see following).

Service consumer

If the SAP NetWeaver Application Server Java functions as a service consumer, a calling application can be created in just a few steps with the help of a WSDL file. The emphasis of this chapter is on this user case, and is particularly referred to in Section 5.3, *Consuming a Service*.

5.2   Services Registry

In service-oriented software development, the service provider must be distinguished from a service consumer. In a simple case, one can assume that the service provider — the one providing the service — knows the service consumer and communicates to the latter where services can be found. To give both providers and consumers a market place for Enterprise Services, there are central directory services available. These have become possible through the development of the UDDI standard that was passed by the standardization committee OASIS (Organization for the Advancement of Structured Information Standards).[1]

With each AS Java, a Services Registry is installed. This then represents a registry for Web services. It contains entries for all services and service definitions with references to the WSDL metadata and the service provider end points that can be called. A query user interface has been integrated into the corresponding tools in the development environment in

---

1 For more information, refer to the UDDI Web page under *http://uddi.org*.

order to simplify the search for services in the registry. Developers can search through the registry directly and call the WSDL file of the selected service.

The Services Registry can be used as follows:

▸ By service providers to publish services
▸ By service users to find a service that meets special requirements
▸ By administrators to find available service end points and manage the links between the consumer and provider systems
▸ By SAP and non-SAP applications

The Services Registry puts users in the position of being able to find services and also use these, for example, in composite applications. Services are called by applications and can be combined into coherent business scenarios.

5.2.1 UDDI Server and Classification Service

The Services Registry is based on a UDDI-v3.0-compatible UDDI server. **UDDI server** The UDDI server is set up in the following way (Figure 5.2).

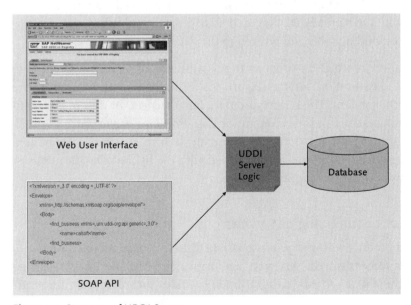

Figure 5.2 Structure of UDDI Server

Web user interface ▸ The Web user interface for a UDDI server is the UDDI client. It enables you to search for and publish data on the UDDI server with the support of the browser. The Web user interface can be used whenever a JEE engine has been started and the UDDI server has been configured on this application server.

▸ You can call the UDDI client through the URL *http://<host>:<port>/index.html.* For *<host>*, enter the required host name, and as the name for the *<port>* enter "50000"; this is the standard port. Finally, choose **UDDI Client**.

SOAP API ▸ UDDI servers can be operated either manually through the browser or through client programs that use SOAP APIs. To access the data on a UDDI registry, the client software uses SOAP through HTTP. In accordance with the specifications, UDDI provides an Inquiry API and a Publisher API in the form of a Web service. The registry calls that search through the registry form the Inquiry API. These include calls such as find_business and find_service.

Database ▸ The UDDI Registry data is usually stored in a relational database.

UDDI server logic ▸ The UDDI server logic implements the search and publication functions that are defined in the UDDI standard. The data searched for through a SOAP API or a Web user interface is read from the database with the help of UDDI logic. Similarly, data is published with the corresponding tools and written to the database.

Classification service The Services Registry supports the classification of services with the help of a classification service (Figure 5.3). This service is not part of the UDDI standard. The service provides the metadata for different classification systems and the content for classification systems, such as possible values with descriptive texts and hierarchical structure information. The registered services are organized with the help of classification systems in order to simplify the search.

5.2.2 Structuring of Services

In a productive registry, it is possible to have a considerable number of data records stored. Here you need a system that allows the structuring of these data records. *Categorization* provides such an option for struc-

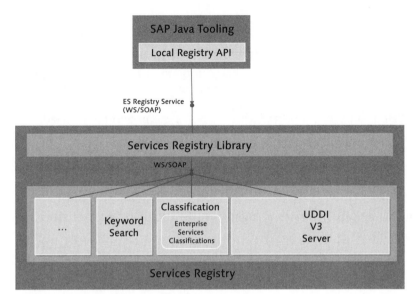

Figure 5.3 Structure of the Services Registry

turing data. Categories are characterized by a set of features that is common to all elements.

For example, different services are recorded in a registry. They all serve the same function, but they are available in different languages. The distinguishing feature in this case is the language. Other categories in the SAP environment would be features such as the deployment unit, the process component, and so on.

The categorization of data enables the data search in the respective data records just as it would be possible in a catalog. In addition, it is possible to combine categories and implement these as categorization groups. This option is used in the Services Registry. In this way, you can accelerate the search for services and simplify it through the combination of various categories.

SAP uses the concept of *Value sets*[2] for the technical implementation of categories. Value sets are part of the UDDI standard and are used for modeling categories, categorization groups, and their relationships.

---

2 This concept is described in detail in: Providing a Value Set for Use in UDDI Version 3 (*http://www.oasis-open.org/committees/uddi-spec/doc/tns.htm*).

To support the classification and search functions on the user interface, the Services Registry requires, as previously mentioned, an additional classification service. The APIs of the classification service are part of the APIs of the Services Registry. They can be used for the following purposes:

▸ Calling a list of supported classification systems and their metadata

▸ Calling the full content of a classification system

▸ Publishing classification systems and values of classification systems

▸ Deleting classification systems and values of classification systems

Types The classification service recognizes three different types of classification systems:

▸ **Flat List**
A flat classification system is a flat list with codes. If you select this kind of classification system in the Services Registry, you will get a results list with all the valid values. By selecting a value, you will get a list of all suitable services displayed to you.

▸ **Hierarchy**
A hierarchical classification system is a tree. If you choose a hierarchical classification system you will also get a list of all subordinate classifications. You can continue navigation from this list.

▸ **Group**
A group classification system is a way of combining values from other flat or hierarchical classification systems.

Classification systems SAP supplies the following classification systems as part of a Services Registry in its very first version:

▸ **Deployment Unit**
Deployment units are logical systems. They are contained in the meta model of the service-oriented architecture for business processes. A deployment unit contains a set of process components, for example, SP_HR.

▸ **Process Component**
Process components implement business processes and make their functions available for use as services. A process component contains

one or several business objects. A business object belongs to exactly one process component. Process components can be used in different integration scenarios, for example, in HCM Compensation Management.

▶ **Business Object**
A business object is a group of entities with common features and behaviors that are uniquely defined in the world of business processes. The group of entities is generally accepted in the business world, for example, HCM Salary Adjustment.

▶ **Life Cycle Status**
The life cycle status informs customers about the development status of objects. The release status specifies whether the customer can use a particular service or whether limitations are in place.

▶ **Service Operation**
Service operations are part of the meta model of service-oriented architecture for business applications. Operations are groups of messages that belong to a single service action.

▶ **Service Interface**
A service interface is a named grouping of operations in the Enterprise Services Repository. A service interface specifies offered (Inbound Service Interface) or used (Outbound Service Interface) functions.

▶ **Software Component Version**
The software component version is the smallest delivery unit for design objects of the Enterprise Services Repository development objects in the respective application system. Software component versions are contained in the software catalog of the System Landscape Directory.

5.2.3 Searching for Service Definitions

The search for service definitions can be refined by entering classification groups and physical systems where the service is located. If you already know the classification of the required service, you can search for this service.

1. Open the user interface of the Services Registry on the start page of the JEE Engine. You can also call the Services Registry through the following address: *http://<hostname>:<port>/sr.*

2. Choose the tab page **Browse & Search** (Figure 5.4).

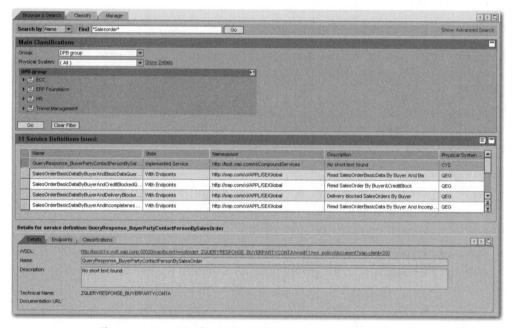

Figure 5.4 Searching for Service Definitions

3. If you know the name of the service definition being searched for, enter it under **Find** and then choose **Go**.

   If you do not know the exact name of the service definition, you can replace part of the name by a placeholder:

   ▶ Asterisk (*) for an indefinite number of characters

   ▶ Question mark (?) for a single character

4. Choose a classification and a physical system in which you wish to execute the search.

   The group DPB consists of the classifications Deployment Unit — Process Component — Business Object. Each deployment unit contains process components and each process component contains business objects.

5. Click **Go**. All the service definitions that match the specified criteria are displayed.

6. Select a service definition and look at the corresponding information in the lower part of the screen:

   ▸ The **Details** tab contains information such as the name and the description of the service definition, as well as a link to the WSDL document. You require the authorizations for the selected physical system in order to be able to access the WSDL document.

   ▸ In the **End Points** tab you will find a list of all end points (configurations) of the service definition.

   ▸ In the **Classifications** tab you see the classifications of the service definition.

7. Using **Show Advanced Search** (upper right of the tab page **Browse & Search**), you can limit the search by services. Choose a service status (Figure 5.5) or additional classifications.

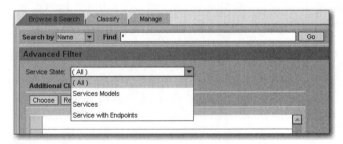

Figure 5.5 Choosing the Service Status

A service model is modeled either in the repository or in the backend system. If you are dealing with a service whose operations perform an implementation function, that is, were filled with the respective coding, it can be found under the heading **Services**. Services with end points are implemented, configured services that can be called.

1. Click on **Choose** in order to add additional classifications.

2. Select a classification system (Figure 5.6). All the available values are listed in the **Values** table.

3. Choose one or several values, and then press **Add** and **Go**.

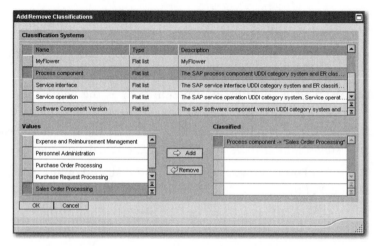

Figure 5.6 Additional Classifications for the Search for Service Definitions

5.2.4 Classifying Services

On the **Classify** tab page, you can arrange services with the help of existing classification systems (Figure 5.7):

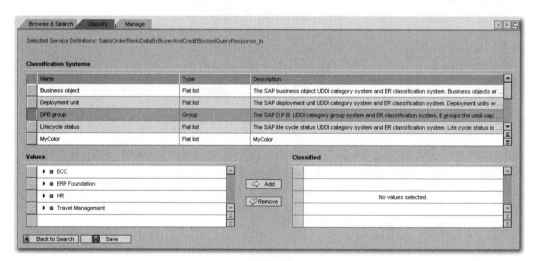

Figure 5.7 Classification of Services

1. Enter the name of the service and click on **Go**.

2. Choose **Classify Selected**. All the classification systems are then displayed.

3. Search for a classification system and a value.

4. Click on **Add** and **Save**.

5. In the **Manage** tab page, you can create and manage classification systems. Choose **New**, and then enter the name and the descriptions of the classification systems as well as the classification type (**Flat List** or **Hierarchy**) and the required values.

Searching through classifications for finding service definitions

5.3 Consuming a Service

The SAP NetWeaver Composition Environment supports different options for consuming services. The consumption of services that have already been delivered by SAP in a user interface scenario or a composite application is of central importance.

A common scenario in this context is the provision of a customer application for an enterprise service through an independent software vendor (ISV), which uses the host SAP system landscape in the Enterprise Services workplace (ES workplace). The ES workplace in the SAP Developer Network (SDN) is the central information source in order to get to know the latest enterprise services that SAP delivers for the SAP Business Suite.

Enterprise Services Workplace

With the help of the ES workplace, Enterprise Services are tangible and real. They can also be tried and tested, in which case customers can familiarize themselves both with the technical aspects and the semantic groupings in the process components. The search options cover an alphabetical index search and a semantics-oriented search on the basis of business contests. Each service is documented in detail, up to the actual WSDL document of the service operation. An ERP backend system hosted on the ES workplace even allows you to test the actual implementation of each service. In addition to the ERP system, a publicly accessible Services Registry is integrated in the ES workplace.

You can call the ES workplace under the address *https://www.sdn.sap.com/irj/sdn/esworkplace*. The Services Registry is available through the following link: *http://sr.esworkplace.sap.com*. The integration option of the Registry with the Developer Studio now allows you to import

WSDL documents directly from the ES Workplace Registry for processing in a consumer application. Figure 5.8 shows, in diagram form, the interaction of the ES workplace, the Services Registry, and the Developer Studio in the Composition Environment.

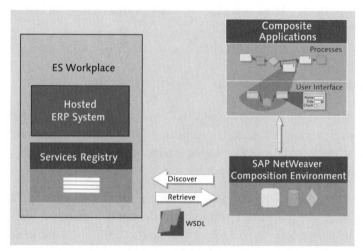

Figure 5.8 Import of a WSDL Document from the Enterprise Services Workplace

5.3.1 Does the Required Service Already Exist?

Example of a customer application for an enterprise service

The following scenario is to form the basis of a typical customer application example. The business process expert of a company has determined that the existing function for creating purchase orders should be enhanced to include an additional option: with the help of an enterprise to be able to query purchase orders by entering an ID.

1. The first step for putting this idea into practice is to check whether this service is already provided by SAP. For this purpose, you can use the Enterprise Services workplace. The URL *https://www.sdn.sap.com/irj/sdn/esworkplace* brings you straight to the initial screen, where you have various search options (Figure 5.9).

2. A look at the alphabetical list of the process components shows that there already is a process component called **Purchase Order Processing**. Further investigation into this process component shows that it contains two service interfaces: **Query Purchase Order In** and **Manage Purchase Order In**.

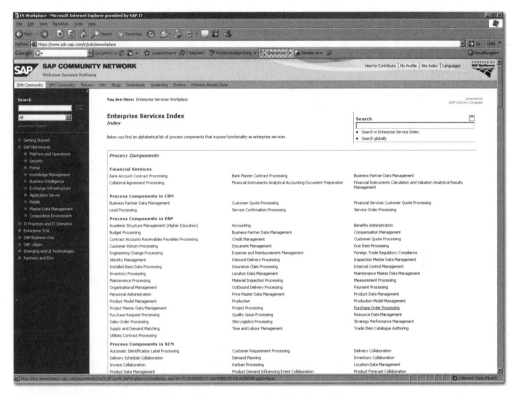

Figure 5.9 Enterprise Services Index of the Enterprise Services Workplace

3. Under the second service interface, there is a service operation called **Read Purchase Order**. This is defined as follows:

A request to and response from Purchase Order Processing to provide the data of a purchase order. The inbound operation Read Purchase Order By ID is used by the buyer to display a purchase order.

The display of the detailed field descriptions confirms that entering an ID returns details on the purchase order (Figure 5.10).

5.3.2 Creating a Web Dynpro Project

This service meets the requirements and will now be used in a Web Dynpro user interface. The SAP NetWeaver Composition Environment provides the necessary tools as it offers direct integration with the Services Registry available on the Enterprise Services workplace.

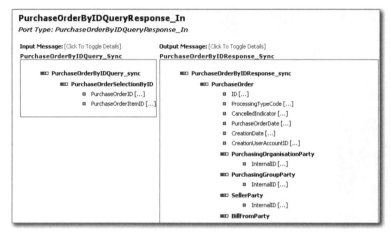

Figure 5.10 Input and Output Messages from Read Purchase Order

In this way, the WSDL of the enterprise service is downloaded directly and can be used for creating the consumer application. These steps are described following in detail:

Connection between Developer Studio and Services Registry

1. First, you should check whether the connection from the Developer Studio to the Services Registry is configured correctly. You do this through the path **Window • Preferences • Web Services • SAP Services Registry**.

2. The following parameters must be set: **Server Name** and **Server Port** of the UDDI-**Inquiry Path** as well as **Publish Path** and **Security Path**. Figure 5.11 shows the necessary settings. In addition, the division of the Services Registry we have already described into a standard-based **UDDI Service** and an SAP-specific classification service (**Classification Service**) is clearly visible.

3. After you have maintained the proxy settings, you can begin with the Web Dynpro project in the next step. For this, you must first open the Web Dynpro perspective through the path **Window • Open • Perspective • Other • Web Dynpro**.

4. With **File • New • Web Dynpro Project**, you open an Editor window in which you enter the name of the new project. In this case, the project should be called "ReadPurchaseOrder". By clicking on the pushbutton **Finish**, you create the empty Web Dynpro project — as seen in Figure 5.12 — complete with application and component.

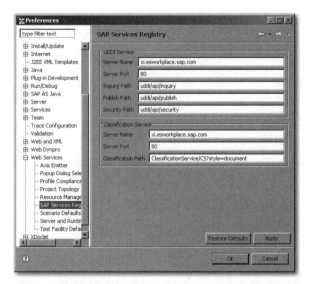

Figure 5.11 Maintenance of Connection to the Services Registry

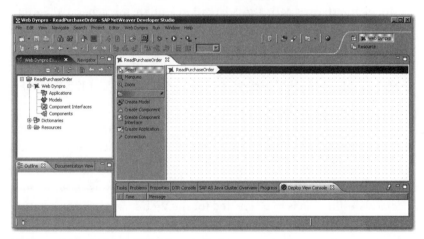

Figure 5.12 Newly Created Web Dynpro Project

5. In the next step, you choose the Web Dynpro model for the enterprise service you selected previously on the ES workplace. This will serve to query a purchase order.

The model is the logical application that represents the interface in the existing back end. Local and external Web services, JavaBeans, and function modules represent reusable model objects that can be used by different Web Dynpro components. The Web Dynpro model is thus responsible for the connection to the selected enterprise service.

6. If you click on the pushbutton **Create Model** and then on the work area to the right, a popup will appear with the following model types for selection:

  ▶ Adaptive RFC Model

  ▶ Adaptive Web Service Model

  ▶ JavaBean Model

Adaptive Web-service Model

7. The functions are provided by the enterprise service Read Purchase Order. Therefore, choose the option **Adaptive Web Service Model**. The Adaptive Web service Model represents the interface to a Web service back end and is the enhancement of the Web service model used until now.

This enhanced Web service model is characterized by a few new functions, including the metadata support at runtime using the Common Model Interface (CMI), the adaptation option for generated design metadata using runtime metadata, and, in particular, the option for configuring destinations and performing security settings. The two last functions will be discussed soon. To be able to use the Adaptive Web Service Model, the service provider must support the Web Service Inspection Language (WSIL).

8. Click on the **Next** button and to get to the next screen where you must define the **Name** ("PurchaseOrderModel") and **Package** ("com.sap. purchaseorder.model") of the model. Enter both and click on **Next**.

Principle of logical destination for Web services

9. In the following screen, you must make a selection as to whether a logical destination is to be created for the Web service call, or whether the URL for the WSDL document of the service to be called should be used directly. This configuration of Web service settings is one of the core new functions of the Adaptive Web Service Model.

At runtime, the model uses Web service configuration settings that are performed in the SAP NetWeaver Administrator (NWA), such as, for example, the maintenance of Web service destinations and proxy settings. The creation of logical ports at design time becomes superfluous because the mapping of logical ports to destinations takes place in the NWA.

10. The selection window first shows the default settings for logical destinations that you can modify later in the NWA. One destination for the metadata and one for the service call are provided by default.

    If you do not wish to work with logical destinations, choose **No logical destinations**. In this case, you use the URL of the Web service WSDL document directly in order to call both the metadata as well as the Web service itself. Additional settings in the NWA are not necessary; however, you will lose the flexibility that logical destinations provide.

11. In the current case, a logical destination should be used. So, change the name of the default value DEFAULT_WS_METADATA_DEST in PO_META DATA_DEST and DEFAULT_WS_EXECUTION_DEST into PO_EXECUTION_ DEST, as shown in Figure 5.13.

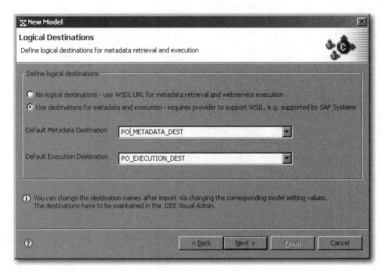

Figure 5.13 Maintaining a Logical Destination

12. When you have created the logical destination, which must be entered in the SAP NetWeaver Administrator later, you proceed to the next step where you are queried as to the source for the WSDL document. At your disposal you have the **Remote Location/File System** or **Services Registry**. Choose **Services Registry**, and then enter the required login data.

UDDI service and
classification
service

13. In Figure 5.14, you see the dichotomy of the registry into a UDDI service and a classification service, which was previously described. If, in addition to the SAP classification service, a UDDI server of a different provider were to be used, then the logon data would be different at this point.

Figure 5.14 Authentication at the Services Registry

5.3.3 Connection to the Services Registry

Download of
WSDL file through
the Services
Registry

The connection to the Registry on the Enterprise Services Workplace is now established, and the user has a similar range of search options available as in the standard user interface of the Registry.

1. Choose **Advanced Search**, and enter "*purchaseorder*" in the field **Search by Name**.

2. To limit the number of hits, also choose **With endpoints**. The list of found services, as shown in Figure 5.15, will be displayed.

3. The correct choice here is the service `PurchaseOrderByIDQuery Response_In`. This has already been checked on the ES Workplace.

4. After you have selected the service and clicked on the **Finish** button, an authentication step will again be necessary at the backend system where the WSDL is called. Finally, the WSDL document is downloaded.

5. After the download, it is quite possible that name conflicts will arise in the model classes, as is the case here with **Price** and **Delivery Terms.** These conflicts need to be removed manually. As soon as this has happened, the classes of the new model are automatically generated (Figure 5.16).

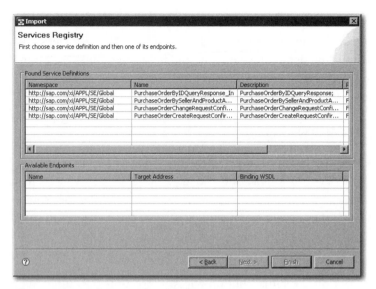

Figure 5.15 List of Services found in the Registry

Figure 5.16 Generated Model Classes

231

5.3.4 Definition of Data Flow and Creation of Web Dynpro UI

The model for the enterprise service is now created. The next steps now show you how you define the data flow and how you set up a user interface for this enterprise service. The central architectural concepts, such as the Model View Controller architecture, will be assumed to be familiar to you. For more information, refer to Chapter 6, *Developing Business Applications with Web Dynpro*.

1. First, in the Web Dynpro project **Read Purchase Order**, you must create a Web Dynpro application called ReadPurchaseOrder App in a package with the name com.sap.demo.readpurchaseorderapp. You do this through the context menu using the entry **Create Application**.

2. In a similar fashion, you create a new component called ReadPurchaseOrderComp in the package com.sap.demo.comp.

3. Simply click on the **Finish** button and you create the required Web Dynpro application and component with a window and an embedded view.

Web Dynpro
Data Modeler
4. Now open the **Data Modeler** in the context menu of the new component in order to display the objects created so far. The newly created Adaptive Web Service Model should be embedded in the Web Dynpro component.

5. To do this, choose **Embed Model** to the left in the actions list and then click on the work area to the right.

6. In the selection window you now see, select the **PurchaseOrderModel** and click on **OK**. The objects created so far are, as shown in Figure 5.17, displayed graphically in the **Data Modeler**.

Now you need to define the data flow between the individual elements. For this, apply a template to the service controller. A controller contains a so-called context, that is, the active part of an application unit, such as a component, a view, or a custom controller. The application has several controllers that are responsible for the data and control flow in the application.

The transport of data between the model and the controller is termed as model binding. Here a reference is kept from the controller context to the backend data. The data flow between the controller contexts is termed as mapping, where a data copy is passed from one context to another.

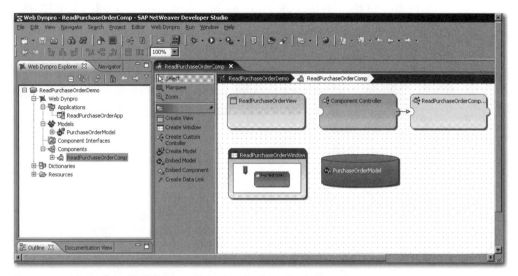

Figure 5.17 View of the Web Dynpro Objects in the Data Modeler

We will now leave the concept and look at the steps required.

1. In the context menu of the component controller, choose **Apply Template** and then **Service Controller**.

2. From the list of executable model classes now displayed, select the operation `Request_PurchaseOrderbyIdQuery Response_In`. Due to the prescribed length limitation, you should shorten the operation name to "Read Purchase Order".

3. Now the model binding will take place when you define the input data for the operation. The entry you make should read "Purchase Order Number".

4. Now you need to select the values that should be returned after the purchase order number has been entered. Here you choose the name of the user who created the purchase order, the description of the ordered articles, and the price and currency. Finally, you determine the date when the purchase order was created.

5. Complete the selection of parameters by clicking **Next**. The system automatically generated a method for executing the model.

5.3.5   Initialization of the Web Service Model

So that the Adaptive Web Service Model can be initialized correctly, the coding of the method `wdDoInit` of the component controller needs to be modified somewhat.

1. To do this, open the context menu of the component controller and choose **Open • Java Editor**. The coding of the `wdDoInit` method must look like the coding displayed in Listing 5.1. This supplement to the generated coding ensures that the model will be initialized correctly as soon as the application is started.

```java
public void wdDoInit()
  {
    //@@begin wdDoInit()
    //$$begin Service Controller(74186106)
    PurchaseOrderModel model = new PurchaseOrderModel();
    Request_PurchaseOrderByIDQueryResponse_In request =
      new Request_PurchaseOrderByIDQueryResponse_In(model);
    PurchaseOrderID orderId = new PurchaseOrderID(model);
    PurchaseOrderSelectionByID selection =
      new PurchaseOrderSelectionByID(model);
    PurchaseOrderByIDQueryMessage_Sync queryMessage =
      new PurchaseOrderByIDQueryMessage_Sync(model);

    selection.setPurchaseOrderID(orderId);
    queryMessage.setPurchaseOrderSelectionByID(selection);
    request.setPurchaseOrderByIDQuery_Sync(queryMessage);

    wdContext.nodeReadPurchaseOrder().bind(request);

    //$$end
    //@@end
  }

  //@@begin javadoc:wdDoExit()
  /** Hook method called to clean up controller. */
  //@@end
```

Listing 5.1 Modified Coding of Method wdDoInit of the Component Controller

2. In the following step, the mapping of the view context to the component controller context takes place through the **Create Data Link** button. First, click on this button and make a connection from ReadPurchaseOrderView to the component controller.

Context mapping between view and component controller

3. An editor window now opens up and there you can perform the corresponding mappings. On the right-hand side, you see the component controller context. This is the data that you previously mapped from the Adaptive Web Service Model onto the component controller context.

4. You define the mapping between the view controller context and the component controller by pulling the context from the right side to the left side using drag & drop — that means, from the component controller to the view controller.

5. Finally, you can choose the data that should appear in the view. In the same way as in the previous selection, choose the name of the user who created the purchase or, the article description, the price, the currency, and the date when the purchase order was created. Figure 5.18 shows the selection required.

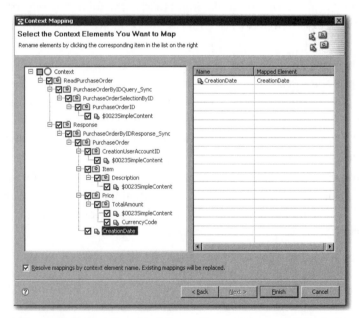

Figure 5.18 Context Mapping Between View and Component Controller — Selected Fields

With this, the definition of the data flow between the model, view, and controller is complete. However, there is still no user interface for the enterprise service, so in the next step you should create the view layout.

5.3.6   Development of Web Dynpro User Interfaces

View layout of
User Interface

The Web Dynpro tools provide support for developing interfaces during the design and implementation phase. The view layout is designed in the view editor. The required user interface elements are divided into various categories to provide a good overview. For each element, there are also several properties, so the usage options and the appearance of the individual elements in a screen are extremely varied. Examples of simple interface elements are labels and input fields; a complex element such as the table provides nesting options. You should first create a simple user interface with one input field.

1. In the context menu of the view, choose **Apply Template** and then **Form** for the input data.

2. Because the ID of the purchase order is required as input, select the element PurchaseOrderId for the input field in the following selection window, and assign "PurchaseOrderId" accordingly as the name for the UI element.

3. Likewise, you need to create UI elements for the output data. To do this, open the context menu of the view again and choose **Apply Template**, then **Form**. Select the same fields again as before, that is, user name, price, and so on, and assign the corresponding name. Under **Editor** you define all fields as **TextView**. You can see the completely filled list in Figure 5.19.

4. Because the output data are to be displayed in table form, a further template needs to be applied to the view. Again, choose **Apply Template** in the context menu of the view, but then choose **Table** instead of **Form**.

5. The data for the table should come from the article list of the purchase order. Therefore, click on **Description**, then **Next**, and, after you have entered **Item** as a description for the UI field, finally, click on **Finish**.

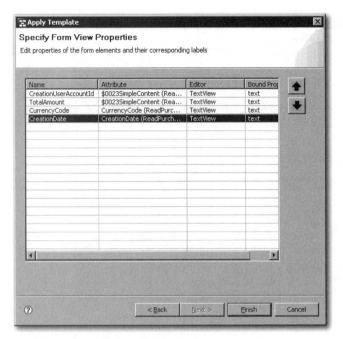

Figure 5.19 Definition of Output Fields

6. As a final UI element, all you need now is a button that enables the execution of the enterprise service. For one last time, now use a template and choose **Action Button**. As a label, assign the description "ReadPurchaseOrder".

7. Finally, specify the method to be called by activating the checkbox **Call Method**. In the controller field, choose `ReadPurchaseOrderComp`. The corresponding method is then displayed automatically since because in this example only one method is available (Figure 5.20).

8. Finally, click on **Finish** to complete the view layout.

The Web Dynpro development is thus completed. As already described in the overview of the individual development steps, you now need to execute the configuration of the Web service destination in order to be able to call the Web Dynpro application.

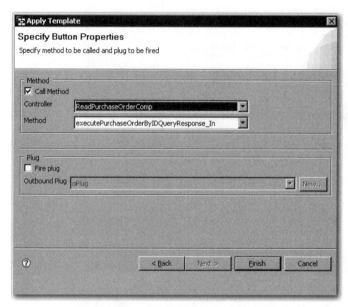

Figure 5.20 Method Call Through ReadPurchaseOrder Button

5.3.7 Maintenance of the Web Service Destinations in the SAP NetWeaver Administrator

The creation and configuration of the logical Web service destinations takes place in the SAP NetWeaver Administrator. To start the NWA, you can enter either the alias *nwa* after the host name and the port number of your local SAP NetWeaver Application Server Java, or follow the link on the start page of the Composition Environment. To use the NWA, you need administration authorization.

1. In the SAP NetWeaver Administrator, choose the tab page **Configuration Management** and then the entry **Infrastructure**.

2. From the list of functions under **Infrastructure**, select **Web Service Configuration**.

3. First, check under **Web Service Global Settings** whether a HTTP proxy server is configured. This is required in order to be able to access the Enterprise Services Workplace through the Internet. As host, proxy.wdf.sap.corp should already be created, as port 8080.

In the next step, you now create the Web service destinations under **WS Destinations**. You will remember that two destinations need to be created — one for the metadata and one for the service execution. Start with the metadata destination.

1. Click on **Create Destination**.

2. As **Destination Type**, use **WSIL** for the Web Service Inspection Language.

3. At design time, you named the destination PO_METADATA_DEST; therefore, enter this name now under **Destination Name**.

4. Some more specifications need to be entered here:

   ▶ URL for the backend system — here, for the ES Workplace

   ▶ Selection of ABAP or Java system

   ▶ System name

   ▶ Host name

   ▶ Installation number

   ▶ Client

   ▶ Details on authentication

In Figure 5.21, you see the completely filled template for the first destination.

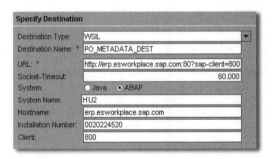

Figure 5.21 Maintenance of Metadata Destination

5. In precisely this manner, you now create the second destination for the execution of the service. The only difference is the name for the destination: PO_EXECUTION_DEST.

The configuration of the logical destination is now finished.

5.3.8 Testing the Enterprise Service Consumer Application

To test the service, you must first deploy the application.

1. To do this, choose **Deploy New Archive and Run** in the context menu of the `ReadPurchaseOrderApp` application and confirm this with **OK** as soon as the deployment is complete.

2. The view defined before will now be displayed. In order to be able to test the Web Dynpro application, you must enter a valid purchase order number. Therefore, enter "4500018023" and click on the **Read-PurchaseOrder** pushbutton.

3. The enterprise service was executed successfully and returns the detailed information on the purchase order: the name of the user who created the purchase order, the amount, the creation data, and the ordered articles. The purchase order consists of only one article.

   Figure 5.22 shows the user interface, as you defined it, that means, without additional effort for design, labels, and so on.

Figure 5.22 Successful Test of Enterprise Service from the Web Dynpro Application

4. Web Dynpro is a very effective tool for designing user interfaces so that you can greatly improve this generated user interface with only a few simple steps, for example, adjust the field labels, and so on. For an example, refer to Figure 5.23.

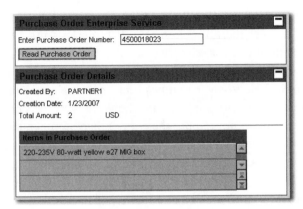

Figure 5.23 Revised Interface

Now the example for consuming an enterprise service is finalized.

5.4 Outlook: Provision of a Service with the Enterprise Services Repository

So far, the consuming of services with the SAP NetWeaver Composition Environment was the primary topic of this chapter. Naturally, of course, providing Web services — based on Java EE 5 standard — is also possible. This option covers mainly the technical conversion of Web services, as defined at the beginning, the option of remotely calling functions with the help of open Internet standards. This purely technical definition does not do justice to the concept of the enterprise service in the way it has been developed by SAP. Rather, enterprise services are defined using the following attributes:

▸ An executable entity that provides business functions

▸ Structured on the basis of a harmonized enterprise model that is built on global data types (GDT), process components, and business objects

▸ Published by SAP in the Enterprise Services Repository

▸ Guaranteed quality and stability

▸ Documented in a detailed fashion

▸ Based on open standards

The release delivered at the end of 2007 for the Enterprise Services Repository (ESR) will meet these requirements. It represents the next generation of provision of enterprise services at SAP. In addition to the delivery with SAP NetWeaver Process Integration 7.1, the ESR will also be available for the SAP NetWeaver Composition Environment. Thus, customers and independent software vendors who work with the Composition Environment but do not require the entire range of integration functions of SAP NetWeaver PI will be able to provide enterprise services in accordance with SAP methodology. Figure 5.24 shows the interaction of the ESR as design environment, the Composition Environments as service provider, and the services registry that contains both the reference to the design WSDL as well as the WSDL — complete with the binding and end-point information.

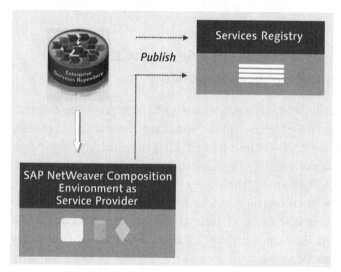

Figure 5.24 Provision of Services with the Enterprise Services Repository

SOA Design Governance What does SAP methodology actually mean and how does it relate to the Enterprise Services Repository? All the enterprise services delivered by SAP follow a uniform methodology with regard to their definition within a business context, their interface design, and their implementation. The most important corner points of this methodology are a common meta model for all services, based on the SAP concept of global data types and service interfaces, the embedding of each service into a business context, the graphic modeling of all relevant entities, including the business processes as well as central storage of all design objects in the Enterprise Services Repository. Accordingly, the Enterprise Services Repository provides the following range of functions relevant for service enabling:

▶ Definition of service interfaces that represent the basis for Enterprise Services

▶ Creation of modeling objects that express the SAP concept of business-oriented process modeling

▶ SAP-wide, defined global data types (GDT) that build on Core Component Technical Specification (CCTS) standards. This ensures that the data types are adapted to each other and can be reused.

While the Enterprise Services Repository contains the design information, it is the task of the registry to manage the information that is necessary for calling a service.

In contrast to the standard method of creating Web services in the SAP NetWeaver Developer Studio, the actual provision of the service does not start in the IDE, but in Enterprise Services Repository. The service interface is modeled independently of language, and only in the next step you have the generation of the Java proxy — JavaBean Skeleton — from the WSDL document of the service interface. Only the proxy contains the actual implementation of the business functions. Figure 5.25 shows the example of the service interface for the enterprise service `ReadPurchaseOrder` consumed previously.

Service provisioning scenario with the Enterprise Services Repository

The proxy generation from the service interface is done using the ESR browsers, which will be available as of the next service release of the SAP NetWeaver Composition Environment. With this you will be able to access objects of the Enterprise Services Repository directly from the Developer Studio and thus greatly simplify the provision of enterprise services.

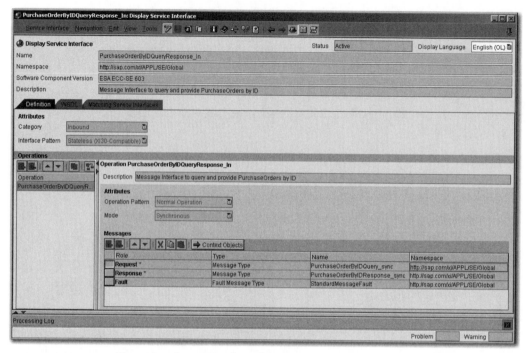

Figure 5.25 Service Interface of the Enterprise Service ReadPurchaseOrder in the Enterprise Services Repository

In this chapter you will learn about the Web application frame-work Web Dynpro Java that is integrated into SAP NetWeaver Composition Environment 7.1. This chapter introduces a component-based tutorial application for displaying stocks data using an external Web service to illustrate the most important concepts and advantages of Web Dynpro.

6 Developing Business Applications with Web Dynpro

Before developing a tutorial application for displaying stocks data, you are first given an introduction to the most important aims, principles, and concepts of the Web application framework *Web Dynpro*. Included in this are features such as the MVC-based (Model View Controller) programming model, model-driven and declarative development supported by automatic code generation, client independence by using a comprehensive library of interface elements, and the component model for modularizing business applications.

Introducing the principles and concepts of Web Dynpro

To make it easier to understand the Web Dynpro tutorial application introduced below, the following two sections will focus on the general anatomy of a Web Dynpro component and its interfaces. You will become familiar with the various visual and programmatic entities of a component and learn to distinguish between the different controller types and controller interfaces. Finally, you will be introduced to the interfaces of Web Dynpro components, as well as the concept of local and standalone component interface definitions

Component architecture and interface concept

This introduction represents the foundation for developing the component-based tutorial application that displays stocks data performed in the main part of this chapter.

Tutorial application for displaying stocks data

The tutorial application is developed in two stages. In the first practical part of this chapter (Section 6.2, *Web Dynpro Calls a Web Service*) an external Web service is called to read stocks data after the stock ticker symbols have been input. Using this tutorial application, you learn the important Web Dynpro development steps such as, for example, importing an adaptive Web service model, defining the context-to-model binding, context mapping, the view layout (including data binding and actions binding), as well as implementing application logic in the generated controller classes.

Integrating a component to search for stock ticker symbols

In the second practical part of the chapter (Section 6.3, *Integrating Web Dynpro Components for Searching for Ticker Symbols*), the tutorial application is enhanced by a pop-up dialog box for searching for stock ticker symbols. This is achieved by reusing a separate Web Dynpro component that implements this search function and exposes its local component interface. The aim of this section is to demonstrate a realistic and component-based Web Dynpro development process that incorporates separate Web Dynpro development components and their public parts, embeds components by defining component usages, and calls the external component interface controller API in the controller code of the embedded component.

Web Dynpro tools in SAP NetWeaver Developer Studio

Moreover, the tutorial application clarifies the strong support provided by Web Dynpro tools, which facilitates the quick, model-driven development of Web Dynpro applications in SAP NetWeaver Developer Studio (in SAP NetWeaver CE 7.1). Included in this, in particular, is the Web Dynpro Code Generator for automatically generating controller classes and interfaces, the new Component Modeler for developing component-based Web Dynpro applications, the Data Modeler for defining context mapping relationships, displaying binding chains (data binding, context mapping) beyond component boundaries, and the Navigation Modeler for embedding component interface views and modeling navigation links between the views embedded in a window.

6.1 Principles and Concepts

Before starting with the actual development of a Web Dynpro tutorial application, the fundamental features of Web Dynpro UI technology and its differences from other Web UI technologies should first be introduced. It is important for everyone who develops professional business applications with Web Dynpro to have a solid grasp of these features because it forms a crucial basis for utilizing the strengths and advantages of Web Dynpro in the best way possible. It is also important to recognize its limits and differences regarding other UI technologies.

6.1.1 Fundamental Features of Web Dynpro UI Technology

The following objectives were set in 2001 when SAP developed a new UI technology for Web-based applications:

Objectives of Web Dynpro UI technology

▶ Stateful MVC[1] programming model for developing transactional and Web-based business applications

▶ Minimization of application coding by automatically generating comprehensive code components

▶ Model-driven, declarative development to reduce the development effort required in a special Web Dynpro development environment

▶ Client abstraction for the unified design of user interfaces regardless of a specific client technology

▶ Consistency of the user interface and a unified look and feel by providing a comprehensive library of user interface elements

▶ Model abstraction for unified connectivity of a business application to different backend technologies such as RFCs, Web services, or Enterprise JavaBeans

▶ Automatic data transport between client, Web Dynpro frontend server, and backend server

▶ Generic UI services for recurring application components, such as input helps, type validation, or error messages

▶ Component model for logical separation, disconnected linkage, and the reuse of application components

---

1 MVC is for *Model View Controller*. A fundamental aspect of this is the division of a Web application into various areas or components according to three aspects: *Model* (business logic), *View* (user interface), and *Controller* (presentation and application logic).

▶ Dynamic programming for adapting a Web Dynpro application to requirements only recognized at runtime

▶ Multilingual capability and translatability by removing language-dependent texts and automatic text filling according to the user

These aims were regularly, and increasingly, implemented and revised in Web Dynpro UI technology, beginning with SAP NetWeaver 2004 and 7.0 through to SAP NetWeaver CE 7.1.

Model View Controller

MVC-based programming model

The Web Dynpro programming model is based on the Model View Controller paradigm used in numerous other Web technologies for the architecture of Web applications, such as JSF or Struts. In addition to this, it is results-based, which means that *requests* sent from the Web Dynpro client to the Web Dynpro runtime environment are processed in predefined phases (Web Dynpro phase model).

Special Development Tools

Model-driven, declarative development and code generation

The development of Web Dynpro applications is based on an abstract model that relieves the application developer from fundamental tasks and reduces large parts of the development to simply defining the properties of various Web Dynpro entities and their relationships to each other. This declarative development takes place using Web Dynpro tools[2] without actually having to implement any application code.

Examples of this include the user interface design in View Designer, the definition of navigation links in Navigation Modeler as well as the definition of automatic data transports using data binding, context mapping, and model binding. Data binding here refers to the declarative, bi-directional transport of data between interface elements at the client side and the context as a structure data store as the server side. Context mapping means the referencing of the context above and beyond controller limits; the model binding relation deals with the relationship between a controller's context structure and the model classes that belong to the model.

---

2 Web Dynpro tools are provided in SAP NetWeaver Developer Studio as own perspective.

In Web Dynpro, the source code to be implemented manually by the application developer is reduced to the actual application logic, including handling user actions, activating navigation links, or calling business logic. All remaining code elements, such as various controller classes or interfaces, are automatically created by Web Dynpro generation framework. This approach significantly reduces the occurrence of errors and the amount of development effort required for the application.

Client Abstraction

In addition to this, Web Dynpro also relieves the application developer of the difficult task of adapting the user interface (called *view layout*) to different clients. This is achieved through an interface element description (such as properties and events)[3] that is abstract and separate from specific client technologies[4] and even from certain end devices (such as desktop PCs or mobile devices). A Web Dynpro developer only has to embed and define user interface elements in view layout and at no time has to deal with implementing HTML, CSS, or JavaScript code. At runtime, Web Dynpro itself renders the user interface for different Web Dynpro clients on server side, such as the Web Dynpro HTML browser client, the Web Dynpro Flex client,[5] or the Web Dynpro client for mobile devices.

Abstract description of interface elements

On the one hand, a *client abstraction* or *client independence* of this type makes it possible to call the same Web Dynpro application without modifications on different end devices and with different client programs, which of course is a great advantage and significantly reduces the development costs. On the other hand, it is worth nothing that Web Dynpro interface elements can only be changed as far as the supported clients and requirements for international business applications allow.

---

3 This technique is also known as *client agnostic UI*. This means that the application developer constructs the user interfaces without knowledge or presumption of the client technology to be used at runtime.

4 Client technologies here include the different browser clients such as Mozilla Firefox or Microsoft Internet Explorer of which there are multiple versions.

5 The *Web Dynpro Flex Client* is first delivered with SAP NetWeaver CE 7.1 Service Pack Stack 3. Note that the first version of the Web Dynpro Flex Client does not yet support the entire Web Dynpro UI Element Library.

This means, for example, that you cannot specify the pixel-precise position[6] of interface elements or develop any additional interface elements[7] of your own. This difference of Web Dynpro should not, however, be seen as a disadvantage, but rather it should be understood more as the price to be paid for the considerable advantages of client independence with Web Dynpro.

User Interface Elements

Library of pre-defined user interface elements

Closely connected with client abstraction is the well-stocked library of more than 100 Web Dynpro UI elements that you can use to develop Web user interfaces that appear consistent and include a significant level of user interaction. Tables, trees, context and pop-up menus, tools, or calendars are also included here.

Generic UI Services

Pre-prepared by Web Dynpro

Repeating parts of the user interface, such as displaying input help in the form of selection fields or help windows, as well as displaying error messages, are provided to the application developer *generically* using special interface elements and services, that is, they are predefined by Web Dynpro. A further generic UI service is the personalization of the user interface by the administrator or end user.[8]

Model Abstraction

Common Model Interface

In Web Dynpro, connectivity to business logic takes place when the application developer imports the corresponding data model. Depending on the backend technology used (whether it be RFC, Web service, or EJB 3.0), special model classes are created for this model import, which all implement a unified interface, known as a Common Model Interface.

---

6 Because texts are different lengths in different languages and font sizes, interface elements are aligned automatically by the Web Dynpro runtime environment making pixel-precise positioning by the application developer unnecessary.

7 It is not possible for application developers to develop own interface elements due to the high-level technical demands of client abstraction, accessibility, and other technical aspects.

8 The personalization of Web Dynpro applications requires that they be included in SAP NetWeaver Portal because this handles the persistence of personalization data.

Next, the application developer creates a corresponding data structure from the imported data model in the controller context, known as *context-to-model binding*. However, the context structure created only represents the data model itself and is independent from the underlying backend technology. The context structure is used in a controller to bridge the gap between the user interface and the model and to be able to define the automatic data transport based on the data binding, context mapping, and model binding.

Communication and data transfer between an application and the backend system is wrapped by the Common Model Interface and is executed by the generated model implementation and Web Dynpro runtime environment. This means that as a result, the implementation effort for the application developer is reduced to just triggering backend calls in the controller implementation.

Components

Web Dynpro components are the building blocks for developing Web Dynproapplications. A component-based architecture makes it possible to split complex applications into individual, functionally separated components and then to develop, maintain, and later enhance them separately with a clear division of tasks.

Component model for modularizing business applications

This is possible due to some fundamental features of the Web Dynpro component model, such as its interface concept, its capability for defining component interfaces abstractly, its ability to modularize large applications, and the facility for reusing Web Dynpro components.

The functionality implemented in a Web Dynpro component can be reused by other components. For reasons of simplicity, reuse is only possible in the Web Dynpro programming model at the component level: This increases the efficiency of the development process and reduces the occurrence of errors in Web Dynpro applications by avoiding redundancies at both the definition and implementation levels.

Components and reusability

By using component interfaces to separate design from implementation, it is also possible to separate the close relationship between component user and component implementation. In *loose coupling*, a Web Dynpro

Loose coupling with component interfaces

component uses an abstract component interface at design time without needing to be aware of the component implementation that will be connected to it at runtime: This can be selected later as a runtime plug-in concept and does not need to be known at design time.

6.1.2 Anatomy of Web Dynpro Components

Component architecture

The architecture of a Web Dynpro component is based on the MVC design model to make a clear distinction between a business data model, the user interface, the controller implementation, and application logic. Every Web Dynpro component consists of different visual and controller-specific or programmatic parts and, in addition, exposes interfaces for providing the functions[9] it implements to other components. To make it easier to understand the application example introduced below, the fundamentals of Web Dynpro component architecture will first be dealt with here.

Visual entities in a component

First, the view layouts for organizing interface elements (also called UI elements) belong to the visual entities within a component. At the next level up, windows provide the opportunity for combining multiple views in one complete user interface (by connecting inbound and outbound plugs at the view level, the navigation schema is defined in a window (Figure 6.1)).

Programming entities in a component

The programming entities of a Web Dynpro component can be divided into different controller types and the message pool. The component controller existing by default, the optional custom controller that can be added multiple times, the window controller, and the view controller belonging to a view layout all count as controllers.[10] Language-dependent texts and notifications are defined in a component in the message pool and can be read from both interfaces IMessage<Name of Component> and IWDTextAccessor at runtime. The use of a model (such as an adap-

---

9 Implemented user interfaces are exposed in the form of component interface views. Context data structures, methods, and events implemented inside a component can be exposed in the Component Interface Controller for external access by other components.

10 You can find a comprehensive description of the Web Dynpro Controller and interfaces concepts in the SDN article *Web Dynpro Java Controller and Interface Concept* under *http://www.sdn.sap.com* or in SAP online help for SAP NetWeaver CE 7.1.

tive RFC model or an adaptive Web service model, for example) can be defined to connect a Web Dynpro component to the backend layer more easily.

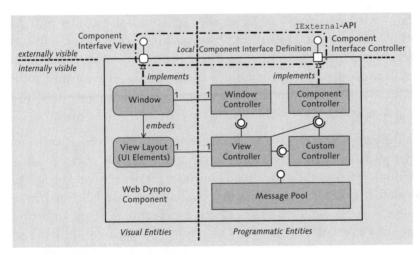

Figure 6.1 Anatomy of a Web Dynpro Component

All the controller classes contained in a Web Dynpro component are created and enhanced by the Web Dynpro generation framework in accordance with the declarations made by the application developer, and thereby accelerate the implementation of the application coding in the user coding areas.

By default, every Web Dynpro component has a *component controller* that is created and deleted as required by Web Dynpro runtime. The component controller acts as the central controller instance in the whole component and implements the exposed *component interface controller*. Cross-view data can be stored globally in the component controller context. In addition, it represents the intermediate layer between model(s) and view(s) without actually transferring any of the tasks related to presenting data. A component controller is accessible to all other controllers (window, custom, and view controller) in a component with its `IPublic` interface, which is created automatically by the Web Dynpro code generation framework and then adapted to the definitions made by the application developer (for example, by adding public methods or results).

Component controller

Custom controller   Custom controllers may be added by the application developer as additional controller instances in a component. They are best suited for encapsulating different controller tasks, such as configuring, connecting models, or using cross-controller functions, and as a result they are an important step toward achieving the separation of requirements. As with component controllers, the functionality of custom controllers is determined by the user interface. The context of a custom controller is available to all other controllers of a component as an additional global data store. A custom controller is accessible to the remaining controllers of a component by its IPublic interface.

View controller   In the view layout (known as *view* for short), the view controller has its own visual interface. Aside from providing the user interface, its task is to display data in the view, receive any user entries made there, and to react to user actions. Based on a data binding definition between UI element properties and context elements, the context of a view controller provides a view with all the data and information required. The business data displayed in the view should normally be provided to the view context from the context mapping to a custom context or controller context.

Window controller   The window controller[11] implements the presentation logic of the windows that belong to it. The presentation logic mainly includes the handling or triggering of different navigation events in a Web Dynpro application, such as starting or leaving an application or displaying windows. A window controller can also implement one or more component interface views defined as visual component interfaces of a Web Dynpro component.

Controller interfaces   Web Dynpro puts into effect for its controllers a special, multi-level interface concept that is integralfor implementing application logic in the individual controller classes. A special IPrivate<Name of Controller> API (IPrivate API for short) is created for each Web Dynpro controller and can be accessed by the wdThis instance variable with which the application developer can use other generated and generic controller functionality. The generated and generic controller code need not be

---

11 The *window controller* was added to Web Dynpro component model in SAP NetWeaver CE 7.1. It implements the now abstract component interface view controller and thereby replaces the the component interface view controller class available in SAP NetWeaver 2004 and 7.0.

implemented itself but is provided by an internally created controller class, such as the Web Dynpro runtime environment.

While the `IPrivate` API of a controller represents the interface to its own functionality, `IPublic` represents the interface for external users, and with it, other controllers. This API is generated automatically and contains the context API, public methods, and access to the generic controller API. Other controllers can then access the `IPublic` API of a controller after its use has been defined.

The `IPrivate` and `IPublic` controller interfaces generated by the Web Dynpro development environment adapt themselves to the declarations made by the developer. In this sense they are *dynamic* and are individually tailored to the specific controller of an application. These generated controller APIs do not, however, include the entire controller functionality available at runtime. They include only that part directly related to the definitions made by the application developer (controller uses, context structures, actions, results, inbound and outbound plugs, or public methods).

Web Dynpro controllers implement one or more generic interfaces (interfaces that are predefined by the Web Dynpro programming model) that can be used to access controller-relevant information, components, and further generic functions and services in your own application coding. All Web Dynpro controllers implement the `IWDController` API; component controllers use the `IWDComponent` interface; view controllers use the `IWDViewController`; and window controllers use the `IWDWindowController`.

Generic
controller APIs

6.1.3 Interfaces of a Web Dynpro Component

A Web Dynpro component has two types of interface that it exposes to another component: the *component interface view* and the *component interface controller*.

A component interface view makes an internal window visible externally. Another component can then embed this visual interface as a normal view into a window of its own and define navigation links: start-up plugs for starting Web Dynpro applications, exit plugs for ending them,

Component interface view as visual interface

and inbound and outbound plugs for defining navigation links. Each Web Dynpro component can either specify none, one, or multiple component interface view(s) as visual interfaces.

The component interface controller allows an external component to interact with the embedded component at controller level; this can, for example, take place by calling methods, reacting to events, or exchanging context data using an *internal* or *external* interface context mapping. The component interface controller can be called at Java API level by controllers in other Web Dynpro components by using its IExternal API.

The Web Dynpro component model defines these component interfaces in two different ways: *Local* and *standalone* component interface definitions.

- ▶ **Local Definition of a Component Interface**
  The *local component interface* (*local component interface definition*) is defined in one of the implementing components. The implementation of the component interface controller takes place in the component controller and the defined component interface views are implemented by Windows and their window controllers. The local component interface is not separated from its implementing component and is therefore to be understood as its self-defined interface for external users.

- ▶ **Standalone Definition of a Component Interface**
  In the Java programming language, an interface represents a type just as a class does. As with classes, Java interfaces define methods without actually implementing them themselves. An interface is therefore an abstraction of a class released from its implementation. The advantage of this interface approach is that the use of an interface can take place separately from its implementation (meaning that the implementation can be changed independently of its user). As a result of this standalone Web Dynpro component interface definition concept), the loose coupling approach between the interface user and the interface implementation is transferred to the Web Dynpro component model. It makes it possible at design time to define usage relationships at the component level without needing to know about the Web Dynpro components to be implemented. The separation of the

definition and implementation in the Web Dynpro component model makes for more flexible application architecture.

The diagram in Figure 6.2 sets out multiple usage and implementation relationships between a Web Dynpro component and other Web Dynpro objects, such as other components, a component interface definition, or a model.

Web Dynpro component diagram

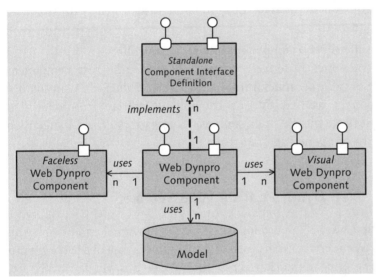

Figure 6.2 Implementation and Usage Relationships of a Web Dynpro Component

A component can implement multiple standalone component interface definitions and it can use other components. It is necessary to use a model in a Web Dynpro component to define the backend connection. Components of this type are called *model components*.

A Web Dynpro component and its interfaces are shown in the diagram and in the *Component Modeler* of the Web Dynpro tools in support of the component diagram introduced in UML 2.0. With both of its interfaces, a Web Dynpro component has two special access points (called ports[12] in UML 2.0) that connect its outer environment with its inner:

---

12 To make it easier to distinguish between UI ports and controller ports, UI ports (component interface views) are shown with rounded corners. Controller ports (component interface controllers) are shown as squares as defined in UML 2.0.

- **UI Port = Component Interface View**
  Component interface views represent the visual interfaces of a Web Dynpro component for the modular construction of Web Dynpro user interfaces (previously known as UI ports). A visible Web Dynpro component exposes at least one component interface view that is implemented within the component by one or more *windows* and their associated window controllers. It is also possible for there not to be a component interface view, as in the case of non-visual (faceless) components.

- **Controller Port = Component Interface Controller**
  The component interface controller of a Web Dynpro component represents the second port type at controller level. Each Web Dynpro component has exactly one component interface controller that exposes context, methods, and events to external users (other Web Dynpro components).

6.2   Web Dynpro Calls a Web Service

In the first tutorial application, you will see how easily and quickly an existing Web service can be used to display stocks data in a Web Dynpro UI after entering the stock ticker symbols. To do this, you use a Web service from an external provider to read the stock data (called stocks Web service for short). As input parameter, the Web service needs a list of stock ticker symbols (these are used to uniquely identify the stocks listed at a stock exchange).

In the second practical part of this chapter (see Section 6.3, *Integrating Web Dynpro Components for Searching for Ticker Symbols*) you will enhance the example by adding a separate Web Dynpro component for searching for multiple stock ticker symbols.

The development of the first part of the tutorial application takes place in the following five steps (Figure 6.3):

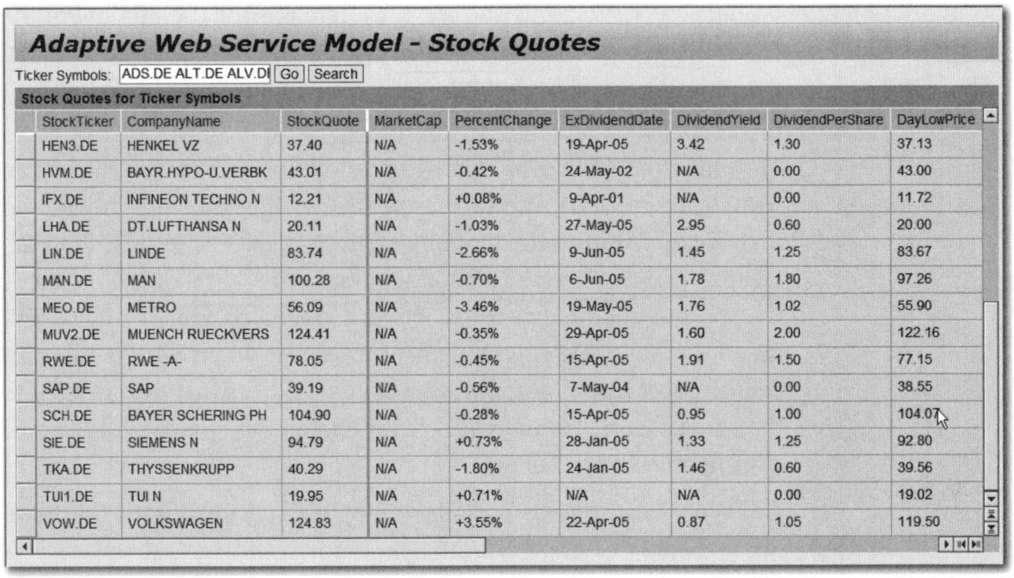

StockTicker	CompanyName	StockQuote	MarketCap	PercentChange	ExDividendDate	DividendYield	DividendPerShare	DayLowPrice
HEN3.DE	HENKEL VZ	37.40	N/A	-1.53%	19-Apr-05	3.42	1.30	37.13
HVM.DE	BAYR.HYPO-U.VERBK	43.01	N/A	-0.42%	24-May-02	N/A	0.00	43.00
IFX.DE	INFINEON TECHNO N	12.21	N/A	+0.08%	9-Apr-01	N/A	0.00	11.72
LHA.DE	DT.LUFTHANSA N	20.11	N/A	-1.03%	27-May-05	2.95	0.60	20.00
LIN.DE	LINDE	83.74	N/A	-2.66%	9-Jun-05	1.45	1.25	83.67
MAN.DE	MAN	100.28	N/A	-0.70%	6-Jun-05	1.78	1.80	97.26
MEO.DE	METRO	56.09	N/A	-3.46%	19-May-05	1.76	1.02	55.90
MUV2.DE	MUENCH RUECKVERS	124.41	N/A	-0.35%	29-Apr-05	1.60	2.00	122.16
RWE.DE	RWE -A-	78.05	N/A	-0.45%	15-Apr-05	1.91	1.50	77.15
SAP.DE	SAP	39.19	N/A	-0.56%	7-May-04	N/A	0.00	38.55
SCH.DE	BAYER SCHERING PH	104.90	N/A	-0.28%	15-Apr-05	0.95	1.00	104.07
SIE.DE	SIEMENS N	94.79	N/A	+0.73%	28-Jan-05	1.33	1.25	92.80
TKA.DE	THYSSENKRUPP	40.29	N/A	-1.80%	24-Jan-05	1.46	0.60	39.56
TUI1.DE	TUI N	19.95	N/A	+0.71%	N/A	N/A	0.00	19.02
VOW.DE	VOLKSWAGEN	124.83	N/A	+3.55%	22-Apr-05	0.87	1.05	119.50

Figure 6.3 Web Dynpro Application for Reading Stocks Data with an Adaptive Web Service Model

1. **Importing the Adaptive Web Service Model**

   Model import

   Web Dynpro tools provide a special wizard for importing an adaptive Web service model.[13] This means that all the classes and files required for communicating with the stocks Web service are created automatically in accordance with the WSDL description addressed by the URL. If the imported model is used in a specific Web Dynpro component, then the connection or binding of a controller context to the adaptive Web service model can be defined in the next step.

2. **Binding the Context to the Model**

   Context-to-model binding

   To display the stocks data returned by the stocks Web service in the model on the user interface, you must define the context-to-model binding in the second step. The context in the Web Dynpro programming model is a hierarchically structured storage place in a controller

13 An *adaptive Web service model* is a special Web Dynpro model type that is used for connecting a Web Dynpro application to Web services. The term 'adaptive' implies that connection, authentication, and encryption settings can be made in SAP NetWeaver Administrator using logical Web service destinations without code modification or redeployment.

on the server side. This storage place remains for the lifetime of the related controller and its components as Web Dynpro is included in the class of stateful Web framework. The context structure consists of elements called context nodes and context attributes.

The phrase *model binding* refers to the definition of a hierarchical context structure according to the classes contained in the model and their relationships to each other at design time. At runtime, the Web Dynpro runtime environment automatically ensures that data is transported in both directions between model, controller context and user interface. This automatic data transport only requires minimal coding effort from the application developer because it is restricted to the context initialization with executable model objects and the processing of Web service calls.

The Web Dynpro tools provide you with a specific wizard for defining a model binding relation. The model binding takes place at a declarative level at design time and does not include any application code.

Context mapping
3. **Defining the Context Mapping**
Context mapping relations can be defined for accessing context data across the controller, and even Web Dynpro component boundaries. In this way, global context data is stored centrally and can be referenced from other contexts. After the model binding of a controller context has taken place, the view controller contexts required for transporting data to the user interface can also be connected with the same model using context mapping. The business data stored centrally in the model can be used in multiple contexts without the need for programming.

In this tutorial application for reading stocks data, a context structure connected to the adaptive stocks Web service was previously defined in the component controller. To display the corresponding model data on the user interface at runtime (view layout), you must define at design time a context structure mapped to the component context in the corresponding view controller.

View layout and data binding
4. **Designing the User Interface**
An automatic, bidirectional data transport between the user interface at the client side and the controller context at the server side can be

defined using the data binding of UI element properties to the context. The user interface for entering stock ticker symbols and the table for displaying the related stocks data in the view layout can be created easily by using specific template wizards.

5. **Implementing Controller Code**

The implementation of the tutorial application includes both a view controller part and a component controller part. The view controller covers the event handling of the Go action triggered by the user to call the Web service.

Communication with the stocks Web service is encapsulated in the tutorial application in the component controller. It exposes the Web service call for getting stocks data with a suitable controller interface, so that the method can be called from the view controller.

At design time, the definition of the model binding takes place at the level of model classes, model class relations, and a corresponding hierarchical structure in the component controller context. At runtime, the adaptive Web service model comprises a graph of model object instances, which are referenced from the context. The code in the component controller includes the actual Web service calls and the binding of model objects to the context for initialization.

The functionality of the tutorial application has been kept very simple and is limited at first to entering a ticker symbol, triggering the Web service call using the pushbutton, and displaying the stocks data that are returned in a table.

This tutorial application is enhanced in Section 6.3 by a separate Web Dynpro component to search for multiple ticker symbols for specific stock indexes. If multiple ticker symbols are transferred to the stocks Web service, then this returns a corresponding number of stocks data that is then displayed in rows in the stock quotes table.

6.2.1 Preparation

When you develop the example, use the pre-prepared, local Web Dynpro development components (or Web Dynpro DCs) included on this book's DVD. The DVD contains the fundamental components of the application. This means that you do not have to create a local Web Dyn-

Controller implementation

Function scope of the tutorial application

Local Web Dynpro DCs as a template

pro DC containing a component and an application that can be addressed by URL. In addition to this, the template already contains the StockQuotesView view embedded in the StockQuotesWin window.

Importing the Local Web Dynpro Development Component as a Template

Execute the following steps to import the pre-prepared local Web Dynpro DCs to SAP NetWeaver Developer Studio:

1. Unpack the entire contents of the *WDAdaptiveWSSample_NWCE.zip* ZIP file from the *WebDynproSamples* DVD directory to the *C:\<workspace root folder>\<workspace name>.jdi\LocalDevelopment\DCs* directory. This directory must belong to the workspace defined by you when you first started SAP NetWeaver Developer Studio. The ZIP file must, for example, be unpacked to the *C:\Workspaces\WebDynpro_NWCE.jdi\LocalDevelopment\DCs* directory for the workspace directory *C:\Workspaces\WebDynpro_NWCE*.

2. Start SAP NetWeaver Developer Studio.

3. Open the **Perspective Development Infrastructure** using the menu options **Window • Open Perspective • Other • Development Infrastructure**.

4. In the **Component Browser** perspective view, select the nodes **Local Development • My Components** and select the context menu entry **Refresh**. As a result the four local Web Dynpro DCs tc/wd/demo/tisy, tc/wd/demo/ws, tc/wd/demo/wsa, and tc/wd/demo/wsb are added as entries to the **My Components** node (Figure 6.4).

5. With the toggle button, select all four local Web Dynpro DCs and select the context menu entry **Sync/Create Project • Create Active Project**.

6. Next, the four imported Web Dynpro DCs in the table are displayed in Web Dynpro Explorer.

Figure 6.4 Displaying the Local Web Dynpro DCs for the Tutorial Application in the Development Configuration Perspective

Name of the Local Web Dynpro DC	Description
[LocalDevelopment] tc/wd/demo/ws	Local Web Dynpro DC that implements the completed tutorial application for the adaptive Web service model (stocks Web service).
[LocalDevelopment] tc/wd/demo/wsa	Local Web Dynpro DC that contains the first template for the tutorial application. You will start the development in this local Web Dynpro DC.
[LocalDevelopment] tc/wd/demo/wsb	Local Web Dynpro DC that contains the second template for the tutorial application. You will later define the use of a separate Web Dynpro component for searching for ticker symbols here.
[LocalDevelopment] tc/wd/demo/tisy	Local Web Dynpro DC that contains a reusable Web Dynpro component for searching for ticker symbols. This development component is required for the second tutorial application on the subject of Web Dynpro components.

Table 6.1 Local Web Dynpro Development Components for the Tutorial Application

When working with tables in the View Layout Designer, it can be an advantage[14] (see Section 6.2.6, *View Layout and Data Binding*) to modify certain settings of Web Dynpro tools.

1. Open the window for changing the settings using the menu entry **Window • Preferences...**.

2. In the top left entry field, enter the text "Web Dynpro" and select the filtered **Web Dynpro** node.

3. Deactivate the checkbox **View Designer • Context data • Show full binding path** so that the data binding to the context is only displayed by its attribute name in View Designer (Figure 6.5).

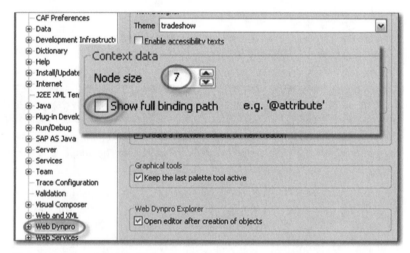

Figure 6.5 Changing Specific Settings for the Web Dynpro Tools

4. In addition, set the setting **View Designer • Context data • Node size** to the value **7** so that the tables in View Designer are filled with more dummy data records.

---

14 Due to missing backend data, context data in View Designer is replaced by context attribute addresses at design time; however, their lengths do not normally match those at runtime. A possible advantage of adapting settings is that, as a result of the shorter context attribute addresses (by concealing the entire binding path), the actual widths of table columns are shown in View Designer.

6.2.2 View of the Pre-Prepared Local Web Dynpro Development Components

Before developing the Web Dynpro tutorial application for the adaptive Web service model, first take a look at the pre-prepared local Web-Dynpro DC called [LocalDevelopment] tc/wd/demo/wsa. The Web Dynpro tools offer more perspectives for use when modeling different Web Dynpro entities:

▶ **Web Dynpro Explorer**
Web Dynpro Explorer displays all the entities that belong to a Web Dynpro DC in a tree structure: Web Dynpro applications, models, standalone component interface definitions,[15] Web Dynpro components, Java dictionaries, and various resources (including MIME objects, resource files, or own Java classes) count among those entities (Figure 6.6).

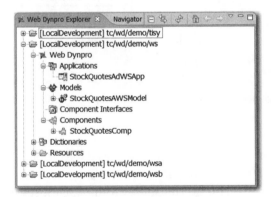

Figure 6.6 Displaying Imported Web Dynpro DCs for the Tutorial Application in Web Dynpro Explorer

▶ **Component Modeler**
Component Modeler is a graphical modeling tool for easily creating Web Dynpro components, defining usage relationships between multiple Web Dynpro components, for defining Web Dynpro applica-

---

15 A *standalone component interface definition* is the abstract description of an interface exposed by a Web Dynpro component (component interface view and component interface controller) without implementation. With this it is possible to define loosely coupled usage relationships between multiple Web Dynpro components, as with Java interfaces between Java classes.

tions, and for importing different Web Dynpro models. Component Modeler can be opened in Web Dynpro Explorer by double-clicking on a Web Dynpro DC.

Figure 6.7 shows the initial Web Dynpro DC [LocalDevelopment] tc/wd/demo/wsa in the Component Modeler: The Web Dynpro application[16] StockQuotesWSApp points to the StockQuotesComp component, more specifically to the start-up plug of the StockQuotesCompInterfaceView component interface view[17] exposed by the StockQuotesComp component.

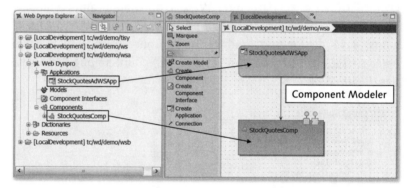

Figure 6.7 Pre-Prepared Web Dynpro DC in Component Modeler

▶ **Data Modeler**

Data Modeler is another graphical modeling tool used for various definitions in a specific Web Dynpro component: Adding new views, models, windows, optional custom controllers to the logical separation of the application, and for using other Web Dynpro components, such as for defining mapping relationships between the controller context included. Data Modeler can be opened easily in Component Modeler by double-clicking on a component.

---

16 A *Web Dynpro application* is an entity for starting a Web Dynpro application with a URL. It points to a start-up plug exposed by an interface view of the root component to be displayed. The term *root component*, therefore, means that a Web Dynpro application can consist of multiple hierarchical components of which one component begins with the embedding.

17 The *component interface view* is a visual interface of a Web Dynpro component that can be embedded by other components in their own view layouts, or addressed by a Web Dynpro application.

Figure 6.8 shows the initial Web Dynpro component Stock-QuotesComp, which, along with component controller, contains the StockQuotesView view embedded in the StockQuotesWin window.

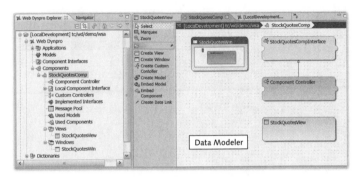

Figure 6.8 View of Pre-Prepared Web Dynpro Component StockQuotesComp in Data Modeler

▶ **Navigation Modeler**

Navigation Modeler is the third graphical modeling tool used for defining view compositions. The term 'view composition' covers all those view assemblies in a window that can be reached using navigation links. A view assembly, on the other hand, is an arrangement of a views displayed in a browser window at a particular time.

In its simplest form, a window contains only one view, but multiple views and even component interface views[18] of other visual Web Dynpro components are nested within it.

To navigate across window and component interface view borders, inbound and outbound navigation plugs can be defined in a window. These window plugs can then be used to define navigation links to and from views and component interface views inside the window. Data Modeler can be opened in Component Modeler simply by double-clicking on a component.

Figure 6.9 shows the StockQuotesWin window with the embedded StockQuotes View view in Navigation Modeler. Note the breadcrumb

---

18 Using a visual interface, a Web Dynpro component can provide other components in the windows or views it implements as user interfaces. This visual interface is called *component interface view* and it is implemented in a Web Dynpro component in exactly one window.

navigation at the top of Navigation Modeler. This special navigation bar makes it easier for you to move quickly between the three modeling levels **Component Modeler**, **Data Modeler**, and **Navigation Modeler**.

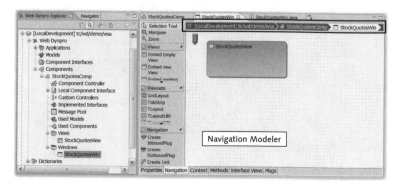

Figure 6.9 View of the StockQuotesWin Window in Navigation Modeler

▸ **View Designer**

At the lowest level, the View Designer enables the design of the user interface in a Web Dynpro view using WYSIWYG (*what you see is what you get*), known as a view layout. An extensive library of UI elements that are subdivided into different categories is available to you for this. View Designer can be opened in Navigation Modeler by simply double-clicking a view.

Figure 6.10 shows the layout of the `StockQuotesView` view with the `PageHeader` UI element already added.

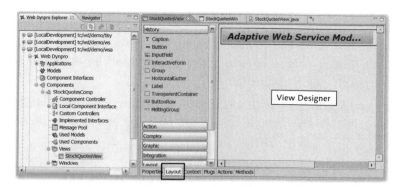

Figure 6.10 Layout of the StockQuotesView View in View Designer

6.2.3   Importing the Adaptive Web Service Model

By developing the first model-based Web Dynpro application, you build upon the pre-prepared template of a local Web Dynpro DC, you can begin by importing the adaptive Web service model for reading stocks data.

In this, and the following steps, you will use the Data Modeler as a simple modeling tool for various definitions related to data flow. Included in this are the import of an adaptive Web service model in the local Web Dynpro DC, the use of this model in a Web Dynpro component, the definition of the context-to-model binding in the component controller, the interface enhancement of the component controller for exporting an adaptive Web service call, the mapping of the view to the component controller context through to the definition of action and its event handling in view controller, and the template-based enhancement of the view layout with integrated data binding. Accordingly, all the definitions required for developing the tutorial application are made from Data Modeler without having to branch to entities in Web Dynpro Explorer.

Modeling step process

1. Switch back to the view of the Web Dynpro component Stock-QuotesComp in Data Modeler (Figure 6.11).

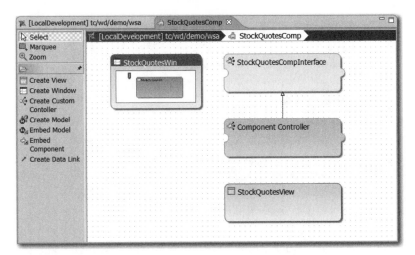

Figure 6.11 Component StockQuotesComp as Seen in Data Modeler

Data Modeler can be opened for each Web Dynpro component by double-clicking on its node in Web Dynpro Explorer, or by the context menu entry. However, the easiest way to access it is using Component Modeler — by double-clicking on the **StockQuotesComp** tab, the Data Modeler then expands to fill the entire workspace in Developer Studio. Another way is to use the **Overview** function in the **Outline** view at the bottom left to select the visible area.

Importing an adaptive Web service model

The models used by a Web Dynpro component are displayed in Data Modeler. Models are first defined in a Web Dynpro DC independent from a specific Web Dynpro component. In a second step an existing model is explicitly used in Web Dynpro component. This means that both the *model import* and the *model use* steps can be combined into one in Data Modeler.

2. To do this, choose the **Create Model** icon in the left-hand toolbar and then move the mouse pointer over the work area in Data Modeler. Click again to open the wizard for importing a model.

3. In the list of possible model types, choose the **Adaptive Web Service Model** entry (Figure 6.12) and use **Next** to switch to the second step where you define the fully qualified name of the adaptive Web service model. This includes the name of the model and the corresponding package name that will contain the generated model classes.

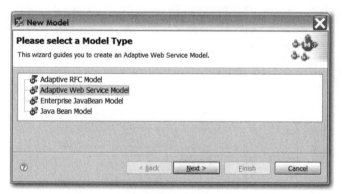

Figure 6.12 Selecting Model Type Adaptive Web Service Model

4. Give the name "StockQuotesAWSModel" to the new model and select **com.sap.tc.wd.demo.ws.model.sqws** as the package name. Because the template already contains the related directory, you can just select

the package name using the **Browse** pushbutton. Ensure that you import every imported Web Dynpro model into its own package namespace; the sub package name *.model.<logical name>* can be used for this.

5. In the next step, you specify the source where the WSDL description belonging to the Web service is to be read from. In this tutorial application, you use an external Web service provider for this that implements the stocks Web service. First, select the **No Logical Destinations — use WSDL URL for ...** radiobutton in the **Logical Destinations** dialog box and then switch to the next dialog step (Figure 6.13); this step is not executed for the used external stock Web service.[19]

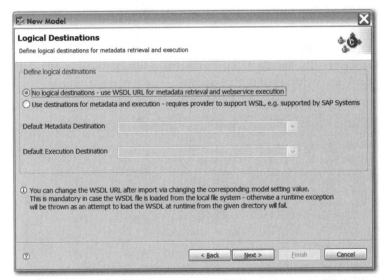

Figure 6.13 Defining Logical Destinations of an Adaptive Web Service Model

6. In the next step you specify the WSDL address of the external stock Web service used, *http://www.swanandmokashi.com/HomePage/Web-Services/StockQuotes.asmx?WSDL*, then click **Next** (Figure 6.14). If it is

---

19 Note that it is not explained in the current example how to define logical Web service destinations. For details on this, see the *How to Consume an Enterprise Service from the ES Workplace in Web Dynpro* guide in the new SAP NetWeaver Composition Environment 7.1 blog *(https://www.sdn.sap.com/irj/sdn/weblogs?blog=/pub/wlg/6281)* or the SDN Wiki *Web Dynpro Java: FAQ — Models — Adaptive Web Service (https://wiki.sdn.sap.com/wiki/x/IhU)*.

not possible to read the external WSDL description, check whether the **proxy host** and **proxy port** settings are defined correctly in the **Internet Proxy Settings** for SAP NetWeaver Developer Studio.

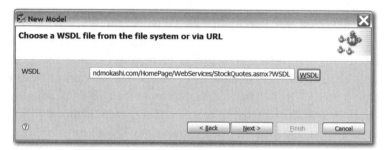

Figure 6.14 Entering the URL of the External Stock Web Service Description

7. After importing the external WSDL description, rename the package namespaces and names of model classes in the next dialog box (Figure 6.15). This option is not demonstrated in the current example.

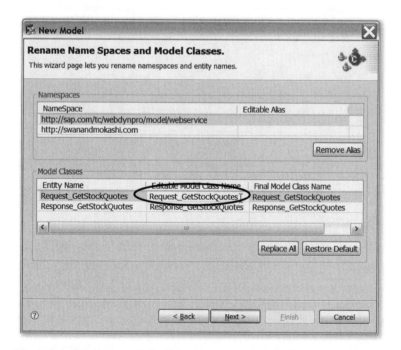

Figure 6.15 Employee Web Service Model Added to Web Dynpro Component in Data Modeler

8. After this dialog step, the XML files needed to describe the external stocks Web service in an adaptive Web service model are generated automatically. The imported adaptive Web service model called StockQuotesAWSModel used by the StockQuotesComp component is then represented by a model symbol in the Data Modeler belonging to the component (Figure 6.16).

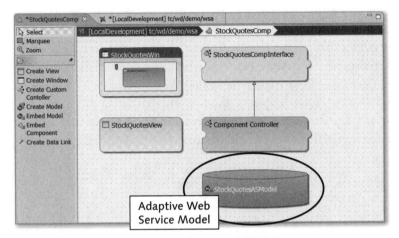

Figure 6.16 Adaptive Web Service Model in Data Modeler

Generated Model Classes and Their Relationships to Each Other

At first, the adaptive Web service model exists only in the form of an XML description, based on the Web Dynpro meta model that is sufficient for declarative development. The related typed model classes (Java classes) that are used by application developers for implementing controllers are created in a separate build step by Web Dynpro generation framework before they are bundled into the deployment archive (EAR file).

The model classes generated for an adaptive Web service model enhance the generic interfaces IWDWSModel ClassExecutable, WSTypedModel-ClassExecutable, WSTypedModel Class and WSTypedModel of the adaptive Web service model API as part of the Web Dynpro runtime API in the packages com.sap.tc. webdynpro.model.webservice.api, and *.gci. The IWDWSInvocationModifier interface that allows a Web service model object to be modified dynamically before execution is also included in this API.

Adaptive Web service model API as enhancement of the Common Model Interface

The adaptive Web service model API, on the other hand, is a special enhancement of the Common Model Interface[20] to the unified model interface for connecting different model implementations to Web Dynpro.

Adaptive-
Web service model
classes and their
relationships

After a model import is completed, the classes contained in the model, and their relationships to each other, are displayed in Web Dynpro Explorer. The example model called StockQuotes AWSModel contains six model classes in total, some of which have relationships to other model classes. Note the two different symbols for model classes (Figure 6.17): The circles that are set slightly to the right with the green dashes to the left represent executable model classes (*Executable Model Classes*). You will later be able to trigger the actual Web service calls for executable model class type objects. In the current example, this is the Request_GetStockQuotes class for receiving the stocks and bond data related to the stock ticker symbols that were transferred.

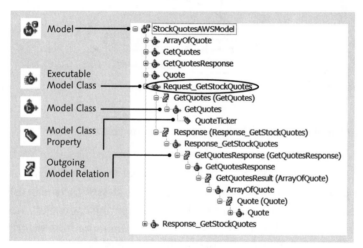

Figure 6.17 Model Classes of the Adaptive Web Service Model and Their Relationships to Each Other

So, how does the existing data model actually look in the adaptive Web service model called StockQuotesAWSModel? You can answer this ques-

---

20 You can find the documentation on the Common Model Interface API in SAP NetWeaver CE 7.1 either in the SAP NetWeaver Developer Studio help under **SAP NetWeaver CE Developer Studio Documentation • API Reference • Common Model Interface** or online under *https://help.sap.com/javadocs/nwce/current/cmi/index.html*.

tion by looking at the properties of the model classes involved and their relationships to each other. These are displayed by selecting a node in the model tree at the bottom right in the perspective view called **Properties** (Figure 6.18). You can see more details on this model class by double-clicking on a class in the model tree.

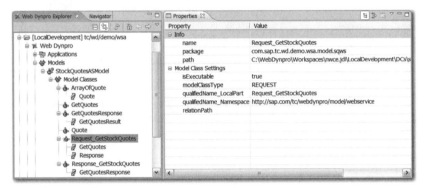

Figure 6.18 Model Classes, Model Relationships, and Their Properties as Seen in Web Dynpro Explorer

The executable model class `Request_GetStockQuotes` does not contain any properties itself; however, the two `GetQuotes` and `Response` relationships come from here. The `GetQuotes` relationship points to the `GetQuotes` class of the same name, which contains a list of the stock ticker symbols to be transferred to the stocks Web service in its single `QuoteTicker` property of type `String`. The second relationship with the name `Response` points to the `Response_GetStockQuotes` class, which contains the response of the Web service. The response basically consists (three further relationships, see Figure 6.17) of a list of `Quote` type objects that contain data relating to a stock.

Two Sides of a Model — Difference Between Design Time and Runtime

It is particularly important for the application developer to understand the Web Dynpro model at both design time and runtime. The two perspectives represent two sides of the same model. At design time, the model classes and their relationships to each other are defined in a Web Dynpro model. Properties are defined in the model classes and the relationships are identified by the associated model classes and their cardi-

Observing model at design time

nalities (0..1, 1..1, 0..n). You must switch from class level when modeling at design time to model instance level at runtime, as illustrated in Figure 6.19.

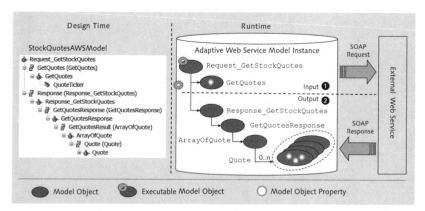

Figure 6.19 Model Classes and Their Relationships at Design Time in Contrast to the Model Object Graph at Runtime

Observing model
at runtime

The first thing to do at runtime is to create an object instance of type StockQuotesAWSModel for the used adaptive Web service model. An instance of the related executable model class also has to be created to call a stock Web service; in this case this is the Request_GetStockQuotes class. In the current model, the QuoteTicker input parameter (a string with a list of ticker symbols) required by the stocks Web service is defined as a property of the GetQuotes class associated with the executable model class. First, a GetQuotes instance needs to have been created at runtime to be able to transfer this parameter to the Web service and to then associate it with the executable instance Request_GetStock-Quotes with a setter method call (Figure 6.19, Point ❶).

Model at runtime =
model object graph

If this *input part* of the adaptive Web service model was created at the object instance level, then the actual Web service call can take place with the execute() method. The adaptive Web service runtime environment now communicates with the external Web service, receives its results as *output,* and then stores them at the instance level in the model object graph of the adaptive Web service model. This part then takes over the adaptive Web service runtime so that there is no further programming effort required of the application developer. Figure 6.19, Point ❷, shows which model objects were created for the output list of stocks data returned by the Web service. The stocks data itself is saved in a list of `Quote` type model objects.

6.2.4 Defining the Context-to-Model Binding in Component Controller

After this detailed examination of the structure of the imported adaptive Web service model, the next step is to define a connection of a suitable context structure to the model (*context-to-model binding* for short). This involves connecting the Web Dynpro UI layer or application logic declaratively to the business logic represented in the adaptive Web service model.

For the sake of simplicity, you implement communication with the stocks Web service partially directly in the pre-existing standard component controller. Alternatively, you could also include the Web service call in an optional *custom controller* (this is advisable when separating extensive application logic). View controllers can also communicate directly with the stocks Web service, but the separation of various interests (view control and user interaction as well as the connection to the model layer) in different controllers (view controllers as opposed to custom controllers) would no longer be included with this direct access to business logic.

Implementing Web service calls in component controller

Component controllers can expose its Web service call using a public service method exposed to its `IPublic` API. In this way, the connections to the model layer and Web service calls are included in component controller and are made accessible for view controller and custom controller in the same component. Access to the stocks data in the context of the component controller takes place later with context mapping. It is first relevant here to connect the custom context to the imported Web service model, what is named *context-to-model binding*.

A custom controller or component controller with a context-to-model binding and service methods for triggering Web service calls is known as a service controller in the Web Dynpro tools. Data Modeler includes a special wizard to create a service controller of this type, which combines the following steps:

Template wizard for defining a service controller

- Adding a new custom controller (or service controller), the wizard can also be used directly in the existing component controller
- Defining the context-to-model binding
- Adding a public service method to trigger a Web service call

1. For the `StockQuotesComp` component switch to Data Modeler and move the mouse pointer over the **Component Controller** area. Select the **Apply Template** context menu entry.

2. By clicking **Next,** you complete the first step with the **Service Controller** icon in the wizard window. Then the single executable model class `Request_GetStockQuotes` of the `StockQuotesAWSModel` is displayed (Figure 6.20).

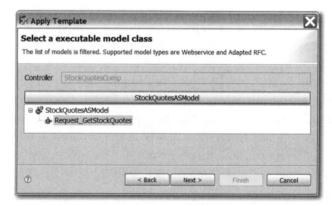

Figure 6.20 Selecting the Executable Model Class Request_GetStockQuotes in the Service Template Wizard

Defining a context-to-model binding

3. Select this model class and then click **Next.**

4. In the next step you will define the actual context-to-model binding. Context-to-model binding means mapping the class model shown in Figure 6.17 to a suitable hierarchical context structure. In this way the data model contained in the model is transferred to the context and is then made available for further use in the Web Dynpro component (for example, for context mapping or data binding). This step happens to a large extent automatically, you just have to select which levels or elements are to be included in the model binding.

5. As shown in Figure 6.21, select all the checkboxes in the context hierarchy and click **Next.**

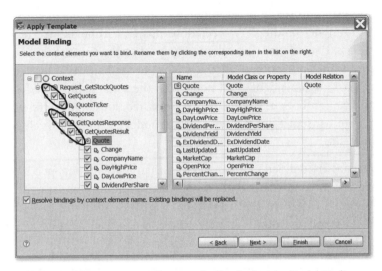

Figure 6.21 Selecting Context Elements for the Context-to-Model Binding

Before starting the next step, we should first take a closer look at the development of the context structure created by the model binding (Figure 6.22). First, an independent[21] context node of the same name is created for the executable model class `Request_GetStockQuotes`.

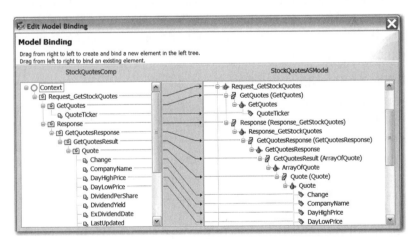

Figure 6.22 Representation of the Context-to-Model Binding with Web Dynpro Tools

---

21 Context nodes at the highest level, that is, directly below the root node, are termed independent. All nodes that appear lower in the hierarchy are dependent nodes, as their content normally depends on a node element in the parent node.

Dependent context node for each relationship

It is interesting to see how the model relationships are handled in the context-to-model binding. Two relationships exit from the executable model class: one relationship called GetQuotes to the GetQuotes class of the same name and another called Response to the Response_GetStock-Quotes class. A dependent child node with the same name is added to the context for both relationships. At runtime, this node references model object instances of the type of the model class that the relationship points to.

If properties are defined in a model class, then these are mapped in the context to new context attributes in the corresponding context node. In this example, these are the properties QuoteTicker in the GetQuotes model class and the other 15 properties Change, CompanyName, ... for identifying stocks data in the Quote model class.

The cardinality of the context node created in the context-to-model binding always corresponds to the target cardinality of the underlying relationship in the model. In the current case, a successful search of stocks data by the Web service for the ticker symbols (model object property QuoteTicker of type String) saved in the GetQuotes model object returns a list of Quotes that are stored in the model as a list of Quote type objects. These model objects are referenced from the context by the context-to-model binding and can be displayed on the user interface using standard Web Dynpro data transport mechanisms, context mapping, and data binding.

Adding a service method in component controller

1. In the final service controller wizard step, you add a public service method in the component controller, whereby other controllers, particularly the view controller, can trigger the stocks Web service call externally.

2. Leave the method name executeGetStockQuotes already entered in the input box unchanged (Figure 6.23) and confirm with the **Finish** pushbutton. By simply enhancing the component controller interface in this way, other controllers (such as the view controller) that use the component controller can trigger the Web service call implemented by the new method externally. Method parameters not transferred as the data exchange (list of ticker symbol) are set up between the controller contexts by the context mapping.

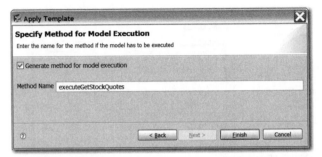

Figure 6.23 Adding a Public Method for Calling a Web Service from Other Controllers

3. The resulting definition of the context-to-model binding between component controller and the adaptive Web service model is shown by an arrow in Component Modeler and Data Modeler (Figure 6.24).

Displaying the context-to-model binding in Component Modeler and Data Modeler

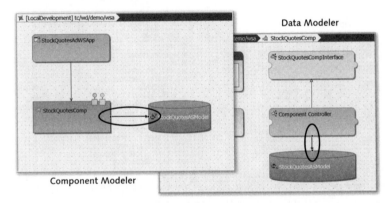

Figure 6.24 Arrow Representing the Context-to-Model Binding in Component Modeler and Data Modeler

4. In Web Dynpro Explorer, select the `StockQuotesComp` component controller component followed by the **Methods** view. You will then see the `executeGetStockQuotes` entry for the service method previously added by the wizard (Figure 6.25).

5. Also, note the structure of the context created in the component controller after the context-to-model binding. The representation of this in the context perspective view (Figure 6.26) corresponds to that shown in Figure 6.22. The model used is displayed hierarchically on the right side.

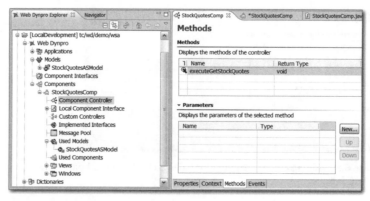

Figure 6.25 Component Controller in Web Dynpro Explorer and New Service Method executeGetStockQuotes

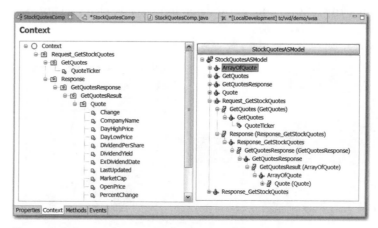

Figure 6.26 Context Structure in the Context of the StockQuotesComp Component Controller After Defining the Context-to-Model Binding

6.2.5 Defining the Context Mapping

Context mapping The next step creates an access to the data context in the view controller context based on context mapping. The data context is defined in the StockQuotesComp component controller and is bound to the adaptive Web service model. In Web Dynpro terms, a data context refers to a context (or context node and attribute) that has not been mapped; mapped context elements point to context elements in the data context. This means that the component context connected to the stocks model should be referenced from the view controller context so that this context data can then be transported to the view layout (and back again) using a data binding (this contains the form for entering ticker symbols and the table for displaying the corresponding stocks data).

1. The context mapping of the view context to the component context in the Data Modeler can be defined easily with a data link. To do so, reopen Data Modeler for the `StockQuotesComp` component and use the arrow icon in the left toolbar to add a data link. **Data link**

2. Holding the mouse button, drag an arrow (data link) from the `Stock-QuotesView` symbol to that of the `StockQuotesComp` component controller, then release (Figure 6.27).

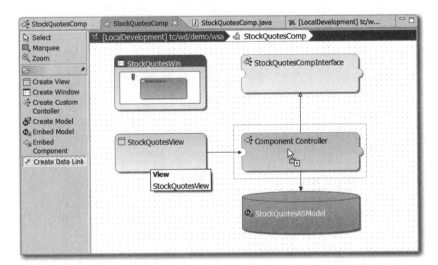

Figure 6.27 Drag a Data Link to the Context Mapping Between View Context and Component Context

3. Next, a window for defining the context mapping (Figure 6.28) opens. The data context in the component controller is displayed on the right side; the context in the view controller is still empty. Using drag and drop, drag the symbol of the upper model context node in the component context from right to left and release it over the root node symbol (context) in the view context.

4. A second window similar to the one you just saw now opens for the context-to-model binding. On the left-hand side, select the selection fields for all the context elements (Figure 6.29).

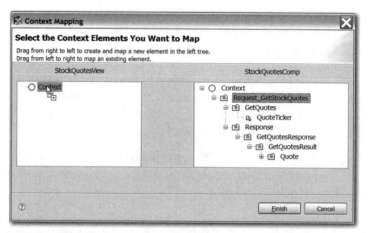

Figure 6.28 Defining the Context Mapping

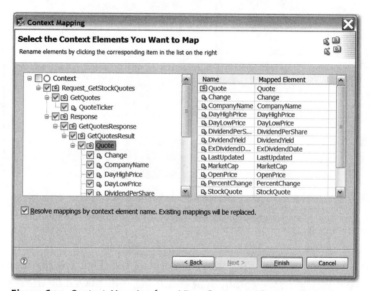

Figure 6.29 Context Mapping from View Context to Custom Context

It is possible to rename a mapped context node

Note that in this dialog box you can rename the mapped context element (context nodes and context attributes); however, this is not recommended in this particular example. To do so, you would first select the corresponding context element on the left side and then click to the right in a field in the **Name** column. This makes the name of the model node or model attribute editable; note that this step does not have any effect on the name of the original node in the component context.

5. Finally, click **Finish**. In the next wizard window you will see the context mapping as shown in Figure 6.30. In the view context, note the arrow shown in the icons of the mapped context elements: The mapping direction is determined as the connection from the view context to the data context in the component controller. The mapping arrow represents the fact that the mapped context elements reference the related elements in the data context.

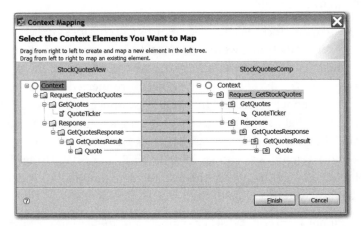

Figure 6.30 Context Mapping from View Context to Custom Context

6. After choosing **Finish**, the new data link is shown in Data Modeler (as a symbol for the defined context mapping) as an arrow between the StockQuotesView view and StockQuotesComp component controller (Figure 6.31).

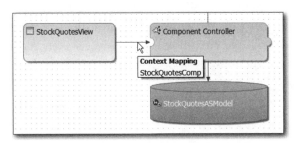

Figure 6.31 Context Mapping from View Context to Custom Context as Seen in Data Modeler

6.2.6 View Layout and Data Binding

Data binding   Using the context mapping definition from the view context to the component controller context, you can make the stock ticker symbols defined in the StockQuotesView view context editable in the view layout using a related form field: You can then display the stocks data that is returned in a table. In the context, the child node GetQuotes of the executable Request_GetStockQuotes model node contains a single QuoteTicker context attribute that is connected to the property of the same name in the GetQuotes model class. In the next step, you will connect an input field to this attribute.

After the search, the stocks Web service returns a list of stocks data relating to the ticker symbols that were entered and which are stored at runtime in the model object graph as a list of Quotes type objects of the type GetQuotesResult. The GetQuoteResults object is connected by the GetQuotesResponse model object and this in turn is connected by an object of type Response that itself is connected at the highest level by the executable model object of type Request_GetStockQuotes; the structure of the model object graph was shown in detail in Figure 6.19. Using the model binding, context mapping, and also the data binding, the stocks data can be displayed in a table of the StockQuotesView view.

Form template   Adding the input form for the ticker symbols and the definition of the data binding all takes place by simply using the form template of the Web Dynpro tools:

1. First, open the layout window of the StockQuotesView view and select the UI element RootUIElementContainer in the **Outline** area. Now you add the new input form to this container UI element using the **Apply Template** context menu entry.

2. In the wizard window, select the **Form** icon and in the subsequent wizard dialog box select the checkbox for the QuoteTicker context attribute in the corresponding Request_GetStockQuotes.GetQuotes node (Figure 6.32). The Response node and its child elements are not selected.

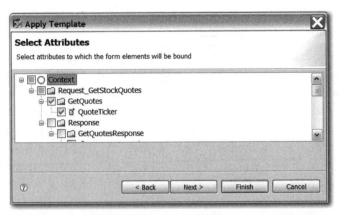

Figure 6.32 Selecting Context Elements when Creating a Search Form
Using the Form Template Wizard

3. In the next step, you can change the type of the editor UI elements to
be used and the order of the corresponding fields in the view layout
when selecting multiple context attributes with the arrow buttons
(Figure 6.33, Point ❶).

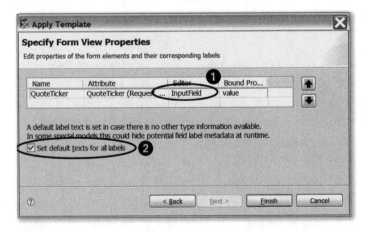

Figure 6.33 Defining Type and Order of Form Editor UI Elements

4. To do this, leave the **Set Default Texts for All Labels** (Figure 6.33,
Point ❷) checkbox selected and ensure that the label texts with the
names are pre-entered for the corresponding context attributes that
your editor fields connected.

5. In this case you can leave all the settings unchanged and quit the wizard with **Finish**.

6. Next, view the input form you added in the view layout. The embedding of a form field of type InputField, the labeling, and the binding of the value properties to the QuoteTicker context attribute were already completed automatically by the form template wizard. You just need to change the label text of the context attribute name to the correct label "Ticker Symbols" and define the tooltip property ("Enter list of ticker symbols separated by empty spaces or semicolons") (Figure 6.34).

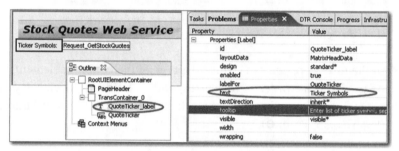

Figure 6.34 Editing UI Element Properties in the Outline and Properties Perspective Views

Defining the action binding

In the view layout you can now enter a list of stock ticker symbols in the search field; however, you cannot send these to the Web Dynpro runtime environment yet on the server side. To be able to do so, you require an Action in the view controller, which is connected to the onAction event of a pushbutton (action binding). There is also a wizard just for this declaration step.

1. First, open the tab page for the layout of the StockQuotesView view and select the TransContainer_0 interface element in the **Outline** area. In the context menu, select the **Apply Template** entry again followed by the **Action Button** icon (Figure 6.35).

2. Add a pushbutton connected to an action using the appropriate wizard. It can be defined at the same time which method of another controller is to be called in the event handler of the action. In the current case, this is the executeGetStockQuotes() public method of the StockQuotesComp component controller for triggering the Web ser-

vice call. With this wizard, you can preempt a large part of what needs to be implemented.

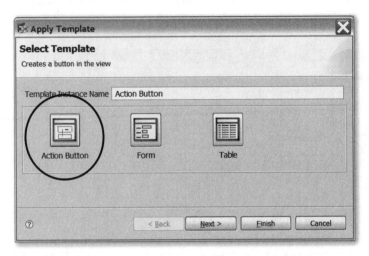

Figure 6.35 Selecting the Template Wizard for Adding a Pushbutton Connected to an Action

3. In the first wizard step, enter the text "Go" in the **Button Label** (Figure 6.36). The names of the actions to be created and the associated action event handlers are formed automatically from the text entered in the **Button Label**. If actions were already defined in the view controller, then you can connect the pushbutton to be added to these.

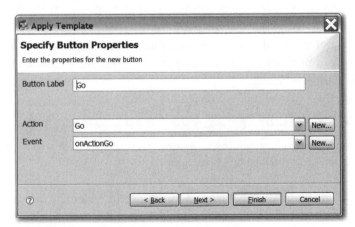

Figure 6.36 Defining the Button Label and Adding a New Action of the Same Name

4. After entering "Go", proceed to the next wizard step and define the controller method to be called in the event handler. In this case, this is the `executeGetStockQuotes` of the `Stock-QuotesComp` component controller after selecting the **Call Method** checkbox (Figure 6.37).

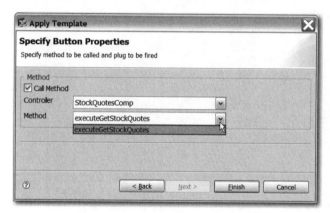

Figure 6.37 Defining the Button Label and Adding a New Action of the Same Name

5. Quit the wizard after choosing **Finish**. Then, in the **Outline** area, move the new button interface element to the container called `TransContainer_0` using drag & drop.

6. Figure 6.38 shows the interface element added for the input for: A label, an input field for the stock ticker symbols, and a pushbutton. The `@QuoteTicker` declaration in the input field expresses that the `value` property is bound to the context attribute called `QuoteTicker`, whereas the corresponding node path `Request_GetStockQuotes.GetQuotes` is not shown due to the setting made at the beginning in the Web Dynpro preferences: **View Designer** • **Context Data** • **Show Full Binding Path** (`false`).

Figure 6.38 Simple Form for Inputting Ticker Symbols

Advantages of the action concept

At this point, you might ask yourself why an interface element event is bound to an action and not directly to an event handler in the view controller in the Web Dynpro programming model. Even though this *indi-*

rection might seem unnecessary at first because of the additional declaration effort that it requires, it actually offers some distinct advantages that would not be possible if the UI element event and the event handler were bound directly.

First, take a look at the Web Dynpro action binding concept shown in Figure 6.39. The view layout contains a UI element in which an event is defined with a parameter, if required. This could, for example, be the event `onColSelect` in the table UI element (`IWDTable.IWDOnColSelect`) with the parameter `col` (`IWDTable.IWDOnColSelect.COL`). The UI element event is now bound to an action defined in the view controller. In turn, the action is associated with a maximum of one related action event handler in the view controller; this is called at runtime on the server side after the user at the client side has triggered the action with an interaction.

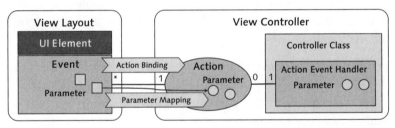

Figure 6.39 Defining the Button Label and Adding a New Action of the Same Name

This concept offers the following advantages:

▶ Different UI element events can be bound to the same action event handler. In the current example, you can use this to your advantage by binding the `onEnter` event of the `QuoteTicker` input field (in the input form created above) to the same `Go` action to which the pushbutton is also bound. In this way, the user can trigger the stocks Web service by using the **Go** pushbutton in the view layout and by pressing the enter key on the keyboard.

▶ Action objects whose status can be changed dynamically exist for actions at runtime. If, for example, an action object is set to `disabled` in the application code, then all the UI elements bound to this action are automatically shown as deactivated in the view layout; a pushbutton may no longer be used.

▶ By defining a parameter mapping relationship[22] between the parameter of the UI element events and the related action parameter or action event parameter, the Web Dynpro runtime environment can transfer parameter values of UI element events (for example, the ID of the triggering UI element) to the action event handler. This means that an action event handler can be completely separated from the triggering UI element event. Events of different UI elements (using a pushbutton, clicking a link, or selecting a menu entry) can therefore be connected to the same action in this way.

▶ Actions can be created dynamically at runtime using controller code so that UI element events can later be bound to them dynamically.

Embedding tables with stocks data Once you have defined a simple input form for stock ticker symbols in the view layout, use the next step to add a table to the stocks data output. You can also use a special template wizard for this step, which makes it considerably easier to add UI elements for tables, table columns, table headers, and table cell editors UI elements, as well as define the context binding.

1. Open the layout window of the `StockQuotesView` view and select the `RootUIElementContainer` interface element in the **Outline** area. A table is now added to this container UI element using the context menu entry **Apply Template**.

2. In the wizard window, select the **Table** icon and select the checkbox of the dependent **Quote** context node (or `Request_GetStockQuotes. Response.GetQuotesResponse.GetQuotesResult.Quote`) in the next wizard dialog box (Figure 6.40).

For reasons of simplicity, select the **Quote** node directly so that all of the context attributes contained within it are also selected. You can restrict the width of the table (despite the number of columns) by simply adapting specific table properties in a later step.

---

22 A *parameter mapping relationship* can be defined in Web Dynpro tools for a UI element selected in the outline view using the **Parameter Mapping** context menu entry. A wizard window opens where you can map parameters from UI element events to action events using drag & drop. This saves implementing the parameter mapping in the view controller method `wdDoModifyView()`.

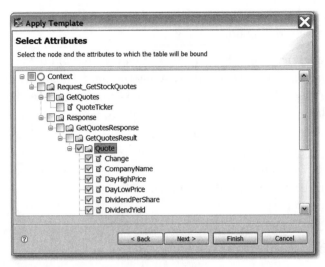

Figure 6.40 Binding a Table to the Quote Context Node

3. In the next wizard step, be sure to select the **Set Default Header Texts for All Columns** checkbox. Otherwise, the column headers would remain empty instead of being filled with the technical name of the related context attribute. In practice these column headers are usually defined in the simple data types of a Java dictionary, but context attribute names are sufficient as column headers for this tutorial application.

4. Move the rows `StockTicker`, `CompanyName`, and `StockQuote` to the highest position. In this wizard step, you can also define the cell editors to be used in the individual columns; however, you will not make use of this here.

5. Close the table template wizard with **Finish**.

6. In the **Outline** perspective view, select the table UI element that you just added with the ID `Table_0` and make the following settings in the **Properties** view:

   ▶ `scrollableColCount` = **6**

   ▶ `width` = **100%**

   ▶ `visibleRowCount` = **15**

7. Set the `fixed-Position` property to the value **left** for the first three tableColumn UI elements (`StockTicker`, `CompanyName`, and `Stock-`

Quote). As a result of this, the first three table columns will remain visible even when scrolling horizontally.

After this development step, the fully defined view layout of the Stock-QuotesView is displayed in the WYSIWYG View Designer[23] (Figure 6.41). At design time, the table content is made visible using context attribute addresses (defined by the data binding) of the <nodename> @...@<attributename> form. By changing the Web Dynpro settings at the start of the example, the full context attribute address is shown shortened to just the attribute name and the table is therefore shown with more realistic column widths in the View Designer.

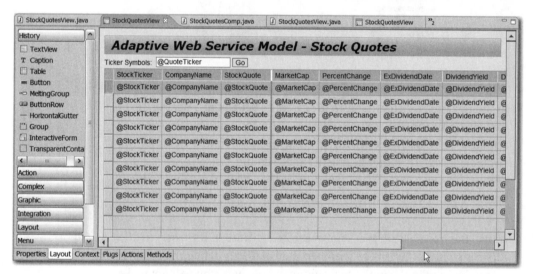

Figure 6.41 Displaying the Table for Stocks Data in the View Designer

Data transport   At this point, make yourself clear on how the definition of the data transport looks between the view layout, view context, component context, and model at design time (Figure 6.42).

▸ After inputting the ticker symbols in the StockQuotesView view form, they reach the context of the related view controller using the data

---

23 Note that the view layout, along with any missing business data, is displayed in the View Designer just as it is rendered at runtime in the Web Dynpro HTML client. An iterative build, deployment, and start of the application for viewing the Web Dynpro user interface in the browser is therefore no longer required at view level.

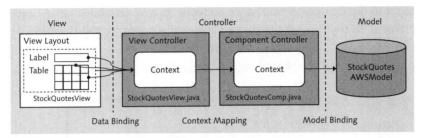

Figure 6.42 Defining the Data Transport

binding. View controller context elements reference elements in the context of the component controller based on the defined context mapping relation. Context data is not transported this way, but saved directly in the data context (known as the component controller context here). A simple reference to the component context is defined in the view context with the context mapping.

▶ The component context is now connected with a model binding to the adaptive Web service model `StockQuotesAWSModel`. In this way, the stock ticker symbols entered by the user and stored in the context at runtime reach the model and they then, using the Web service client, reach the actual Web service, which in turn deals with retrieving the related stocks data.

▶ The stocks data is stored in the model (object graph) as a list of related model objects of type `Quote` and referenced by the component context (context-to-model binding). Based on its mapping relationship to the component context, the view context also references the `Quote` objects stored in the model.

▶ The stocks data is finally displayed on the user interface as a table as a result of the context data binding between the table in the view layout and the view context.

Web Dynpro tools make it possible to track the binding chains[24] defined for the data transport with the special **Binding Chain** perspective view. You can open this **Binding Chain** view by first selecting an interface ele-

Displaying binding chains

---

24 Binding chain here refers to the combination of data binding between the user interface and context, context mapping between multiple controller contexts, and model binding between context and model.

ment in the **Outline** view of a view layout (in this case, the `QuoteTicker` element in the `StockQuotesView` view) and then selecting the **Binding Chain** context menu entry. The **Binding Chain** perspective view then opens a graphical display of the defined binding chain (Figure 6.43).

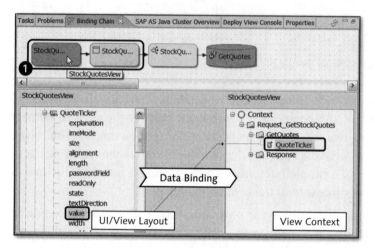

Figure 6.43 Perspective View for Displaying a Binding Chain — Data Binding

The upper section of the view shows all the entities that are involved connected by arrows, that is, the view layout, view controller, component controller, and model.

The lower section shows the related binding and mapping relationship specific to the selected entity:

▶ Figure 6.43 shows the data binding of the `value` property of interface element `QuoteTicker` in the layout of the `StockQuotes View` to the `Request_GetStockQuotes.Get Quotes.QuoteTicker` context attribute.

▶ Figure 6.44 shows the context mapping of the `Request_GetStock-Quotes.GetQuotes.QuoteTicker` attribute in the view context to the attribute of the same name in the component context.

▶ Figure 6.45 shows the context-to-model binding of elements of the component context to the respective relationships, model classes, and model attributes.

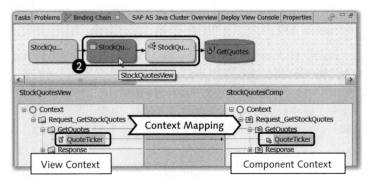

Figure 6.44 Binding Chain Display — Context Mapping

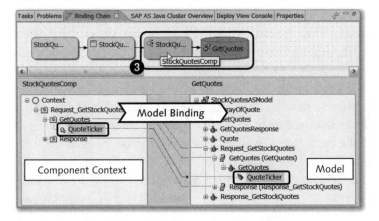

Figure 6.45 Binding Chain Display — Model Binding

It is particularly important to be able to visualize binding chains to be able to quickly understand the transport of data in a Web Dynpro component and also across Web Dynpro component boundaries.

6.2.7 Controller Implementation

After the declarations made earlier, the question now remains as to which code lines still have to be added by the programmer in the view controller and custom controller. The answer: Not many! This means that the application code implemented in the tutorial application was created almost entirely by the Web Dynpro code generation framework according to the declarations that were made. Now you can explore in detail which Java code was already added automatically to the related controller positions and what still needs to be enhanced.

Creating a new model instance

The runtime instance of an imported adaptive Web service model is not itself managed by the adaptive Web Service runtime environment integrated in Web Dynpro. Accordingly, a model instance of type `Stock-Quotes AWSModel` is created in the first controller code line where the related model class was automatically generated when importing the model.[25]

Binding an executable model object to the context

The model binding, that is, the definition of a context structure according to the classes and relationships contained in the model, takes place at design time solely at metadata level. Metadata is, for example, the context hierarchy (the contained nodes and attributes according to the model classes and their relationships to each other), the cardinalities of the context nodes, or the model classes[26] belonging to the node as the supplying relationship roles.[27] At runtime you have to imagine a model as a graph of model objects, that is, as a number of object instances for different business data that can be related to each other.[28] The model binding at design time does not yet include the direct connection of a context to the model at object level. For this you have to ensure that the uppermost context node (here the `Request_GetStockQuotes` model node) contains a node element that references an executable model object of type `Request_GetStockQuotes`. In other words, you first have to instantiate such a model object before you connect it to the uppermost model node. For this, you have to ensure that the constructor belonging to this model class requires the transfer of the adaptive Web service model instance (this is also the case for all other model classes).

---

25 Explicit model instance creation using controller code was not required for the predecessor of the adaptive Web service model in SAP NetWeaver 2004 and 7.0.

26 At runtime the node elements contained in a context node, depending on the node cardinality, reference the object instances of this model class contained in the model.

27 A *supplying relation role* specifies the relationship between two model classes required at runtime to determine object instances in the model object graph. This is determined automatically by the Web Dynpro runtime environment and causes an update of the controller context.

28 This important difference between the model at design time and the model object graph at runtime was already covered (see Figure 6.17).

In the component controller, this coding was already added by the wizard for the model binding to the wdDoInit() method (see Listing 6.1).

```
public void wdDoInit() {
   //@@begin wdDoInit()
   //$$begin Service Controller(-1758556445)
   StockQuotesAWSModel model =
     new StockQuotesAWSModel();
   wdContext.nodeRequest_GetStockQuotes()
     .bind(new Request_GetStockQuotes(model));
   //$$end
   //@@end
}
```

Listing 6.1 Initializing the StockQuotesComp.java Component Controller

At runtime, the uppermost model node in the context of the Stock-QuotesComp component controller now references an executable model object. It is clear now that the controller code previously implemented in wdDoInit() is still not sufficient. It is not the executable model object of type Request_GetStockQuotes that contains the QuoteTicker input parameter as a property but its associated model object of type Get-Quotes. Therefore, you must also create a model object of type Get-Quotes in the wdDoInit() method and transfer it to the executable model object. Only then is the model object graph correctly initialized and appears as shown in Figure 6.46. On the one hand, it contains an executable model object instance of type Request_GetStockQuotes that references a second object of type GetQuotes with a single string attribute as input parameter for ticker symbols. On the other hand, the context is connected to this model object, meaning that one node element in the Request_GetStockQuotes node in the controller context references the executable model object in the model object graph and another node element in the GetQuotes context node references the second model object. Finally, the QuoteTicker context attribute indicates the property of the same name in this second model object of type GetQuotes. As a result of this, the binding chain required for the automatic transport of data between user interface (view) and model is also created at runtime at instance level.

Second model object for saving ticker symbols

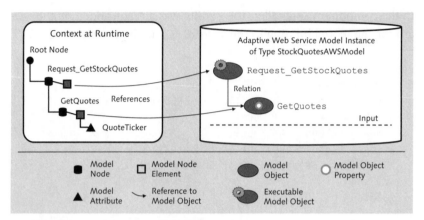

Figure 6.46 Context-to-Model Binding at Runtime

The Java code method from Listing 6.2 is to be implemented in the wdDoInit() method. Using the data binding and the context mapping, the form data or stock ticker symbols entered on the view interface then get to the object instance of type GetQuotes that is associated with the executable model object at runtime directly.

```
public void wdDoInit() {
  //@@begin wdDoInit()
  //$$begin Service Controller(-1758556445)
  StockQuotesAWSModel stockQuotesModel =
    new StockQuotesAWSModel();
  Request_GetStockQuotes requestStockQuotes =
    new Request_GetStockQuotes(stockQuotesModel);
  requestStockQuotes.setGetQuotes(
    new GetQuotes(stockQuotesModel));
  wdContext.nodeRequest_GetStockQuotes()
    .bind(requestStockQuotes);
  //$$end
  //@@end
}
```

Listing 6.2 Complete Initialization of the StockQuotesComp.java Component Controller

Organizing imports When looking at the component controller coding, you will be able to see that the compilation of the class will still fail due to missing import lines. Therefore, add these lines automatically using the **Source • Organize Imports** context menu entry.

How does the actual Web service call take place? When creating the component controller, its interfaces were enhanced by a public method called `executeGetStockQuotes()` and it was automatically implemented by the wizard for model binding. You can trigger the Web service call for employee registration by calling the `execute()` method for the executable model object. You can access this object instance in the context using the selected node element in the uppermost model node. You get the node element that is currently selected by `wdContext.current<Name of Node>()` and reach the model object by attaching `.modelObject()` (see Listing 6.3).

Web service call

```
public void executeGetStockQuotes() {
    //@@begin executeGetStockQuotes()
    //$$begin Service Controller(-327308351)

    IWDMessageManager manager =
        wdComponentAPI.getMessageManager();
    try {
        wdContext.
            currentRequest_GetStockQuotesElement()
              .modelObject().execute();
        wdContext.nodeResponse().invalidate();
    } catch (Exception ce) {
        manager.reportException(ce.getMessage());
    }
    //$$end
    //@@end
}
```

Accessing message manager, executing model object, invalidating response nodes

Listing 6.3 Executing Web Service Call in the executeGetStockQuotes() Method of the StockQuotesComp.java Controller

What does the code line mean after executing the `wdContext.nodeResponse().invalidate()` model object (invalidating the response node)? To answer this, you need to know that the executable model object is not stored in the context but rather in the model itself.

Invalidating response nodes

After calling a Web service, the model objects delivered by (and associated with) the Web service are stored in the model. Figure 6.47 shows exactly which model objects this involves.

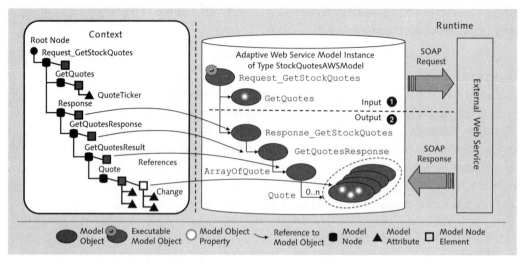

Figure 6.47 Context-to-Model Binding at Runtime After Executing the Web Service Call

The actual stocks data is received in a list of model objects of type `Quote`. The context first points to the executable model object (see code in `wdDoInit()`) and does not observe anything of the new response objects of type `Response_GetStockQuotes` in the model object graph or the objects associated with it in the model. Therefore, you first have to *invalidate* the response node in the context using the application code; this means you have to declare its contents (node elements) and any model objects that it references as invalid.

Once these invalid context contents are accessed on the user interface (with a data binding) or in the application code (in this case when displaying the stocks data returned by the Web service or the model objects of type `Quote` in the `Quote` mode node), the Web Dynpro runtime environment validates the context. *Validate* here means the connection of the object instances in the current model to the context. The context contents are then brought up to date regarding the current model status. This data comparison between context and model is completely automated by the Web Dynpro runtime environment in that it executes the supplying relationship roles contained in the context metadata as associations between model classes.

The Web service call takes place in a `try-catch` block, where the message returned by the Web service in case of an error is displayed on the interface by the Web Dynpro message manager.

The third place where the wizards have already added application code is the `onActionGo()` event handler for the `Register` action for sending the form data by the user. You already know that you only have to call the public method `executeGetStockQuotes()` of the `StockQuotesComp` component controller at this point to execute the Web service call. Nevertheless, the question of how you get to the API of the component controller in the view controller implementation remains.

Action event handling in view controller

According to the *information hiding* principle, all controllers for general use are hidden by default for all other controllers. If, however, in one controller (the controller of the `StockQuotesView` view in this case) you want to use the public API of another controller,[29] or you want to define a mapping for its context, then there needs to be a suitable controller usage defined. The use of the `StockQuotesComp` component controller was already added to the `StockQuotesView` view controller based on the context mapping from the view context that was previously defined for the custom context.

Defining controller usage

How do you access the API of the component controller in use in the action event handler? To answer this question, take a look at the `StockQuotes View.java` controller class that contains the user coding areas for the application code. Here you will find the hook methods `wdDoInit()` and `wdDoExit()` for initialization when creating and clearing before the deletion of the controller by the Web Dynpro runtime, `wdDoModifyView()` for dynamic modification of the view layout, `wdDoBeforeAction()` for nongeneric validation[30] of user entries using application

Controller API: IPrivateStock QuotesView and wdThis

---

29 Public APIs of Web Dynpro Custom Controllers and Web Dynpro Component Controllers are created automatically by Web Dynpro Generation Framework and begin with the prefix `IPublic`. This API is visible externally and is therefore also known as the `IPublic` API of a Web Dynpro Controller.

30 Not generic regarding generic type validation with the Java Dictionary Runtime. Generic type validation merely checks whether a user entry is dealing with a valid date and not whether this is in the future (which can, for example, be relevant for dates of birth).

code, the action event handler, and other defined methods. At the end you can add further code such as private instance variables or methods. All these areas contain their own application code.

Web Dynpro controller and its interfaces

Should this class already contain the complete controller implementation? The answer to this is no, because with the `InternalStockQuotes-View.java` class there is a further part of complete controller generation that is generated entirely automatically. So, where then should the controller context and action objects be stored, for example? Or where should the interfaces of other controllers used be accessible?

Because you will not ever actually add any code to this, you do not need to know what this internal controller class looks like in detail. However, you do need to know that an interface is provided as the access point for all important parts of the complete controller implementation using `IPrivateStockQuotesView`. The `wdThis` variable (which every Web Dynpro controller has) is of the type `IPrivateStockQuotesView`. This interface is generated automatically by the development environment and is adapted to the definitions made by the application developer. This means that the view controller API `IPrivateStockQuotesView` automatically expands as soon as you define the view context or add actions, outbound plugs, methods, and especially when you add new controller usages.

The `IPrivate<Controller>` interface also provides access to the interfaces of all the controllers used, in this case using the generated `wdGet-StockQuotesCompController()` method. This method delivers the `IPublic` API of the component controller used, which in turn contains the `executeGetStockQuotes()` method for determining stocks data. The coding in Listing 6.4 is then produced in the action event handler.

Calling public methods using IPublic API

```
public void onActionGo(
    com.sap.tc.webdynpro.progmodel.api.IWDCustomEvent
        wdEvent ){
//@@begin onActionGo(ServerEvent)
//$$begin ActionButton(-759600870)
wdThis.wdGetStockQuotesCompController()
    .executeGetStockQuotes();
```

```
//$$end
//@@end
}
```

Listing 6.4 Event Handler of the Go Action in the StockQuotesView.java Controller

6.2.8 Building, Deploying and Starting an Application

To display stocks data with the Web service application you just developed, proceed as follows:

Display Web service results

1. Open Component Modeler for the local Web Dynpro DC [Local Development] tc/wd/demo/wsa, move the mouse pointer over the StockQuotesAdWSApp rectangle (Figure 6.48), and then select **Deploy New Archive and Run** entry in the context menu.

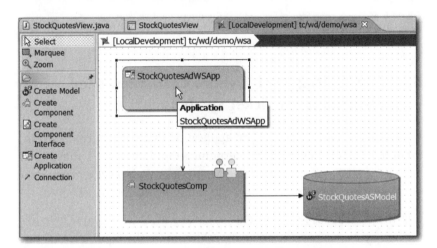

Figure 6.48 Building, Deploying, and Starting the StockQuotesAdWSApp Application in Component Modeler

2. The tutorial application is opened in the Web browser after creating the Web Dynpro EAR files (*Enterprise Archives*) and deploying them on the SAP NetWeaver Application Server Java.

3. After entering a ticker symbol into the form and pressing the **Go** pushbutton, the stocks data record returned by the external stocks Web service is displayed in the table (Figure 6.49).

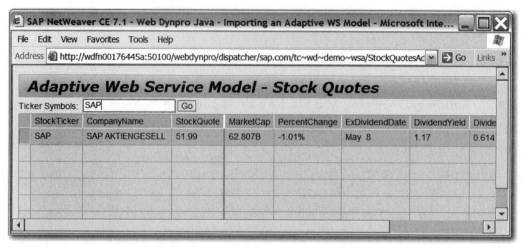

Figure 6.49 Displaying Stocks Data in the Running Adaptive Web Service Tutorial Application

6.3 Integrating Web Dynpro Components for Searching for Ticker Symbols

A weak point in the Web Dynpro application that you just created is the input help that is missing for determining multiple ticker symbols. The QuoteTicker parameter provided by the stocks Web service permits the transfer of multiple ticker symbols separated by commas or blanks.

It is, therefore, possible to provide the user with a special value help dialog box by means of an additional pushbutton in the input form (Figure 6.50, Point ❶), here the user can then search for and choose from multiple ticker symbols from different stock indexes such as Euro Stoxx 50, NASDAQ, or DAX (Figure 6.50, Points ❷ and ❸). After closing the search window (Figure 6.50, Point ❹), the selected ticker symbols are transferred to the input field in StockQuotesView and then the Web service call is triggered to display the related stocks data in the table (Figure 6.51, Point ❺).

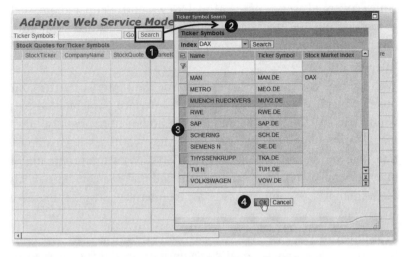

Figure 6.50 Using the Dialog Box to Search for Ticker Symbols

Adaptive Web Service Model - Stock Quotes

Ticker Symb ⑤ MUV2.DE RWE.DE SAP [Go] [Search]

Stock Quotes for Ticker Symbols

StockTicker	CompanyName	StockQuote	MarketCap	PercentChange	ExDividendDate
MUV2.DE	MUENCH RUECKVERS	129.82	N/A	+1.26%	29-Apr-05
RWE.DE	RWE -A-	81.91	N/A	+1.78%	15-Apr-05
SAP.DE	SAP	38.65	N/A	+1.66%	7-May-04
SCH.DE	BAYER SCHERING PH	102.99	N/A	-0.14%	15-Apr-05
SIE.DE	SIEMENS N	88.15	N/A	+1.65%	28-Jan-05
TKA.DE	THYSSENKRUPP	40.09	N/A	+1.42%	24-Jan-05

Figure 6.51 Displaying Stocks Data After Selecting Multiple Ticker Symbols in the Dialog Box

Executing a search function such as this makes use not only of the Web Dynpro component concept functions but also helps you come to recognize its strengths and advantages:

Advantages of Web Dynpro components

▶ **Componentization**

For the development of substantial Web Dynpro applications, it is very important to separate it into smaller development components. Web Dynpro provides the Web Dynpro component entity for this,

307

which covers all aspects of the Model View Controller paradigm, such as forming the user interface view layouts, implementing application logic in controllers, or connecting to the business logic using models.

▶ **Interfaces**
Web Dynpro components have clearly defined interfaces. The component interface view exposes the user interface implemented by a window in a Web Dynpro component. Another component can then include this *visual* interface as a view of its own in its view composition. The component interface controller exposes the programming interface of a Web Dynpro component and makes a context publicly accessible for user components as a data interface as well as methods and events.

▶ **Reusability**
A considerable advantage of Web Dynpro components is their scope for reuse, which in turn drastically increases productivity during the development of large applications and their maintainability. Examples of reusable Web Dynpro components are the `TickerSymbolSearch` components used in the current tutorial.

▶ **Loose Coupling with Component Interfaces**
A component interface[31] merely describes the abstract interfaces of a Web Dynpro component triggered by the component implementation. When using component interfaces to separate design and implementation, it is possible to separate the close relationship between component user and component implementation. For *loose coupling* of this sort, a Web Dynpro component simply uses the abstract definition of another Web Dynpro component without needing to be aware of the component implementation at design time. This can be selected later at runtime according to a plug-in concept and need not be known at design time.

Symbol search component
The following shows how simply the existing tutorial application can be enhanced to include a search dialog box for stock ticker symbols with the help of a Web Dynpro component. The main focus here is the inclu-

---

31 The technical term for a Web Dynpro component interface is *component interface definition*.

sion of a second Web Dynpro component, not its implementation, which will be dealt with later in brief.

First, look at the simple specification (Table 6.2) of the Web Dynpro component to use for searching for stock ticker symbols (simply called 'symbol search component' below).[32]

Web Dynpro Component for Searching for Stock Ticker Symbols	
Description	Reusable, visual Web Dynpro component that displayed a search dialog in a pop-up window for selecting multiple stock ticker symbols and which returns this in a single `String` value to the calling client component
Name	`SymbolSearchComp`
Web Dynpro DC	`[Local Development] tc/wd/demo/tisy`
Component Interface Controller	
Methods	▶ `void popupSymbolSearchWin (IWDAttribute-Pointer appAttributePointer)`: Methods for display a pop-up dialog box (search window) for search for stock ticker symbols
	▶ Parameter `appAttributePointer`: Reference to the context attribute in the calling client component in which ticker symbols selected by the user in the search window are to be written. Precondition is that the related context attribute is of type `String`.
Events	None
Context	Empty
Component Interface Views	
None	

Table 6.2 Specification of Symbol Search Components

---

32 It is worth noting that the symbol search component itself is displayed in a pop-up window. It is not possible at this time to display another view or component interface view in a pop-up window using a navigation link in Web Dynpro navigation modeler. Instead, pop-up windows are opened programmatically calling the `IWDWindowManager` API which the symbol search component uses itself. It opens itself in a pop-up window so that this task does not have to be taken over by the calling client component.

As you can see, the definition of the component interface is restricted to the single method `popupSymbolSearchWin (IWDAttributePointer appAttributePointer)` in component interface controller. By calling this method, the client component[33] can delegate the complete functionality for searching for, selecting, and returning stock ticker symbols to the service component without having to implement it itself. It simply has to transfer a reference to its own context attribute of type `String` to the symbol search component in which the ticker symbols selected by the user in the search window are to be displayed.

Data is exchanged, therefore, using a method call with parameter exchange, however it would also be possible for an alternative approach using interface context mapping.[34] For reasons of simplicity, the data exchange in the current example is achieved using a method call. The example here, therefore, introduces the classic case for efficient developing by reusing an existing component implementation.

In Figure 6.52, you can see how the symbol search component is shown in Component Modeler after it has been included in the `StockQuotesComp` component. The usage relationship between the two components is represented by a line from the client interface to the connector symbol at the component interface controller of the service component.

---

33 *Client component* means those Web Dynpro components that use another Web Dynpro component as a service. In the tutorial application, the component `StockQuotesComp` is the client component and `SymbolSearchComp` is the service component.

34 Interface context mapping means the definition of context mapping relationships between a client component and the interface controller context of a service component. It facilitates the declarative, bidirectional data transfer across Web Dynpro component boundaries.

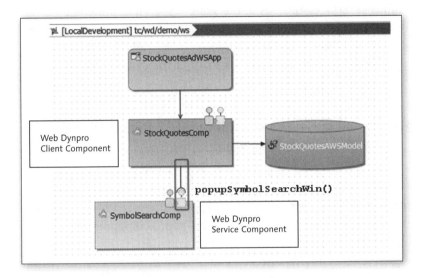

Figure 6.52 Displaying Symbol Search Components Used in Component Modeler

The required steps will be introduced in brief before actually including the symbol search component for searching for stock ticker symbols. This overview should clarify how simple it is to enhance the functionality of an existing Web Dynpro application by including a reusable component. Three of the following four steps are declarative and the programming step is restricted to just a few lines of application code in the view controller.

Overview of including the symbol search component

1. **Defining the Usage of a Separate Web Dynpro DC**
   Because the symbol search component is contained in a separate Web Dynpro DC, you must first define a usage relationship for a public part of this Web Dynpro DC.

2. **Defining the Usage of the Symbol Search Component**
   Including the symbol search component in the stock quotes component requires you to define a corresponding component usage relationship.

3. **Adding a Pushbutton in the View Layout**
   To open the symbol search component in a pop-up window, you need to add a pushbutton in the view layout and connect it to a new Search action.

4. **Calling Interface Methods of the Symbol Search Component**
   In this last step, open the symbol search dialog box in the event handler of the `Search` action. It is enough to call method `popupSymbolSearchWin()` in the `IExternal` API of the symbol search component used.

6.3.1 Defining the Usage Relationship Between Web Dynpro Development Components

Web Dynpro development components

The component model of SAP NetWeaver Development Infrastructure (NWDI) provides a special development component type (namely, the *Web Dynpro DC*) for storing Web Dynpro entities in a NWDI development system. To be able to reuse a Web Dynpro component in multiple client components, then it needs to be separated from this at file or Web Dynpro DC level. In this tutorial application this means that the symbol search component is not stored in the local Web Dynpro DC [Local Development] `tc/wd/demo/ws`, but in a separate Web Dynpro DC called [Local Development] `tc/wd/demo/tisy`.

In contrast to other Web Dynpro projects, it is also possible to define usage relationships between Web Dynpro DCs, whereby the visibility of development components to each other is limited to the exposed components in the *public parts*. A public part should, therefore, be seen as the interface of a development component for its external user. It is also possible to define multiple public parts for a development component.

Figure 6.53 shows how a Web Dynpro component can be used by another Web Dynpro component across DC boundaries:

1. The outbound Web Dynpro component `TickerSymbolSearchComp` provided for reuse is added to a public part of the related Web Dynpro DC [Local Development] `tc/wd/demo/tisy`. A *DC build* then needs to be triggered to create the related public part.

2. The other Web Dynpro DC [Local Development] `tc/wd/demo/ws` defines the usage (*DC usage*) of the first Web Dynpro DC. The content of all public parts exposed by the Web Dynpro DC used is available for use in the own Web Dynpro DC. The reusability of the public parts

exposed by a development component in other development components can be determined or restricted as necessary by defining *Access Control Lists* (ACL).

3. The stock quotes component can define the use of the symbol search component by means of a component usage relationship as if it were contained in the Web Dynpro DC [Local Development] tc/wd/demo/ws itself.

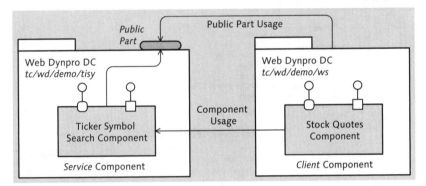

Figure 6.53 Public Part Definition and Usage Relationship Between Two Web Dynpro DCs

Start by including the symbol search component in the StockQuotesComp component (subsequently known as stock quotes component).

1. To be able to use the symbol search component exposed in a public part[35] of the Web Dynpro DC [Local Development] tc/wd/demo/tisy, in the first step you must define a DC usage relationship between the two Web Dynpro DCs.

2. The symbol search component is included in the tutorial application in a second pre-prepared Web Dynpro DC called [LocalDevelopment] tc/wd/demo/wsb. This Web Dynpro DC is based on the complete version of the first Web Dynpro DC template called [LocalDevelopment] tc/wd/demo/wsa. This means that you can execute the following steps even if you have not completed the first application tutorial.

Defining public-part usage relationship between Web Dynpro DCs

Using the second Web Dynpro DC template

---

35 Because the reusability of an existing Web Dynpro component is the main priority here, the definition of the corresponding public parts in the Web Dynpro DC [Local Development] tc/wd/demo/tisy is not described but is required as given here.

3. In Web Dynpro Explorer, select the node [LocalDevelopment] tc/wd/
demo/wsb and open **Development Component • Show in Component
Properties** in the context menu (Figure 6.54). The special perspective
view **Component Properties** to set DC metadata then opens.

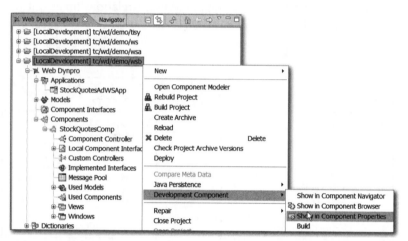

Figure 6.54 Displaying DC Properties for Web Dynpro DC
tc/wd/demo/wsb in Web Dynpro Explorer

4. Select the **Dependencies** tab page and press the **Add...** button to add
the public part of another Web Dynpro DC (Figure 6.55).

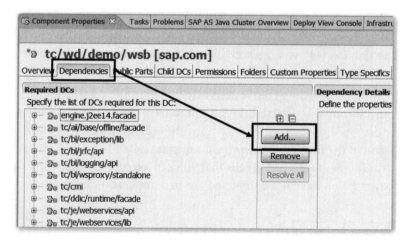

Figure 6.55 Adding a DC Relationship

5. In the **Adding Dependencies** dialog box, enter the name "tc/wd/demo/tisy" of the Web Dynpro DC to be used (Figure 6.56).

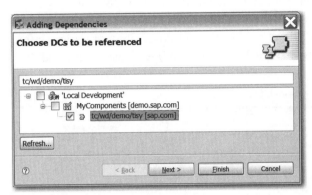

Figure 6.56 Selecting Web Dynpro DC tc/wd/demo/tisy to be Used

6. The display of the relevant development component is continuously updated as you enter the DC name until only the Web Dynpro DC tc/wd/demo/tisy to be used is displayed.

7. The public parts defined in the Web Dynpro DC to be used are displayed in the next dialog step. In this example, this is the public part called SymbolSearchPP, which makes the reusable symbol search component reusable for other Web Dynpro DCs (Figure 6.57).

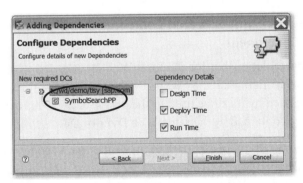

Figure 6.57 Displaying Public Parts Defined in Web Dynpro DC tc/wd/demo/tisy Used

8. Quit the definition of the DC usage relationship with the **Finish** pushbutton.

9. The perspective view **Dependencies** now shows the added use of the local Web Dynpro DC called `tc/wd/demo/tisy` and the public part `SymbolSearchPP` contained within it (Figure 6.58). Move the mouse pointer over a public part node and additional information such as header, description, public part purpose, or deprecation information[36] (along with a quick-fix, if defined) is displayed as a tooltip.

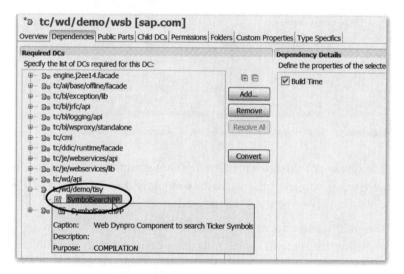

Figure 6.58 Displaying New DC Usage Relationship

6.3.2 Including the Symbol Search Component in the Stock Quotes Component

After the public part relationship for the local Web Dynpro DC `tc/wd/demo/tisy` has been defined, the Web Dynpro component `SymbolSearchComp` exposed by it can be used in the `Stock-QuotesComp` component as if it were contained in the same Web Dynpro DC.

1. First, in Web Dynpro Explorer, go back to the Component Modeler of the local Web Dynpro DC `tc/wd/demo/wsb` by either double clicking on the DC node or by selecting its context menu entry **Open Component Modeler**.

---

36 Public parts of development components can only be set to `deprecated` as of SAP NetWeaver CE 7.1. The developer can use a special quick-fix function to replace a deprecated public part with its successor.

2. To define a usage relationship in the stock quotes component (*component usage*) for the symbol search component, use the **Connection** function in the tools list to draw a line to connect the two component symbols.

Defining a component usage relationship in Component Modeler

3. First, select the **Connection** function in the tools list of the Component Modeler (Figure 6.59, Point ❶). In the work area, move the mouse pointer over the image of the StockQuotesComp component (Figure 6.59, Point ❷). Hold the mouse button down and move the pointer over the image of the SymbolSearchComp component (Figure 6.59, Point ❸).

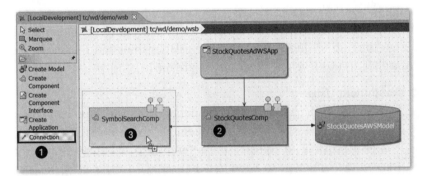

Figure 6.59 Displaying New Usage Relationship 1

4. After releasing the mouse button, the stock quotes component is connected with the port symbol of the component interface controller for the symbol search component by a line (Figure 6.60).

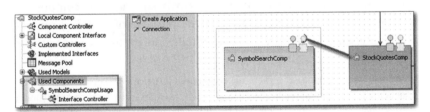

Figure 6.60 Displaying New Usage Relationship 2

5. In addition, the defined component usage relationship is shown in Web Dynpro Explorer as a new node called **StockQuotesComp • Used Components • SymbolSearchCompUsage**.

Web Dynpro Component Usages

Before proceeding with including the ticker symbol search component, we should first take a look at the highly important entity of component usage. In the Web Dynpro component model, component usage acts as a *variable* that the embedded component uses to define the use of another component. At design time it is a placeholder for another used Web Dynpro component. At runtime, a component usage is associated with a related component instance. If a component is used more than once, then two separate component usages need to be defined. At runtime, the embedding component would have two component instances of the same type.

After defining a component usage in an embedding component, at design time up to three types of usage relationships can be defined at controller and UI level, as shown in Figure 6.61.

❶ **Component Usage**
A controller of the embedding component uses the component usage to control the lifecycle of the component instance associated with it.[37] It is also possible to transfer the reference to another component usage of the same type to a component usage. This *referencing mode* of component usages can first be used for visual components in SAP NetWeaver CE 7.1.[38] Using the IWDComponentUsage API, a controller can access the component usage used.

❷ **Component Interface Controller**
A controller of the embedding component uses the component interface controller of the component associated with the component usage. In this way the context (for the purpose of defining context mapping chains) along with its methods and events exposed in the

---

[37] Manually *controlling the lifecycle* of the component instance associated with a component usage is only required in special application scenarios, such as when using model components as singletons. Web Dynpro runtime controls the lifecycle of the components used by default.

[38] The component usage referencing mode could only be implemented for nonvisual components, such as model components, in SAP NetWeaver 2004 and 7.0. For visual components, referencing mode can be used for the development and use of layout components which reference other UI components for arrangement in ViewContainerUI elements, but do not control their lifecycle themselves.

component interface are visible to the controller. The component interface controller provides a user with its `IExternal` API as interface.

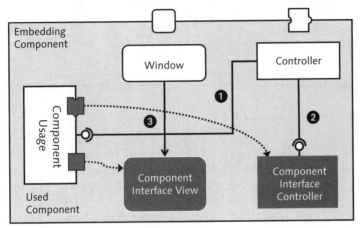

Figure 6.61 Usage Relationships After Defining a Component Usage

❸ Component Interface View (Optional)

A window or ViewContainer UI element can use or embed the component interface view of the component instance associated with the component usage in itself. By using the inbound and outbound plug defined by the component interface view, navigation links can be defined across component boundaries. This usage relationship is not possible for UI components as nonvisual components do not have any component interface views.

Lifecycle Properties of a Component Usage

A good comprehension of component usages requires a clear distinction between the entity of the component usage itself and the component instance that it references. The component usage represents the usage relationship between the parent component and embedded child component at design time. This is comparable to a variable in Java that represents the use of another object instance. The entity of the component usage is, however, not identical to the actual component instance. This difference can be seen in Figure 6.62 where alongside the component usage, both of the interfaces of a Web Dynpro component, component

Difference between component usage and associated component instance

interface view and component interface controller can also be used directly.

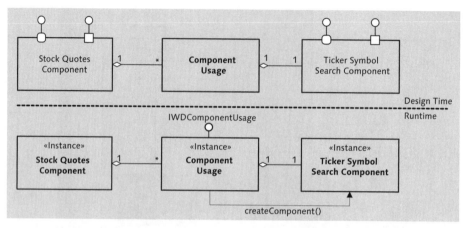

Figure 6.62 Display of a Component Usage Game in Web Dynpro Explorer

Component usage and lifecycle of a component instance

At runtime, an instance of the component usage of type `IWDComponent-Usage` references the instance of the component used. At design time, the `Lifecycle` property can be defined for a component usage to determine how the creation and deletion of the related component instance is to be controlled at runtime.

▶ `Lifecycle = createOnDemand`
The Web Dynpro runtime environment takes over the Lifecycle Management of the component instance that belongs to the component usage. The component instance is created automatically if required and then deleted if necessary. For example, a UI component is created automatically as soon as its component interface view is contained for the first time in a *view assembly* or displayed on the user interface.

▶ `Lifecycle = manual`
The Lifecycle Management of the component instance belonging to the component usage is implemented explicitly in the application code. The component usage gives a controller and its interface `IWD-ComponentUsage` the chance to control the lifecycle of the associated component instance, that is, to create it if necessary using `IWDComponentUsage.createComponent()` or delete it using `IWDComponent-Usage.deleteComponent()`.

Inverse Search Function for Web Dynpro Entities

The new useful inverse search function for individual Web Dynpro entities, such as components, controllers, context nodes, context attributes, or model classes, makes it easier to develop a componentized Web Dynpro application. This makes it possible to list all users (other components and controllers) of such a Web Dynpro entity both within and outside of a Web Dynpro development component. The inverse search function is provided by the Web Dynpro tools in Web Dynpro Explorer using the two context menu entries **References • Workspace** and **References • Project**. This function is particularly useful when finding the components that have defined a usage relationship (*component usage relationship*) to a reusable Web Dynpro component.

Finding use relationships in componentized Web Dynpro applications

Example

The inverse search for the component `SymbolSearchComp` in the second Web Dynpro development component `[LocalDevelopment] tc/wd/demo/ws` results in the hit list shown in Table 6.3.

Element Name	Element Type	Main Object	Refer-enced Via	Project
SymbolSearch-CompUsage	Component Usage	Stock-QuotesComp	Component Usage	...demo/ws
StockQuotesComp	Controller	Stock-QuotesComp	Component Usage	...demo/ws
StockQuotesView	Controller	Stock-QuotesView	Required Controller	...demo/ws

Table 6.3 Hit List of Web Dynpro Entities in a Usage Relationship with Component SymbolSearchComp

6.3.3 Adding a Pushbutton to Search for Ticker Symbols

Let's return now to including the symbol search component in the stock quotes component:

1. To open the search dialog box in the input form of the `StockQuotes-View` view, add an action button in the next step as you already did for the **Go** pushbutton.

Getting to the
View Designer
using forward
navigation

2. A quick access to the View Layout Designer permits forward navigation in Component Modeler and Data Modeler. First, open the Component Modeler of the local Web Dynpro DC `tc/wd/demo/wsb` and double click the `StockQuotesComp` component (Figure 6.63, Point ❶).

3. Now navigate forward in the Data Modeler in the same way to View Designer of the `StockQuotesView` view (Figure 6.63, Point ❷).

4. After the **Go** pushbutton in View Designer, add a second pushbutton for opening the search dialog box for stock ticker symbols (Figure 6.63, Point ❸).

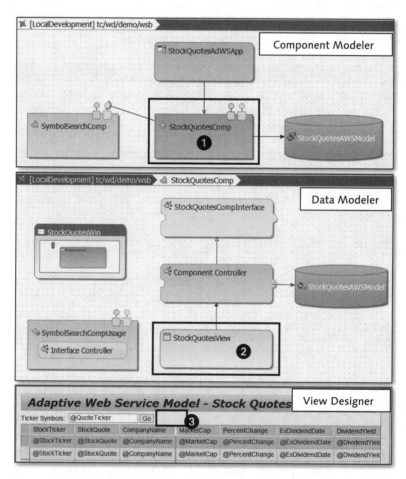

Figure 6.63 Step-by-Step Navigation to View Designer Using Component Modeler and Data Modeler

5. In the **Outline** area select the interface element `TransContainer_0`, in the context menu open the **Apply Template** entry and select the **Action Button** icon. In the next dialog step, enter the text "Search" in the **Button Label** field and then click **Finish**. Then in **Outline** area move the new button interface element using drag & drop to the container called `TransContainer_0`.

6. Figure 6.64 shows the **Search** pushbutton added to the view layout for opening the search dialog for stock ticker symbols.

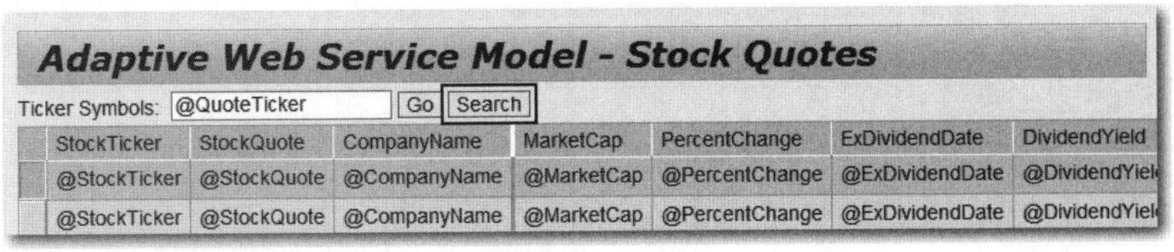

Figure 6.64 Simple Form for Entering Ticker Symbols

6.3.4 Using the Interface Controller of the Symbol Search Component in the View Controller

The search dialog implemented in the symbol search component is called in the action event handler of the `Search` action (to which the **Search** pushbutton you just added is connected). The call takes place using the public `IExternal` API of the component interface controller of the symbol search component.

Because there is not initially any usage relationship to another visible controller in every Web Dynpro controller, you first have to define such a controller usage relationship from the view controller to the component interface controller. Web Dynpro tools offer two alternatives:

▸ Implicit definition of a controller usage relationship using the **Draw Data Link** function in Data Modeler

▸ Explicit definition of a controller usage relationship on the **Properties** tab page of the View Controller

The second alternative is better; however, in the current example it can require more work to define the use of the symbol search interface controller in the view controller `StockQuotes-View.java`.

1. Open the **Properties** tab page for this in the stock quotes view and select the **Add** function (Figure 6.65).

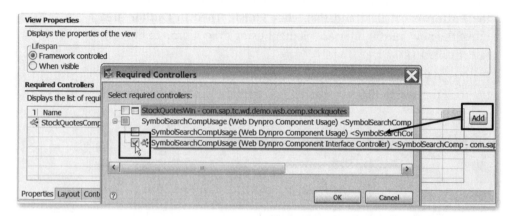

Figure 6.65 Defining Interface Controller Usage in View Controller

2. In the **Required Controllers** dialog box, select the **SymbolSearchComp-Usage — SymbolSearchCompUsage (Web Dynpro Component Interface Controller)** checkbox and then press **OK**.

3. As a result the newly defined usage relationship is displayed in the **Required Controllers** table of the **Properties** view (Figure 6.66).

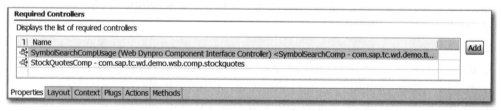

Figure 6.66 Displaying Added Interface Controller Usage on the Properties Tab of View Controller

Implicit definition of controller use-in Data Modeler

A hidden but better chance for the definition of a controller usage relationship from the `StockQuotesView.java` view controller to the symbol search interface controller is offered by Data Modeler. Here you make use of the circumstance that when defining a data link, that is, a context mapping between two controllers, a controller usage relationship is added to the controller with the mapped context automatically and implicitly. In this case, this means that only a data link has to be drawn from the `StockQuotesView` controller in Data Modeler to the symbol search interface controller, without actually having to define a context mapping relationship.

1. As described in section 6.2.5, *Defining the Context Mapping*, select the **Create Data Link** function in Data Modeler (Figure 6.67, Point ❶) and with the mouse draw a link from the `StockQuotesView` to the interface controller of the symbol search component (Figure 6.67, Point ❷).

2. Press the **Finish** pushbutton in the **Context Mapping** dialog box (Figure 6.67, Point ❸) without actually defining a context mapping relationship because this is not possible in this example due to the empty interface context.

3. The result of this second alternative is, however, the same as with the first: The usage relationship of the interface controller for the symbol search component was added automatically to the `StockQuotesView` controller just as it would have been required for the context mapping relationship.

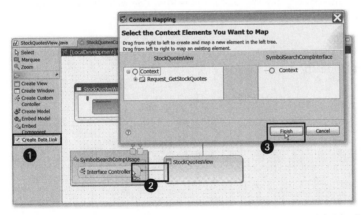

Figure 6.67 Implicit Definition of a Controller Usage in Data Modeler Without Context Mapping

6.3.5 Calling the Symbol Search Component in the View Controller

In the last step in the following directions, you open the symbol search dialog by implementing the action event handler `onActionSearch()` in view controller `StockQuotesView.java`.

1. It is simply enough to call the `popup-SymbolSearchWin()` method in the `IExternal` API of the symbol search component in use.

2. In the Data Modeler of the stock ticker component, open the Java Editor of the `StockQuotesView` view by selecting the **Open with · Java Editor** context menu entry (Figure 6.68).

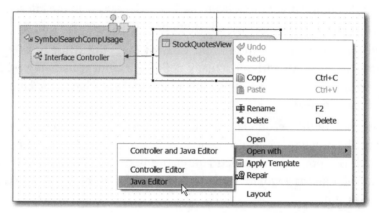

Figure 6.68 Opening the Java Editor to the View Controller Implementation in Data Modeler

3. In the action event handler `onActionSearch()`[39] implement the application code shown in Listing 6.5:

```
public void on ActionSearch(
  com.sap.tc.webdynpro.progmodel.api.IWDCustomEvent wdEvent
) {
  //@@begin onActionSearch(ServerEvent)
  wdThis.wdGetSymbolSearchCompUsageInterface()
    .popupSymbolSearchWin (
      wdContext.currentGetQuotesElement()
        .getAttributePointer(
          IPrivateStockQuotesView.IGetQuotesElement
            .QUOTE_TICKER));
  //@@end
}
```

Listing 6.5 Calling the Symbol Search Component in View Controller

---

39 Use the keys ⎡Ctrl⎤+⎡O⎤ to toggle quickly to the action event handler `onAction-Search()` in the Java Editor. A pop-up window opens showing the methods and variables belonging to the controller class.

4. The symbol search pop-up is opened by calling the `popupSym-bolSearchWin()` method in the `IExternal` API of the symbol search component used. Because you have already defined the usage of the component interface controller of the symbol search component in the `StockQuotesView` controller, the Web Dynpro generation framework automatically enhanced the `IPrivate` API of the view controller by the `wdGetSymbolSearchCompUsageInterface()` method for accessing the `IExternal` API of the symbol search component interface controller. The `IExternal` API exposes the `popupSymbolSearchWin()` method for opening the symbol search pop-up.

How is the data transferred between the stock quotes component (*client component*) and the symbol search component (*service component*) called? Simply put, the question is: How the symbol search component writes the ticker symbols selected by the user to the input field in the `SymbolSearchView` view form.

Alternatives to cross-component data transfer

The Web Dynpro programming model provides different alternatives for this, the simplest of which is demonstrated in the current example: method call with parameter passing.

▶ **External Context Mapping**
   The service component defines a context attribute in its interface context and identifies this as an input element (by setting the property `isInputElement = true`). The client component then maps this context attribute externally to the data context attribute in the component controller, to which the corresponding context attribute in the view controller is also mapped. As a result, a closed mapping chain comes into being that provides the service component with the necessary write access.

▶ **Server-Side Eventing**
   In its interface context, the service component can define an event and related event parameters that the client component then subscribes to. By triggering this event from the side of the service component after the user has selected the ticker symbols, the client component in its event handler can then write the parameter value received back to its own data context.

▶ **Navigation Plugs**

If a client component navigates to the component interface view of the service component used, then it is as a result of triggering a navigation outbound plug. By defining one or more parameters in the inbound and outbound plug, a client component can pass parameter values to the outbound plug event handler of the service component addressed.

▶ **Method Call**

The simplest form of cross-component data transfer is by calling an interface controller method[40] of the service component inside the client component including the transfer of one or more parameters.

Transferring references to attribute pointers

As mentioned previously, data is transferred in the current example by method call. The exact process of this data transfer is shown in Figure 6.69.

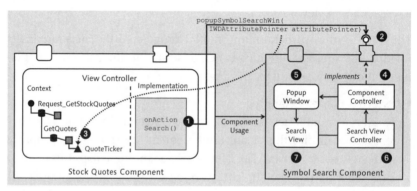

Figure 6.69 Calling Symbol Search Component and Transferring a IWDAttributInfo Parameter Value

The action event handler `onActionSearch()` implemented in the view controller of the stock quotes component (see Figure 6.69, Point ❶) opens the symbol search pop-up by calling the `popupSymbolSearchWin()` method in the `IExternal` API of the interface controller of the symbol search component used (see Figure 6.69, Point ❷). This then transfers as parameter the *attribute pointer* of the context attribute to which the input field of the `SymbolSearch` view is connected. The context attribute

---

40 More specifically, a method in the `IExternal` API exposed by the component interface controller of the service component.

pointer references the QuoteTicker context attribute that is saved at runtime in the node element of the GetQuotes node (see Figure 6.69, Point ❸). Therefore, the component controller saves the attribute pointer it received in a private instance variable (see Figure 6.69, Point ❹) and opens the pop-up window to display the ticker symbol search dialog box (see Figure 6.69, Point ❺). After the user has selected ticker symbols on the user interface of the search view (see Figure 6.69, Point ❼), the action event handler implemented in the view controller causes the component controller to write the selected ticker symbols back to the data context of the calling client component (stock quotes component) as shown in Listing 6.6 (see Figure 6.69, Point ❻).

```
public void applyResult( ) {
  //@@begin applyResult()
  // Write String with selected symbols into the
  // application context attribute using attribute pointer
  if (appAttributePointer != null)
    appAttributePointer
      .getNodeElement().setAttributeValue(
        appAttributePointer.getAttributeInfo().getName(),
        this.getSelectedSymbols());
  if (symbolSearchPopup != null)
    symbolSearchPopup.destroyInstance();
  this.resetContext();
  //@@end
}
```

Listing 6.6 Writing Ticker Symbols Back to the Context Using the Attribute Pointer

The string value for the selected ticker symbols is written by the generic context API method IWDNodeElement. setAttributeValue() where in addition to the string value itself, the name of the context attribute is also transferred. This name can be determined by the attribute information of the type IWDAttributeInfo associated with the attribute pointer.

6.3.6 Building, Deploying, and Starting the Enhanced Tutorial Application

Proceed to start the Web service application enhanced for searching for ticker symbols as follows:

1. Open Component Modeler for the local Web Dynpro DC [Local Development] tc/wd/demo/wsb and move the mouse pointer over the rectangle **StockQuotesAdWSApp**, select **Deploy new Archive and Run** in the context menu.

2. The tutorial application opens in the Web browser after the Web Dynpro EAR files have been created and deployed on the SAP NetWeaver Application Server Java.

3. The pop-up window for searching for ticker symbols can be opened by the user by pressing the **Search** pushbutton in the input form of the StockQuotesView view. After selecting a stock index and any optional filter criteria, multiple ticker symbols can be selected in the results table and transferred to the input field by pressing the **OK** pushbutton (Figure 6.70).

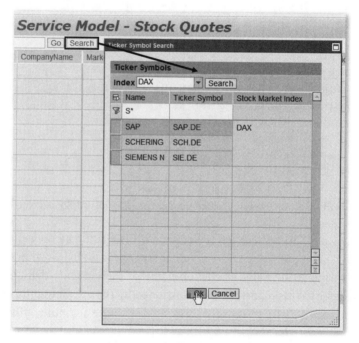

Figure 6.70 Opening the Symbol Search Pop-Up in the Enhanced Tutorial Application

Using a portal, business users can reach and search all types of enterprise information they need to complete their daily tasks, through a single point of access in a Web-based environment. Therefore, Web Dynpro applications should be integrated into the Portal in a last step to provide a unified role based access to enterprise content.

7 Running Web Dynpro Applications in SAP NetWeaver Portal

Web Dynpro Content Administrator

The Web Dynpro Content Administrator can be used for browsing and administrating all the deployed Web Dynpro applications, for example, starting and stopping the applications. It can also be used for defining and maintaining JCo destinations for Web Dynpro applications that use Adaptive RFC models. You can also define additional JCo destinations that are not part of the development component. The Web Dynpro Content Administrator is available in the portal and is assigned to the Content Administrator role by default.

Standard portal navigation controls

As shown in Figure 7.1, the standard portal interface enhances the Web Dynpro interface with enterprise features. The top-level navigation area, a navigation panel on the left side of the screen, and a page title bar navigation area at the upper right of the screen. A content area shows the customizable Web Dynpro pages, containing one or more Web Dynpro iViews.

On the left side of the Portal page you find the *Detailed Navigation Panel*, which is a tree display of the available Web Dynpro Applications. The remaining content area displays the Web Dynpro pages that are composed from various Web Dynpro applications. In this figure, an administrative application is shown, where you can maintain the properties and connectivity settings of Web Dynpro applications.

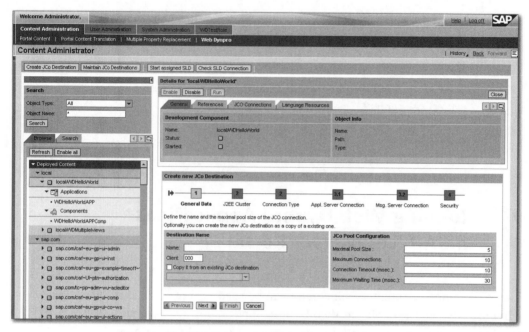

Figure 7.1 The Web Dynpro Content Administrator Page

Top Level Navigation
: The top-level navigation lists the roles assigned to the user or the group the user belongs to. Additionally, it shows in the second row the Worksets assigned to these roles. The roles typically combine the tasks for a specific user-group. For example, every user can create leave requests in his role, but only managers can approve or reject these and therefore only managers should have this role assigned and access it in their top-level navigation.

Detailed navigation
: The detailed Navigation pane on the left offers additional entries below the Workset hierarchy. It is typically used, if a role contains more than five Web Dynpro pages. The page title bar navigation area contains a history list box, a forward and back button, which the user has to use if he navigates in a Web Dynpro application that consists of more than one page, and a page personalization menu.

7.1   Creating Web Dynpro iViews in the Portal

iViews based on Web Dynpro applications are exposed as pages in the Web Dynpro Applications GPAL repository. To use these pages in the portal, you copy them from the repository and paste them into the Portal Catalog.

Web Dynpro applications are accessible in the Portal via the Generic Portal Application Layer (GPAL) Repositories. The GPAL repositories provide portal content administrators with access to content developed outside the portal.

Generic Portal Application Layer

For creating a Web Dynpro iView, you have to copy the Web Dynpro application from the GPAL to the Portal Content Directory (PCD). In order to do so, you have to perform the following tasks:

Portal Content Directory

1. Right-click your Web Dynpro application icon in the GPAL repository, and choose **Copy** (Figure 7.2).

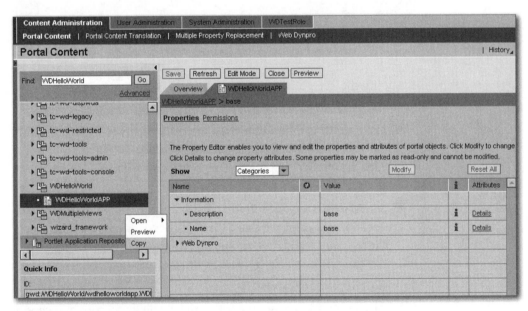

Figure 7.2 Web Dynpro Applications in the Portal Generic Application Repository

2. Right-click any target folder under **Portal Content**, and choose **Paste as PCD Object**. As a result the **Paste as PCD Object** Wizard opens in the Content Studio (Figure 7.3).

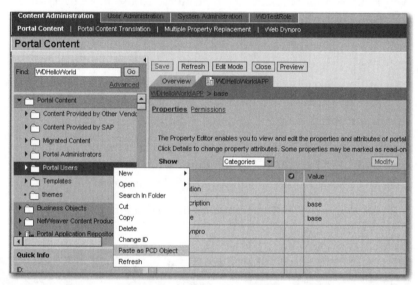

Figure 7.3 Create a Portal Page out of a Native Web Dynpro Page

3. Specify the general properties of the new page (Figure 7.4):

   ▶ The **Page Name** is the display name that appears in the Portal.

   ▶ The **Page ID** is the unique page identifier that will be registered in the Portal Content Directory. The Page ID may have an optional **Page ID Prefix**, helpful for naming conventions in large portal landscapes.

   ▶ The **Master Language** defines the language on which all translations in the Portal are based. The last description in wizard step 1 allows you to add comments, which appear in the tooltip when you hover over the page name in the Portal.

4. At the end, choose **Next**.

5. In the confirmation pane, check that the details are correct and choose **Finish**. The result is technically a Web Dynpro portal page, containing the Web Dynpro application (Figure 7.5).

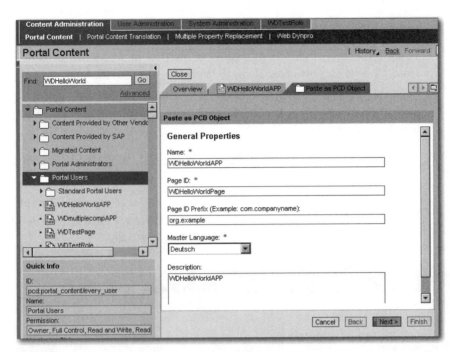

Figure 7.4 Provide Name and ID for the New Portal Page

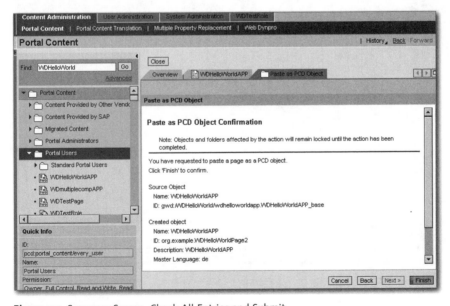

Figure 7.5 Summary Screen, Check All Entries and Submit

7.2   Creating a Web Dynpro Page

You cannot add content to, or remove content from, pages that originate from external repositories such as Web Dynpro. To add content to a Web Dynpro page you have to create a new page. Portal Pages also support pages that contain more than one Web Dynpro application, organized in a page layout.

Wizard-based page creation

Creating a Portal Web Dynpro Page in the Portal is supported by a 4-step wizard.

1. In the Content Administration role, open the Workset **Portal Content**, choose a folder of your choice and choose **New • Page** via context menu (right mouse click) as shown in the Figure 7.6.

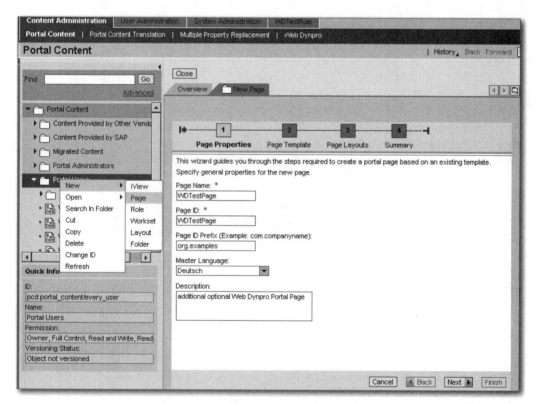

Figure 7.6 Create a Portal Web Dynpro Page with Portal Custom Layout, Step 1

2. Wizard Step 2 offers several different Web Dynpro Page Templates:

▶ **Default Page Template**
Creates a page based on the regular portal page template.

▶ **Web Dynpro Page**
Creates a page based on Web Dynpro technology.

Select one of the predefined templates on which to base your **Web Dynpro page** and click **Next**.

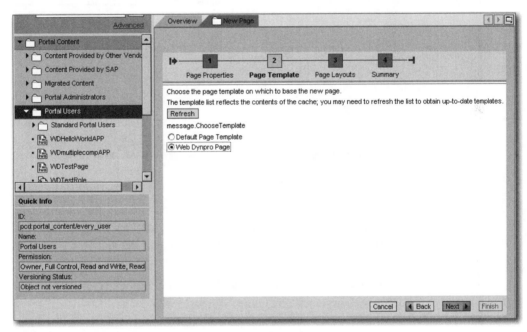

Figure 7.7 Choose Web Dynpro Page as Page Template, Step 2

3. In Wizard Step 3, you have to choose one or many of the predefined Page Layouts and click **Add**. The Portal offers several predefined layouts by default. You can also create custom layouts. Please refer, therefore, to the SAP documentation. Each layout offers a certain setup of iView containers, which can be assigned to Web Dynpro iViews.

Choose layout

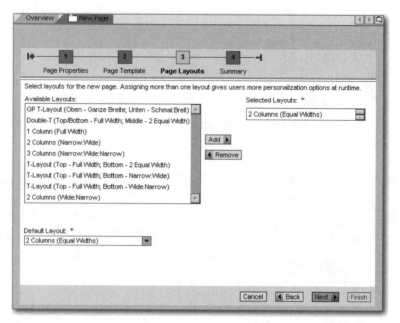

Figure 7.8 Choose a Portal Page Layout, Step 3

4. Choose **Next**. In the Summary Review you can see the options you selected for the new page. You can use the Back button until you return to the appropriate screen to do changes. When you are ready to create the page, click **Finish**.

5. As a result a new Portal Page will be created. Choose **Open Object for Editing** to assign Web Dynpro iViews to the page.

7.3 Adding Web Dynpro iViews to the Portal Page

Page Editor For populating a page with iViews, you first have to open the page. In the Portal Catalog, double-click the name of the page to which you want to add content, or right-click and choose **Open Page**. The Page Editor opens.

1. In the Portal Catalog, right-click the name of the object you want to add and choose **Add Page to Page • Delta Link** (Figure 7.9). The object is added as a delta link. You may also add the page as copy, which creates a new copied page.

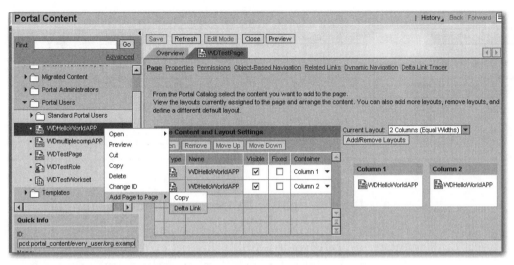

Figure 7.9 Add a Web Dynpro Page to a Two-Column Portal Page Layout

2. The page/iView appears in the page content list.

   Mixing Web Dynpro iViews and portal pages, and vice versa, generates a warning message concerning the isolation mode of the iViews. The Isolation Method property of iViews defines how an iView or page is encoded in a page. It determines whether iView content is collected at the server or at the client, and how the PageBuilder component displays the content. The value of this property can affect the performance of a page.

   iViews can have one of the following isolation methods: **Embedded** or **URL**. Web Dynpro usually uses **URL**.

3. To see how the added item appears on the page, choose **Preview**; the page opens in a new window. When you have finished, choose **Save**.

7.3.1 Creating a Role and Worksets

To test the newly created Portal Page you have to assign the page to Role and optionally to a Workset. You can either choose an existing one or create new one. For testing purposes, choose a folder in the PCD, right click and create a Workset and Role, and assign this to your user. Mark the Role property **Entry Point** as true. As a result, you can see the newly created page and navigation entries (Figure 7.10).

Test role

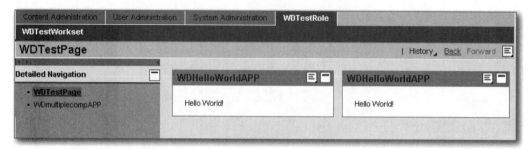

Figure 7.10 Test the Result in a Test Role

7.3.2 Developing Web Dynpro Applications for the Portal

The portal embeds the Web Dynpro UI technology and offers enhanced features to the UI such as personalization of Web Dynpro Application Properties. Administrators and Users personalized data are stored in the Portal Content Directory (PCD) and not in the application itself.

You can also develop multiple iViews directly in your Web Dynpro Application and deploy them on the portal as one application with several iViews, which can be personalized differently.

7.3.3 Creating Personalizable Properties

Create application properties
Application properties that you create in Web Dynpro can be personalized by portal users and/or administrators. When the Web Dynpro application retrieves the value of such an application property, the personalized value is returned.

1. In the Web Dynpro application, create application properties by clicking your application (in this example, Figure 7.11, WDHelloWorldAPP), and then selecting the **Application Properties** tab.

2. In this design time view, you can add now properties to the Application Properties table. In this example, we choose myProperty and the value 100.

Get Application Properties
3. If you want to retrieve the properties, the Web Dynpro code in Listing 7.1 retrieves application properties in the method wdDoModifyView of your Web Dynpro view.

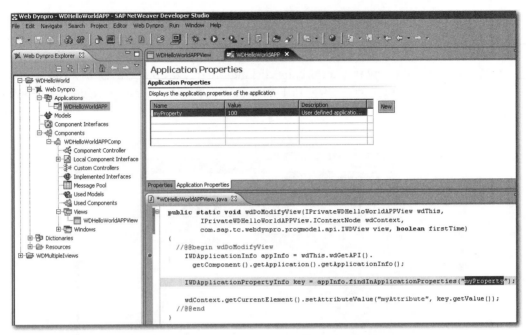

Figure 7.11 Create an Application Property in SAP NetWeaver Developer Studio

```
public static void wdDoModifyView(...)
{
  //@@begin wdDoModifyView
    IWDApplicationInfo appInfo =
      wdThis.wdGetAPI().getComponent()
      .getApplication().getApplicationInfo();
    IWDApplicationPropertyInfo key =
      appInfo.findInApplicationProperties("myProperty");
    wdContext.getCurrentElement().setAttributeValue
    ("myAttribute", key.getValue());
  //@@end
}
```

Listing 7.1 Retrieve a Personalizable Attribute in Web Dynpro

4. The next step is to deploy the application on the portal and create a Portal Page out it. After that, a content administrator can view the page's properties. The custom Web Dynpro properties are displayed in the Web Dynpro category. The content administrator can decide which user groups are allowed to modify the application property:

portal users, administrators, both, or none of them. By default, the property is personalizable for the user.

Personalize application properties

5. If a property can be changed by a portal user, he can access it via the iView tray service, by clicking the tray drop down list box and selecting **Personalize**. In Figure 7.12 `myProperty` and its value `100` shows up.

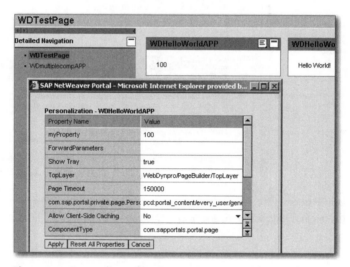

Figure 7.12 Personalize an Application Property on the Portal Page

7.3.4 Enabling Multiple iViews from a Web Dynpro Application

A Web Dynpro application can be designed in a way that a Web Dynpro view can be split in the Portal into different iViews. With different iViews, a Portal Web Dynpro Page can be completely rearranged to the users' preferences and each iView can be personalized on its own.

Implement user interface controls

To achieve that, a Web Dynpro view has to implement `ViewContainerUIElement`. Each `ViewContainerUIElement` on a Web Dynpro page will be a iView on its own in the Portal.

1. To do so, create a new Web Dynpro project and create a new component. The component automatically includes a view and a window, in which the view is embedded. The view is the root view. In this example, it has the name `MultipleCompView`.

2. Now create additional views that implement the portal user interface. In this example, we name them `ViewOne` and `ViewTwo`. These views will be visible in the portal, in contrary to the root view that will not be visible.

3. For each additional view created in the previous step, add a `ViewContainerUIElement` object to the root view where you want the additional views to be displayed.

4. Give meaningful IDs to the `ViewContainerUIElement` objects because the IDs are used as the default iView titles when an administrator creates iViews from this application (Figure 7.13).

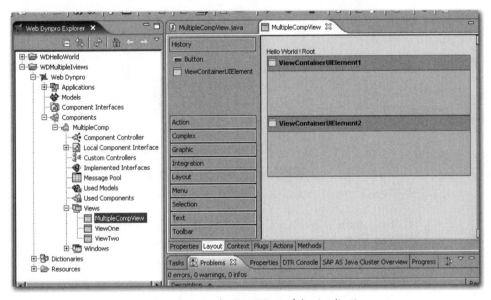

Figure 7.13 Create Two View Containers in the Root View of the Application

In the root view, you may define other UI elements. However, these UI elements are displayed only when the application is run as a single iView, and not when the application is split into individual elements. So, add an application property to indicate that the application's views can be split into different iViews.

Add application properties

1. Right-click the application, and select **Edit**.

2. Select the **Application Properties** tab. To the table of properties, add the property `sap.canBeSplitInIViews` and set the value to `true`.

3. After that, open the Web Dynpro window, in this example `Multiple-CompView`, and drop the two Web Dynpro views to the `ViewContainerUIElements` (Figure 7.14).

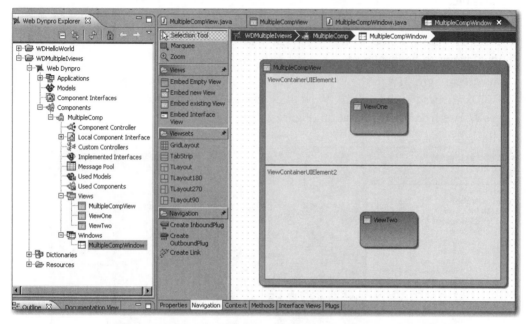

Figure 7.14 Drop the Web Dynpro Views into UIContainer in the Windows Designer

4. Now create a Web Dynpro application, if not having done so yet and deploy the application in the Portal. Create a Portal Page out of the application. The result will show `ViewOne` and `ViewTwo` as two separate iViews. The root view is not visible. `ViewOne` and `ViewTwo` are seen in Figure 7.15.

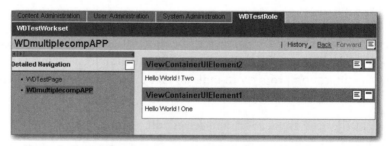

Figure 7.15 Test the Result in the Portal Environment

5. If you test the application as single iView or outside the portal via the **Multiple iViews** Web Dynpro content Administrator, for example, the result will be simply the text elements defined in the three views:

```
Hello World ! Root
Hello World ! One
Hello World ! Two
```

You have finished your first Web Dynpro Multiple iView project.

SAP NetWeaver Visual Composer provides you with a graphical user interface for the quick and easy creation of applications and prototypes, without having to write code manually. Instead of having to rely on technical skills and programming knowledge, you simply link graphical elements together in a flow diagram. This chapter gives you an overview of the functions available in Visual Composer and explains what they make possible.

8 SAP NetWeaver Visual Composer

SAP NetWeaver Visual Composer is a fully browser-based modeling tool offered by SAP for the UI layer, suitable for both business process experts and for developers. Visual Composer aims to provide users with a tool for creating applications as quickly as possible without having to write a single line of code.

This chapter explains Visual Composer in depth, including its background theory and technical details. The chapter also includes a step-by-step example for creating an application in Visual Composer.

8.1 Model-Based Development

A full discussion of model-based development would go beyond the scope of this chapter; however, it does handle the question of how you can benefit from it, in particular by using Visual Composer. The main benefits of model-based development result from the level of abstraction in the models.

▶ When you use models, you abstract them from your technology, so it allows you to change the technology later without any problems. When you decide to switch technologies, you no longer have to carry out a new implementation of all your current applications: You merely need to compile the existing models again. This can reduce

Technology independence

the costs involved in switching technologies dramatically. These savings in costs and effort become particularly significant when upgrading technologies.

▶ In addition, technology-independence means you can use different technologies in parallel. This can become a decisive factor when the application focuses on different target platforms. Model-based development avoids the costs incurred by developing on more than one platform.

Implementation in Visual Composer

Visual Composer makes use of all the advantages we have just discussed. Visual Composer models are independent of technology and can also be created using two different technologies (SAP Web Dynpro for Visual Composer and Adobe Flash). Visual Composer Kits are available for the implementation of any additional technologies you require.

Models as a common language

▶ The implementation of models creates a medium that can be understood by different groups of users. The business process expert mentioned earlier is just as capable of understanding a Visual Composer model as a developer or application designer. This common language ensures a shared understanding of the final application as early as the development phase.

Implementation in Visual Composer

As well as benefiting from this aspect of model-based development, Visual Composer goes one step further by providing boards. For example, business process experts use the design board to define and control the flow of an application. Application developers, on the other hand, use the layout board to display and develop the user interface of the application.

Reusability

▶ When you use models, you implement certain standardized elements, which are abstracted from the technology you use. This also has the following advantage: The models you construct from these elements can be reused, either in part or as a whole.

▶ Theoretically, you could use this aspect of models to reduce new development work to a minimum. Practically, however, new developments are difficult to avoid completely, even if the consistent use of models is guaranteed. Despite this, the implementation of model libraries can exploit significant synergies.

Implementation in Visual Composer

Visual Composer supports the reuse of models at various levels. As well as import and export functions, it makes consistent use of the SAP NetWeaver Development Infrastructure (NWDI), including Design Time Repository (DTR), which is used to construct model libraries.

SAP NetWeaver Composition Environment is provided without an NWDI installation; however, this does not mean that you cannot use an already installed NWDI. NWDI also offers complete lifecycle management for Visual Composer applications, including versioning, packaging, and the mapping of dependencies and compatibilities.

▶ Technology independence removes the need to familiarize yourself with new technologies, and also circumvents most of the problems that can occur at the technology level. In addition, the use of a commonly understood medium reduces the need for constant coordination and discussions. Reusing existing models or fragments of models condenses development time down to the development of new features. Finally, models can be handled intuitively, which also speeds up the development work performed by individuals.

Speed of development

Implementation in Visual Composer

As discussed, Visual Composer makes consistent use of the benefits of model-based development, increasing the speed of development significantly. Visual Composer also places great emphasis on the intuitive nature of the tool, therefore making development even faster.

We could list the many benefits provided by model-based development, but let's concentrate instead on the practical implementation of these principles as realized in Visual Composer.

8.2 Visual Composer in the SAP NetWeaver Composition Environment

SAP NetWeaver Visual Composer is not a new tool, and was first introduced before the advent of SAP NetWeaver Composition Environment. Its suitability as a model-based development tool for creating applications was first spotted several years ago at SAP; this idea has matured over time and the tool has been implemented accordingly.

SAP Visual Composer for NetWeaver 7.0

We will not dwell on the details of previous versions of Visual Composer; instead, we will emphasize its role in the Composition Environment. For an in-depth look at Visual Composers for SAP NetWeaver 7.0, we recommend the book *SAP NetWeaver Visual Composer* (SAP PRESS 2007).[1]

8.2.1 What's New?

Those users who are familiar with older versions of Visual Composer will spot several new features:

▶ **New user interface**
The UI has undergone a thorough redesign, without any of the familiar elements being removed and without losing its intuitive nature.

▶ **New concepts**
At the same time, the concept of reusable components in Visual Composer for SAP NetWeaver Composition Environment 7.1 has been taken to a new level. New elements and concepts have been introduced throughout to make it easier to incorporate existing models or components within other models.

▶ **New focus**
The focus of Visual Composer has also shifted. Older versions centered on Portal iViews; Visual Composer for Composition Environment, on the other hand, emphasizes the use of composite applications.

---

1 At this time, SAP NetWeaver Visual Composer was still known as Visual Composer for SAP NetWeaver 2004s. When SAP NetWeaver 2004s was renamed as SAP NetWeaver 7.0, the name of Visual Composer changed as well.

▶ **New technology**

From a technology perspective, the shift in focus has resulted in support for Web Dynpro as the UI runtime technology throughout Visual Composer. The support for Adobe Flex (familiar from previous versions) has not vanished; however, Web Dynpro, Web Dynpro HTML, and Web Dynpro Flex are all supported as runtime technologies.

> **Note**
>
> This shift in emphasis means that applications are deployed as Web Dynpro applications on the server, and no longer directly in SAP NetWeaver Portal. Support for the integration of the application is still guaranteed, however. The backend integration of the applications has also changed; they are integrated directly and no longer through the portal.

Other new features include full support for SAP NetWeaver Development Infrastructure (NWDI), support for Enterprise Services, and the implementation of various business requirements in Visual Composer (such as the introduction of new UI elements).

8.2.2 Prerequisites

Fundamentally, any prerequisites that are valid for SAP NetWeaver Composition Environment also hold for Visual Composer. Consequently, once you have installed SAP NetWeaver Composition Environment successfully, you have already completed the main step required to use Visual Composer.

There are still a few aspects to consider; however, there are some configuration steps to complete, as described in the configuration guide for Visual Composer, and you must also ensure that every user has the `VisualComposerUser` role.

"Visual-ComposerUser" role

The computer used to access Visual Composer must have the following software installed: Microsoft Internet Explorer 6.0 SP1 or higher, Adobe SVG Viewer 3.0, and Microsoft XML Parser 4.0 or higher.

Adobe SVG Viewer and Microsoft XML Parser

> **Note**
>
> Support for Microsoft Internet Explorer 7.0 on Windows Vista is planned, alongside the existing support for Microsoft Internet Explorer 6.0 SP1. No official statement had been made about this at the time of going to print, however. For up-to-date information on the supported clients, see the current Product Availability Matrix (PAM) for clients on SAP Service Marketplace (*http://service.sap.com/pam*).

You must register backend systems by defining them in SAP NetWeaver Administrator before you can access these systems from Visual Composer. The same applies to any Web services and Enterprise Services that Visual Composer uses as data sources.

8.2.3 Architecture

We could dedicate a whole chapter to the architecture of Visual Composer, but despite the restricted space available we would still like to present its different components. In this way, you will get a better sense of its architecture as a whole. Figure 8.1 shows the schema of the Visual Composer architecture in SAP NetWeaver Composition Environment.

Consolidated architecture
There have been no major changes made to the architecture in Visual Composer for SAP NetWeaver 7.0. The changes that have been made are intended to consolidate the architecture and create defined interfaces. Most noticeably, SAP NetWeaver Portal services have been decoupled as part of the switch to uniform support for composite applications.

> **Note**
>
> SAP NetWeaver Portal is missing from the architecture, but do not interpret this as meaning that the portal strategy has been discontinued. On the contrary, at UI level, all applications are displayed either in SAP NetWeaver Portal Client (browser) or in SAP NetWeaver Business Client (smart client), which itself runs on the portal infrastructure.

Let's take closer look at Figure 8.1. The main components of Visual Composer are as follows:

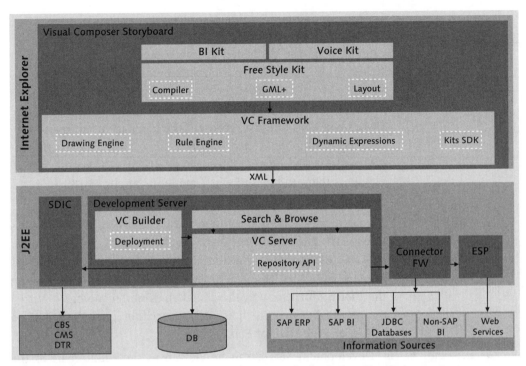

Figure 8.1 Architecture of SAP NetWeaver Visual Composer in the Composition Environment

▶ Visual Composer Storyboard runs entirely in Internet Explorer. This storyboard gives Visual Composer users all the tools they require to model an application.

Visual Composer Storyboard

▶ From an architecture perspective, the storyboard for Visual Composer in the Composition Environment is an important component from the Free Style Kit. The Free Style Kit is the basis for all modeling tasks in Visual Composer and has the following components:

▶ **Layout**

The Layout component is responsible for all tasks that concern the graphical representation of the storyboard. As well as the representation of the tools used in Visual Composer, this component also has the important role of representing graphically the elements that are put together as models. Technically, all graphical elements are displayed either in HTML (for example, the tools) or SVG (the models).

▶ **GML+**

All models in Visual Composer are described using XML. In addition to XML, the dedicated language *Generic Modeling Language* (GML) is also used. New in comparison to the SAP NetWeaver 7.0 version, Visual Composer for the Composition Environment uses an updated version, GML+. In the architecture discussed here, the GML+ box does not just represent the language used; it also represents a component that ensures the correct construction of GML+ DOM (Document Object Model). GML+ DOM describes all elements that can be used when modeling applications.

▶ **Compiler**

If your model is complete and you want to test it, you must compile it first. The compiler transforms the description of the model (in GML or GML+) to a different format, known as *Xgraph Language* (XGL). This language has the special task of transforming the models for use with the actual runtime technologies. Visual Composer gives you a choice of two technologies: Web Dynpro HTML or Web Dynpro Flex.

Development Server ▶ The Development Server can be viewed as the counterpart to the Visual Composer Storyboard, which runs on the client (browser). The server provides the components required by the storyboard and also guarantees persistency and communication with other components on the server. The three most interesting components of the Development Server are as follows:

▶ **Search & Browse**

This is the component you generally use when you first start to model applications. As indicated by the name, it provides basic functions for searching for and browsing through data sources.

▶ **VC Builder**

VC Builder is a service on the Development Server that stores the logic for the components modeled using Visual Composer.

▶ **VC Server**

VC Server contains all important infrastructure elements. It provides the elements shown on the Visual Composer Storyboard and makes them accessible to the client. VC Server also has the task of providing and administering the Visual Composer Kit.

▶ Server Development Infrastructure Client (SDIC) provides access to the Development Infrastructure, so guaranteeing a link between Visual Composer and NWDI.

▶ Connector Framework is a framework for the development of connectors and enables abstract access to almost any backend system.

▶ Enterprise Service Protocol (ESP) enables Visual Composer to consume Enterprise Services. SAP provides its own Enterprise Services Repository, which can be used by Visual Composer.

8.2.4 Creating Applications

When you develop an application with SAP NetWeaver Visual Composer, you always follow these six basic steps:

1. **Create a model**
   The first step is to create a new model. Section 8.3, *Example Scenario*, examines the creation of a model in Visual Composer and the subsequent steps in depth.

2. **Find a data service**
   Every Visual Composer application is based on the usage of existing services. Accordingly, the second step involves the application developer finding the right service for his or her application.

3. **Add UI elements**
   Once the right data service has been found, the developer adds UI elements that enable the end user to enter data or view the results of the service.

4. **Model a data flow**
   Before the UI elements can get the data they need, they need to be associated with the services. In most situations this step can be automated, because Visual Composer is capable of generating many UI elements automatically from the data services.

5. **Create a layout**
   In the fifth step, the application developer (or a layout specialist) uses the Layout Board in Visual Composer to tailor the layout to the requirements identified for the end user.

6. **Deploy and test the application**

Once all the preceding steps have been completed, it is advisable to deploy and test the application. This either completes the development of the application, or new functions are implemented by going back to step 2.

The following section uses a practical example to show how these steps are performed.

8.3 Example Scenario

In the following example scenario, you use Visual Composer to model an application. This application enables a user to create employees in an ERP system, delete them, and modify their data. Exposed Enterprise Services are used to do this.

> **Note**
>
> The aim of this example scenario is to highlight some of the basic functions offered by Visual Composer to application developers. It is not intended to be completely comprehensive, however, and certain parts of the example model's design could be made more efficient. For reasons of simplicity and clarity — and to emphasize certain concepts — we have decided not to include this in the model.
>
> Note that the services used in the example are not included in the standard shipment of the Composition Environment. The example does allow you to use a service of your choice, however. For more information about services and how to use them, see Chapter 9, *Developing Composite Applications*.

8.3.1 Creating the Start Page

Creating a website in Visual Composer

We begin by generating a start page from which various functions can be accessed. You can help the user here by using the familiar look and feel of his or her Web browser. Accordingly, you use links to enable the user to navigate from the start page to the functions.

Creating a model

In the first step, you create a model for a composite view in Visual Composer. Models must be assigned to a development component (DC), which you can create yourself.

1. Figure 8.2 shows the dialog where you create a model, with the model type for this example already selected. The model is called `hr_model` and is assigned to the development component `demo`.

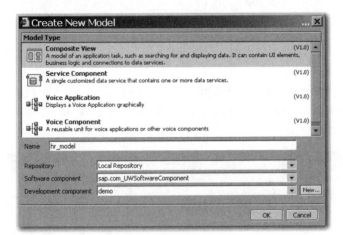

Figure 8.2 Dialog for Creating a New Model in Visual Composer

2. Drag the **User Data** connector into the model so that it can be used later. You need the connector at this stage already because you now need to link to its fields. Figure 8.3 shows the open model with the components that you can use in it. **User Data**, for example, can be dragged and dropped to the model easily.

Connecting to user data

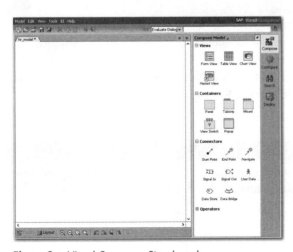

Figure 8.3 Visual Composer Storyboard

357

Creating forms 3. One important element on the start page is a form. In Visual Composer, this is provided by Form View, listed under **Views**. Drag **Form View** to the model and rename it as `main`, either by choosing **Rename** in the context menu of the form, or by selecting Form View and pressing F2.

Layout Board In the next step, you create a personalized welcome text for the end user.

1. To do this, switch to the Layout Board — up until now you have been on the Design Board — by choosing **Layout**. The new board is displayed (Figure 8.4).

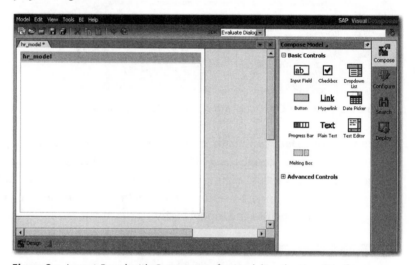

Figure 8.4 Layout Board with Components for Modeling the User Interface

Basic controls 2. Drag the **Plain Text** control from the **Basic Controls** list. To enter your preferred expression, press **F2** (Figure 8.5):

```
="Hello, "&[userdata]@NAME&"what do you want to do today?"
```

> **Note**
>
> Experienced users of Visual Composer will notice that the syntax has changed. Expressions in **Dynamic Expression Editor** must now always start with an equals sign (=).

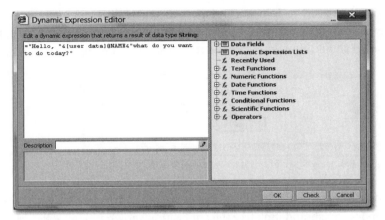

Figure 8.5 Dynamic Expression Editor with a Simple Expression

3. You can also go to the Dynamic Expression Editor by selecting **Config-ure** in the context menu of the component and choosing the **fx** icon next to the **Text** field. Browse through the **Data Fields** until you find the **NAME** field of the **User Data** connector; insert it into the expression so that you get the same expression that you created in the previous step. The editor also enables you to check expressions by choosing the **Check** button.

Dynamic Expression Editor

4. Create three hyperlinks that the end user of the application can use. To do this, drag three **Hyperlink** components from the **Basic Controls** list to the model, and give them the following names:

Creating hyperlinks

▶ "Update employee data"

▶ "Create a new employee"

▶ "Delete an employee"

To make these hyperlinks work when clicked, you define actions for them.

Creating actions

1. You create the first action by selecting the first hyperlink, opening its context menu, and choosing **Action**. Choose the **Plus** icon (**+**), select **Custom Action**, and give the action the name "update".

2. In this example, the action you just created will be used as the basis for navigating to a new component. To enable this, go back to the **Design Board**. Drag the **Navigate** connector to the model. The **Create New Model** dialog opens. Give it the name "update" and choose **OK**.

Navigation between components

3. You now need to join the **out** port of the **Main** component to the **update** component and rename this connection as "update". Your model should now look like the model shown in Figure 8.6.

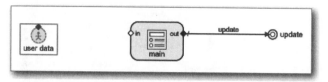

Figure 8.6 Early Stage of the Start Page Model

Deploying an application

4. You can now deploy and test your application for the first time. The application should look like the application shown in Figure 8.7. Here you can see that the name of your login user appears automatically (in this case, **administrator**).

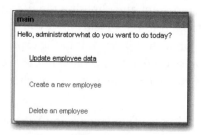

Figure 8.7 Deployed Application

8.3.2 Updating Employee Addresses

The following part of the example involves implementing a function for updating employee addresses.

1. Simply by double-clicking **update**, you open a new tab page with the model that you created previously.

Finding and using a service

2. You can search for a data provider service by choosing **Search**. In this example, you search for the GetEmployee1 service in the **employeeWS** system. Once you have found this service, drag it to the model.

3. This service does not include a representation at UI level, so you now need to create the required elements. To do this, configure another input form. Select the **Input** node of the service. When you release the mouse button, a context menu appears. Choose **Form View**.

4. Once you have created the input form, go back to **Layout Board** and create two **Input Field** elements here. Give the first **Input Field** the name "Employee ID". This field is used for entering the employee ID for the service and was already created automatically. The second **Input Field** is for the name of the employee. Enter another expression as the value of this element:

Creating input fields

```
=[getemployee1.GetEmployee1Response]@name
```

This expression is used to find the name of the employee. As already explained when creating the start page, you can enter the expression directly or select it in Dynamic Expression Editor.

5. The Layout Board should now look like the image in Figure 8.8.

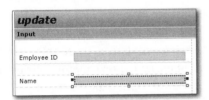

Figure 8.8 Layout Board of the Update Model

6. You can now deploy and test your application again. The application should look like the application shown in Figure 8.9.

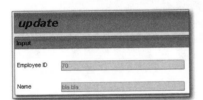

Figure 8.9 Deployed Application of the Update Model

Before you add more functions, organize the user interface by using tab-strips.

Creating tabstrips

1. To do this, go back to the Design Board and drag a **Tabstrip** container to the model.

2. Create four tabs (**Add Tab**) by choosing the icon in the top left corner of the **Tabstrip** container. Your model should now look like the model shown in Figure 8.10.

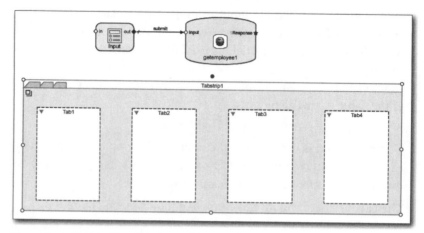

Figure 8.10 Model with a Tabstrip and Four Tabs

Creating tables 3. Create a table for the address data of the employee. To do this, select the **Response** node of the service, open its context menu, and then choose **Table View**. This opens the **Define Data** dialog box, in which you select address_Address (as shown in Figure 8.11). Close the window.

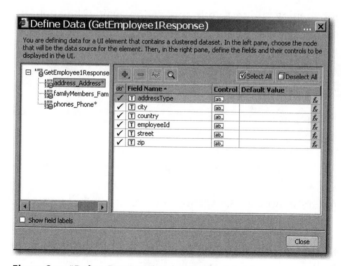

Figure 8.11 "Define Data" Dialog for the Service

4. Move the new table to the first tab (**Tab1**). Rename this table as "Addresses".

5. Because you do not want to open this table in edit mode in the first step, change the **Editable** property from `true` to `false` in the configuration menu; the entries in the table are then no longer editable.

6. To enable the entries to be edited when required, you now add some buttons to this table. First, you create a **Toolbar** for this table by selecting the **Show toolbar** property.

Creating a toolbar

7. To create buttons for the toolbar, switch to the Layout Board and drag three buttons (**Button** elements) to the toolbar:

Buttons for the toolbar

   ▶ Update Address

   ▶ Create Address

   ▶ Delete Address

8. Before you associate the buttons with actions, you can choose to rename the table columns and rearrange them to meet your requirements. The Layout Board should now look like the image in Figure 8.12.

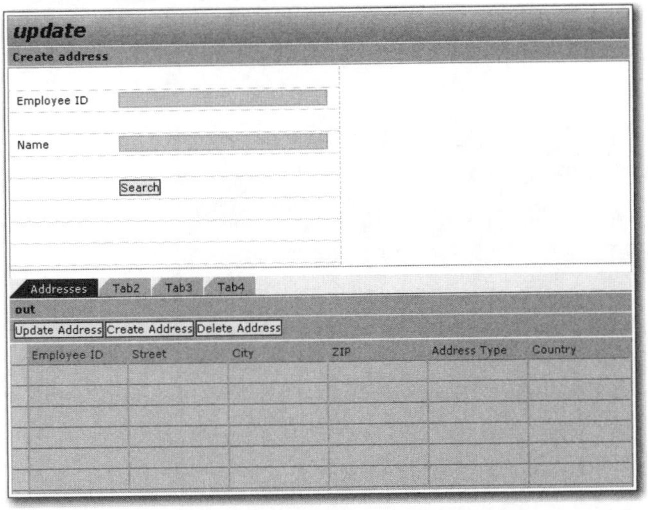

Figure 8.12 Layout Board with Rearranged Address Tab Page

You now want to give the end user the chance to update his address by using a form.

Creating data fields

1. To do this, drag a form view to the first tab page on the Design Board and call it "Update Address".

2. In this form, create a field for each column of the table (except the employee ID): On the Design Board, open the context menu of the form, and choose **Define Data**. Define the fields as shown in Figure 8.13. Also, create a **Toolbar (Bottom)** with a **Button** element called OK.

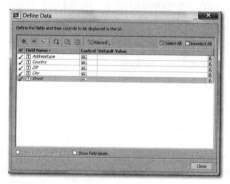

Figure 8.13 Fields Defined for the "Update Address" Form View

3. Repeat this final step for a second form view called "Create Address". The Layout Board should now look something like the image in Figure 8.14.

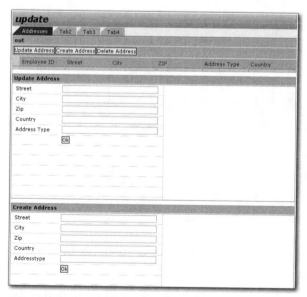

Figure 8.14 Layout Board with the New Forms "Update Address" and "Create Address"

These forms should only be offered to the user when he presses the appropriate buttons. To realize this, you must communicate the state of the buttons.

1. Start by creating a data store. To do this, just drag the relevant connector into the model. The location is not important, because the entire model can access the entries in the data store.

2. To create fields in **Data Store**, open the context menu of the data store and choose **Define Data**. A dialog opens where you can use the **Plus** icon to create a new field with the name "address" and type "string".

3. Now fill the "address" field with appropriate values. To do this, open **Action Editor** (choose **Action** in the context menu) for the **Update Address** pushbutton.

4. Use the **Plus** icon to create a new action with the type ASSIGN. Enter all other values as shown in Figure 8.15.

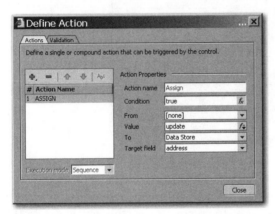

Figure 8.15 Action Editor with the Properties of an "Assign" Action

5. Repeat the last step for the **Create Address** button, but assign "create" under **Value**.

6. You now need to communicate to the forms when they should be visible and when not. To do this, use the **Visible** property of the forms to define the conditions for visibility. Instead of true, you require expressions that reflect the states of the buttons:

- ▶ For "Update Address": =store@Address=="update"
- ▶ For "Create Address": =store@Address=="create"

Filling form fields If you now deploy the application, you can see that the forms can be hidden and unhidden as required. However, you will also notice that, when you update addresses, the data from the table is not copied to the form.

1. To change this behavior, go back to the **Update Address** button, create further `ASSIGN` actions, and use them to fill the form fields.

2. To be able to create or update table entries for real, you must associate the **OK** with actions. This is simple for the **Update Address** form: To fill the form fields, you just have to define the same actions that you used in the previous step, only in the opposite direction. Figure 8.16 shows the dialog.

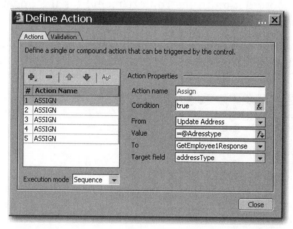

Figure 8.16 Action Editor with Actions Defined for the "OK" Button

New table row 3. You have to insert an additional step for the **Create Address** form, because you want to use it to create a new table entry. To do this, define an `INSERT ROW` action as the first action for the **OK** button; you apply this action to the table. All other actions that you define for this button are the same as for **Update Address**.

4. In addition, use the `ASSIGN` action to pass the employee ID from the input field back to the table automatically. This guarantees that the relevant field in the table is filled.

Deleting a row from the table 5. Finally, define a `DELETE ROW(S)` action for **Delete Address**, as shown in Figure 8.17.

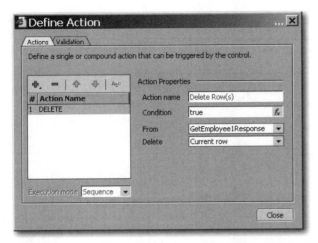

Figure 8.17 Using a Predefined Action to Delete a Row from a Table

6. You should now deploy and test your application. The application should look like the application shown in Figure 8.18; the model should look like the model shown in Figure 8.19. The asterisk next to **update** on the top left of the following second figure indicates that the model has not yet been saved.

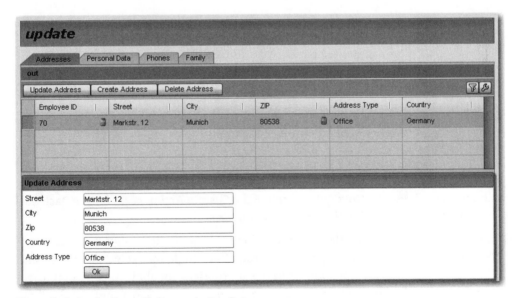

Figure 8.18 Application with Demonstration Data

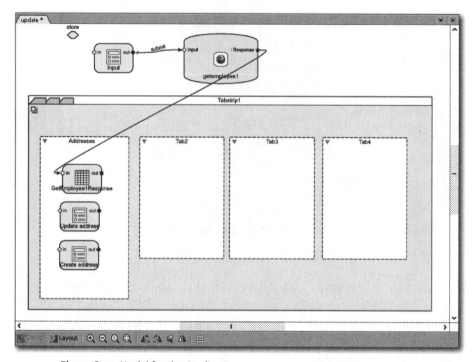

Figure 8.19 Model for the Application

Navigation between tab pages

There are two things left to do before you edit the next tab page: First, you need to enable navigation between the tab pages; second, the addresses need to be saved.

1. To enable navigation between the tab pages, start by creating a **Toolbar (Bottom)** element for the **Tabstrip** container.

2. Configure two buttons in the toolbar:

   ▸ **Back**

   ▸ **Next**

Creating a custom action

3. For the **Next** button, define the **Custom Action** next; for the **Back** button, define the **System Action** BACK.

Transition between two tab pages

4. To activate the **Custom Action** next, go to the Design Board and connect the tab pages with a **Transition**. To do this, select a tab page, and drag the dot above it to the appropriate dot above the next tab page. In the context menu that now opens, choose **New Event...** and call the event next.

5. This context menu only opens for the transition between the first and second tab pages. It does not open for the others because they do not yet have any content. In these cases, simply drag the connections and rename them. The model should now look like the model shown in Figure 8.20 (once the second tab page has been renamed).

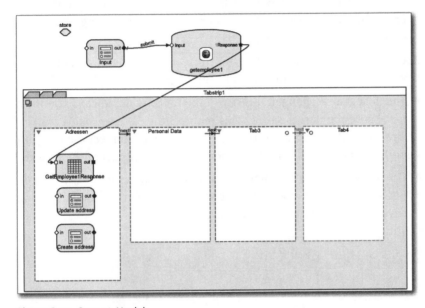

Figure 8.20 Current Model

You can use the SaveAddresses service to save the updated addresses. This should always be done before navigating to a new location.

1. Start by dragging this service to the first tab page.

2. You must now connect the **out** port of the table with the **addresses** port of the service. Visual Composer (in its standard configuration) is responsible for mapping the fields expected by the service to the fields of the table. You should check this, however. For the employee ID, connect the **out** port of the table with the **input** port of the service.

3. To guarantee that the data is always saved when you navigate away from the tab page, associate your new connections with the *next event by renaming them as "*next". The asterisk prefix (*) guarantees that the data is always changed when a next action is executed in the model.

Holistic event handling

8.3.3 Updating the Personal Data of an Employee

On the first tab page, you can now enter the addresses of an employee; the second tab page is intended for the administration of an employee's personal data.

1. Start by dragging the **Response** node of the service. This opens a context menu where you can choose **Form View**. In the dialog that opens, select the node for personal data.

2. On the **Layout Board**, adapt the form to your requirements, after which it should look like the form in Figure 8.21.

Saving the data
3. The data can be changed directly in the form, which means you must make sure the data is saved. This requires the `SavePersonalData` service. After dragging the service to the tab page, connect the **out** port of the form with the two input ports (**data** and **Input**) of the service.

4. Check the mapping and make any required changes manually. You do not associate your new connections with an event yet; however, you have the option of testing them with *next.

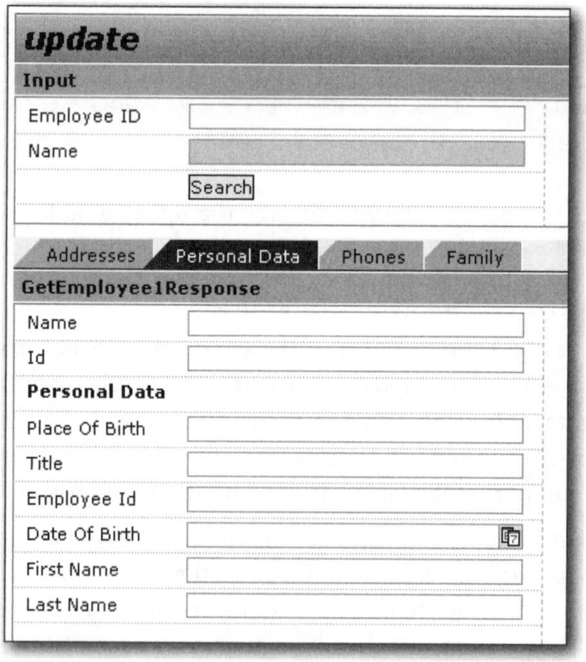

Figure 8.21 Tab Page Layout for the Personal Data of an Employee

8.3.4 Editing the Telephone Numbers of an Employee

The third tab page is used to edit the telephone numbers of the employee.

1. Rename the tab page as "Telephones."

2. Now display a table of the employee's telephone numbers. Start by dragging the **Response** node of the service. This opens a context menu where you can choose **Table View**. In the **Define Data** dialog, select `phones_Phones` and close the window.

3. As before, create a **Toolbar (Bottom)** for this table. Configure two buttons in the toolbar: **New Telephone** and **Remove Telephone**.

   Creating and removing telephone numbers

4. For the **New Telephone** button, define the INSERT ROW action (as described previously). This time, however, set the **Insert** property to `last`, so that the new row is inserted at the bottom of the table.

5. For the **Remove Telephone** button, define the DELETE ROW action (also as described previously).

6. The data can be changed directly in the table, which means it needs to be saved. This can be done using the service `SavePhones`.

7. After dragging the service to the tab page, connect the **out** port of the form with the two input ports (**phones** and **Input**) of the service.

8. As far as mappings are concerned, the same applies as for personal data. Again, the connections are not associated with an event.

8.3.5 Editing the Family Members of an Employee

The fourth (and final) tab page is interesting from a data protection perspective, because it is used to enter and edit the family members of an employee.

1. Rename the tab page as "Family".

2. Just as in the preceding examples, generate a table from the basis service, but this time use the `familyMembers_FamilyMembers` node.

   Creating and removing family members

3. Once more, incorporate an option to create new entries. You can save the employee's family details using the `SaveFamilyMembers` service.

8.3.6   Final Steps

If you now try to deploy the application, Visual Composer will display several errors. This is because certain events have yet to be defined; however, we will do this in the next step.

Saving all data

1. Start by creating a new button in the **Toolbar** of the **Tabstrip**, preferably between the two existing buttons. Call this button **Save Data**.

2. Define actions for the new button that save all data. To do this, create four custom actions (as shown in Figure 8.22):

   ▶ SAVEADDRESSES

   ▶ SAVEPHONES

   ▶ SAVEFAMILYMEMBERS

   ▶ SAVEPERSONALDATA

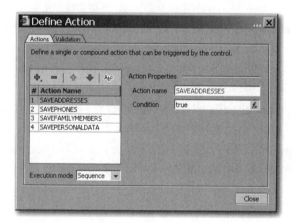

Figure 8.22 Action Editor with Actions that Save Personal Data

3. Rename all connections between the forms and tables so that they match the actions defined above:

   ▶ *saveaddresses for the connections on the **Addresses** tab page

   ▶ *savephones for the connections on the **Telephones** tab page

   ▶ *savefamilymembers for the connections on the **Family** tab page

   ▶ *savepersonaldata for the connections on the **Personal Data** tab page

8.3.7 Creating Employees

You already learned how to modify the data of an employee; the next step is to associate actions with the two remaining links on the start page. Just a short glimpse at **Create a new employee** should tell you that there is a lot of common ground with actions that update employee data. We have already emphasized the reuse benefits of using model-based developments, and we are about to examine this in more depth in the following. We will not create a completely new model, however, and will use a different method instead.

1. Go to the model on the start page and define a `create` action for the **Create a new employee** link.

   Creating a new employee

2. Then create a new connection between the form and the existing navigation element **update**. Give this connection the same name as the `create` action. You model should now look something like the model shown in Figure 8.23.

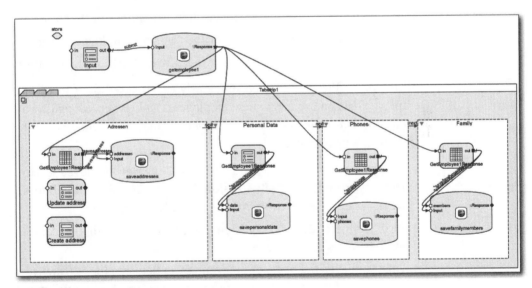

Figure 8.23 Model After the Latest Update

3. You also perform the next few steps in the **update** model.

4. You use the `NewEmployee` service to create an employee. Drag the service to the model and then create an input form for it. To do this, drag

the **Input** node of the service. This opens a context menu where you can choose **Form View**.

Dynamic user interface

Right now, the user can see both input forms, regardless of whether the user wants to update an existing employee or create a new employee. You start by arranging the input forms on the **Layout Board** so that one is directly above the other. More importantly, however, you need to define the visibility of the forms. We have already looked at the visibility conditions for elements, but you still need to learn how to define which link was used.

Start point

1. To decide which link was used by the user, create a **Start Point** connector. A connection to a form is optional, rather than mandatory.

2. Define a new field, app_mode, for the **Start Point**.

3. Go back to the start page model. You can now define a mapping for the two connections create and update. For both mappings, set the name of the connection as the value of the field app_mode.

4. In the **update** model, define the visibility conditions of the forms:

   ▶ =start@app_mode=="update" for the "Update Employee" form

   ▶ =start@app_mode=="create" for the "Create New Employee" form

All tab pages that you created previously can be used both to update employee data and to create new employees. Only when saving do you need to decide whether the data is being updated or whether a new employee is being created.

1. To create a new employee, you need to call the **NewEmployee** service. Start by opening the **Define Action** dialog for the **Save Data** button. Here, create a new **Custom Action**, called "newempsave".

Guard conditions

2. Also, define a **Guard Condition** for this action, with the content =start@app_mode=="create".

3. Finally, change the name of the connection between the "Create New Employee" form and the service to *newempsave. At the same time, you can remove the **Submit** button from the input form.

Extended data mapping

4. You now need to define the mapping for the "Save" operation, while ensuring that a distinction is again made between updating an employee and creating a new employee. In connections to "Save" operations, any references to the employee ID must be replaced by

the following expression. This expression refers to the new employee or an existing employee, depending on the mode:

```
=if(start@app_mode=="update",
 GetEmployee1Response@employeeId,
 [newemployee.newEmployeeResponse]@newEmployeeResult)
```

8.3.8 Deleting Employees

Now associate a function with the remaining link on the start page: a function to delete an employee.

1. Go to the model on the start page and define a `delete_employee` action for the **Delete an employee** link. A simple `delete` cannot be used here because there is already a system action with this name.

   Deleting employees

2. Now create a new connector of the type **Navigate**. Define a new **delete** model in the dialog that now opens.

3. Configure a connection between the form and the connector. Call this connection `delete_employee`. Your model should now look something like the model shown in Figure 8.24.

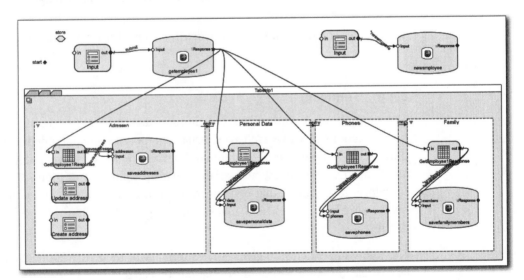

Figure 8.24 Model After the Latest Update

4. To open the new model, double-click the **delete** connector.

5. You now need the `GetEmployee1` service again. Drag this service to the model and then create an input form for it.

6. Continue by dragging the **Popup** container to the model.

7. Drag the **Response** node of the service into the **Popup** container and select the personal data of the employee that you want to display in a form.

8. You need a further service, `DeleteEmployee`. Connect the input node (**Input**) of this service with the output node (**out**) of the form in the pop-up dialog.

9. Select the pop-up and choose the Layout pushbutton (on the bottom left) to see a preview of the pop-up dialog. You will see that two buttons have already been defined, **OK** and **Cancel**. Actions have been defined for both buttons. For the **OK** button, define a **Custom Action** called `OK`. Change the name of the connection you created in the last step to `*ok`.

10. Define the data mapping for the new connection.

11. Go to the **Response** node of the `DeleteEmployee` service and generate a form. This form is sent to the user and tells him whether the employee was deleted.

12. Finally, create a transition between the input form and the pop-up dialog.

8.3.9 Summary

The example we have just worked through demonstrates some of the basic functions of SAP NetWeaver Visual Composer and is intended as a quick start in the world of model-based development. We have deliberately omitted some steps, such as an enhanced validation of input. We, therefore, recommend that you construct your own example with your own choice of services, and invest some energy into fine-tuning the details.

The following conclusion gives you a summary of the entire application as created in the steps shown throughout this chapter.

Start page
Figure 8.25 shows the model of the **Start Page**. At the end of the example, all links on the start page should be associated with actions. The start page should look like the start page shown in Figure 8.26.

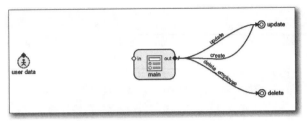

Figure 8.25 Final Model of the Start Page

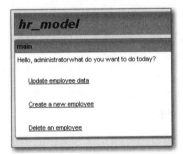

Figure 8.26 Start Page After Deployment in SAP NetWeaver Portal

The model for **updating and creating employees** has not changed. Depending on which link you choose on the start page, the application either looks like the application in Figure 8.27 (for creating employees) or like the application in Figure 8.28 (for updating employee data). You can open the new model by double-clicking the **delete** connector.

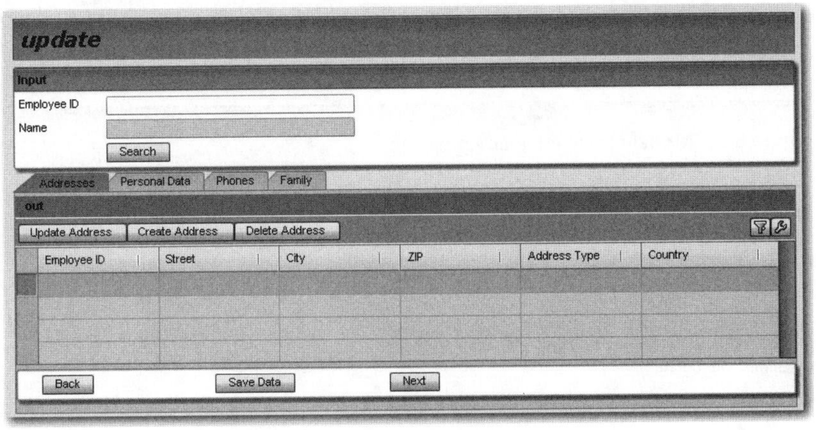

Creating employees and updating their data

Figure 8.27 Application View for Creating a New Employee

377

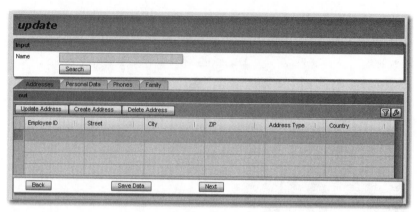

Figure 8.28 Application View for Updating Employee Data

Deleting employees
Figure 8.29 shows the model for **deleting employees**. Figure 8.30 shows the application with an opened pop-up dialog.

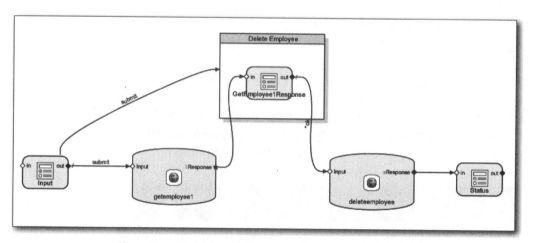

Figure 8.29 Model for Deleting an Employee

delete	
Input	
Employee ID	[ ]
	Delete
Status	
☐ Employee Deleted	

Figure 8.30 Application View for Deleting an Employee

We've already talked a lot about composite applications in this book, but haven't really discussed how to implement these ideas in actual programs. This chapter sheds some light on how to develop composite applications.

9 Developing Composite Applications

Composite applications are a new generation of business applications. Until now, applications concentrated mainly on the input of data and the processing of this data in (more or less) monolithic systems; composite applications, on the other hand, take a completely different approach: Existing functions are reused deliberately in new business processes. And in the places where functions are missing from standard applications, they are added by the composite applications' own business logic.

Properties of composite applications

A further important difference is the separation of business processes in their own architecture layer. Business processes in today's applications are mostly hard-coded, but composite applications move them to a separate layer, which makes them easier to modify. The often criticized lack of flexibility in business processes becomes a thing of the past. On top of this, people are consciously included in these business processes, which is when they become *collaborative business processes*. This new application architecture is accompanied by a development process that focuses on modeling rather than on programming.

This quick overview of a composite application's most important characteristics gives you an indication of the possibilities available when developing applications based on SOA (service-oriented architecture) principles. Accordingly, the aim of this chapter is to follow a short introduction to the philosophy and benefits of composite applications with details of their concrete implementation. We will illustrate this in a simple example, while also studying some typical characteristics of the architecture and best practices for development work.

9.1 Philosophy and Benefits

There remains little doubt about the efficiency with which business data can be handled and analyzed by traditional business applications, or about the effectiveness of fully automated business processes. However, the coverage of the already mentioned collaborative business processes, leaves much to be desired.

Weaknesses of classical applications One weak point of classical applications is the lack of support for inexperienced or occasional users who come into contact with standard applications only when performing administrative tasks, such as entering travel expenses or logging their working hours. Even today, the results of business processes are entered manually in ERP (Enterprise Resource Planning) systems, but the processes themselves lack structure and coordination, due to the use of word processing and spreadsheet programs and documents being exchanged in emails. In addition, the monolithic architecture of existing ERP systems does not exactly lend itself to the flexible implementation of the new and innovative processes that provide enterprises with a competitive edge.

Finally, we must not forget that classical applications are presented as sealed units that demand exclusive access to their data and have unrestricted control over their own processes. Customers and end users, however, both have requirements that are no longer covered by these applications. These include:

End user expectations ▶ Provision of consistent and intelligent user guidance, across varying applications and systems (and even across enterprises)

▶ Provision of new functions across applications, systems, and enterprises

▶ Global view of the enterprise and its processes (and not just of functional units such as CRM (Customer Relationship Management) or SCM (Supply Chain Management) systems)

- ▶ Support for enterprise-wide cooperation between people and systems
- ▶ Creation of new solutions, primarily by reusing existing services
- ▶ Simplification of customizing for existing applications by process experts

End users have a special significance in a composite application: The applications must enable easy access to the relevant information for a task. This generally requires data to be retrieved from various sources, without this being noticed by the end user. The combination of a consistent user interface and integrated applications across system boundaries is the decisive factor in using composite applications.

Role of the end user in a composite application

A further argument for this new generation of applications is the quick and effective way you can customize them to an ever changing environment. The special layered architecture of composite applications, which we will discuss in detail later, makes them ideal for quick customizing. After all, collaborative processes in particular generally have short lifetimes and need to be modified often.

Efficient customizing of composite applications

Standard applications concentrate on standard business processes and accommodate these processes extremely well, even across different industries; competitive factors, however, have also produced a great demand for industry-, country-, and region-specific solutions, as well as applications tailored to individual customers. Against this background, the customizability of an application with regard to individual customer requirements becomes particularly significant.

Competitive advantages of composite applications

In conclusion, we see that the flexibility and independence of the existing system landscape are important aspects of composite applications. These aspects allow software vendors to develop solutions fully independently of where the standard applications in their landscapes are in their release cycles.

9.2 Basic Assumptions

The following is a short definition of the important aspects of a composite application, as discussed in the introduction:

Definition of composite applications

A composite application is an application that uses service calls to access the existing data and functions provided by the solutions already in the system landscape. It combines these elements into new (primarily collaborative) business processes, enhanced by custom user interfaces and business logic.

More properties of composite applications become apparent when you look at the requirements of end users, enterprises, and software vendors from a technological viewpoint:

Technological properties of composite applications

▶ **Composite applications are based on services provided by other systems.**
They combine available services with new business logic and user interfaces to produce innovative business processes. Services can be provided by

- ▶ SAP's Business Process Platform (BPP)
- ▶ SAP ERP 6.0 with predefined services
- ▶ the new SAP solution for medium-size businesses, SAP Business ByDesign
- ▶ third-party vendor services.

▶ **Composite applications are user-oriented solutions that support collaboration across system boundaries.**
They offer a consistent custom user interface, with additional automated steps (that do not require user interaction).

▶ **Composite applications are process-oriented applications that access one or more systems in the landscape to perform their tasks.**
Individual steps within the processes can be performed by software from third-party vendors or by proprietary solutions developed by customers.

▶ **Composite applications have their own lifecycle and are independent of the system landscape.**
Composite applications use external functions, but they should not be made dependent on the associated systems and the lifecycles of these systems. The most important idea here is the *required function*: For example, a composite application could require the function "Create

Purchase Order." The actual system that provides this function, and the release of this system, is of secondary importance.

To enable you to construct a composite application with these properties, a framework must provide the abstraction of the IT landscape with respect to the composite application. Composite Application Framework (CAF) is responsible for this task in the toolset of the SAP NetWeaver Composition Environment. This framework guarantees that the composite application has its own lifecycle and is independent of other systems and their release levels.

▶ **Composite applications are developed primarily as model-driven applications.**
This model-driven approach reduces the amount of code that has to be written by hand, while increasing the proportion of generated code used. This makes developers significantly more productive and improves quality at the same time.

9.3 Basic Architecture

Composite applications, as shown in Figure 9.1, initially have a universal architecture, regardless of the tools used to develop the different layers. The figure shows a recommended way of organizing a composite application, with (as the central components) separate layers for processes, user interfaces, and business objects and services.

Layers of a composite application

Figure 9.1 emphasizes effectively the idea of a composite application as an independent standalone application, constructed on existing services from the backend systems. Always keep in mind the independent nature of a composite application and, consequently, how it is split from the system landscape.

Independence of a composite application

As you can see from the architecture, service enablement is not part of a composite application. Composite applications always assume the availability of these services, which comprise the core business logic and core data of the systems.

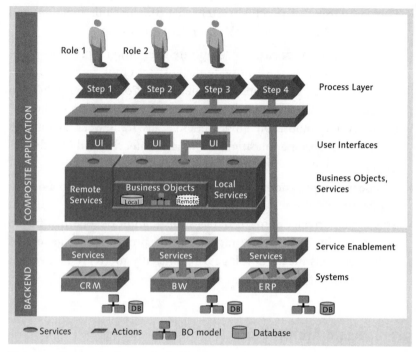

Figure 9.1 Layers of a Composite Application

9.3.1 Business Objects and Service Layer

The objects and services required by the composite application are developed in the business object and service layer. This layer is also an abstraction layer with respect to the associated systems. It includes all functions that enable the composite application to be adapted for use with concrete systems.

You do not have to develop these functions yourself because these capabilities are included in the runtime environment of Composite Application Framework. This means that developers do not have to worry about the technical details of Web service communication and can concentrate on the business content of their applications instead.

Business objects as a basis for composite applications

You generally start by developing your business objects. Once you have identified your required set of composite applications, you can start working on the details of the objects. For developers of composite appli-

384

cations, it is important to know that they can rely on a uniform interface of their objects for implementing the new business logic.

As you can see in Figure 9.1, there are two categories of business objects: local and remote. Each composite application works with a well-defined set of objects, such as a *customer*, a *purchase order*, or a *project*. You will always encounter objects that are already available in existing systems, for example a customer in a CRM system or an order in an ERP system. Why do we need to store this data again in the composite application? This is where the remote objects come into play: those objects that control access to the data in the system landscape without duplicating the data in the composite itself.

Conversely, you also need to consider the objects that are designed especially for use by the composite application. A good example of this is the *product idea* as the business object in a product definition process. Objects like this cannot be associated with a particular system, which means their data must be stored in the database of the composite application itself. These objects are known as local business objects.

Regardless of which object type developers use in their business logic, they want a uniform interface for access to their objects. The repository of the objects, whether local or remote, is of secondary importance at design time. Developers are only concerned with their own objects when programming, and do not want to worry about implementation details. This is the service that Composite Application Framework provides in the business object layer.

Once the objects have been identified, you can give them the attributes relevant for use in the composite application. This aspect of "composite application-relevance" cannot be stressed strongly enough: An order object in an ERP system, for example, is certain to have an overwhelming number of attributes, but composite applications need to concentrate on the *relevant* attributes only, and can ignore any others when modeling objects. Don't be tempted to incorporate all the attributes available in the backend system and overload your object model with characteristics; instead, keep the object model simple. Of course, you are allowed to reuse existing models and import them into your development environment, but don't forget to remove any fields you don't need.

Attributes of business objects

Composite applica-
tion-specific busi-
ness logic
Once you have created an object model, you can start to develop your new, composite application-specific, business logic. Programming work is required here, but this is made easier by the simple and uniform interfaces provided to the business objects. The new business logic can itself be provided to the surrounding environment as a Web service.

As you can see again in Figure 9.1, there are both local and remote services. Unlike the new local services just described, remote services are themselves wrapped only in order to provide developers with a uniform interface for the implementation of their logic. Later, this remote service implementation can even be swapped for an alternative solution.

The next layers in the stack, the UI layer and process layer, benefit immediately from this abstraction. As long as they make consistent use of the services in the business object layer and service layer, they do not need to worry about the dependencies on the existing system landscape. We, therefore, recommend that you always link the higher layers to the backend systems through the business object and service layers, and do not skip them in your programming.

> **Practical Example**
>
> A customer appraisal service can be offered by various different vendors. If you chose vendor A in the first version of your composite application, the wrapper enables you to switch to vendor B at a later date, even if this provider uses a complete different interface from vendor A.
>
> Because you programmed your composite application on the basis of the stable interface, you, as a developer, do not notice any changes. The composite application is independent of the service implementation.
>
> This demonstrates how important the business object layer and service layer are for standalone composite applications.

9.3.2 User Interface Layer

Consistent UIs for
composite applica-
tions
The UI layer must ensure that the user interface of the composite application is consistent. The preferred tools for this task are SAP NetWeaver Visual Composer and Web Dynpro, described in detail elsewhere in this book. Visual Composer is generally the tool of choice for less complex forms, whereas Web Dynpro's more program-driven approach is best

suited for interfaces with a lot of UI logic (where a model-driven approach would be less appropriate).

Both tools focus on the use of service interfaces in UI design, where the definition of the UI elements is based on the attributes of the inbound and outbound interfaces. In this way, simple structures in the inbound interface can be mapped to form fields and lists mapped to tables. The data types of these fields or tables then determine the individual UI components: For example, a field with the data type `Date` is associated with a date picker on the UI.

This chapter does not go into the details of the tools, because they were explained in depth in Chapter 6, *Developing Business Applications with Web Dynpro*, and Chapter 8, *SAP NetWeaver Visual Composer*.

9.3.3 Process Layer

The integration of the user interfaces into the next layer in the architecture, the process layer, is even more important than the individual functions of the tools. This layer is responsible for fitting the services and UIs into an appropriate flow model. As discussed in the introduction, collaboration is a particularly significant aspect here and, accordingly, different roles are responsible for different steps. During the process itself, roles are kept informed by notifications (*work items*). Guided procedures (GPs) are responsible for this task from a tool perspective.

Modeling the process flow

Integration Between the Process Layer and the User Interface Layer — The Guided Procedures Context

You may now be asking yourself how a user interface is integrated with guided procedures. It helps if you think about it as follows: In a process flow, multiple people contribute to the process, for example, by filling out data in forms. This data has to be collected and, at the end of the process, saved to applications in the backend systems or the composite application itself.

This data must be cached somewhere during the process; it does not make sense to create separate business objects for incomplete data. The

Data flow from the GP context

GP framework has a cache for this data, known as the guided procedures context.

This context is similar to servlet sessions in the Java EE environment; these sessions also retain data states between servlet calls. The lifetime of the GP context always matches the lifetime of the process. These processes can have extremely long lifetimes (weeks or sometimes months) and the content of the contexts is therefore continued in a database, helpful when developers need to recover data in the event of a crash.

There are no limits on how complex the data can be (combinations of structures, tables, and nested structures and tables are all permitted). The associated services and UIs must cooperate with the GP context to enable it to manage the data, a simple task for service calls due to their clear interface definitions.

But how does this cooperation work for UIs? This is the point where UIs start to collaborate with a guided procedure: The UIs are required to implement a special Java interface. In Web Dynpro, this is done manually; in Visual Composer you model start points and end points (as you'll see in detail later). The interface information for the guided procedures is then generated from these models, which will then be used for the data exchange between guided procedures and the UIs.

Basic Process Modeling Steps

If all agreements made between the guided procedures and the associated steps are honored, there are three major steps you have to perform in the GP development environment:

Process flow
1. **Modeling the process flow**
    The first step defines the order of the process steps. As well as the basic sequence, you can include further modeling options, such as parallel steps, loops, alternatives, or jumps. Each step must be mapped to an interactive step or a background step, using the UIs and services developed in the steps described earlier.

Process roles
2. **Assigning process roles to the individual steps**
    You must then assign the process roles. Each step must be assigned to an appropriate role. (Note that process roles are not the same as the

roles you are probably familiar with from the portal or other user databases.)

Initially, the guided procedures contain only simple names for the process roles. Only at start time does a guided procedure define which specific user, group, or role from the portal or user database is mapped to the process role in question. Of course, multiple users, groups, or roles are allowed, or combinations of any of the three.

3. **Consolidating the parameters in the GP context**

All that remains is to consolidate the data of the GP context. Once the individual steps have signaled their collaboration with the guided procedures (using their interfaces), GP runtime needs to know which data to pass from step x to step y. This is known as *parameter consolidation*. The process does not use a step-to-step mapping (as you might imagine); instead, you tell the GP framework which parameters to handle identically in the GP context, that is, which parameters are to be regarded as the only variable.

Parameter consolidation

Practical Example

The example here is a simple confirmation process in which an employee enters data about his leave of absence in step 1. The employee's manager has to confirm this data in step 2, possibly while adding a remark. Step 3 completes the process by calling a Web service to update the data in a standard application. Based on this description, the following interfaces can be determined between the steps:

▶ **Step 1**
   Input parameters: None
   Output parameters: First and last names, period of absence (from-to date)

▶ **Step 2**
   Input parameters: First and last names of the employee, period of absence (from-to date)
   Output parameters: Approved (yes/no), remark

▶ **Step 3**
   Input parameters: First and last names of the employee, period of absence (from-to date), approved (yes/no), remark
   Output parameters: Saved business object "Leave of Absence"

These interfaces can be used to explain the parameter consolidation. It is obvious that all output parameters from the first step must be passed to the inbound interfaces of both the second and third steps.

This is guaranteed by consolidating the parameters, for example, by consolidating the output parameter of step 1, Last Name, with the same input parameter of steps 2 and 3.

This is where the difference from traditional mappings becomes clear: instead of the two mappings Last Name(1) = Last Name(2) and Last Name(1) = Last Name(3), there is just one consolidation, Last Name(1) = Last Name(2) = Last Name(3), where the number in parentheses indicates the parameter of the step in question. This consolidation must be repeated for all parameters stored in the GP context, to ensure that the parameters are passed from step to step at runtime.

Once the process has been defined, it can be instantiated and the process flow initiated. At this point, each process role must be assigned fixed users, groups, or portal roles. The users assigned to the process roles are sent appropriate notifications by the process framework. These notifications contain a link that takes the user to the pending step. After the user has entered his or her data, the framework notifies the next user in the process or executes any background steps required. This enables the process to be monitored at every stage.

9.4 Example Scenario: Project Management

In Section 9.3, *Basic Architecture*, you familiarized yourself with the fundamental elements of composite applications; we now move on to how to develop a composite application. To demonstrate this, we have chosen a simple scenario (a project management process) that is quick and easy to implement, but also covers all the important components of a composite application.

Example scenario: Project management

As you can see in Figure 9.2, there are two different project management roles: a *program lead* who coordinates the projects in a particular program and creates new projects, and a *project lead*, who is responsible for project management tasks.

The aim of this scenario is to outline how a new project is created. The program lead starts by entering the basic data of the new project, first selecting the project lead from a list of employees.

This list is filled by a Web service call to a backend system. Once the program lead has entered all the required project data, the chosen project lead has to confirm the new project in the next step. In this example, this step consists only of confirming that all resources needed are available. The project lead also has the option of entering remarks in comment field. The final step uses a Web service call to save all the project data to a specially developed business object.

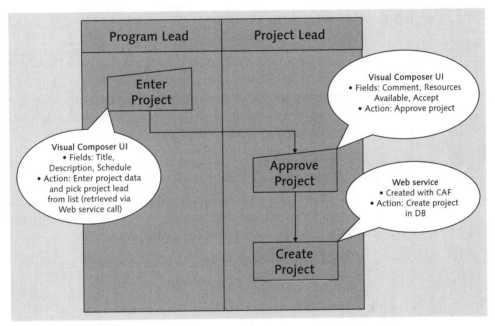

Figure 9.2 Project Management Example Scenario

This example is a particularly good introduction to composite application development because it emphasizes the way that the technologies involved cooperate with the available tools:

Technologies used in the development process

▶ Composite Application Framework for modeling business objects (with persistency) and providing the CREATE method as a Web service

▶ SAP NetWeaver Visual Composer for modeling UIs; the program lead's UI consumes a Web service, but the project lead's data is provided in full by the GP context.

▶ Guided procedures for modeling the process flow

Our example composite application is implemented in precisely this order.

9.4.1 Modeling Business Objects with Composite Application Framework

Composite Application Framework (CAF) enables you to model business objects and implement business logic. To implement the modeling artifacts in executable code, the framework uses session beans (familiar from the Java EE 5 environment) for all service calls, and also the Java Persistence API (to persist the business objects).

The implementation details are, however, hidden from the developer. Developers are only concerned with modeling their application components, which are then saved in metadata files. CAF then generates the Java source files from this metadata, which themselves are then translated (in a build process) and constructed as deployable files.

We'll now take a look at this development process in more depth.

Creating a Composite Application in SAP NetWeaver Developer Studio

We start with the new business object `Project`. In our example, this object consists of the following fields:

Attributes of the Project business object

- `title`: String (project name)
- `description`: String (short description of the project)
- `schedule`: String (estimated time frame of the project)
- `firstname`: String (first name of the project lead)
- `lastname`: String (last name of the project lead)
- `comment`: String (remark from the project lead)
- `resourcesAvailable`: Boolean (All resources needed to complete the project are available.)
- `accepted`: Boolean (The project proposal has been accepted.)

Launch SAP NetWeaver Developer Studio and open the specially designed **Composite Application** perspective by choosing **Window · Open Perspective · Other....** To create a new project, open the **New Project Wizard** by choosing **File · New · Project....** Enter data in the wizard as follows:

1. Under the **Development Infrastructure** node, select the item **Development Component** and confirm by choosing **Next**.

   Creating a project in CAF

2. Select **Composite Application** as the type of the new development component and choose **Next**.

3. We recommend that you develop your composite application locally, so select **MyComponents** under the **Local Development** node. Now choose **Next**.

4. Enter a name for your development component. For the purposes of this example, leave the **Vendor** field set to "demo.sap.com" and give your component the name "xproject" in the **Name** field (only lowercase letters are allowed here). Enter a short description of your component in the **Caption** field (Figure 9.3) and confirm by choosing **Next**.

Figure 9.3 Naming the Development Component (DC)

Subproject of an
application in
Composite Appli-
cation Framework

5. The next dialog step lists the projects created for a composite application, a total of five projects in this case (Figure 9.4).

   ▸ The Metadata project contains additional information about the business objects and services you have modeled. This can include, for example, information about the length of a string assigned to one of your fields as a data type, or information about whether a field is mandatory.

   ▸ The Dictionary project contains detailed data required to create database tables for your business objects.

   ▸ The Permissions project controls access to objects and services.

   ▸ The EJB and EAR projects contain the standard Java EE 5 components.

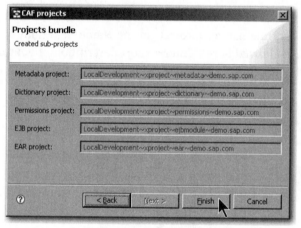

Figure 9.4 Projects in a Composite Application

6. Exit the wizard by choosing **Finish**.

Composite Appli-
cation Explorer

7. The new project is listed in Composite Application Explorer. Open the [Local Development] xproject node. Two subnodes are displayed, external and modeled.

   You can import links to external services under the external node. This is not relevant in this example, however, because you are not using external services to implement a new business logic, nor do you want to implement business objects with persistency in backend systems. We want to model a new business object instead.

8. To do this, open the context menu of the `modeled` node and choose the item **New Business Object** (Figure 9.5).

Figure 9.5 Creating a New Business Object

9. On the next dialog screen, give your new object the name "Project." Exit by choosing **Finish**. You now see two new subnodes in Composite Application Explorer, `Business Objects` and `Data Types` (Figure 9.6).

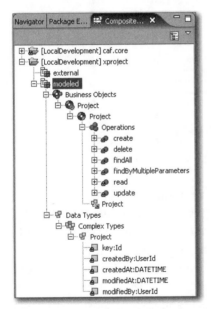

Figure 9.6 New Business Object "Project" in Composite Application Explorer

As you can see, CAF has not just created the business object, it has also generated a data structure for the attributes of the business object and some typical object lifecycle methods (such as `create`, `read`, `update`, `delete`, and `find`). Composite Application Framework administers these

Default fields and methods of a business object

attributes automatically at runtime; it also assigns the primary key (attribute `key`).

You model the actual object on the right half of the screen, in the new "Project" window (Figure 9.7). You may also have noticed a second window called ***xproject**. This window functions in certain aspects as the master project for this application.

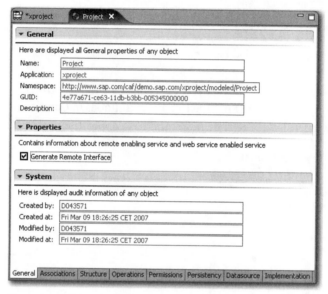

Figure 9.7 Editing the Business Object in Developer Studio

As discussed in the introduction, a composite application consists of five subprojects. The master project keeps you informed about the latest state of the changes made to your application, and saves you from having to track each of the subprojects separately. If an asterisk appears before the application name (as shown in Figure 9.7), then a change has been made to at least one of the subprojects. The master project serves as an umbrella for the entire composite application; consequently, when you save the master project, you also save all changes made to the subprojects.

General object information

You now edit the business object in a series of steps. You are guided through these steps by the tabs on the lower edge of the screen. The **General** tab contains administration information about the object. Of particular relevance for developers is the **Generate Remote Interface** checkbox. You use a Web service call to generate the business object from a guided procedure, which means you need to call a correctly prepared `create` method. An important step here is the activation of the remote interface. (To recap: These methods are provided as session beans that can be called locally or remotely; you need the remote variant in this case.) The relevant checkbox is deactivated by default (as shown in Figure 9.7), so you need to select it now.

Modeling the Attributes of Business Objects

1. You now continue with the definition of the object attributes. Choose the **Structure** tab, which contains the attributes of the object. As you can see, the administrative fields of the object are listed together with the object's primary key.

   Attributes

2. You now add business fields to the object. To do this, choose **Edit Main Structure**. A two-part window is displayed.

3. The left half of the screen shows you the data types you can use in your object definition. The right half shows you the structure of your object and its attributes (Figure 9.8).

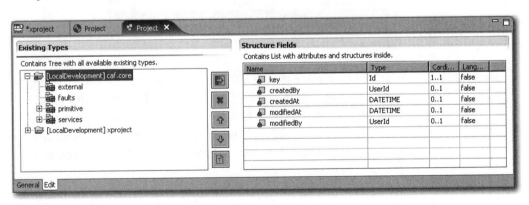

Figure 9.8 Editing the Structure of a Business Object

4. Expand the `primitive` node. This node contains the data type `String`. Select this item and then choose the "Arrow right" pushbutton (⊡).

   Assigning a data type

5. Overwrite the editable name of the attribute in the table. Enter "title" as the name of the project.

Cardinality of an
attribute

6. In the **Cardinality** column, you can define an attribute as a single field or a list of items. You can also classify single fields as mandatory fields; similarly, you can specify that the list must contain at least one element. In this case, `title` is a single field, and it must be filled when the object is created. Therefore, change the cardinality to **1..1**. Mandatory fields are also added as parameters to the `create` method.

7. Repeat these steps for the fields `description`, `schedule`, `firstname`, `lastname`, and `comment` (of the type `STRING`), and the fields `resources-Available` and `accepted` (of the type `BOOLEAN`). Your business object should now look like the object shown in Figure 9.9.

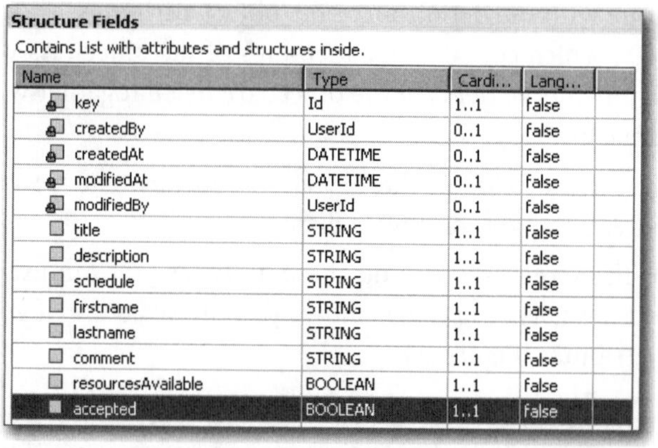

Structure Fields

Contains List with attributes and structures inside.

Name	Type	Cardi...	Lang...
key	Id	1..1	false
createdBy	UserId	0..1	false
createdAt	DATETIME	0..1	false
modifiedAt	DATETIME	0..1	false
modifiedBy	UserId	0..1	false
title	STRING	1..1	false
description	STRING	1..1	false
schedule	STRING	1..1	false
firstname	STRING	1..1	false
lastname	STRING	1..1	false
comment	STRING	1..1	false
resourcesAvailable	BOOLEAN	1..1	false
accepted	BOOLEAN	1..1	false

Figure 9.9 Attribute Definition of the "Project" Business Object

Predefined data
types

You will encounter several different text data types when browsing in the data types provided with Composite Application Framework. For example, the `services` subnode contains the data types `LongText`, `ShortText`, and `xLongText`. The **Properties** window (located directly under the structure definition editor (Figure 9.10)) tells you the differences between these types.

As shown in Figure 9.10, the data type `ShortText` has the length 30 (specified in the attribute `DefaultLength`). The data type `LongText`, on the other hand, has the length 256. The details in the **Properties** window help you to select the data type that best meets your requirements.

8. You can now exit the object definition phase by closing the structure editor.

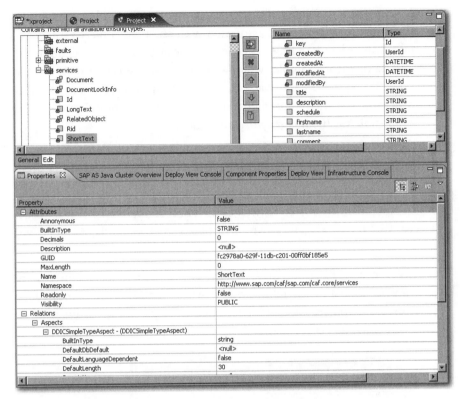

Figure 9.10 Detailed Information About the ShortText Data Type

Relations Between Business Objects

Our example scenario does not require you to model relationships to other business objects, but it is still worth taking a look at the **Associations** tab of the **Project** business object. This window is also split into two parts: The left half shows you the business objects that have already been modeled; the right half shows you how the current object has been related to other business objects. You can model these relations easily by selecting an appropriate object from the list on the left and choosing the pushbutton (⊡).

Relationships to other objects

Once you have created a node in the table of associations, and given it a name, you can define further details, such as the association type (CROSS_BO or PARENT_CHILD) and a cardinality (for example, ONE_TO_MANY or NONE_TO_ONE). PARENT_CHILD indicates a type of association where

399

child nodes are deleted if their parent node is deleted (for example, when an "Order" object is associated with an "Item" object); CROSS_BO, on the other hand, indicates a type of association where the child nodes are retained (for example, when an "Order" is associated with a "Customer"). You can use these associations to model object hierarchies that meet your specific requirements. Composite Application Framework is responsible for the integrity of your model.

Lifecycle Methods of a Business Object

Methods The **Operations** tab page shows you the automatically generated lifecycle method of the object. As well as the familiar operations create, read, update, and delete, there are also two search methods, findAll and findByMultiple Parameters.

1. When you select one of the methods, the associated parameters are displayed below the table. For example, when you select the create method, you see the parameters that were given the cardinality **1..1** when the object was defined (Figure 9.11).

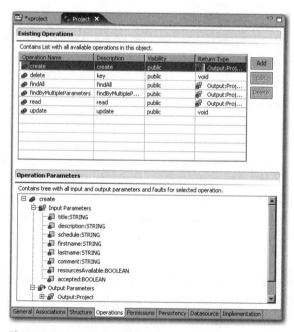

Figure 9.11 Parameters of the 'create' Method

2. You can also define your own finder methods. To do this, choose the **Add** pushbutton on the right side of the table. The dialog box shown in Figure 9.12 is displayed.

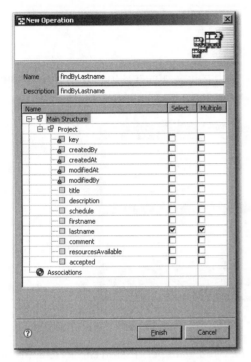

Figure 9.12 Definition of a New Search Method

3. Enter an appropriate name for your new operation and select the object attributes that you want to use as search parameters. In this example, you want to search for the last name of the project lead. Give the method the name `findByLastname` and select `lastname` as a parameter for this method.

The columns **Select** and **Multiple** are also useful. By selecting the appropriate checkbox, you indicate whether you want to pass one (**Select**) or more (**Multiple**) search terms to the method. When dealing with associations, you also have the option of retrieving the attributes of all associated objects for the method definition. This allows you to model, for example, search methods such as "Find all orders whose items include product xyz." This requires a relation to be made between the order and the item, with the product being an attribute of the item.

4. Exit the dialog by choosing **Finish**. You have now defined a new search method.

Permissions for Business Objects

Permissions   The next step in modeling your business object is to define permissions for the object on the **Permissions** tab page (Figure 9.13).

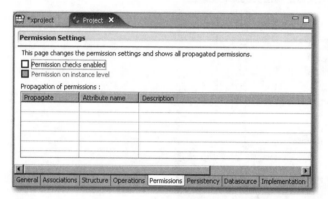

Figure 9.13 Definition of Permissions

1. You must first decide whether you want permission checks to apply or not. To activate checks by Composite Application Framework, select the **Permission checks enabled** checkbox. If you choose to do this, you must use a further tool (**Authorization Tool**) to define permissions for the business object after you deployed the composite application. This goes beyond the scope of this exercise, so deselect the checkbox (it is selected by default).

2. As you can see in Figure 9.13, you can also propagate permissions to related objects. If you had defined associations to our **Project** object, you would see **Propagation of permissions** in the table, and you could choose to apply the same permissions to one or more of the associated objects.

3. The **Permission on instance level** checkbox also has an important role. It lets you fine-tune the permission rules you define in **Authorization Tool** at the level of the individual field content. Using this capa-

bility, you could, for example, model permission rules such as "Customer numbers 0 to 100,000 to be processed by Richard Miller and customer numbers 100,001 to 200,000 to be processed by Donna Armstrong."

Persistency for Business Objects

You can make more settings on the **Persistency** tab page, which summarizes all persistency attributes of the business object (Figure 9.14).

Persistency

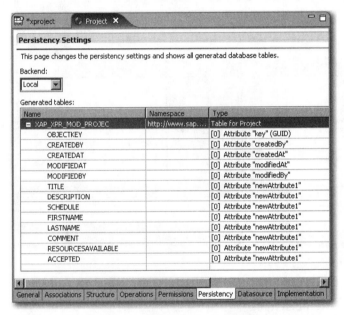

Figure 9.14 Persistency Attributes of a Business Object

1. As already mentioned at the start of the chapter, you can define business objects with local or remote persistency. You make this setting on this tab page.

   Defining local or remote persistency

   The **Backend** dropdown box contains the persistency options **Local** and **Remote**. Our example uses local persistency, so select this option.

2. The table below the dropdown box contains an overview of the database tables used to save the business object and its relations with other objects. A database table for the business object is always created, even in remote scenarios. In this case, however, only the admin-

istration fields are filled and the business fields left empty. Relations also require a join table to be generated for each relation modeled.

Data sources
3. The **Datasource** tab page is only relevant for scenarios using remote persistency. Therefore, if you want to view the modeling options on the **Datasource** tab page, select **Remote** in the dropdown list on the **Persistency** tab page (Figure 9.15).

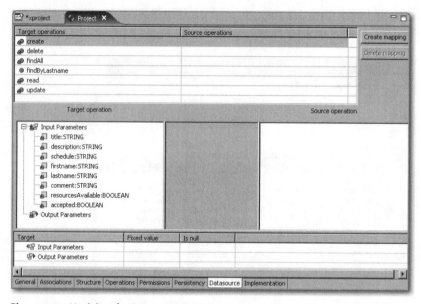

Figure 9.15 Modeling for Remote Persistency

Modeling Remote Persistency

Remote persistency
The central question here is what can we achieve by using remote persistency? In a remote scenario, you want to save the data of the business object to an existing backend system, but you do not know which system this is. This is why you cannot just assume that the object attributes are mapped one-to-one to an existing table in the backend system. This approach would skip the entire business logic of the backend system associated with the business object, and is therefore not a feasible solution.

The following approach is more promising: backend systems generally contain business objects that have lifecycle methods similar to those of your new object and that also mirror its business logic. You can take an ABAP system as an example: These systems contain the business object Salesorder with the associated BAPI (Business Application Programming Interface) BAPI_SALESORDER_CREATEFROMDATA. So, it seems obvious to just use these methods. This is why the **Datasource** tab page offers you a list of the generated lifecycle methods of your business object.

You can now map these methods to appropriate backend methods. This means that there is no mapping between the fields of the business object and its counterpart in the backend; instead, appropriate *methods* from the business objects are assigned to each other, followed by a subsequent mapping of the *method parameters*.

1. In the example in Figure 9.15, you have selected the create method. You can now choose **Create mapping** to open a dialog box where you can select a suitable backend method. This method must already have been imported as an external service. This has not been done in our example, so leave the list empty.

2. If you had selected a backend method, you would now be able to assign the individual parameters of the methods. Figure 9.15 shows you the parameters of the object's create method under **Target operation**. You can use drag & drop to assign parameters between methods.

After this brief excursion into the details of remote persistency, set the **Backend** dropdown list on the **Persistency** tab page back to **Local**.

This completes the definition of your object. You can view the classes you have created on the **Implementation** tab page. You can click the link to the implementation class of the object to display and edit its source code. Figure 9.16 shows you that the model is represented in Java code as stateless session beans.

Implementation

Exposing Methods as a Web Service

Before you generate the application, you must expose the create method as a Web service. This is because the last step of the business process modeling procedure is to use a Web service call to include this method in the process.

Figure 9.16 Generated Code for the Object Implementation

Exposing selected
methods as a Web
service

1. It is important that the object has been given a remote interface on the **General** tab page.

2. To generate Web services, open the context menu of the `Project` node in Composite Application Explorer and choose the option **Expose service as Web Service** (Figure 9.17).

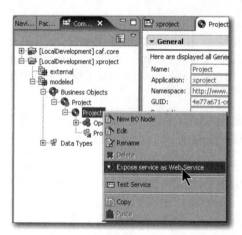

Figure 9.17 Generating Web Services for the Methods of the "Project" Business Object

3. A dialog box opens where you can enter a name for the Web service and select the methods that you want to call using the service. Give your example Web service the name "ProjectWS" and select the `create` method only (Figure 9.18).

4. Confirm your entries by choosing **OK**.

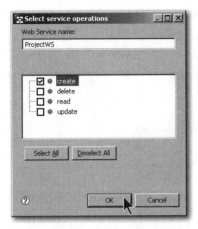

Figure 9.18 Generating Web Services

5. Save the business object by opening the context menu of the project **xproject** in Composite Application Explorer and choosing **Save application**.

The build itself comprises three steps:

1. **Generating the Composite Application**
   Your modeling efforts have created an XML description that now has to be transformed into Java code. To do this, open the context menu of the project and choose **Generate application** (Figure 9.19).

Generating, building, and deploying a composite application

Figure 9.19 Generating the Composite Application

2. Compiling and Creating Deployable Archives

You now need to transform the new Java classes and metadata and compile them as archives. You do this by choosing **Build application** from the same context menu. You can view the progress of the build (Figure 9.20).

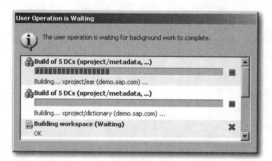

Figure 9.20 Build Progress Indicator

3. Deploying the Composite Application

The archives are now ready to be deployed as a composite application. You copy these archives to the server by choosing **Deploy application** in the **xprojects** context menu.

You may be prompted for the master ID and password you created when you installed the SAP NetWeaver Composition Environment. Enter the logon data and, once the deployment has been completed successfully, confirm by choosing **OK** (Figure 9.21).

Figure 9.21 Confirming a Successful Deployment

You can now test the new application directly from Developer Studio.

1. To do this, open the context menu of the **Project** node in Composite Application Explorer and choose **Test Service** (Figure 9.22).

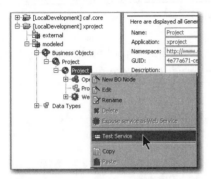

Figure 9.22 Testing the New Business Object

Access denied?

If you encounter the error message *Access denied! The application requires CAF developer's rights!* when you launch the test environment, you must give your test user (generally your administrator ID) the correct permissions. For information about giving user permissions, see the online help for SAP NetWeaver Composition Environment under *http://help.sap.com/ saphelp_nwce10/helpdata/en/b2/4f9b3e1f1e7c7de10000000a114084/con-tent.htm (Administration of Users, Groups, and Roles)*.

The following is a brief overview of the procedure:

1. Launch the user administration tool at *http://<host>:<port>/useradmin*.

2. Search for the user "admin*" and select your administrator ID in the hit list.

3. When you select a user in the hit list, a **Modify** pushbutton appears below the list. Choose this pushbutton. You can now search for special CAF roles under **Available Roles** on the **Assigned Roles** tab page. Use the criterion "*caf*" for your search.

4. You will see the entries **CAF Developer** and **CAF Administrator** in the new hit list. Select both rows by pressing the ⌨Ctrl key and add them both to your administrator ID by choosing **Add**.

5. You should now also take the chance to check whether your user is assigned the roles required to use guided procedures. This is indicated by special GP roles under **Assigned Roles** (such as GP User or GP Runtime WC). If they are not assigned, search for them under **Available Roles**, using the criterion "*gp*".

> 6. If in doubt about which to select, select all hits and add them to your administrator ID.
>
> 7. Save your changes by choosing **Save**. You should now be able to continue testing your business object. (Choose **Refresh** in the browser page where the error message appeared.)

Service Browser
2. **Service Browser** opens. This is a Web-based tool for testing all business objects and services on the server that were modeled using CAF (Figure 9.23).

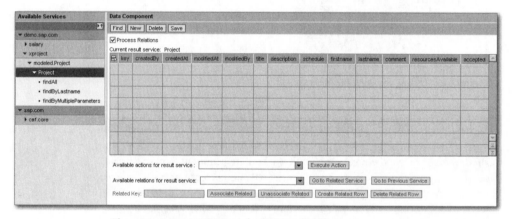

Figure 9.23 Service Browser for Testing CAF Services

The browser screen has a hierarchy on the left side that shows all available services (under the header **Available Services**) and a test area on the right side (with the header **Data Component**).

3. Expand the available services, as shown in Figure 9.23. You can see the new object you have modeled, and its search methods. The create/read/update/delete methods are not listed here, because they are located on pushbuttons on the right side of the browser.

Working with Service Browser
4. To create a new object, click the **New** pushbutton. This activates the first row of the associated table. You can now fill the fields you have modeled with data (as shown in Figure 9.24) and save the data by choosing **Save**.

5. When you save, the data administered by CAF is entered automatically. You can make changes to existing entries by selecting a row and editing its content.

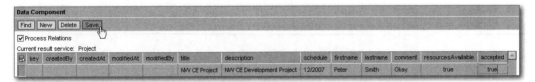

Figure 9.24 Creating a New Object Instance in Service Browser

6. Confirm the new data by choosing **Save**.

7. Objects are deleted in a similar way: You first select a row that you want to delete, choose **Delete**, and then confirm the deletion by choosing **Save**.

8. You can use the **Find** pushbutton to search for entries by primary key. You can enter multiple primary keys in the subsequent dialog. The entries found are displayed in a table.

9. You can also test the various search methods: The findAll method is executed directly after your selection, because it does not require any parameters to be passed. You can use this method to display the entire content of a table very quickly. In all other search methods, you have to enter the search criterion first, and then choose **Execute query**.

Service Browser offers you a practical test environment for your services, leading to shorter turnaround times for your development projects. You can even use it to test complex hierarchies and the business logic you have programmed. This makes it your starting point when testing the functions of your composite application.

Testing Web Services

Before we finish our overview of developing in Composite Application Framework, let's take a look at the Web service we have created.

1. Launch Web Service Navigator (familiar to you from Chapter 5, *Web Services and Enterprise Services in the SAP NetWeaver Composition Environment*) at *http://<host>:<port>/wsnavigator*. The new Web service you developed for the Project business object appears in the list (Figure 9.25)

> Web Service Navigator for testing Web services

2. Click the link of the Web service directly. You can then select the create service under **Operations** (Figure 9.26).

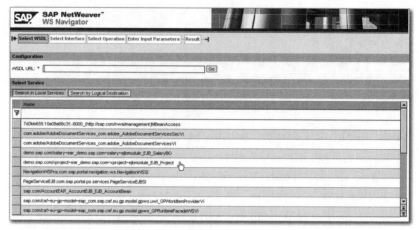

Figure 9.25 Testing the Web Service in Web Service Navigator

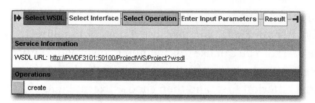

Figure 9.26 Selecting the Operation

3. You can now run the Web service by entering the required input parameters and choosing **Execute**. You can see whether your create method ran successfully in the results dialog (Figure 9.27).

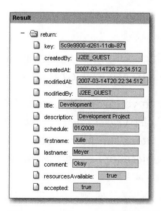

Figure 9.27 Successful CAF Web Service Call

9.4.2 Modeling User Interfaces with SAP NetWeaver Visual Composer

Once you have implemented and tested your business object, as described in Section 9.4.1, *Modeling Business Objects with Composite Application Framework*, you can now move on to the interaction of the object. This is demonstrated by creating two UIs in Visual Composer.

SAP NetWeaver Visual Composer as a modeling tool for user interfaces

1. Launch Visual Composer at *http://<host>:<port>/VC/freestyle.jsp*. The following steps assume that you have familiarized yourself with the basic Visual Composer functions from Chapter 8, *SAP NetWeaver Visual Composer*.

2. You begin by modeling the UI for the program lead. Create a new model and call it **programlead**. Select **Composite View** as the model type (Figure 9.28).

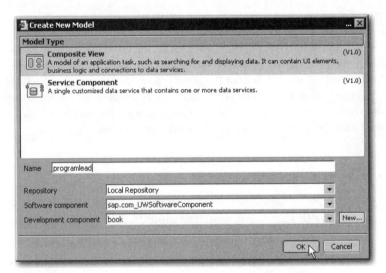

Figure 9.28 Creating the Visual Composer Model for the Program Lead

3. The program lead's process step involves selecting a project lead from a list of employees; this list is filled by a service call. For this example, you use an existing service from the reference applications available with every installation of SAP NetWeaver Composition Environment.

Reference applications in Composition Environment

> **Note**
>
> The reference applications are used to demonstrate the wide range of options available in SAP NetWeaver Composition Environment, using ready-to-run composite applications. One of these reference applications is used specially to demonstrate standard Java EE features, another shows you how to use guided procedures, and a final reference application emphasizes the collaboration between guided procedures, Visual Composer, and Composite Application Framework. This latter application covers a similar range of functions to our example, but is much more complex.
>
> This latter reference application is highly recommended as an advanced example for this scenario, because it goes on to address more in-depth concepts and best practices for composite application development. For more details about this reference application, see the Composition Environment online help at *http://help.sap.com/saphelp_nwce10/helpdata/en/64/fcdf4103c24d469e332c335eea3a2a/content.htm*.
>
> You can also access SAP Help Portal directly at *http://help.sap.com*. Choose **SAP NetWeaver • SAP NetWeaver CE • SAP NetWeaver Composition Environment Library • Developer's Guide**. This is the online help for software development with SAP NetWeaver Composition Environment. You can access the documentation about the reference application by navigating through the following path in the left side of the screen: **SAP NetWeaver Composition Environment Library • Developer's Guide • Developing and Composing Applications • Developing Java EE 5 Applications • Reference • Tutorials • Project Management and Employee Services Application**.

Consuming Web Services

Searching for Web services

1. In our example, we want to reuse the service that gets a list of employees. To locate this service in Visual Composer, choose the **Search** button (on the far right side of Visual Composer).

2. In the **Search** dialog, enter an asterisk ("*") in the **Search for** field, select the logical destination EDMProjectDestination from the **Search in** dropdown list, and select **WSDL** as the **Type**. If you cannot see this logical destination, it has not been created yet. For more details about installing the reference application and creating the logical destination, see Section 9.5, *Installing and Configuring the Reference Application*.

Selecting a service from the results

3. When you choose **Search**, you see a list of all available Web services. Select getAllEmployees and drag it to the work area on the left (Figure 9.29).

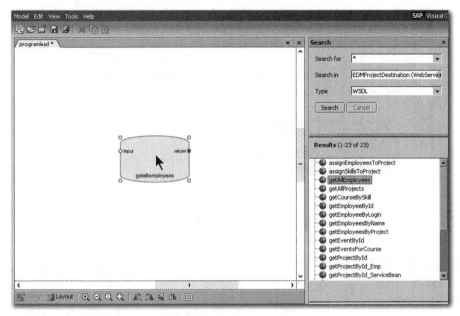

Figure 9.29 Selecting the getAllEmployees Service

Adding UI Elements

As you have already seen in Chapter 8, a service call can be returned either as a form or as a table, depending on the return type. In our case, the service call returns a table of all employees, which is why we have chosen the table variant.

1. Drag a line from the **return** plug of the service to the work area. Release the mouse button and select the **Table View** item from the context menu.

   Creating a table from service return parameters

2. In the next dialog, select the fields `firstName`, `lastName`, and `login` as table fields. These fields are indicated by a checkmark in the column under the spectacles icon.

As well as the table of employees, you need input fields for creating the project. These fields are grouped together in a form.

1. On the right toolbar, choose **Compose**, select **Form View** from the list of available views and drag it to the work area.

   Creating a form

2. Rename the form as "Project Definition Form."

3. You must now add the fields of the project to the empty form. To do this, right-click the form and select the **Define Data...** item from the context menu.

4. Add the text fields `title`, `description`, and `schedule` in the next dialog (Figure 9.30).

Figure 9.30 Defining the Fields for the Program Lead

Editing the Screen Layout

Now switch to the **Layout** view, to complete the form.

Positioning of buttons on the UI

1. To do this, select **Button** under **Basic Controls**, drag it to the work area, directly under the three fields, and rename it as "Submit."

2. Each button must be associated with an action, so assign the standard action `SUBMIT` to this new button. You can also modify the labels of each of the fields to meet your requirements. Here, the aim is to have a UI that is similar to Figure 9.31.

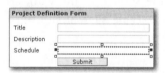

Figure 9.31 Form for Creating a Project

Modeling the Data Flow

Integrating Visual Composer UIs in guided procedures

Switch back to the **Design** view to model the integration of Visual Composer UIs with guided procedures (GPs). In the introduction, we already discussed the importance of the GP context for composite applications, and how it has the task of persisting process data during the process flow. Interactive applications do not work with the GP framework automatically. After all, how are they supposed to know to cooperate with a process framework and send or receive data? This is why, in each dialog application, you need to perform certain steps to ensure a clean integration of the application in the GP framework.

Note

Service calls are not affected by this restriction because they have clearly defined interfaces that can be accessed by guided procedures. These interfaces are usually missing from UI-centric applications. Visual Composer supports the modeling of these input and output interfaces, so enabling the clean integration of Visual Composer UIs into the process framework.

---

1. In the **Design** board, select the **out** plug of the project definition form, drag it to the UI (this makes a connecting line appear) and select the **End Point** item from the context menu (Figure 9.32).

Definition of end points

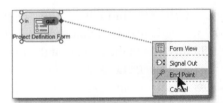

Figure 9.32 Creating an End Point for Integrating Guided Procedures

2. These steps copy the form data to the end point automatically, from where it is available to the guided procedures.

You can check this by selecting **Define Data...** from the context menu of the end point. The dialog that appears lists the three fields of the form. You can also select the **Map Data...** item from the connecting line between the form and the end point. The dialog box that appears here shows you the assignments between the fields in the form and the fields of the end point.

3. Now that you have selected the connecting line between the form and the end point, you can also determine the event that copies data from the form to the end point. Verify that **Configure** is selected in the toolbar on the right of the screen and that the connecting line is selected.

Assigning events

4. Enter "*submit" under **Event name** in the **Configure Data Map** window.

   You may ask yourself why you can't just choose the submit item from the dropdown list. This is because the action name *without* an asterisk is used whenever *precisely one* event (or connection) is to be triggered; the variant with the asterisk, on the other hand, gives the modeler the option of triggering multiple events with a single UI element (such as a button). In our example (as will become clear later), we want to pass both the project data and the project lead to the guided procedure from different parts of the screen. This requires two actions, and we therefore use *submit with an asterisk.

5. We have now ensured that data can be passed from the form to the end point, but the name of the selected project lead is missing in the end point. This name is defined when a row is selected in the table containing all employees. It must now be passed from the table to the end point.

Defining extra fields in the end point

6. You model this connection by connecting the **out** plug of the table to the end point. The data from the selected entry is not passed automatically, however. You must first add this data to the end point (by right-clicking the end point, selecting **Define Data...** from the context menu, and adding the string fields firstname and lastname) and then map the corresponding connecting line (by right-clicking the connecting line between the table and the end point, selecting **Map Data...**, and mapping the relevant fields).

   Only the fields firstname and lastname need to be mapped, because the other fields are already filled by the form.

7. You now need to change the event name for the connecting line; for tables, this is set to select by default. As discussed above, change it to *submit.

8. You have nearly completed the modeling of the first screen. All you have to do now is call the Web service that loads the employee data the first time the UI is displayed.

Start point as a trigger for the service call

You can do this by using a start point, to be found under **Connector**, then **Start Point**, in the tools of the **Compose** view. Drag the start point to the work area, in front of the Web service call icon, and connect it with the **Input** plug of the Web service. Your completed model should now look something like the model in Figure 9.33.

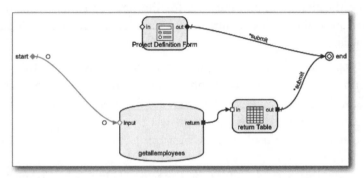

Figure 9.33 Completed Visual Composer Model for the Program Lead UI

9. You can deploy and test your model in the usual way. If your **Deploy** button is gray, make sure that Web Dynpro is configured as the output format for Visual Composer Compiler. The **Options** dialog is in the main Visual Composer menu under **Tools • Options**. Expand the **Compiler** tree in the **Options** dialog and select **Web Dynpro HTML** from the dropdown list of the **Runtime** field. You can see the resulting UI in Figure 9.34.

Option settings in Visual Composer

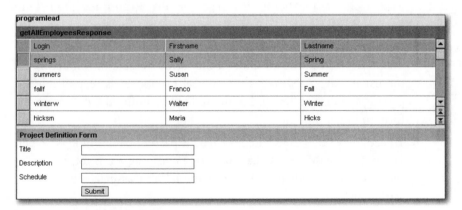

Figure 9.34 Runtime Appearance of the Visual Composer Model

We now move on to the composite application's second screen, which is intended for the project lead and is much simpler than the program lead UI.

Modeling the project lead UI

1. Create a new model and call it **projectlead**. As in the first UI, select the model type, **Composite View**.

2. Unlike the first example, the data for the new UI comes from the guided procedure. This requires you to model an appropriate input interface.

Start point as integrator for guided procedures

In Visual Composer, the start point is again responsible for this, so begin by selecting **Start Point** and dragging it to the work area. The only valid input parameters, however, are fields added to the guided procedure in the previous step, namely firstname and lastname for the selected project lead, and the basic project data title, description, and schedule.

You model this data, as before, by choosing **Define data...** from the context menu of the start point.

3. You then drag a form on to the working area, rename it as "Approval Form" and connect it to the start point. Once this is done, you can choose **Define data...** in the form to check that the data is passed automatically from the start point to the form.

4. To display the data in the form, you must activate it by choosing **Select All** in the dialog (a checkmark appears next to all the fields). Now also add the new fields to be used by the project lead to enter data, namely comment (a String field), resourcesAvailable, and accepted (both Boolean fields).

End point definition

5. Once you have defined the data, you can create the end point. You use drag & drop from the **out** plug of the form to create the end point, in the usual way. This means that Visual Composer is responsible for passing the data to the end point and for mapping the data from the form to the end point.

6. You still have to define when the data is passed, by defining an event. To do this, switch to the **Layout** board and drag a pushbutton on to the work area. Call the button "Submit" and associate it with the action SUBMIT.

7. You can now make cosmetic changes to the form, such as renaming field labels or replacing the comment field control with a text editor. Finally, switch to the **Design** board and assign the new event name submit to the connection between the form and the end point (but without * this time). You can see the results of this modeling in Figure 9.35.

Figure 9.35 Modeling Results in Visual Composer, for the Project Lead

8. Translate, deploy, and test your model. The result should look something like the model depicted in Figure 9.36.

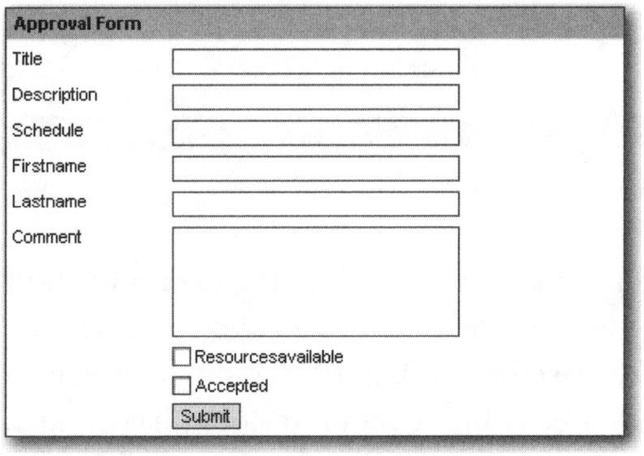

Figure 9.36 Project Lead Form at Runtime

9.4.3 Modeling Processes with Guided Procedures

The final stage in this implementation exercise is to model the actual business process using the guided procedure framework. Guided procedures (GPs) are used to model lightweight, collaborative business processes and are launched as Web applications in the portal.

1. Open the portal at the URL *http://<host>:<port>/irj*. Once you have logged in, you can see the **Guided Procedures** tab at the top of the screen.

   Launching the guided procedures framework

2. Click this tab and choose **Design Time** one level further down. You are now in a section called **Gallery**, which is where you organize your GP development objects (Figure 9.37).

   GP development objects are organized in folders. These folders are not, however, part of a file system where you store your GP artifacts, but an organizational structure under GP design time administration, mapped to corresponding database tables. You can create and nest folders according to your requirements.

   Guided procedures gallery

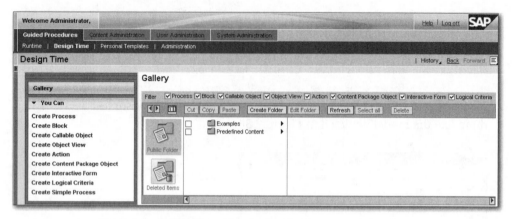

Figure 9.37 Guided Procedures Design Time

3. Create a new folder for your project by choosing **Create Folder** and call it "Project Management Process." (Note that you must also enter a text in the mandatory **Description** field.) Make sure that your new folder has been created directly in the root directory (that is, the **...as member of the root folder** has been selected). The new folder automatically becomes the default folder for holding your new GP development objects.

Guided Procedures Development Objects

Take a look at the available activities listed under **You Can** on the left of the window. This window is also known as **Contextual Navigation Panel**, because the activities it offers you are always context-specific.

Processes, blocks, actions, and callable objects

Because you have selected a folder, all Create operations are available to you. The four development objects Process, Block, Action, and Callable Object are the most important, because they allow you to structure your process.

Here, the process itself functions as an external wrapper and contains only blocks. Also, each process must contain at least one block. The blocks themselves contain logically connected steps, known in GP parlance as actions. Blocks ideally group reusable subprocess steps together, so providing the maximum benefit for other processes. There is no limit on the number of actions in a block.

We have not actually created an executable process yet. An action does not come to life until you have added callable objects to it (where a callable object can represent either a UI or a service). The split between action and callable object allows business analysts to model a process down to the action level. Developers can then enhance the process by adding technical implementations. We can now return to our example process to examine this process in more depth.

1. First, choose **Create Process**. Confirm your chosen development language to display the process editor (Figure 9.38). Creating a process

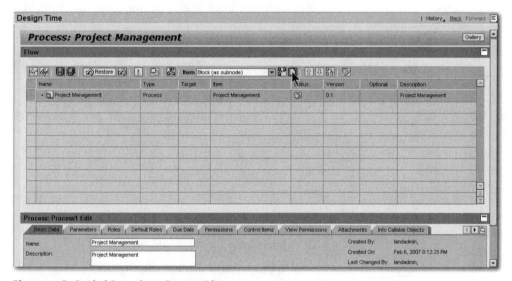

Figure 9.38 Guided Procedures Process Editor

2. The top half of the editor is a table showing the individual GP development objects that comprise the process flow. This table currently only contains a `Process` item, which is selected automatically. The bottom half of the screen consists of a row of tab pages for configuring the selected development object, in this case a process.

3. On the **Basic Data** tab page, change the name of the process to "Process Management." You make the other settings after you have finished modeling the process.

All the other development objects are organized in a hierarchy below the table, with indents indicating that one object contains another. For example, a process contains the block or blocks that are indented below it. Actions and callable objects are structured in the same way. The lower-level objects become child nodes of the parent node in question. This will become clearer in the screenshots later on in the object modeling process.

Objects can have one of two states, `Active` or `In Processing`. These states are indicated in the **Status** column. Active objects show the **Active** icon (⊞) and objects in processing show the **Inactive** icon (⊞). Our process has the state `In Processing` after it has been created.

GP process editor toolbar

For an overview of the editor's toolbar and its functions, see Table 9.1 below.

Icon	Function	Description
✎	**Edit**	Enables you to edit the object attributes. When you open design time for individual objects, it is in read-only mode by default.
✎	**Toggle Multi Edit Mode**	Enables you to edit the selected object, and the objects above and below it. Any objects on the same level as the selected object remain in read-only mode.
ᖚ	**View**	Shows the details of the selected object in read-only mode. This function is disabled if a child node of the selected object is in editing mode.
ᖚ	**View All**	Displays multiple selected objects (and all their child objects) in read-only mode.
🖫	**Save**	Saves the currently selected object. This function also saves all data entered on the object's tab pages.
🖫	**Save All**	Saves all objects of the process or block, and all the data of the callable objects assigned to the actions.
↺	**Revert**	Restores the selected object to its state before it was last saved.
⬆	**Save and Activate**	Saves and activates the selected objects (and their child objects). You can activate an entire process with a single click on the process node.

Table 9.1 Editing Tools in Guided Procedures

Icon	Function	Description
	Update	Refreshes the selected node to its last active state.
	Adjust All	Propagates the changes made to the parameters and roles of the selected node to all parent nodes along the hierarchy.
	Insert	Inserts a compatible existing object below the selected node. For example, you can insert a block below a process, an action (or another block) below a block, and callable objects below actions.
	Create New	Creates a new object and inserts it below the selected node. See also the rules described under **Insert**.
	Move Up	Moves the selected node upwards in the hierarchy. For example, you can move actions within a block or move blocks within a process.
	Move Down	Moves the selected node downwards in the hierarchy. See also the rules described under **Move Up**.
	Remove	Deletes the selected object from the hierarchy.
	Edit Usage Name and Description	Enables you to rename the selected object after you have created it. This requires you to edit the **Name** and **Description** fields on the **Basic Data** tab page.

Table 9.1 Editing Tools in Guided Procedures (cont.)

Process Flow Modeling

We continue to model the process by creating the block.

1. The process is currently selected by default, as shown in Figure 9.38. You can select an object by clicking in the field in front of the object; you can select multiple objects by holding down the Ctrl key while selecting.

2. You create a new block by choosing the ▢ icon (action: **Create New**). You can also see an **Item** field next to this icon. This field is a drop-down list of the objects that you can insert. In our case, this is a block.

   Creating a block

3. A dialog box prompts you to specify a block type (Figure 9.39).

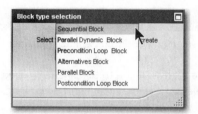

Figure 9.39 Creating a Block: Selecting the Block Type

4. This example requires you to specify a sequential block. In this block type, all actions that you later add to the block are executed in a sequential order. Select **Sequential Block** from the dropdown list and confirm by choosing **Select**. This block is now inserted below the process object and indented (Figure 9.40).

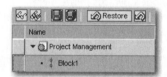

Figure 9.40 Creating a New Block Below the Process

Block types The following block types are available in addition to sequential blocks:

▶ **Parallel block**
All actions or blocks in the process are executed in parallel.

▶ **Parallel dynamic block**
The number of table entries passed to this block specifies the number of instances of this block that are created. This is a good option if you do not know in advance how many parallel instances of a block need to be created.

▶ **Alternative block**
You can configure conditions for a block, and specify one or more alternatives for these conditions.

▶ **Precondition/postcondition loop block**
In this block type, the actions or blocks are executed in a loop until a specified condition applies and ends the block. In a precondition loop block, the condition is checked at the start of the loop; in a postcondition loop block, the condition is checked at the end.

1. Select the row containing the new block in the table. You can now change the name and description of the block to "Project Management Block" on the **Basic Data** tab page.

2. You can now add the three process steps to the block as its content. The block is still selected in the table, which is why the content of the dropdown list in the **Item** field changes accordingly. You can now choose from the items **Action (as subnode)**, **Block (as subnode)**, and **Block (on the same level)**, because they can all be placed within this block. **Action** is selected by default (Figure 9.41).

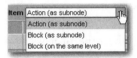

Figure 9.41 Selection List of Objects Within a Block

3. Because you need three actions, click the ☐ icon three times (action   Creating actions **Create New**). This creates three new rows in your table. On the **Basic Data** tab page, rename the actions as follows:

   ▶ Action1: "Enter Project"

   ▶ Action2: "Approve Project"

   ▶ Action3: "Create Project"

Your process flow should now look like the process flow in Figure 9.42.

Figure 9.42 Process Flow After Modeling the Process Steps

Integrating the Visual Composer UIs for the Program Lead

You have now created a process flow for your example process. You now need to assign fixed (and ready-to-run) UIs or service calls to the actions.

1. You start with the **Enter Project** step. Select the action in question in the process table. The dropdown list in the **Item** field shows you the objects that you can bind to the action. Guided procedures distinguish between callable objects (COs) for execution and callable objects for display (Figure 9.43).

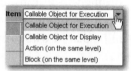

Figure 9.43 Different Callable Object Types for an Action

Callable objects for execution are deployed when the process step is ready to be executed, namely when the user has to input data. Callable objects for display, on the other hand, are used by the GP runtime environment if the current user does not have sufficient authorizations to input data, or if the process step has been completed and you just want to review the data entered. You must create a callable object for execution; callable objects for display, however, are optional.

2. For the purposes of this example, only create callable objects for execution (this type is selected by default in the dropdown list). Click the icon to create a callable object below the action. This launches a wizard for creating a callable object (Figure 9.44).

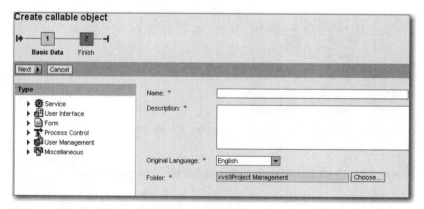

Figure 9.44 Wizard for Creating a Callable Object

3. The left side of the wizard shows you the different CO types shipped by SAP in the GP framework. These types are split into the categories **Service**, **User Interface**, **Form**, **Process Control**, **User Management**, and **Miscellaneous**. An in-depth description of all these CO types goes beyond the scope of this book, but they are explained in detail in the SAP Help Portal (*http://help.sap.com*).

Predefined callable object types

4. For your first action, select the CO type **WD4VC Application** from the category **User Interface**. WD4VC stands for "Web Dynpro for Visual Composer" and indicates how UIs modeled with Visual Composer are transformed to Web Dynpro.

Configuring the CO type WD4VC

5. Enter the same name that you gave to your action. You do not have to use the same name, but it helps you identify which callable objects are associated with which actions in the gallery. Enter this name in the **Description** field as well.

6. Then choose **Next** (Figure 9.45).

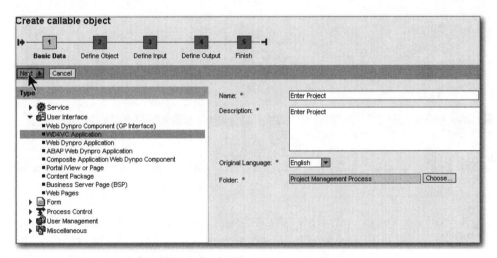

Figure 9.45 Creating a Callable Object for the Visual Composer UI

7. In the second step, allocate the appropriate VC application from the list of available programs to the callable object. You called the UI **programlead**. Find this name in the list, select it, and continue by choosing **Next**.

Selecting VC applications

8. The wizard extracts the information about the VC program's input and output parameters and displays it in steps 3 and 4. You cannot add or remove any further parameters here. You can only do this at the modeling stage in Visual Composer.

   For this reason, check that the wizard recognizes all parameters that you modeled previously in Visual Composer. If any parameters are missing, you must correct the VC program accordingly.

9. The fifth and final step shows you a short summary of what you have done. Confirm this by choosing **Finish**. The process flow should now look like the process flow shown in Figure 9.46.

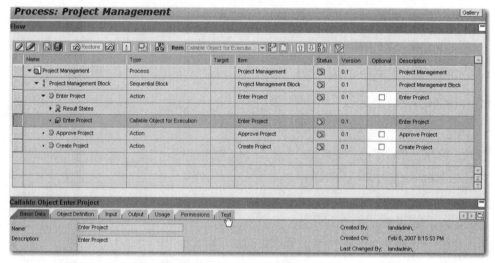

Figure 9.46 Process Flow After Adding Callable Objects for the "Enter Project" Step

Testing the CO type WD4VC

10. You can test every callable object you create directly from the editor. To do this, select the appropriate row of the callable object in the process hierarchy and choose the **Test** tab page on the bottom half of the screen (see Figure 9.46).

11. Because the UI does not require any input parameters, you can choose **Execute** right away. This executes the callable object (that is, the Visual Composer UI is launched).

12. Enter test values for the **Title**, **Description**, and **Schedule** fields and choose an employee from the list of available employees. To complete the test, choose **Submit**.

13. Examine the test results carefully. The test should be successful (as indicated by the message *Completed successfully*) and all output parameters should have been filled correctly (Figure 9.47). Only then do you know that the process has executed properly and the correct parameters have been passed to the GP context.

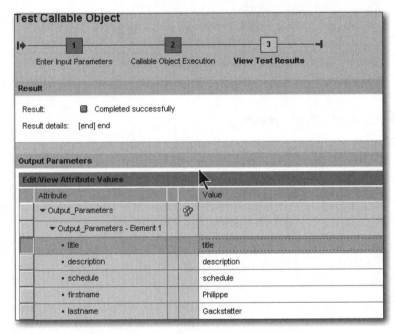

Figure 9.47 Successful Callable Object Test

Integrating the Visual Composer UI for the Project Lead

For the second step in the process, create a new callable object called **Approve Project**.

1. This is another WD4VC callable object, so just repeat the steps described previously, only this time selecting the UI called **projectlead** (Figure 9.48). *Creating the callable object for the project lead*

2. This time, when you test the callable object, you need to provide input parameters. This is because the program lead's data has to be passed to the project lead. Simulate this data by filling out the appropriate fields in the first step of the test wizard.

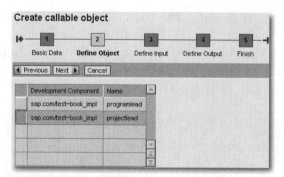

Figure 9.48 Selecting the VC Application when Creating a WD4VC Callable Object

Integrating a Web Service

If the previous test also ran successfully, you can now create the last callable object, namely the Web service call that creates the project in the database.

1. Select the item in question in the process table and launch the wizard for creating a callable object by choosing the ▯ icon.

Configuring the CO type Web service

2. This time, select the **Web Service** item from the category **Service** and give it the name "Create Project." Enter the same name in the **Description** field.

3. Choose **Next** to go to the next step in the wizard. Here you have to enter the address of the WSDL file of the CAF service. To remind yourself, go back to Figure 9.26. You tested the CAF Web service in Web Service Navigator and selected the appropriate WSDL URL from the list of available Web services. Copy this URL and paste it into the **WSDL URL** field (Figure 9.49).

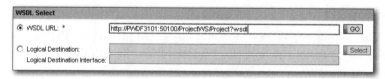

Figure 9.49 Entering the URL for the CAF Web Service

Getting the WSDL address

4. Choose **GO** to extract the WSDL information and display all the available services. In this case, you only see the `create` method in the **Web Service Properties** window.

5. Select this method to display further details about the input and output parameters on the tab pages to the right of the method tree, and also any method exceptions (Figure 9.50).

Selecting the service method

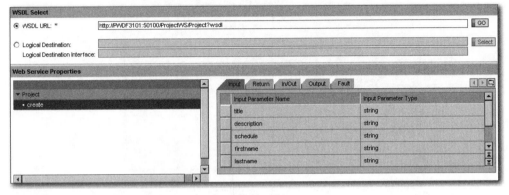

Figure 9.50 Selecting the Web Service for the Callable Object

6. Choose **Next** to go to step 3 of the wizard. This displays the input parameters, as specified by the WSDL information.

7. Choose **Next** to go to step 4, which displays the accompanying output parameters. You cannot make any changes in either of these steps.

8. The final step of the wizard shows you a summary of information about the new callable object. To exit the wizard, choose **Finish**.

9. Again, we strongly recommend that you test the callable object. Select the row containing the Web service callable object in the process flow table, and choose the **Test** tab page. Enter appropriate data in the input parameters of the Web service and choose **Execute**. You can see typical test results in Figure 9.51.

Testing the CO type Web Service

10. This callable object does not have a UI, so the service is executed straight away and the result appears immediately. Examine the results carefully to make sure that the service executed correctly. Also, run the CAF service browser to verify that the new data record was created successfully in the database.

You have now passed a further milestone on your way to creating a business process: The process flow has been defined, and you have associated all the steps involved with executable callable objects.

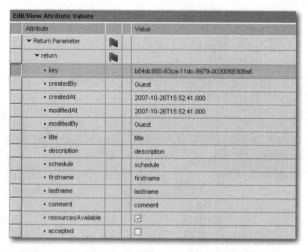

Figure 9.51 Testing the Web Service Callable Object

Parameter Consolidation

Your next task is to ensure that the data entered is passed between the individual process steps, using the GP context. In the introduction to this chapter, we discussed in depth how the GP context works and what tasks it fulfills. We now take a closer look at how the parameters of each step are consolidated.

1. Start by selecting the **Project Management Block** in the GP design time environment, and choose the **Parameters** tab page (Figure 9.52).

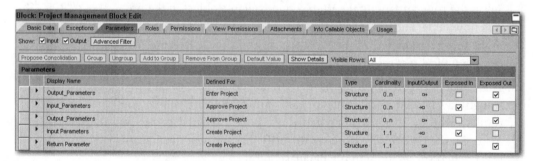

Figure 9.52 Start Screen for Parameter Consolidation

Consolidation at block level

2. First, familiarize yourself with how the consolidation of parameters is presented in this screen.

▶ The **Defined For** column shows you a list of the callable objects in this block. You will notice, however, that **Enter Project** only appears once, while **Approve Project** and **Create Project** are duplicated. This is due to the parameter definitions of these callable objects. You did not define any input parameters for the program lead's Visual Composer UI, but you defined both input *and* output parameters for the subsequent steps of the project lead. Accordingly, you see rows for both input and output in the **Display Name** column for the steps in question.

▶ The other columns show you details about the types and cardinalities of the parameters, and their visibility in higher levels of the hierarchy (namely **Exposed In** and **Exposed Out**). The checkboxes in the **Exposed In** and **Exposed Out** columns are editable, which means you can decide whether to make data visible at higher levels. By doing this, you can reduce the complexity of the parameter consolidation process at higher hierarchy levels significantly. In particular, take the opportunity now to hide any parameters that are not needed at higher levels, by deactivating the relevant checkboxes.

3. We now need to plan the parameter consolidation, placing particular emphasis on the differences between parameter consolidation and parameter mapping.

   Planning parameter consolidation

   When consolidated, parameters are consolidated in the GP context. They are then viewed as one variable, and this variable can be both the input and output parameter for several steps. When parameters are mapped, on the other hand, the output parameters of step x are bound to the inbound parameters of step x+1 only. This is not the purpose of parameter consolidation in guided procedures, however. Before you actually start working with the tool in the GP design time environment, create a rough consolidation plan, specifying how each parameter is handled during the process flow.

4. We will use an example to demonstrate how to create a consolidation plan. First, take a look at Figure 9.53, which lists all parameters involved in each step. Start with step 1, the callable object **Enter Project**. We can see immediately that this callable object has five output parameters; we will use `title` for our example. This parameter

   Consolidating the title parameter

should be used to prefill the identically named field in the project lead's confirmation step. This means that the parameter must be passed to the second step (which represents the approval), using the GP context, and from there pass it on again using the input parameter of the approval step with the same name.

This is our first consolidation: The output parameter title of the step **Enter Project** is consolidated with the input parameter Title of the step **Approve Project**.

Figure 9.53 Parameter of the Process Before Consolidation

5. What do we do with the parameter now? We need to know whether it is possible to make changes to this parameter in the project lead step, and if it is, how to make these changes visible externally.

   Parameter changes

   In our example, the project lead just adds a remark, checks resources, and approves or rejects the project. The program lead does not make changes here (in regard to the `title` field), which means that the associated output parameter of the **Approve Project** step can be ignored in consolidation. If, however, changes do need to be made, we can assume that the output parameter `title` needs to be included in the consolidation so that any changes made in the UI take effect in the GP context as well.

6. Moving through the process flow, we now encounter the step **Create Project**. The task of this step is to save the project title to the database. This means that the Web service parameter to be passed must be filled accordingly from the GP context.

   This becomes our next consolidation: The `title` must be consolidated with the input parameter `title` of the **Create Project** step.

7. In conclusion, we need to consolidate the project title as follows: the output field `title` (from the **Enter Project** step) with the input field `Title` (from the **Approve Project** step) with the input field `title` (from the **Create Project** step).

8. We now put our plan into practice as follows: Expand the nodes in question and select their subnodes by keeping the `Ctrl` key pressed. This enables you to select multiple rows, as shown in Figure 9.54.

   Practical application of the consolidation plan

9. Choose **Group** and give the group an appropriate name in the next dialog. This will be the name of the group one level up in the process, which is why it is important that it describes the purpose of the group properly. In our example, simply accept the default name by choosing **Create**.

   Grouping of parameters

10. A new item at the end of the parameter list indicates that the consolidation was successful. Verify that your consolidation matches the one depicted in Figure 9.55.

11. Repeat these steps for the remaining parameters. Table 9.2 summarizes all the required consolidations.

Parameters							
	Display Name	**Defined For**	**Type**	**Cardinality**	**Input/Output**	**Exposed In**	**Exposed Out**
▼	Output_Parameters	Enter Project	Structure	0..n	▷→	☐	☑
•	title	Output_Parameters	String	0..1	▷→		
•	description	Output_Parameters	String	0..1	▷→		
•	schedule	Output_Parameters	String	0..1	▷→		
•	firstname	Output_Parameters	String	0..1	▷→		
•	lastname	Output_Parameters	String	0..1	▷→		
▼	Input_Parameters	Approve Project	Structure	0..n	→▷	☑	☐
•	Title	Input_Parameters	String	0..1	→▷		
•	Description	Input_Parameters	String	0..1	→▷		
•	Schedule	Input_Parameters	String	0..1	→▷		
•	Firstname	Input_Parameters	String	0..1	→▷		
•	Lastname	Input_Parameters	String	0..1	→▷		
▶	Output_Parameters	Approve Project	Structure	0..n	▷→	☐	☑
▼	Input Parameters	Create Project	Structure	1..1	→▷	☑	☐
•	title	Input Parameters	String	1..1	→▷		
•	description	Input Parameters	String	1..1	→▷		
•	schedule	Input Parameters	String	1..1	→▷		
•	lastname	Input Parameters	String	1..1	→▷		
•	firstname	Input Parameters	String	1..1	→▷		
•	comment	Input Parameters	String	1..1	→▷		
•	accepted	Input Parameters	Boolean	1..1	→▷		
•	resourcesAvailable	Input Parameters	Boolean	1..1	→▷		
▶	Return Parameter	Create Project	Structure	1..1	▷→	☐	☑

Figure 9.54 Selection of Multiple Parameters for Consolidation

▼ 🔲	title	<Group>
•	title	Enter Project : Output_Parameters
•	Title	Approve Project : Input_Parameters
•	title	Create Project : Input Parameters

Figure 9.55 Result of the Parameter Consolidation

Overview of all parameter consolidations

Field	Step
▶ title	▶ **Enter Project**: Output
▶ Title	▶ **Approve Project**: Input
▶ title	▶ **Create Project**: Input
▶ description	▶ **Enter Project**: Output
▶ Description	▶ **Approve Project**: Input
▶ description	▶ **Create Project**: Input

Table 9.2 Parameter Consolidations

438

Field	Step
▸ schedule ▸ Schedule ▸ schedule	▸ **Enter Project**: Output ▸ **Approve Project**: Input ▸ **Create Project**: Input
▸ firstname ▸ Firstname ▸ firstname	▸ **Enter Project**: Output ▸ **Approve Project**: Input ▸ **Create Project**: Input
▸ lastname ▸ Lastname ▸ lastname	▸ **Enter Project**: Output ▸ **Approve Project**: Input ▸ **Create Project**: Input
▸ Comment ▸ comment	▸ **Approve Project**: Output ▸ **Create Project**: Input
▸ Resources_Available ▸ resourcesAvailable	▸ **Approve Project**: Output ▸ **Create Project**: Input
▸ Accepted ▸ accepted	▸ **Approve Project**: Input ▸ **Create Project**: Input

Table 9.2 Parameter Consolidations (cont.)

This completes the consolidation of the parameters. Using the GP context, the guided procedures framework can buffer process states and input data (transaction-secured), without the need for special objects with database connections.

The location of the data in the GP context also benefits any enhancements you make to the process, such as adding new steps. You can extract the data directly from the context and display it or tailor it to your special requirements. There is no need for additional read operations in backend systems or databases. Even if the process is terminated, the GP framework ensures that both the process and the context are cleaned up. These are just a few of the advantages of working within the GP architecture.

Role Assignment

The assignment of roles to process steps is the last modeling task to be performed before we run the process. So far we have defined the order of the steps, but we have not yet specified who is responsible for performing them. The guided procedures' runtime environment needs to know who to send notifications to, and this requires you to group steps to be performed by the same person (or group of people) under a single process role. Initially, a process role is just a name (or string) that describes the role. Actual people or groups of people are assigned to these roles only when a process starts.

Role assignment at block level

1. We have defined the roles *Program Lead* and *Project Lead* in our example. We now define these roles for the block. As far as the visibility of roles in higher hierarchy levels goes, the same applies as when consolidating parameters: Consolidated roles at lower levels are visible at higher levels and can be consolidated again at these levels.

2. Select the block node (if not already selected) and choose the **Roles** tab page on the bottom half of the screen.

3. By default, a separate role is created for each step within this block and given the name **Processor of...** It is recommended that you enter your own role names for your steps, however. To do this, select the first role item called **Processor of Enter Project**, and choose **Rename**. Enter the role name "Program Lead" on the dialog that appears.

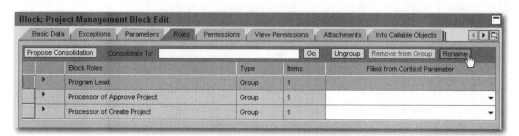

Figure 9.56 Renaming/Consolidating Roles

4. The steps **Approve Project** and **Create Project** are to be performed by the project lead, so select both rows in the table by pressing the `Ctrl` key and enter the role name "Project Lead" in the **Consolidate To** field.

5. Confirm by choosing **Go** and your consolidated roles should look like the roles in Figure 9.57. Also, check the number of steps assigned to each role in the **Items** column.

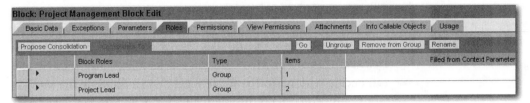

Figure 9.57 Assigned Roles After Consolidation

6. This completes the assignment of roles at block level, but we still need to make some final changes at process level. To do this, select the process node in the process flow table and choose the `Roles` tab page on the bottom half of the screen. You will see the roles you just consolidated, `Program Lead` and `Project Lead`, plus the standard GP roles `Administrator`, `Overseer`, and `Owner`.

Role assignment at process level

As the names imply, these standard roles define which people or groups of people own a process (`Owner`), oversee a process (`Overseer`), or administer a process (`Administrator`). These roles are associated with various permissions, such as the permission to assign your current action to a different person, stop an action, change the deadline of a process or action, or even terminate a process while it is running.

7. We do not want to consolidate roles again though. Instead, you need to define who performs these process roles at runtime. You can, for example, choose the dropdown list of the administrator in the **Role Type** column to see the options from Figure 9.58.

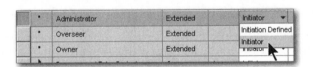

Figure 9.58 Options for Role Assignment at Runtime

▶ The **Initiator** option specifies that the user who starts a process adopts the administrator role at the same time.

▶ If you select **Initiation Defined**, you specify the explicit assignment of fixed users and groups (from User Management Engine in Java EE Engine, for example) when the process starts.

▶ The three standard roles can be associated with these two options only. This is not the case for any new process-specific roles that you define where you can also choose a third option: **Runtime Defined**. This option gives you the greatest flexibility because you can decide who performs specific process steps while the process is running. You can do this manually in a dialog step or it can happen automatically in the background. Both cases require you to define a user ID in the GP context, which can then be assigned to the role. This information is provided by the **Filled from Context Parameter** column.

8. The **Initiator** setting is sufficient for the purposes of this example, so select this option from the dropdown list for all roles. This enables the process to start and run without the user switching constantly.

As the initiator of this process, you also adopt the various process roles. Guided procedures can recognize when a single person adopts different roles. Once the first step has ended, the next dialog screen appears automatically, and no additional notifications are sent. This simplifies the testing of guided procedures significantly, and you benefit directly from this feature in this small demonstration.

Options for passing parameters to a guided procedure

9. You have to make one final cosmetic change on the **Parameters** tab page of the process node. This tab page includes an **Exposed In** column. If you activate this checkbox for a parameter listed in this column, then this parameter can be passed to the process from an external source.

We do not want to pass parameters to the process in this example, so deselect all the checkboxes in this column. This also means that you can start the process without an extra dialog step prompting you to define these parameters.

10. You have now completed all preparations for starting the process. Activate the process by choosing the **Activate** icon (⬆).

9.4.4 Testing Composite Applications

You have now created an activated, executable process. This is indicated clearly by the **Status** column in the process flow table. All rows in the table have changed from inactive (⬚) to active (☑).

1. Make sure that the process node is selected, and choose the **Instantiation** tab page on the bottom half of the screen. To see this tab page, you may need to scroll right, or you can choose the instantiation option from the menu (⬚) on the right of the tabs (Figure 9.59).

Launching the composite application

Figure 9.59 Choosing the Instantiation Tab Page from the Menu

2. On this tab page, select the **Include Default Parameters** checkboxes (so that these parameters are included when the process starts) and the **Start Process Automatically** option (so that the process starts without additional dialog steps for checking roles and parameters).

Starting a process from a URL

3. Choose **Generate Instantiate URL** to generate a URL for starting the process. You execute the process by choosing **Open Instantiate Application** (Figure 9.60).

Figure 9.60 Starting a Guided Procedure

4. A new window opens with the first step of the process. This is because, when you defined the roles, you assigned the initiator to the individual steps as their processor. This is why you see the first step straight away.

In most cases, the initiator and the processors are different people. You as the initiator would have seen a standard message informing you that the process has started successfully, but you would not have been able to perform the step. The guided procedure would determine the current processor in the background and send this person an appropriate notification. These notifications are displayed in the Guided Procedures Runtime Work Center.

Guided Procedures
Runtime Work
Center

You open this work center in SAP NetWeaver Portal by choosing **Guided Procedures** and then **Runtime**. Here, choose the link under the **Tasks that require my action** header (Figure 9.61).

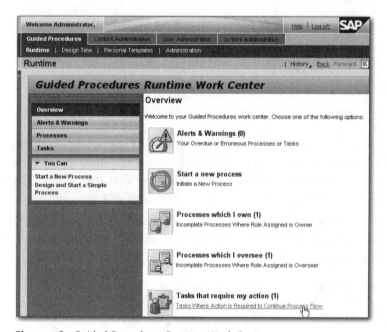

Figure 9.61 Guided Procedures Runtime Work Center

You see a list of all open processing steps. You can go to a step directly by choosing a link in the **Work Item** column (Figure 9.62).

5. Regardless of how you access a step (either directly as the initiator who starts the process or from the work center), you are now in the GP runtime environment. The screen is divided into three basic sections: the process title, a navigation area, and an application area (Figure 9.63).

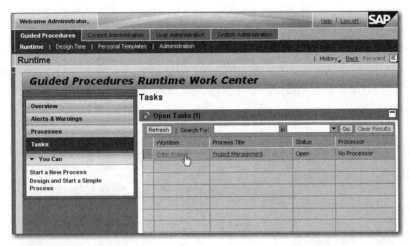

Figure 9.62 Navigating to a Step

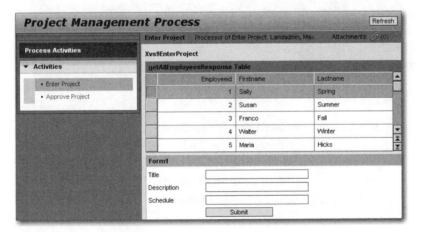

Figure 9.63 Guided Procedures at Runtime

The process title bar gives you information about the process itself: its name and the name of the step, the current processor of the step, and a link to any attachments you add at design time. These documents are usually process documentation provided to help users unfamiliar with the application.

GP runtime environment

The navigation area on the left of the screen shows you a list of pending and completed activities. Here, the first step is active, indicated by a different color highlight. The actual processing of the step takes place in the application area. The callable object associated with the step is called and displayed, in this case a Visual Composer UI for creating a new project.

Program lead UI at runtime

6. Select an employee from the list and enter appropriate data in the fields **Title**, **Description**, and **Schedule**. Then choose **Submit** (Figure 9.64).

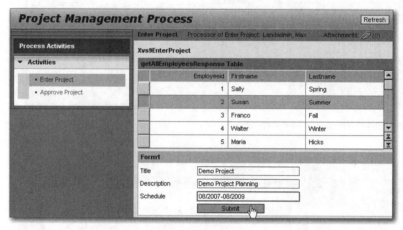

Figure 9.64 Step Processing: Entering a Project

7. The data you have entered or selected is passed to the GP framework and saved in the GP context. The guided procedure determines the next user involved in the process and sends him a notification (as a work item). If the processor of the completed step and the pending step is the same person, he is guided directly to the next step to avoid the work center.

Screen flow versus guided procedure

In this case, the guided procedure operates like a regular screen flow, but there are important differences: In a screen flow, you collect data on the way to completing a transaction; in a guided procedure, on the other hand, each step is a separate transaction. Generally speaking, each UI in a GP process is handled by a different person, whereas in a screen flow, this person does not change.

8. When the next step is launched, the data is passed on and displayed in accordance with the settings made when you consolidated the parameters. The project lead fills out the form with the required data and closes the step by choosing **Submit** (Figure 9.65).

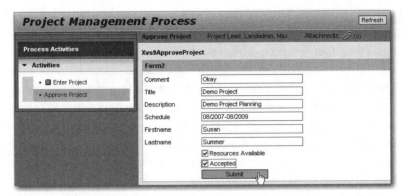

Figure 9.65 Project Lead's Input

9. This completes the visual part of the process. You now see a standard confirmation screen that indicates the step was performed correctly (note the green icon next to the step) and that the process is not yet complete (Figure 9.66).

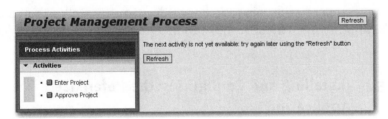

Figure 9.66 Successful Completion of the Dialog Steps

10. Choose **Refresh** and you see a message notifying you that the process has been completed successfully (Figure 9.67).

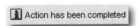

Figure 9.67 Successful Completion of All Actions

11. In the background, the guided procedure passes the data to the service call that saves the data in the CAF business object. As usual, you can check that this service call ran correctly in Service Browser in Composite Application Framework. When you run the findAll method, it should appear as a new row for your business object (Figure 9.68).

Calling Web services as background steps

447

| Demo Project | Demo Project Planning | 08/2007-08/2009 | Summer | Susan | Okay | true | true |

Figure 9.68 New Project Created as a New CAF Business Object

This completes our short look at the world of composite applications. To recap, you have gained an impression of the architecture and functions of this new generation of applications, and familiarized yourself with the steps required to build a composite application. When you developed your composite application, you worked with the development tools Composite Application Framework, Visual Composer, and guided procedures, and also saw how they interact with each other.

Of course, in this chapter we have not been able to explain every function of these tools in depth. We, therefore, recommend that you do some further reading, for example, in *The Developer's Guide to the SAP NetWeaver Composition Environment* (SAP PRESS 2008). However, you should now be able to model and execute your own simple process flows. Equipped with this basic knowledge, you are well prepared to take your first steps in the world of composite application development.

9.5 Installing and Configuring the Reference Application

Before you can implement your example composite application in full, you must make sure that one of the reference applications shipped with the Composition Environment has been installed correctly, and the appropriate users have been created in user administration in the Java Engine. These users must also be given the appropriate permissions, so that they can perform the steps in the process flow. Finally, you must create a *logical destination* for one of the shipped Web services, so that it can be consumed in Visual Composer.

This section explains how you install the reference applications, grant permissions to users, and create logical destinations. You can treat it as a type of checklist, and each step in the checklist makes reference to in-depth information elsewhere in the documentation.

Before you start to go through the checklist, check whether the reference application you want to use is installed already on your server. To do this, go to the URL *http://<host>:<port>/EDMProjectWEB*. The logon screen shown in Figure 9.69 should appear. If you do not see this screen, you must deploy the application from SAP NetWeaver Development Studio.

Launching the reference application

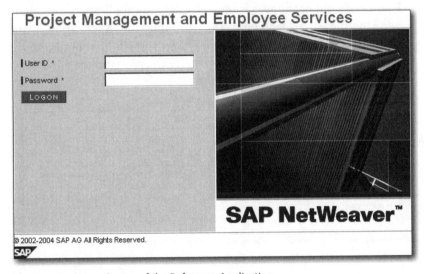

Figure 9.69 Logon Screen of the Reference Application

1. Import the reference application into SAP NetWeaver Developer Studio and use a batch import to load users, roles, and groups into the User Management Engine of the Java server. For more details about this, choose **Help • Welcome** in the SAP NetWeaver Developer Studio menu.

Importing the reference application into NWDS

2. On the new tab page, choose the **Samples** icon (⊞) in the top toolbar.

3. Then choose the icon on the left of the heading **Deploying and Running the Samples** (Figure 9.70).

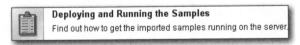

Figure 9.70 Documentation About Installing the Reference Application

4. A new page opens. On this page, find the section called **Project Management and Employee Services**. Then choose the link **Running the Application** (Figure 9.71).

5. This displays the documentation for the reference application. From this page, run the step **Setting Up Application Users**.

6. Two scenarios are possible at this stage: If the logon screen depicted in Figure 9.69 did not appear when you called the application URL, then perform the step **Deploying and Running the Application from NWDS**; if the logon screen appeared, then perform the step **Running the Predeployed Application**. The reference application is now ready to run.

PROJECT MANAGEMENT AND EMPLOYEE SERVICES	
Standards Compliance	Java EE 5
URL	http://<host>:<port>/EDMProjectWEB/
Use Cases	The application represents a solution for maintaining HR data of employees of a department in a company, as well as for defining and staffing projects with appropriate employees.
Preliminary Remark	The application may be already predeployed on your server. That's the case if you find a login screen using the URL http://<host>:<port>/EDMProjectWEB. In this case you need to set up application users (see link below for instructions) to get the application running.
Instructions	Use the following link to get exhaustive information on how to set up application users and how to run the application: <u>Running the Application</u>

Figure 9.71 Link to Installation Description for the Reference Application

Granting permissions for the new users of the reference application

You want one of the new users you created in the reference application to process one of the steps in the process flow. To do this, the user needs permissions to run guided procedures shipped with predefined roles. All you need to do is assign the roles GP User, and GP Runtime WC to the groups ITeloEmployees and ITeloPartners in the UME. You do this as follows:

1. In SAP NetWeaver Administrator, choose **Operation Management • Users and Access • Identity Management**.

2. Select **Group** as a search criterion and restrict the scope of the search by entering "it*" in the input field. You get two results: `ITeloEmploy-ees` and `ITeloPartners`.

3. Select the row `ITeloEmployees` in the table and choose **Modify**.

4. Choose the **Assigned Roles** tab and search for roles by entering "*gp*."

5. Select the items `GP User` and `GP Runtime WC` from the results and assign them to the currently selected group by choosing **Add**.

6. Save your changes by choosing **Save**.

7. Also, do this for the row `ITeloPartners` in the table.

In the next step, you create the logical destination for the Web service.

Creating a logical destination

1. Find out the URL of the WSDL file of the Web service by going to Web Service Navigator at the URL *http://<host>:<port>/wsnavigator*.

2. The list of all available services contains a link to the service of the reference application, called `ProjectDataServiceBean` (Figure 9.72). Choose this item.

sap.com/xapps~ra.edm.prjmgmt.jee.app_xapps~ra.edm.prjmgmt.jee.ejb_EJB_ProjectDataServiceBean

Figure 9.72 Link to the Web Services of the Reference Application in Web Service Navigator

3. Copy the URL of the WSDL file.

4. To configure logical destinations in SAP NetWeaver Administrator, choose **Configuration Management • Infrastructure • Web Service Configuration**. To create a logical destination, choose **WS Destinations • Create Destinations**.

5. You require a destination of the type **WSDL**. Give it the name "EDM-ProjectDestination" and paste the copied URL into this field. The URL generally looks like *http://<host>:<port>/ProjectDataServiceBeanService/ProjectDataServiceBean?wsdl*.

6. Do not change any of the other fields. Make sure, however, that the item **None** is selected in the dropdown box **Authentication**, because the Web services of the reference application do not require authentication.

7. Exit the dialog for configuring logical destinations by choosing **Save** (Figure 9.73).

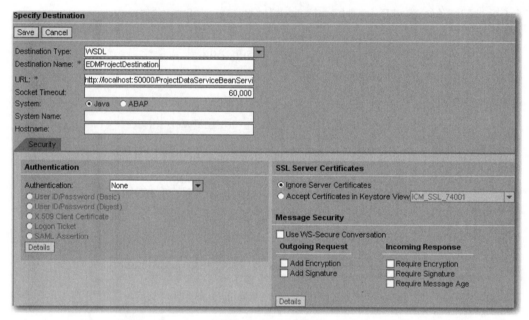

Figure 9.73 Creating the Logical Destination

Large-scale application projects with long lifecycles require efficient and powerful processes for development and maintenance. With SAP NetWeaver Development Infrastructure, SAP has created a development environment for Java-based developments that supports all processes for the entire software development lifecycle. These developments include a new model for structuring software, a centralized development landscape, and a modification concept for Java-based applications.

10 SAP NetWeaver Development Infrastructure and the Component Model — Concepts

SAP develops business applications on a large scale. The size and number of development groups can prove challenging. These groups are responsible for a large number of projects, and are often based in different development locations. The software lifecycle poses yet another challenge. SAP solutions are maintained over a long period of time, during which they are repeatedly modified in customer systems, which may also include large development teams. Our customers now also expect the kind of flexibility for which ABAP-based applications have long since been renowned, from the Java environment. Therefore, we must ensure that the software lifecycle is remarkably stable, and that modification management is possible within the framework of Support Package and release cycles.

10.1 Special Characteristics of Large-Scale Software Projects

Large-scale projects have a broad scope and long maintenance cycles, which exacerbate the problems that usually arise in small development groups. These problems include using libraries in different states, the difficulty of compiling consistent source files and archives, and simultaneously changing and using the same object. All of these problems are dealt with in *SAP NetWeaver Development Infrastructure* (NWDI)[1], either by development concepts that relate to the structure of the software itself, or by predetermined development processes that are implemented in the development tools. NWDI is now used by SAP itself, and by a number of its customers and partners. You can also benefit from the advantages offered by NWDI in SAP NetWeaver Composition Environment 7.1 (CE).

Requirements of a development environment for large-scale software projects
With regard to the development process, this means that the environment must have the following characteristics:

► The goal of the development must be clearly defined. This starts with the definition of the product to be developed and of its components.

► The starting point for the development must be the same for all developers. This applies to source files and to all the libraries and archives used. It should be possible to restore the development landscape in which a product was developed, for example, for maintenance purposes.

► Software should be developed in components that incorporate functions and that can be accessed by one another using interfaces. This reduces coupling between the software components and allows them to be maintained, as changes have no impact on other components — unless the interface is affected — or only impact on them in a precisely defined manner. This makes it a lot easier to reuse all components. This structure also allows a new type of development system to be created that avoids the problems usually associated with large-scale software projects.

Synchronization in a team environment
► The work of developers must also be synchronized during the development process. This must be done automatically while the developers are working, and must not constitute an additional task. Both source files and archives must be taken into account in this context.

---

1 As of SAP NetWeaver release 7.0, the name Java Development Infrastructure (JDI) has been changed to SAP NetWeaver Development Infrastructure (NWDI), to underline that it is part of SAP NetWeaver.

This requirement has not been adequately incorporated into development processes in the past.

▶ The steps after development — central test, consolidation and shipment — must be executed in a predefined manner. Equally, the use of the new source files and archives in the next release and in other products must be guaranteed. This means that development must be guaranteed for several parallel releases. If modifications are planned, the shipment process must also ensure that Support Package versions are reconciled with modifications. One way of achieving this is to include version information at the file level in the shipment.

Development in
release cycles

Some of the features that must be included in large-scale software projects are not a prerequisite for smaller teams. However, the features of SAP NetWeaver Development Infrastructure will also benefit smaller software projects. The following example demonstrates these benefits.

10.1.1 Example of a Typical Development Process Without a Central Infrastructure

Let's say two developers are working on software that is organized into projects. The second developer uses the build results of the first developer, which means that Project 2 depends on Project 1. To coordinate (or synchronize) their work, the developers use a central location to store the source files. They use a central build process for the entire software, to implement the build. We will call this process *nightly build*, because it usually runs at night, so that the runtime objects are available the following morning.

Synchronization
problems in the
development team

First, Archive 1 is built with the runtime objects (RTA1) in Project 1, and then RTA2 is built in Project 2, using the current state of Project 1.

1. Developer 1 now changes the source files (sync) for Project 1.[2] After the local build, the developer runs check-in, but the new state of RTA2 is not yet available centrally, because the nightly build has not yet run.

---

2 If these changes are not compatible with the current state, the developer should now inform all users, so that they can make the required changes. To do this, the developer must know and be able to contact all users on his own initiative. This becomes increasingly difficult as the development increases in size.

2. Developer 2, who uses Project 1, now changes Project 2, also using sync and check-out. This developer receives (the old version of) RTA1, which is being used in Project 2, and implements a new method.

   Developer 2 successfully builds Project 2 locally with the dependency to RTA1 (but still with the old version).[3] After a local test, developer 2 checks in.

3. In the next central build, Project 1 is rebuilt with RTA1. If Project 2 is built, the old signature causes an error. Project 2 cannot be built centrally, even though neither of the developers has done anything wrong. Manual changes must be made before a successful build can be executed. The results of the entire process are not available when the work begins.

This situation can occur irrespective of the developer team's group size. However, the bigger the group, the more likely the situation is to arise. This is due to a lack of synchronization at the archive level. The following sections — in particular Section 10.2.3, *Component Build Service*, — outline how you can avoid this situation using a centralized infrastructure.

The previous example illustrates what happens if the synchronization aspect of development objects at the archive level is not solved. A central storage location is usually available for source files. However, similar problems arise as soon as members of the development team are based in different locations. If source files are to be transported, synchronization becomes difficult as soon as one version of a file is changed in both locations.

Synchronization problems in modification scenarios — A similar problem arises when customers wish to modify shipped software. Although it is easy to ship the source files, it is somewhat more difficult to ship updates and Support Packages, and ensure that the new software can be implemented without losing any customer modifications. This dilemma is solved by Design Time Repository (DTR), which has a built-in feature that recognizes any conflicts between file versions, even after the files have been transported.

---

3 If developer 2 were now to deploy RTA2 on a central test system, inconsistencies would arise, which would be difficult to analyze and would hinder other developers in the central test system.

10.1.2 Software Logistics in Java Development

To solve the problems outlined previously, we need mechanisms of software logistics. Software logistics refers to all steps related to the administration and transport of development objects. Many concepts of SAP NetWeaver Development Infrastructure are the results of decades of experience with ABAP development. Even if you never use an ABAP-based system, the problems and solution concepts you do use are language-independent.

Let's start with a short overview of NWDI's systems and the relevant development processes to obtain an overall picture. *Design Time Repository* (DTR) manages the source files. *Component Build Service* (CBS) manages the development's archives. However, it is important to remember that these objects are used in different versions in development and consolidation systems and again in different versions in Support Packages and new releases. The administrator is responsible for enabling developers to access the correct versions of source files and archives. This is done in *System Landscape Directory* (SLD), in which products and software components — the objectives of the development — are defined,[4] and in *Change Management Service* (CMS), in which access to objects — the source files in Design Time Repository and the archives in Component Build Service — are arranged for all development tasks. Once a developer has released the development, subsequent steps that precede the shipment of the software are also carried out here. The developer's tasks remain more or less the same. However every developer always has access to the current versions of all colleagues in the team.

NWDI services

Figure 10.1 shows the entire Java development process:

Java development process

1. In the first step, a product is defined in SLD. This includes the name, the release and the software components used. In the next step, the

---

4 SLD is not actually part of NWDI. Whereas NWDI is installed separately, SLD is, in fact, part of the JEE Engine standard installation. SLD is also used to manage information on ABAP and Java landscape and software. However, we deal with it here because use of SLD is a prerequisite for the development process with the entire NWDI. SLD includes a Name Service, which checks that object names are unique when objects are created, to prevent problems from occurring at a later stage. In many cases, these names contain prefixes that define namespaces for enterprises.

logical[5] development system is created, which defines access to the source files and archives required for the project. The entity of all logical development systems for a release is referred to as a *track*.

2. The resulting development configuration is imported into each SAP NetWeaver Developer Studio of the developer group. Now the configuration of the local environment of the individual developer is finished. Development steps such as creating and changing source files, compiling the local build, testing, checking-in into DTR, and the subsequent central build in CBS now follow. Once a central test has been successfully conducted, developers release their objects for subsequent steps in CMS.

3. Once all development and consolidation steps have been completed, the Quality Manager releases the entire software application. The software is now assembled and shipped.

4. To develop the next release, it only needs to be defined in SLD and CMS. All physical systems remain unchanged, but may have to be modified to reflect the changes made to a modified target release. The new development configurations are used to separate the different release states.

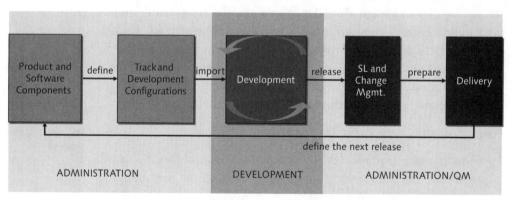

Figure 10.1 Overview of the Java Development Process Using SAP NetWeaver

---

5 A logical development system is a key concept of NWDI. A *logical* system means that rather than installing new systems for new development tasks, memory areas are made available on the server database for the relevant development team. A memory area contains all the required sources and archives, and represents the corresponding development status.

10.2 Elements of SAP NetWeaver Development Infrastructure

This section looks at all elements of SAP NetWeaver Development Infrastructure (NWDI). These include Change Management Service (CMS), Design Time Repository (DTR), and Component Build Service (CBS), which was mentioned previously.[6] System Landscape Directory (SLD) and Name Service are also used. The developer accesses them using SAP NetWeaver Developer Studio. The development follows SAP's component model.

Structure of the development landscape

Figure 10.2 shows all elements of Java Development Infrastructure. The development environment consists of a local part and the central NWDI. The local part is made up of SAP NetWeaver Developer Studio as an *Integrated Development Environment* (IDE), the local file system as the temporary storage location for all new development objects, and usually a local installation of Java EE Engine as the initial test environment.

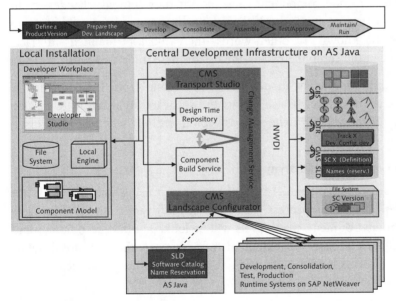

Figure 10.2 Elements of NWDI

---

6 In SAP NetWeaver release 7.0, Support Package Stack 12, transports in CMS can also be combined with transports of Change Management System in SAP NetWeaver AS ABAP. This will be described in greater detail at a later stage.

SAP NetWeaver Developer Studio connects developers to the central NWDI. As a developer, you load the development configuration of CMS into Developer Studio using SLD. Now you can access both source file storage in the DTR workspace, which you use for your work, and archives in the buildspace in CBS. Name Service checks that the names of the objects you create are unique. CMS is used for deployment to the central test systems.

10.2.1 Component Model

A new way of structuring software

The special demands placed on SAP software shipments require a powerful programming model. An essential feature of making software easy to maintain and understand is breaking it down into components that can be changed more or less independently of each other. Once the software has been broken down into components, reusing them is the next logical step. Reuse is made easier, however, if two conditions are fulfilled: First, the individual components must be decoupled, so that changes to one component cause no, or only limited, changes to the other components. Second, the relationship between the components must be known. In other words, there must be defined interfaces between the components and the use of these interfaces must be clear.

The SAP component model meets these conditions. It is designed to structure software. It also allows the software architecture to be precisely planned and provides a basis for an entirely new build process.

The Component Hierarchy

SAP's component model structures software using four levels. As the order mirrors the process used to create software in the SAP development environment, these levels will be looked at in descending order.[7] In SAP NetWeaver Development Infrastructure, the software development process has been adapted to the natural sequence of these steps.

---

7 The entire process is described in detail in Chapter 12, *SAP NetWeaver Development Infrastructure — Developing an Example Application Step-by-Step* which explains how to create an example application.

Products

At the start of development, there is a vision of a product.[8] SAP products are solutions in the business environment. The management decides on new products. A product can be viewed as a software application that is designed to be sold to customers and defines a particular set of functions. A product usually makes use of existing software that provides general functions. Products range from generally available libraries to developments made by the product manufacturer. The remaining software components to be created can now be defined.

As the nature of a product determines the type and features of the software, it also determines the structure. The substructures of a product consist of new and reused parts, and are called software components. These are the product components that can be installed and reused.

Product components

The new functions, which are specific to the new product, form one or more additional units. A new product version is created in *Software Landscape Directory* (SLD). SLD stores information on the system landscape (*Technical Landscape*) and *Software Catalog*, which contains a list of all the products and software components available. The definition of each product contains the name of its owner or *vendor*.[9] The development environment for the new product is created based on the information in SLD.

Software Components

Software components (SCs) are groups of related functions. Examples include generally available Basis libraries that are combined in a software component or a framework that is shared by all applications. These functions are implemented in development components (DCs). A software

Structure of software components

---

8 The product is not actually part of the component model. However, the use of the component model can be understood much better if you start with the definition of the product, which is always the first step in the development process — as it is implemented in SLD — or must already have been carried out before a software component is created.

9 This is important, because products are usually the units that are shipped to the customers.

component can therefore be regarded as a container for development components. Consequently, each development component belongs to one software component. This means that there are no development components outside of software components and that each development component exists only once in a software component. However, these two statements are valid only for the development of one product version (release). In other releases, this assignment may be changed.

The reason for this fixed assignment lies in the way in which software components are used in products. A development component cannot appear twice in the same product. This means that you cannot use software components that contain the same development component within one product.

Software components in development

Software components, like products, are defined in SLD. They belong to a particular product. During development, software components are used in two different ways. Software components that are specific to the product to be developed can be changed during the development process. Apart from this new software component, there are others that you use to build your development. They contain, for example, Basis libraries that are shared by various Java projects. Software components of this kind can (usually) not be changed in this context. Software components themselves do not define mutual dependencies, because they are used unchanged (in the same release) in different products. However, the administrative process determines these relationships between software components for the current product development. Groups of related software components are arranged into software units, to clarify the structure (of the Java components) of large-scale products such as SAP NetWeaver.

Technical implementation of software components

From a technical point of view, a software component is structured into folders and files. All folders are stored in one joint folder *SCs*. The software component structure is made up of the *vendor* or owner name of a software component, the name under which the component is developed, and a folder *_comp*. This folder contains another folder, *TopLevel-DCs* (top-level development components that are not contained in other development components), with the *.dcref* files of all top-level development components. The build result of a software component is a deployable *Software Component Archive* (SCA).[10]

Software components function as units. A product is broken down into general and specific components, which provides the basis for reusability, as described previously. However, software components themselves only provide a framework that is not yet directly used by a development, but is specified by the administration layer. The inner structure must also adhere to the rules of decoupling by encapsulating elements as complete components. This is done in development components.

Development Components

The development components layer lies below the software component level. Although development components are also groups of (development) objects, they directly define their mutual use and therefore represent the units with which developers actually work. Development components contain and encapsulate the development objects. They are also the units on which the NWDI's build process works.

Development components carry the crucial characteristics of the component model. They define the internal structure of the software component, as they contain the actual development objects, which can be any type of file contained in the standard Java development. These can be Java classes and interfaces, image files for icons, and SAP-specific data, from Web Dynpro development, for example.

Characteristics of the component model

Development components constitute the build process units when you develop software based on the component model. In this way, the structure of the software component, which you determine in the development components, is verified during the build. To achieve this, you use a visibility concept and the definition of interfaces and the explicitly declared use of other components. This combination allows and requires that the development be planned with exact precision. However, it does allow you to replace the time-consuming nightly build pro-

Component-based build process

---

10 This structure is displayed in the DTR perspective of Developer Studio, which shows the software at the folders and files levels.

cess of the entire development with a build of those individual development components, at the request of the relevant developer.[11]

Relationships between development components

The left section of Figure 10.3 shows the relationships between development objects (for example, classes and interfaces) in the Java development environment. As soon as an object is marked `public`, it can be used by any other object. Conversely, you must define development component objects that you want to release for use by other development components explicitly in public parts (even if they are `public`, objects that do not lie in the public part of a development component cannot be used outside of the development component). Public parts serve as defined interfaces of a development component. For more information on public parts, see *Developing Objects Based on the Component Model* in Section 10.2.1 later on. As a result, the software has a better structure and can also be evaluated in development processes such as the build process (see the right section of Figure 10.3).

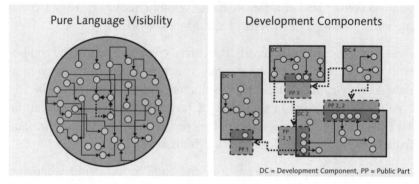

Figure 10.3 Structure and Visibility of Software Based on the SAP Component Model

Figure 10.3 compares Java-based development with and without components.

▸ Without components, development objects (classes, interfaces, text files or image files) are only structured using packages, and relationships between the objects (where-used list) are difficult to identify.

---

11 The explicitly declared dependencies can be used to load all of the required development components and update all dependent development components using another build. In this way, you can consistently manage elements at the archive level, despite the fact that components are assembled individually.

Anything marked `public` can be used without restriction, and as a result, the visibility of objects is only determined using language constructs. As a result, the entire application is built as an entity — usually using a nightly build — and this often causes problems, as an error, for example, the use of a version that is no longer current, can cause the entire build to terminate.

▸ The use of components achieves the following: Development objects remain unchanged, but are packed into development components in such a way that they are invisible from the outside. This means that a development component is a "black box." To allow usage, development components define interfaces or public parts, as described previously. As their use must be specified in another development component — both the public parts and the use dependencies are included in the metadata for the DC project — the application's structure is known and can be verified. In this way, cyclical dependencies that represent an inconsistency, for example, can be avoided. By defining the structure in the metadata, a build can be assembled at the component level, as dependent development components are known and can therefore be rebuilt automatically. SAP provides the build scripts for the automatic build of all development component types.

Development Objects

Finally, the development objects contained in the development components can be any type of object generated during the development process. They are the source files for the build process. They include files from Java development (for example, classes and interfaces) and specific files developed by SAP, such as Web Dynpro files or development metadata. Development objects from the Java and J2EE/JEE standard environment are not changed by the component model and — like SAP-specific components — are managed in development components and other projects.

Content of development components

Developing Objects Based on the Component Model

All objects are created in SAP NetWeaver Development Infrastructure in the order outlined previously. No development components can be cre-

Implementation of the component model

ated and, as a result, no source files can be created, if product and software components are not defined.[12] The relationships between the levels are determined explicitly at each level and are automatically evaluated for the development processes.

Figure 10.4 shows the structure of software, based on the SAP component model. Product Y consists of software components (SCs). These are either used in this product and exist in read-only format (SC X, `read-only`) after the import, or they are developed for the product (SC Y, `changeable`). A software component can be used in various products. Use dependencies must be defined between the software components (shown by the `uses` arrow). As SC Y uses SC X, development components from SC Y can access development components in SC X. Use dependencies for software components are defined in SLD.

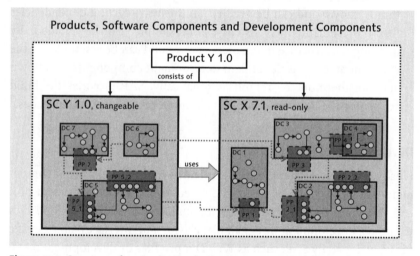

Figure 10.4 Structure of an Application in the Component Model

Nesting of development components Component

Software components contain the development components. These always exist in just one software component. Development components contain the development objects — these also exist in just one development component. In addition to development objects, development

---

12 This is the process usually used to create objects, with the following exceptions: For example, an object such as a Java class can be created outside of NWDI and can be added to the DTR database at a later stage.

components can also contain other development components. This is known as nesting, and is displayed in SC X, for example. The dependencies to other development components are defined in the development components themselves, as depicted by the arrows between the development components.

Each release of a product is defined separately in SLD. This definition determines the versions of the software components used and their uses.

In addition to development objects, development components can contain other development components, thereby structuring the software by hierarchically encapsulating its components. The visibility rules for embedded development components are the same as for the development objects. You use this nesting if a development component makes a function available in a public part, and this function will only be used by other development components in a specific context. Limited visibility of a development component may be interesting, for example, for security-related functions.

Visibility of development objects

We already know that development components are containers for development objects, that is, projects and metadata. They limit the visibility of development objects from the outside. All objects in a development component are initially invisible outside of this development component. Therefore, changes to the invisible development objects have no impact on other components. This results in a perfect decoupling of all development components, but would also make it impossible for development components to use each other. Therefore, to allow mutual use, development components define interfaces that can be used by other development components.

Visibility of objects in development components

The interfaces of a development component are known as *public parts*. In public parts, a development component publishes the development objects that will be visible from the outside, and can therefore be used by other development components. Objects assigned to public parts are known as *public part entities*. Entities can be individual objects such as a class or tree structures such as a package tree.

Interface concept of development components

Two types of public parts

Depending on their use, we distinguish between two types of public parts:

- A public part of the type *Compilation* can be used for the development of other development components and will be used during compilation. This is always necessary if objects from one development component are used to compile another development component.

- A public part of the type *Assembly* provides a build result that can be packed by other development components. This type is required, for example, if a development component type (such as a Java development component) does not produce deployable build results. Parts of this development component can then be packed in a public part of this type, and uploaded to the server as a J2EE Java library file or an enterprise application, for example.

In principle, a public part of the type compilation can also contain entire development components. However, in this case, each object of the development component could be used and the advantage of function encapsulation would be lost. By limiting public parts to a few entities, inner structures of a development component can be modified without forcing the development components that use them to react to this change.

Build results of a development component

DC 1 in Figure 10.5 defines, for example, a public part API with the usage type *Compilation* and a public part ASSBL of the usage type *Assembly*. API only contains the objects C1 and C2. ASSBL, on the other hand, contains all objects of the development component, to pack them into another development component for deployment. The build result is always a JAR file. A ZIP file is also created for public parts of the type Assembly. The development component itself is packed as an SDA file.

Use dependencies between development components

Use dependencies — or *dependencies* — between development components constitute the second part of the component concept. Another development component can only be used if this use if defined in the metadata for using a development component. The new build process in CBS checks this information, which is the basis of the build, because development components can be built individually instead of as a software entity in a nightly build if the dependencies between development components are known. When the use dependencies are known, specific dependent components can be rebuilt. Each time development components are used, you must decide how they will be used. You define this use in the relevant wizard in SAP NetWeaver Developer Studio. The following use types exist:

▸ **Build time dependencies**
You allow the use of another development component at the time the build process is executed.

▸ **Deploy time dependencies**
You ensure that the deployment of a used development component is verified when the using development component is deployed.

▸ **Runtime Dependencies**
You ensure that the used development component is correctly referenced at runtime.

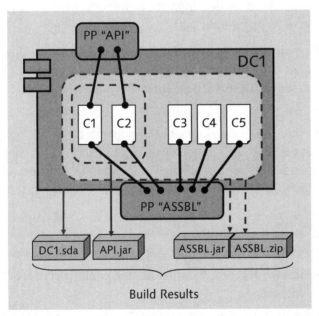

Figure 10.5 Public Parts of the Types Compilation and Assembly with Build Results

A number of restrictions apply to the use, however, based on the software component to which the development component belongs, and on the hierarchy of development components due to nesting. The used development component must fulfill the following conditions:

Use dependencies between nested development components

▶ The used development component must be in the same software component as the using development component. If this is not the case, the use of the software component that contains the used development component must be defined in SLD by the software component of the using SC.

▶ The used DC must be visible for the using development component. This is the case if:

  ▶ It is on the same nesting level

  ▶ It is a child development component in the using development component

  ▶ The embedding development component can use the development component

If these conditions are not met, it can only be used if the development component that embeds the development component to be used adds its public parts to its own public parts.

Use dependencies between nested development components

Even if a use dependency has been defined, only the objects of a development component (DC) that belong to one of its public parts can be used. Figure 10.6 shows the use dependencies between nested development components:

▶ DC 1 contains three other development components: DC 1.1, 1.2, and 1.3. Continuous arrows represent allowed dependencies, an X shows that these dependencies are not allowed in the present situation.

▶ DC 1 itself is allowed to use all three embedded DCs, for example, DC 1.1 in this case.

▶ Development components on the same level are allowed to use one another. For example, DC 1.1 uses DC 1.2 or DC 1 uses DC 3.

▶ DC 4 can only use DC 1.3 if DC 1 propagates the public part of DC 1.3 in its own public part.

▶ DC 2 cannot use DC 1.2, because as a child DC of DC 1, it is not visible for DC 2.

▶ In this example, DC 1, therefore, defines the visibility of particular functions and structures the software component with this encapsulation.

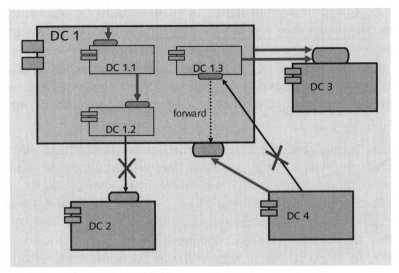

Figure 10.6 Use Dependencies Between Nested Development Components

Access control lists can define further restrictions by setting limitations using nesting. Here, you can explicitly define which development components are allowed to access a specific development component. If development components are specified here, use is denied to all other development components.

Access control list

Cyclic dependencies are not allowed. A cyclic dependency exists, for example, if there is a use relationship of the following type: DC A uses DC B, which uses DC C, which uses DC A. The build process of a development component cannot prevent the definition of dependencies of this kind. However, it detects these dependencies and terminates the build process. As a result, this type of dependency will never be activated. In a build process as it was used up to now, dependencies of this kind have been possible. If DC A from our example is built before the cyclic dependency is defined, then the build process can be executed. However, this results in inconsistent states, if both DC A and DC C are changed in a process. In this case, the old state of DC A, and not the current one, is used.

Cyclic dependencies

It is possible to grant other components access to development components, to which nesting would usually deny access. A development component can declare a *public part entity reference* to any public part that

Entity references

adds the content of the public part to the development component's public part. This public part can then be used by other development components. You can use this technique to grant any development component access to any public part (in all available software components). It reverses the effect of nesting development components. You can use a permission, to prevent unrestricted access to certain development components.

Types of development component

When you create development components, you must always determine their type. The type is used to automatically control the build process. In addition, the structure of the development component is created in accordance with its type, and type-related settings are generated. For a development component of the type Java, this means that metadata is created, in addition to the development component files usually required for a Java project. In SAP NetWeaver Developer Studio of SAP NetWeaver releases 2004 and 7.0, this data is displayed in a folder of the development component project called *DCMetaData*. In SAP NetWeaver CE, this metadata is displayed as *properties* of the development component in the **Component Properties** view. The following types of development components are available.

- ▶ **Composite Application Services DC**
  A Composite Application Services DC contains all elements required for a Composite Application Services project. These are dictionary objects, metadata, and Java classes. If you select a Composite Application Services DC, the system creates four projects of the types Dictionary, Metadata, EJB Module, and Enterprise.

  The product of a Composite Application Services DC consists of three archives. These are a Software Deployment Archive (SDA) for the Dictionary project, and one Enterprise Archive (EAR) each for the Metadata and Enterprise projects. They can be deployed on the server.

- ▶ **Dictionary DC**
  A Dictionary development component defines global data structures that are created in the database on the server where the development component will be deployed. As the data structures will be created in a central database, it is important to use unique names. To ensure this, the name server will allow only certain prefixes for table names.

Up to now, you had to add the simple types, structures or tables to a public part, to use the structures created in a Dictionary DC in another development component. In SAP NetWeaver CE, this development component type is the exception to the rule, as this is no longer obligatory.

The product of a Dictionary DC is a Software Deployment Archive (SDA) that can be deployed on the server. (To create the archive locally, use the development component build or choose **Create Archive** from the context menu of the Dictionary project in the Dictionary Explorer.)

▶ **J2EE/JEE DC**

Development components correspond to projects that also contain specific metadata. There are now different project types — the standard types that you know from J2EE/JEE development and SAP-specific types. The following list specifies the development component types that you can create in SAP NetWeaver Developer Studio:

▶ **Java Enterprise Application DC**

An Enterprise Application DC combines Web Module DCs and EJB Module DCs for an Enterprise Application. The product of an Enterprise Application DC is a deployable *Enterprise Application Archive* (EAR) file. The build result is an EAR file that contains the WAR files from the Web Module DCs and the EJB files from the EJB Module DCs.

▶ **EJB-Module DC**

An EJB Module DC contains the model classes (that is, Message-Driven Bean, Container-Managed Persistence Bean (CMP), Bean-Managed Persistence Bean (BMP), Stateful Session Bean, or Stateless Session Bean) for an Enterprise Application DC. SAP NetWeaver Developer Studio automatically creates public parts for assembly and compilation. Results of the build are compiled classes that can be used by an EJB Assembly DC.

▶ **Web Module DC**

A Web Module DC contains the files that belong to the view and view controller of an enterprise application project, that is, JSPs, servlets, and proxy classes for beans defined in an EJB project. The build result is also a WAR file.

▶ **J2EE Server Component Library DC**

A J2EE library is a special add-on for Java EE Engine. A J2EE library project is easy to use. You refer public parts (that will be used for assembly) of Java DCs (build time dependency) or other J2EE library DCs (runtime dependency). The build result is an SDA file.

▶ **Java DC**

A Java DC can contain arbitrary Java code. It does not generate a deployable or installable build result. (The class files generated from the source code are only stored in a temporary folder and removed after the build.) It is up to the developer to define a public part for the assembly, if a JAR file is to be generated.

▶ **Web Dynpro DC**

A Web Dynpro DC is a container for one or more Web Dynpro components. The build result is an EAR file that contains a Web Dynpro Archive (WDA).

▶ **Web Services**

A Web Service Client Proxy is a special Java DC that contains client code that accesses a Web service. Unlike a standalone proxy, for a deployable proxy, the application of the Web service client must be deployed on Java EE Engine. A standalone proxy, on the other hand, can be executed without Java EE Engine.

You can choose between the standard types Java and J2EE — the latter is broken down into Enterprise Application, EJB Module, Web Module DC — and SAP-specific types such as the Web Dynpro or Java Dictionary. Of course, combinations of SAP-specific and standard types are allowed and are useful.

Using development components in the build process

Development components are the units that are built in Component Build Service. During this process, all rules of use dependencies and visibility are checked. If, for example, a development component method is used without being specified as a used development component, the build process terminates. This guarantees that the structure of the software component remains clearly defined.

The development component type defines the build process. The appropriate build script for each type is available in the build tool and is used automatically. This is possible because the development component

474

metadata is evaluated. This ANT-based tool is used both in the development component build of SAP NetWeaver Developer Studio and in Component Build Service. As a result, the build support is available in the local and in the central build, and any deviations in the build results are excluded as long as the source files and archives used are identical.

From a technical point of view, each development component — just like a software component — is a structure that contains folders and files (for example, the folder _comp, class files and files for managing the development component, such as .dcdef), with the granularity of an eclipse project. The name of a development component defines a folder hierarchy. Related development components that have names with the same beginning are assigned to the same branches in the folder hierarchy. The files .classpath and .project, which are also displayed in the structure, have been added by Eclipse to project management. Each of these files are therefore generated when you use NWDI, and excluded from being saved in DTR by being designated *Ignored Resources* in Developer Studios preferences.

Technical basis of development components

All development components have a common _comp folder, which always contains folders for binaries (*bin*) and the public parts. These are stored as XML files (even though they are displayed in Developer Studio as folders, to provide a clear overview of the data). The folder also contains the development component definition with used development components and child development components. The *gen* folder contains generated files. Here, you can view deployable build results, for example. All other folders depend on the development component type.[13]

Support in IDE, SAP NetWeaver Developer Studio CE 7.1

SAP NetWeaver Developer Studio provides wizards for all steps in component-based development. You create your development components directly in the software component that you are developing, and you can see all the software components that you may use. To create development components, you use a wizard that guides you through all the

Wizard concept

---

13 Chapter 12 contains figures depicting development components and the tools that you will have to use. This chapter describes the development of an example application using NWDI.

settings required for the development component. The structure of the development component is then created automatically. In this process, the use dependencies required for the selected type are also generated automatically.

Development components and Eclipse projects

As SAP NetWeaver Developer Studio is based on the Eclipse framework, which has been enhanced by SAP plug-ins, Eclipse projects must be defined for development. One development component corresponds to one project.[14] The Eclipse user interface is organized into perspectives and views. The view of a development component in Developer Studio depends on the selected view.

Figure 10.7 displays two central views of the Development Infrastructure Perspective — the perspective in which you always start in component-based development. The displayed views are the Component Browser, in which you connect with the development landscape and create development components, and the Component Properties, in which you mainly define development component metadata, based on the component model. To create development objects, you open perspectives based on the type of development component being processed.

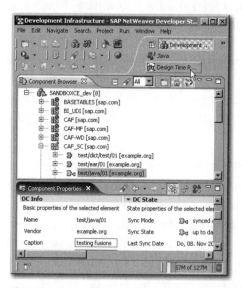

Figure 10.7 Development Infrastructure Perspective

14 For more details on Eclipse projects, see Chapter 12.

To edit development components, different views are available for different tasks in the development process.

Perspectives and Views for Working with the Component Model

These perspectives show a view of the development components that corresponds to the respective task. For example, information that is not required is hidden, and most actions are controlled in the context menu.

User interfaces for component-based development

▶ **Development Infrastructure Perspective**

You create all development components here and connect to the development landscape. The following default views are available:

Starting point for component-based development

▶ **Component Browser**

The development configurations, software components, and development components are contained here. In other words, this view contains the basic elements for your work in the component model. If you work with NWDI, you load development configurations here. You can also find software components and create development components here. You always create a development component in the context of a software component. Software components and connections to central systems are defined in *development configurations*.

When you work in a local scenario, you can create all three object types here. (For more details, see Section 10.4.2, *Component-Based Development with a Local Development Configuration and Optional External Infrastructure*). For display purposes, you can toggle between all development components, all activated development components (for more information on activation, see the section on *Build Processes — Activating Changes* in Section 10.2.3), all inactive development components (development components that can be changed), and development components that are only available locally on the PC. This last view is useful if you want to quickly find your own development components. The other views display the development components of all developers working on the team.

▶ **Component Properties**

Here, you check and change the properties of your development components, in particular the metadata of the component model, which are dependencies and public parts. For more details on the component model, see Section 10.2.1, *Component Model*.

► **Open Activities**
Here, you manage your changes in Design Time Repository. You also change and check in activities here. For more details on DTR, see Section 10.2.2, *Design Time Repository*.

► **Infrastructure Console and DTR Console**
Here you find messages of NWDI services.

The following optional views are also available in this perspective: To open the **Component Navigator**, go to **Window • Show View • Other... • Development Infrastructure • Component Navigator** (Figure 10.8).

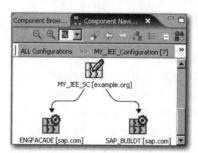

Figure 10.8 Component Navigator

► You need the following views in the NWDI development process. To incorporate these views, select **Window • Show View • Other... • CBS** or **CMS**, to integrate these directly in the Development Infrastructure Perspective or any other perspective.

► **Activation View**
In this view, as a developer, you trigger the central build for your development components in Component Build Service (CBS). DCs that have been successfully activated in this way are displayed in the Active DCs View.

► **Transportation View**
Here, you can release activities for further processing in Change Management Service (CMS).

If you are only working locally, these two views are not of interest to you. For more information, see Section 10.4.1, *Scenarios for Component-*

Based Software Development in Composition Environment. There are other perspectives, based on different development component types.

Use of Perspectives and Views with and Without the Component Model

Examples of perspectives and views that are used with and without the component model include the following:

▶ **DTR Perspective**
This shows all objects in the repository as folders and files. For example, public parts are shown as XML files.

▶ **Web Dynpro Perspective**
The Web Dynpro Explorer view of this perspective displays all Web Dynpro projects.

▶ **Java Package Explorer View**
This view displays all Java projects for the type. You need this view to create Java packages.

You can configure SAP NetWeaver Developer Studio in such a way that it corresponds to your way of working. You also use SAP NetWeaver Developer Studio to make settings for development work that concerns the storage of file types in DTR, for example.[15]

In Developer Studio, development components are displayed in development-component-specific views as folders and files. For each development component, **metadata** is displayed as properties in the **Component Properties** view (in Developer Studio versions prior to SAP NetWeaver CE, these were displayed in the *DC Meta Data* folder). It contains those properties of a development component that go beyond an Eclipse project.

Displaying development components in Developer Studio

▶ **Access List**
Here, you can define which development components can access your development component. If you do not specify components, all development components for which your development component is visible are allowed to access it.

---

15 The settings may vary, depending on whether you use only DTR or the entire NWDI. More details will be provided at a later stage.

► **Child DCs**

Here, the lower-level development components for this development component are listed.

► **Folders**

This node contains a list of folders in this development component, for example, Java Packages.

► **Used DCs**

Here, you define all use dependencies to development components that you want to use. All development components that are used by default in a particular development component type are automatically inserted in this list.

► **Public Parts**

These are displayed as folders to keep the layout clear and simple (they are XML files). The folder contains the individual public parts. Each of them displays its own **Access List**, the contained **Entities**, and **Entity References** in SAP NetWeaver Developer Studio 7.0. In SAP NetWeaver Developer Studio 7.1 public parts are shown in the *Components Properties* view as a register card containing the same information.

Development Objects

In the context of component-based Java development in an SAP environment, the term *development object* is used for classes and interfaces, EJBs, and user interface icons from the standard development, for example, and for tables in Java Dictionary or in Web Dynpro files. They are stored as *versioned resources* in DTR.

10.2.2 Design Time Repository

Tasks and architecture of DTR

Design Time Repository (DTR) is NWDI's central source file management system. In principle, it can manage all types of files, however. DTR is a J2EE application, which runs as a service on SAP NetWeaver's J2EE Engine. It uses a database to store and create versions for development objects. In this context, it performs several tasks:

► All versions of files must always be available.

▸ Access should always be restricted to those objects that are needed in the relevant software development project.

▸ Versioning information must be kept, even after the transport of objects into other DTR instances.

Examples of such transports include the scenarios described in the introduction, which cover the shipment of source data to customers, to enable modifications and the synchronization of development laboratories in different countries. For both processes, there must be a mechanism for avoiding conflicts between versions during parallel developments within a product.

Figure 10.9 illustrates the architecture of DTR, which is made up of the server and different user interfaces (clients). The server saves all files as *Versioned Resources* in the form of *Binary Large Objects* (BLOBs) in a database (which can be shared with CBS and CMS, for example), but presents them to the user interfaces in the form of files and folders. Communication is based on standards, and is conducted between clients and servers using HTTP, based on WebDAV and DeltaV.[16]

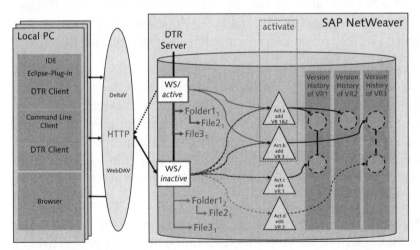

Figure 10.9 DTR Architecture

16 DeltaV is an enhancement of the WebDAV standard for versioning. WebDAV defines a standard method of using the Web to access and manage files. DeltaV adds versioning to this concept by defining a protocol for tasks related to configuration management and version control. DTR uses workspaces and activities to implement concepts from the DeltaV standard.

Storing objects in the database

To access all objects in the database, you use logical storage locations, known as DTR workspaces. These are usually created using CMS. For the central build, the source files managed in DTR workspaces are sent to CBS, which in turn triggers specific actions in DTR, if a build has run successfully. Individual objects or the state of a workspace can be propagated or exported to a number of targets such as CMS.

Storing file versions in the database

DTR's functions support the development process in SAP NetWeaver Development Infrastructure. DTR is embedded into the development infrastructure in such a way that it cannot be replaced by other versioning tools. SAP NetWeaver CE also provides development scenarios that offer specific services for component-based development but do not require the central services of NWDI. For more details, see Section 10.4.1, *Scenarios for Component-Based Software Development in Composition Environment.*

For DTR, all databases that are supported by SAP NetWeaver in this release can be used. A database allows access to any object stored within and provides an ideal means for backing up data. DTR uses its own database schema; it can share the physical database with all other development services — CBS, CMS, and SLD — that also use a database. The objects DTR stores do not have to fulfill any requirements. Basically, it can store any file.

All objects created for all releases of all products are saved in DTR database tables.[17] This includes all objects in Support Packages. This means that new objects are continuously being created for previous releases. Access to these objects must now be designed in such a way that it reflects the task of the developer. In other words, it must only access the objects of a particular software version. The concept of DTR workspaces serves this purpose.

Check-in/check-out mechanisms

Figure 10.10 shows the check-in and check-out mechanisms of DTR. The actions described here are integrated into most of the perspectives of SAP NetWeaver Developer Studio. The PC of a developer with SAP NetWeaver Developer Studio and a local file system is shown on the left, the DTR server appears on the right. Its database contains all source files. You use the DTR client to access specific objects in the DTR data-

---

17 It is possible to use more than one database.

base. Objects are accessed using DTR workspaces. All changes — new or changed versions or deletions — are grouped into activities. All changes as an entity define the workspace state.

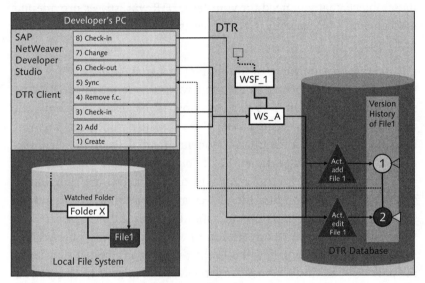

Figure 10.10 Check-In and Check-Out Mechanisms in DTR

The process flow is as follows:

1. You have created an object *File 1*.

2. You have selected the file to be inserted into the DTR database. For this, you have created the activity add File 1. This is open and can be changed. At this stage, the file within the activity is only available in the local file system.

3. You check in *File 1*, to add it to the database. Your activity is now closed and can no longer be changed. The version which was checked in last is the active version in the workspace.

4. You can now delete the local file.

5. You can use the Sync command, to load the files from DTR at any stage. This also happens automatically for all files in a development component when you create a project.

6. You create a new activity for changes.

7. Make your changes.

483

DTR Workspaces

Accessing objects in the database

If all versions of all development objects of all product releases are in one database, developers need an access mechanism that shows (only) those objects that you need for your task. DTR workspaces provide this mechanism. You can only access objects in the database using these workspaces.

DTR workspaces are views of the content of a DTR database. They work like folders and are created in the same way as folders. Each DTR workspace contains references to database objects. For every file, only one version can be referenced at a time. This is because workspaces are used to define states of software components (and development components). As outlined in Section 10.2.1, *Component Model*, each file — or the function it defines — can only exist once in a software component. With each new version of a file you create, the reference in the workspace in which you work is automatically set to the new version. As soon as you check in a new version of a file into DTR — in the DTR workspace in which you develop — the reference is automatically set to the new file, and this becomes the active version in your workspace. All other versions of this file may be the active file in other workspaces, however.

It is important in this context that database objects can be used in any number of workspaces. If a file version is required in more than one source code line, then several references to the same physical object are used. This saves storage space and prevents inconsistencies from occurring.

DTR workspaces in development

As workspaces represent a specific collection of file versions, separate workspaces are created for development phases in which files are changed (which, because of referencing, only marginally increases the data volume). These phases are usually development and consolidation (dev and cons).[18] We recommend this distinction for all development scenarios in which DTR is used. These phases are represented by workspaces with the same names, if only DTR is used by the entire NWDI.

---

18 For more information on workspaces in development, see Section 10.2.4. You can also define the workspaces manually if you only use DTR for development.

In addition to the typical workspaces dev and cons, you can create other workspaces as required. You can, for example, create a workspace for each Support Package, or to restore software states (a set of particular versions of source files) at a specific time. You can then use such a workspace, for example, to find errors resulting from modifications in a state created at a customer site, or to recover an earlier release state.

If DTR is used with CBS and CMS[19] two workspaces are created for each of these phases, to separate objects checked by a successful central build process from those that have not yet undergone this step. These workspaces are called inactive and active. The reason for this separation is that the central build involves an additional check of the objects. If you use objects from the active workspace that are created by other developers, you can ensure that you use the most up-to-date versions that have been reconciled with all other versions. To create new objects, you always use the inactive workspace. The development phases dev and cons are also required here, and are represented by another level of workspace folders that contains workspaces.

Inactive and active workspaces

Typically, there are therefore almost always several interrelated workspaces. The names of these workspaces are the same in every release and for every development object. To organize these workspaces more clearly, additional folders known as workspace folders contain the information on the project and release. These folders form a hierarchy: For example, there is one workspace folder for each project, and this folder contains another workspace folder for all releases, which again contains the different workspaces, depending on the development scenario.

Workspace folder organize workspaces

If DTR is used with CBS and CMS, the lowest workspace folder level is always called dev and cons, each of which contains the two workspaces inactive and active. This is the scenario that is used by SAP and the one recommended to customers. In this scenario, workspace folders and workspaces are no longer created manually by the administrator, but are defined and then automatically generated in Change Management Service when creating a track — a logical development system for a new

---

19 This is a typical use of DTR. Other uses are possible, but they will not be described here in detail, because this book focuses on the use of the entire NWDI. Another use would be the creation of versions for all types of files.

release. As a result, there is a direct relation between the software project and the folder structure in the development system.

DTR workspace and Eclipse workspace

Development environments based on the Eclipse framework also use the term *workspace*. Do not confuse the Eclipse workspace with the DTR workspace. The Eclipse workspace is a folder in the local file system, and is controlled by the development environment. This concept is also used in SAP NetWeaver Developer Studio. Here, you use Eclipse workspaces for the local management of file versions that you access using DTR workspaces. (For more information, see Section 10.2.2, *Design Time Repository*).

Activities

Changes to the database content

We have seen that all source files are stored in the database and that they are accessed in the context of workspaces that are defined according to the task of the development team. Now the question arises as to how objects can be created or changed. In other words, how are new file versions managed? DTR uses lists of changes, the *activities*. Activities organize related changes. Each time you create a new file (that is, its first version) or change a file, you use an activity to perform these changes. If you have worked with ABAP, you are familiar with the concept of transport requests. Activities are based on a similar concept. They contain all changes and form the (smallest) units for a transport.

Open and closed activities

Activities are open until they are checked in. You change open activities by adding or deleting files, by renaming the activity or by deleting empty activities. Open activities contain new versions in the local file system. Files must be available locally in order to be changed. New files are created locally. To change files that already exist on the server, synchronize them to the local file system (using the command Sync) and check them out again, to flag them as changeable. Once you have changed the file, you check in the content of an activity — that is, all new file versions — on to the server to make the changes generally available. The new version automatically becomes the active version in the DTR workspace in which the activity has been created and checked in.

As soon as an activity has been checked in, it is closed and can no longer be changed. Closed activities can be transported or activated by a central build. This kind of transport is performed, for example, into the consolidation workspace after a file has been released in the development workspace.

The following sections provide some examples of assigning objects to activities.

Assigning files to activities

▶ When you create a new development component, you always create several files. As these files are related and will therefore also be transported together, you will assign all files of a new development component — both the automatically created elements and each class created in the first version of the development component — in the same activity.

▶ If, at a later stage, you want to add another class to the development component or you change an existing class, you can use a new activity (you can also use the same activity in which the development component was created, provided that it has not yet been checked in). If several changes are related, they should be transported together, to create a new working version of the development component with one single transport.

▶ If two development components are closely related, you can include them both in one activity. This may happen, for example, if a Java J2EE library DC without any source code of its own packs a specific Java DC.

Activities, therefore, contain individual or several file versions from one or more development components. Note that objects in the same activity can no longer be transported individually. Therefore, consider assignments carefully, to allow you to easily handle objects at a later stage. If you still need to transport objects separately, you can create dummy versions — without actually making changes — in a new activity that only contains a subset of the former objects.

Deleting files in workspaces is a special case. Versions that are stored once in the DTR databases are never lost. However, it is of course often necessary to delete files from workspaces. To do this, you create a deletion version of a file that you also store in an activity. When you check in this activity, the reference to this file is deleted and it will no longer

Deleting files in workspaces

be used in this state of the software component. You can use this procedure for individual files or folders and for entire subtrees.

Defining workspace states All new versions are contained in activities. Activities are always created in the context of a particular workspace and are initially only effective in this workspace. Other states — or workspaces — of the same software component are not affected. Therefore, the state of a workspace and, as a result, the state of the software component, is defined by the activities it contains. You use transports, to make these changes available in other systems. The sequence in which the transports are executed is irrelevant. The name of an activity contains a GUID and a timestamp. Using this information, the versions can always be inserted at the correct position in the version tree. This implies that the most recent version of a file in a workspace is always the active version. The integration of activities changes the state of a workspace. This means that development is always directed forward. In other words, you can synchronize any version that is or was active in the workspace. However, older versions can no longer become active versions in this workspace.

Copying Changes to Other Workspaces

Integrating activities into workspaces Changes must often be copied from one workspace (that is, a software state) to another. One example is the integration of development objects from the development state into the consolidation state. The organization of copied objects is determined by the activities. You copy the activities into other workspaces. Copying files into a workspace, that is, setting a reference in the workspace to the object in the database, is known as integration. If the source and target workspaces are in the same repository, integration is possible without a physical transport, as each workspace consists of just references. If the workspaces are in different repositories, for example, a DTR at SAP and a customer workspace, the objects must first be exported into a resulting file; this file must then be imported into the database of the target DTR, and then integrated into one or more workspaces.

Propagation lists If you want to transport several activities at once — for example, an entire state of a workspace — you can combine several activities in propagation lists that can then be transported. You can create propagation lists in a number of ways. For example, you can retroactively export a workspace state at a specific time into a propagation list. By integrating this state into a new workspace, you can restore an earlier state.

Conflicts

At the start of this chapter, we mentioned the three prerequisites that the development process at SAP must meet: long-term maintenance of the software, the possibility of simultaneous development at different locations, and modifications at the customer site. All of these processes share one characteristic: They use source files in various states. Versions may be changed concurrently, that is, one version is changed at two locations so that two new versions are created that exist in parallel.[20] This is not permitted in the same workspace, because each workspace can only contain one version of any file.

Parallel development can result from checking out the version in a workspace more than once or from integrating two versions into the same workspace (of course, parallel created versions of one file in different workspaces do not cause a conflict, because each of them belongs to a different state of the software and they will therefore not be installed together).

How conflicts arise

▶ The first case occurs when a second user checks out the same file version as the first user, and does so before the first user has checked it in again.[21] Checking in the first parallel version does not cause any problems. However, a check-in conflict occurs when the second developer tries to check in the parallel version. (It is irrelevant who checked out first — only the person who checks in last is relevant.) The second developer must then choose one of the following options:

Check-in conflict

  ▶ Accept the currently active version and ignore your version

  ▶ Use your version as the new active version in the workspace

---

20 Existing in parallel means that both versions are based on the same *root version*, but neither of them is the predecessor of the other. If this were the case, the more recent version would simply replace the less recent version as the active version.

21 You can avoid this situation by using the exclusive check-out option. This is not always the best choice, however.

▶ Merge the two versions into one joint version. SAP NetWeaver Developer Studio supports this option by displaying the differences between the two file versions and making it easier to create the new version, which contains the changes from both versions.

Integration conflict and modifications

▶ The second case occurs when the two versions have been created in different workspaces, but are then brought together into the same workspace. This may happen within an enterprise, if, for example, changes have been carried out simultaneously in the development or consolidation workspace, and these are integrated from dev into cons, or if changes from Support Packages are copied into another release in which these objects have also been changed.

This kind of conflict often occurs if changes are made at the customer site. The customer creates its own workspace for modifications and usually updates this workspace using changes contained in Support Packages, shipped by SAP, for example. If the same files are affected by the changes, an integration conflict occurs, and this can be resolved using the mechanisms for solving check-in conflicts. Changes are not automatically overwritten.

Global version history

To synchronize several development locations — within an enterprise or between a software company and the modified customer system — the information that enables a conflict to be recognized must be retained during transport. This is always the case when you use DTR to *move* objects, regardless of whether the files are integrated into other workspaces in the same DTR or whether they are exported and re-imported into other installations of DTR. Therefore, we refer to the *Global Version History*.[22]

DTR User Interfaces

To access DTR, you use different user interfaces (or *clients* — not to be confused with the DTR client, which determines which DTR is used by a DTR user interface). The Hyper Text Transfer Protocol (HTTP) is used for

---

22 For more information about dealing with conflicts, go to *Conflict Resolution — How to Analyze, Handle, and Avoid Integration Conflicts in SAP NetWeaver Development Infrastructure* in SAP Developer Network (*http://sdn.sap.com*).

communication. The choice of the user interface depends on the user's task and role:

▸ **DTR perspective in SAP NetWeaver Developer Studio**

This is the user interface used by developers. In Repository Browser, the objects are displayed on the server. In the local file system, they appear in the part that is used (*mounted*) by DTR. Icons display the corresponding state of each object, and indicate whether an object is checked out, available *only* locally or *only* on the server, or is checked out by another user, for example. The default layout of this perspective shows the open and closed activities of the DTR console. For example, you can display the **Version Graph** view, which shows a version history of the selected object and allows access, for example, the synchronization of particular versions or a check of its content.

SAP NetWeaver Developer Studio

▸ **DTR Administrator Plug-In**

All views and perspectives in SAP NetWeaver Developer Studio are plug-ins. The DTR Admin plug-in enables you to perform a number of administrative tasks such as creating workspaces and integrating activities, and above all, granting permissions to access objects in the DTR database.

DTR Admin plug-in

▸ **DTR Command Line Client**

This client is called in the command line editor. It is used exclusively for DTR administration. You can also use it to create workspace folders and workspaces. Above all, as an administrator you can use it to create propagation lists, start exports, and start tasks as a batch job. You cannot use it to maintain permissions.

DTR command line client

You can use any of the user interfaces described previously to access various DTR instances, which is why you must restrict access to one specific DTR. You do this by creating a DTR client.

Creating DTR clients

From a technical point of view, the definition of a DTR client is also an XML file. It contains a name, the URL of the DTR server and the local root, which is a folder that you create or select. This folder stores all files that you work with. In other words, all files that you synchronize are copied to this folder. You also use this folder to create new files that you will save in DTR at a later stage.

DTR monitors the local root. Any objects that you create here are also visible in the Repository Browser. To facilitate the assignment to particular development projects and states, during file synchronization DTR creates a folder structure that corresponds to the structure of workspace folders and workspaces. A DTR client usually also contains a filter definition that restricts access to specific workspaces. In addition, access can be restricted to read-only.

DTR client and the development scenario

Clients are created based on the selected development scenario. If you only use DTR, each developer creates a client in DTR. If you use Change Management Service, however, *development configurations* are used for development. They determine access for all systems, and the DTR client is therefore also defined in the development configuration. (For more information, see Section 10.2.4, *Change Management Service*.) In these DTR client definitions, write access is restricted to the `inactive` workspace, and read access to the `active` workspace. This is the technical basis that ensures that only files that have been checked by a central build are available in the `active` workspace.

Integrating DTR into NWDI

In addition to the user interfaces that belong directly to DTR, other NWDI systems also access DTR. These include CMS, in which the workspace folders and workspaces are created, and CBS, which retrieves source files for the central build process directly from DTR, and triggers the activation of source files if a build process is successful.

Permission Concept in DTR

Authentication and authorization

In DTR, there is a distinction between authentication and authorization. Authentication determines whether you are allowed to access DTR. This is ensured by checking the user/password combination with SAP NetWeaver's *User Management Engine* or with another SAP system. Authorization enables a very fine-tuned check. The administrator can control access specifically for each object in DTR. This allows you to determine that certain critical objects can only be changed by certain developers but still remain visible for all.

Access control lists

These fine-tuned checks are carried out by *access control lists* (or ACLs). An ACL defines the privileges each user or group has for a particular file. Technically speaking, an ACL consists of *access control entities* (or ACEs).

These assign one or more privileges to a user or a group. These privileges define basic permissions required by all developers, such as for read and write access to files or for check-in. Privileges also contain permissions that are usually reserved for administrators, such as exporting, importing and integrating activities, and creating users and workspaces. ACLs and ACEs define user and group access to objects in DTR.

The file path is used to determine permissions. Permissions do not need to be defined for all files. A child hierarchy level inherits all permissions granted to a parent folder, unless permissions are assigned to it directly. Figure 10.11 shows the structure for managing permissions in DTR.

Inheriting permissions

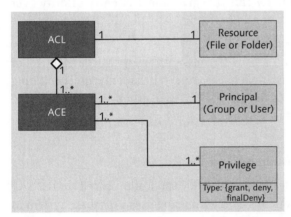

Figure 10.11 ACL Class Diagram — Organization of Permissions for User and Group Resources

You do not need to define ACLs for all files. However, you can define ACEs that exclude one another for the same resource, even if it does not make sense to do so. To ensure that a permission is unique for contradictory situations, permissions are interpreted according to a set of rules that is applied for all privileges independently of each other, but always in the sequence in which they are numbered.

▸ **Rule 1 — finalDeny before all children**

A privilege granted with `finalDeny` undoes all other ACEs that grant this privilege to this resource or to a child resource.[23]

Hierarchy of permission rules

---

23 You can use this rule to temporarily set a DTR workspace to read-only, without having to change each privilege individually.

▶ **Rule 2 — inheritance ignore**
This rule allows you to interrupt the inheritance hierarchy. A resource for which an `inheritance ignore` ACL is defined does not inherit any permissions from parent folders.

▶ **Rule 3 — child before parent**
This rule allows you to refine the permissions for resources in child resources.

▶ **Rule 4 — user before group**
This rule defines the priority for contradictory ACEs that are defined for the same resource. (As this rule is defined after Rule 3, it can only affect the same resource.) This rule gives the user entry priority over the group entry.

▶ **Rule 5 — deny before grant**
If there is a `grant` and a `deny` permission for a privilege, `deny` takes priority. As this rule is applied after rule 4, it can only affect colliding permissions for the same user or for user groups with a common member.

10.2.3 Component Build Service

Architecture and task of CBS

Component Build Service (CBS) is a J2EE application based on the SAP component model. It contains a build tool and uses a database system to manage archives. CBS is the central build environment of SAP NetWeaver Development Infrastructure. The build process is component based and is triggered for individual components at a developer's request. Figure 10.12 shows the Component Build Service architecture.

Managing build events in the database

Like DTR, CBS also runs on Java EE Engine and uses a database to store archives. The archives are organized in buildspaces. HTTP is used for communication. The CBS Web user interface and the **activation** view in SAP NetWeaver Developer Studio are available as user interfaces. A command line tool is also available for special administrative tasks. In addition, CMS can be considered as a user interface for CBS, because you can use it to control important actions in CBS, such as creating buildspaces.

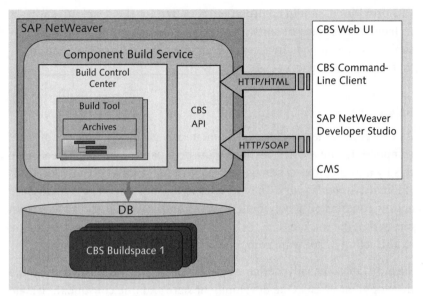

Figure 10.12 Architecture of CBS — Organization of Database Archives in Buildspaces, Client Accesses Using HTTP

In addition to building archives, CBS manages all archives that are required during development. These archives include the build results of the source files that are created by building source files, and the archives that already exist for the development. Archive management includes keeping them up-to-date. This is achieved by rebuilding all development components that depend on a specific development component whenever this development component is built. This is possible as the dependencies between the components are defined using the component model.

The built units are the development components. During the build, the dependencies between development components are checked. Use dependencies to all used development components must be defined, and they must be available in a usable software component. Cyclic dependencies are not allowed and will be detected. If the rebuild of dependent development components fails due to a change in the interfaces of the used development components, the development component receives the state Broken. This status is displayed in the Web user interface of CBS and must be corrected by the responsible developer.

Units of the build process

CBS provides the build environment required for the development tasks in hand. The choice of software components matches the product version to be developed. To access the archives, logical storage locations — that is, the buildspaces — are used.

Buildspace

Buildspace tasks

As CBS allows the parallel development of various versions of software components, the archive versions must be separated in CBS. You achieve this by defining logical storage locations in the database. These locations are known as *buildspaces*. They serve as virtual build servers. A buildspace always contains all newly built archives and all the used archives from one part of the track, either dev or cons. In other words, this can be a state of a selection of software components that together form a product.

Such a state is usually defined by the release of a product and by the development phase. One development state and one consolidation state is created for each product release, both of which are represented by one buildspace. A product consists of software components. A buildspace contains one *compartment* for each software component. Software components can be used in two ways.

▶ **Used software components**
These contain, for example, Basis libraries. They exist only in the archive state and cannot be changed.

▶ **Software components that are developed in this product version**
For these software components, there are source files in DTR and archives in CBS. The archives are generated by building development components that were created in this software component.

A buildspace, therefore, usually contains several software components that are stored in a compartment (a container for physical instances of components). In SLD, use dependencies are defined between the software components.

Workspaces and buildspaces

For each buildspace, there is a pair of workspaces in DTR. This pair of workspaces is called inactive and active, as described in Section 10.2.2. These workspaces are closely connected with the build process in CBS. Unlike the workspace, which contains pointers to objects in the database, each buildspace actually contains the archive files.

Build Processes — Activating Changes

The build process in CBS is not a build that tries to build the entire product. Instead, each developer decides when to build his changes — based on the respective activities. Activating an activity starts the build process for the relevant development components. This is possible because the use dependencies to other development components are known based on the metadata of each development component. Based on this information, the dependent development components of any development component can be determined and updated by an automatic build as soon as the used development component is changed. The nightly build, which can only build the dependent development components by building all development components, is no longer necessary because the dependencies are not transparent.

Tasks of the build process in CBS

The advantage of the component-based process is that you can build each section of the entire software individually. This is the technical prerequisite for conducting a build at the developer's request. This optimizes the waiting period of the individual developer for the results of the central build of his or her development components. It also has the following important effect. A failed central build of one component hardly affects other developers working on the same software project. Until the build is successful, the latest version of the archive remains active for all users, as does the source files, thanks to the activation concept. If the development situation so requires, you can also build all development components together in CBS.

The CBS build process uses the development component concept to perform three essential tasks:

- It creates the runtime objects. An essential advantage for the developer is that manual build scripts are no longer necessary. They are already available in the build tool and are used depending on the type of development component to be built.

Build scripts

- It introduces an extra check of the development. This is important because the build process checks whether the component model rules are adhered to. This also happens in the development component build in SAP NetWeaver Developer Studio, which uses the same build tool as CBS.

Checking the development components

▶ The main difference to the local build is that the objects required for the build process are retrieved exclusively from the central systems DTR and CBS.[24] This means that the system always checks whether the most up-to-date versions of all objects — source files and archives — are used.

Let's now look at an example of a build process (see also Figure 10.13): Assume that you want to build DC 2, which depends on DCs 1, 3, and 4. DC 2 consists of the four development objects a, b, c, and d and has already been successfully built once before (this is why it exists in both the inactive and active workspaces). You have an activity d, which contains changes to the development object d.

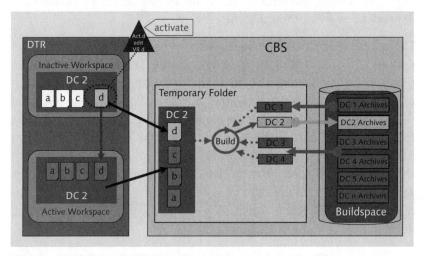

Figure 10.13 Build Process in CBS

The build process is as follows:

1. Choose Activate for activity d, which contains a new version of the file *d*.

2. A temporary folder is created for the build task.

3. Object d is retrieved from the inactive workspace.

---

24 Unlike the local build, the archives (or runtime objects) a developer has copied to his or her local file system can be changed during his or her work (provided that they are in a changeable software component).

4. Objects a, b, and c are retrieved from the `active` workspace. This ensures that the new version is compatible with the previously activated parts of DC 2.

5. Archives of the DCs A and B are retrieved from the buildspace. This ensures that the new version is compatible with the currently activated versions of the used development components.

6. The build process builds the new archive for DC 2.

7. The archives in the buildspace are updated. This is now the reference status for all developers on the team.

8. Once the build has been successfully completed, CBS automatically triggers the integration of activity d into the workspace `active`.

9. CBS then automatically starts the build process for development components that use the changed development component.

Figure 10.13 outlines the concept underlying activation. By retrieving all unchanged objects from the `active` workspace, these objects are successfully built. Only the new versions in the activated activity are added. All used development components that serve as archives are retrieved from the *Archive Pool* in the buildspace. This means that the latest version of all archives is automatically used.

Overall, the build process in the temporary folder of the build task provides a *preview* of the new state of the buildspace. This state can only be written to the database if the build process runs without errors.

Now, just one step in the activation process is missing: the activation of the source files. You already know that for each buildspace, there are two workspaces in DTR, the `inactive` and `active` workspaces. New objects are always created in the `inactive` workspace. Once these objects are successfully built in an activity, they are automatically integrated into the `active` workspace. As you mainly use source files from this workspace, you can be sure that this state is consistent with the latest state of the entire software project. Therefore, all development for a product is synchronized both at the source file and the archive levels.

Activating the source files

A few questions arise regarding the size of the developer team:

Provision for large teams

▶ Build processes are costly. What happens if several developers want to activate their changes?

CBS can form clusters. For very large teams, several instances of CBS that serve a common buildspace can be called via a dispatcher, which balances the load.

▶ What happens if a used development component is changed during a build process?

CBS automatically deals with this case. It identifies the change, builds the used development component first, and then restarts the build process of the dependent development component.

This question also crops up if a used development component is changed after the build process of the using development component. In this case, existing dependencies are determined by CBS and using development components are rebuilt if a relevant change has been made to a used development component. If the change was compatible, the using development component is now in the new state again. If not, the status of the using development component can be easily identified in the CBS Web user interface.[25] These automatic build processes that are triggered by CBS itself are known as *follow-up requests*. For more details, see Chapter 11, *SAP NetWeaver Development Infrastructure — Configuration and Administration*. These follow-up requests allow the status of the buildspace to be kept current at all times.

Build Variants

Tasks of build variants

CBS can generate different variants from the sources of a compartment (however, at least one variant must be defined for each compartment).

▶ Variants that differ in the choice of special parameters for the used compilers, for example, one *optimized* and one *debugging* variant.

▶ Variants that are designed for different operating systems or runtime environments. An example of this is the use of an NWDI for SAP NetWeaver release 7.0 for the development of applications for SAP NetWeaver CE. (The creation of this variant is described in detail in Section 12.3.4, *Creating, Configuring, and Preparing the Example Track*.)

▶ Variants that take account of special country-specific or language-specific characteristics.

---

25 For more details on dealing with DCs whose CBS-internal build has failed, go to *CBS Secrets Unveiled — Understanding Broken and Dirty DCs* in SDN (*http://sdn.sap.com*).

The development configuration defines a list of variants for each compartment — at least one variant must exist. Not all compartments must offer the same variants. If variants are defined for a compartment, the compartment provides specific libraries and deployable archives for each component and each variant (*build variants*). See Section 10.2.4, *Change Management Service*, for details on development configurations.

For example: A compartment determines that a software component SC X creates a *debugging* and an *optimized* variant. The only difference between the two variants is that the compilers and generators are called using different options. The variants have the identifiers dbg and opt. The component is also designed to support two different operating systems so that a total of four variants must be built: linux/dbg, linux/opt, win/dbg, and win/opt. Finally, the component is translated into different languages so that the number of variants must be multiplied by the number of supported languages: de/linux/dbg, en/linux/dbg, de/linux/opt, and so on.

Examples of build variants

When activating changes in the Build Service, all variants defined for a component compartment are built. However, all variants may not necessarily have to be built error-free to ensure successful activation.

Required variants

User Interfaces of Component Build Service

A number of different clients are available for CBS users.

▶ Developers use the following views in SAP NetWeaver Developer Studio:

Integrated CBS user interface for developers

  ▶ The **Activation View** shows the changes that can be built. Here, you can directly start the build process for all activities. As changes are only generally available after activation, you are prompted to start the activation when you check in an activity. (You can postpone this, however.)

  ▶ You can monitor the build process in the **request view**.

▶ In a Web browser, you can carry out administrative tasks in the CBS Web user interface. Here, you can view all available buildspaces and details on the following objects:

User interface for administrators

► **Buildspaces**
You see all compartments and their states (ready to accept input, building of build requests activated, etc.). Here, you can change the specified buildspace and compartment settings or delete buildspaces.[26] In the details, you see information on the development components, such as top-level DCs, broken DCs,[27] and so on.

► **Development components**
Here, you can search for development components that fulfill specific criteria such as name, buildspace, or vendor. You see details on the selected DCs, such as build status, child DCs, public parts, used development components, and you can also build the development components.

► **Activities**
Here, you can search for activities that fulfill specific criteria, for example, the timestamp, and call activities that are not yet activated. You can also enforce this even if the build fails.

► **Activation requests**
You find the build requests here.

► **Compartments**
You find information on buildspace compartments here.

► **Development components**
Here, you can search for development components that fulfill a number of different criteria.

CBS command
line client

► The CBS command line client is only used by administrators. Here, you can create buildspaces or build all development components of a compartment. However, most of these functions are usually performed in the CBS Web user interface or in CMS.[28]

► CMS can be regarded as a client of CBS as it is used by administrators to create buildspaces, which may be partially filled by imports.

---

26 You usually do this by deleting a track in CMS.

27 This information is important, because incompatible changes to interfaces in CBS also cause problems in the build process, which are recognized there.

28 In particular, this includes the creation of buildspaces, which is automatically carried out when a track is created.

10.2.4 Change Management Service

Change Management Service (CMS) is the environment used by administrators and quality managers of NWDI who look after development work in NWDI.

Architecture and Tasks of CMS

We have already seen that management mechanisms are available both for the source files and the archives and that they are tailored to the needs of the development task in hand. The workspaces and buildspaces required for the development phases *Development* and *Consolidation* must be created and the buildspaces must be filled. For both phases, test systems are also defined, and allow extensive testing of the entire application at an early stage. Like DTR and CBS, CMS is a J2EE application that runs in Java EE Engine of SAP NetWeaver. It also uses its own database schema, which can run on the same physical database with DTR and CBS.

As we can see in Figure 10.14, CMS also runs on Java EE Engine — like DTR and CBS — and it uses a database to store development configurations and transport requests. HTTP is used for communication. The user interfaces are the CMS Web user interface and the Transport View in Developer Studio. In addition to the API for CMS clients, SAP NetWeaver 7.0 Support Package Stack 12 also contains a connection to Change and Transport System (CTS) of the ABAP stack, which may also be used. For more information, see Section 11.3.4, *Non-ABAP-Based Transports in a Mixed System Landscape*.

All objects for each development phase of a product release (as a typical application example) are collectively known as *logical systems*. We refer to them as logical because no physical system is required for each of these systems. Instead, the workspaces and buildspaces of many development states may be in the same DTR or CBS. As the development and consolidation systems always belong together, we refer to these collectively as a *track*. Tracks are organized into *domains*. A domain is created for each vendor, and is managed in this vendor's CMS. Each CMS manages one domain. Domains are an organizational criterion for tracks. Domains contain the data required for the track management environment: Which SLD is used, on which server does CMS run?

Logical systems, domains, and tracks

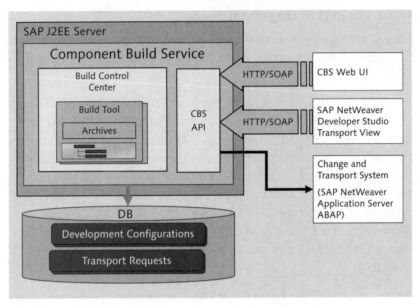

Figure 10.14 Architecture of CMS

Administrators are responsible for defining these logical systems and defining transport management into and between these systems. We can distinguish between two comprehensive tasks:

Landscape Configurator

▶ One area is comprised of the creation of logical development systems. They provide the development landscape for the respective development tasks and consist of the DTR workspaces, the buildspaces with the appropriate archives, and the related test systems. You carry out these tasks in CMS *Landscape Configurator*.

Transport Studio

▶ The second area is comprised of transports and processes related to software logistics. You use CMS *Transport Studio* for these tasks.

Before we discuss the individual tasks in detail, let's take at look at the software logistics process as a whole. Figure 10.15 shows the structure of the logical development systems and the transport tasks in the development process. Section 11.3.4, *Non-ABAP-Based Transports in a Mixed System Landscape*, describes how these elements are integrated into a transport landscape that also comprises ABAP systems. The sections that follow focus solely on a Java-based landscape.

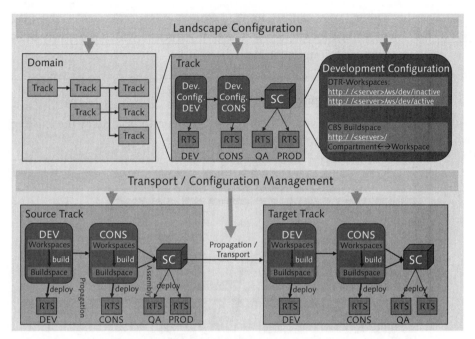

Figure 10.15 Software Logistics Processes

We will first look at *Landscape Configurator* in CMS:

1. Start by defining a domain for the development.

2. In this domain, you define tracks for each product release.

3. Tracks contain logical development systems for development and consolidation. Each of these systems is defined in a development configuration. This, in turn, determines workspaces, buildspaces, and the runtime systems used.

   Track

   ▶ Once you define a track, the following tasks must be carried out in Transport Studio. The used software components are checked in and imported into the buildspaces as archives.

   ▶ When the new software component is being developed, the consolidation state is supplied from the development state.

   ▶ After approval and assembly, the result of a track is a Software Component Archive that is deployed in runtime systems (RTS: Request to Send) for testing purposes and will be shipped at a later stage.

▶ Other tracks can be supplied from one (source) track — this may be a track for the next release, or a track in which the newly built software component is used.

Landscape Configurator

Settings in Landscape Configurator As administrator, you use Landscape Configurator to display the existing tracks and to create new ones (Figure 10.16).

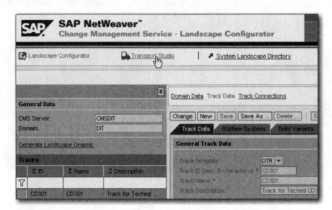

Figure 10.16 CMS Landscape Configurator — Track Data

In the introduction to NWDI, we stated that development always starts from the product point-of-view. Consequently, software logistics in CMS also adhere to this model. You create a new track for each new product release.

All the settings required for development are contained in the track. (See Section 10.3.1, to fill in the values.)

Step 1 1. **Creating the domain**

You create the domain once when you set up CMS during the installation process. The domain defines the vendor's CMS area. The vendor owns a software component. A domain definition contains the following elements:

▶ **Name of the domain**

This value is entered in the Configuration Wizard (see Section 11.1).

- ► CMS name, description, and URL

- ► **CMS user and CMS password**
  A CMS user is required for communication between NWDI components. Once a user has logged on, the user ID is used to connect to DTR, CBS, and CMS. To be able to do this, a user requires configuration permission in SAP User Management Engine.

- ► **Transport directory**
  Files for the import into a track are stored here.

When you define the domain, you also download information on the existing software components. You need this to receive information on the available (usable) software components, as you need these to create the track.

2. **Defining the track**
   As an administrator, you define the logical systems for the development and consolidation of a release, as follows:

   Step 2

   - ► **Track name and description**
     This information helps you obtain an overview in the administrator's Web user interfaces. You also define the name of the resulting development configurations here, which will help guide development.

   - ► **Repository type**
     Here, you can choose between the DTR and the XI repository (the latter is only required if you are using CMS to transport Exchange Infrastructure objects).[29]

   - ► **URL for DTR and CBS**
     The workspace folders, workspaces, and buildspaces are automatically generated based on these entries. The DTR client is generated. It has the same name as the track, with the extension _D for development and _C for consolidation. It contains a filter that only displays the inactive and active workspaces that belong to this development phase. The write permission is only valid for the inactive workspace. Both the inactive and active workspaces are in a hierarchy of workspace folders with the (a) name of the

     Default URLs for DTR and CBS

---

29 Before you select the second option, note the transport options described in Section 11.3.4.

track, (b) name of the software component to be developed, and (c) the development phase. The buildspace names include (a) the track ID, (b) the track name, and (c) the identifier of the development phase as the extension. You can change these settings for each track. As demand increases, you can add DTR and CBS servers to NWDI.

You now define the software components that make up the product release. You use two tables to do this:

▶ The table of software components for the development: Here, you select the software components that contain the functions specific to this product. These software components include the release information, and were only selected from the software components that were loaded from SLD. As of Support Package 13, you can also enter a temporary definition in CMS (see Section 10.3.4). You also define one of the following shipment formats: archives, source files, or source files and archives.

▶ The table for the used (required) software components: The dependencies are defined in and read from SLD. You are only allowed to select the available software component releases from a list of existing software components in special cases. In this case, you must manually modify the defining XML file.

Step 3   3. **Defining the runtime systems**
You can define runtime systems for all four development phases. These phases are development, consolidation, test, and production. You define the systems by entering the following information:

▶ **SDM host name and port number**
SDM stands for Software Deployment Manager, which deploys the runtime objects (archives) into the runtime systems. The Composition Environment server contains the server deploy tool instead of SDM.

▶ **Information on J2EE Engine**
This is required to enable you to correctly use Java Support Package Manager (JSPM) with NWDI.

▶ **Password**
Only some users are allowed to deploy into all systems. Enter the valid password for the target system.

4. **Defining the track connections**

Step 4

We have already described two different statuses of software components in development: used software components and new software components. There are two cases in which new software components are used in a different track:

▶ The product extends into the next release: The same software component is developed further, and the same software components continue to be used.

▶ The new software component becomes the used software component in another track that is developed in parallel: During the development phase, versions of the software component developed in the source track are continually imported as used software components into the target track.

Transport Studio

Once the logical development systems have been defined, you switch to Transport Studio (Figure 10.17), because your next task is to use these systems to provide the used objects centrally to all developers on the team that develops this product release.

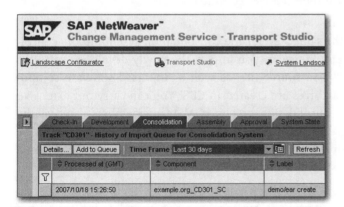

Figure 10.17 Transport Studio — Test and Production are Optional

In this studio, the user interface reflects the order in which the required steps must be executed:

Setting up a development landscape

1. **Check-in**

   In this step, you check in all used software components as archives, as they will not be changed. Specify the name of the *Software Component Archive* (SCA) file of each software component used. The archives must be available in the transport directory of CMS. You select them from a list. The software component details contain the following information:

   ▶ **Component**
   Name of the software component

   ▶ **Release**
   The release is determined by the information in the track definition.

   ▶ Patch level, Support Package number and version of the archive

2. **Development**

   The selected archives are now listed for the development system. You can import the archives that you checked in the last step. They are now available in the buildspace for the development phase. Developers can test their activated results here, if a runtime system is assigned to this phase. As deployment is usually carried out at activation, the state of the runtime changes continually.

3. **Consolidation**

   You repeat the same step for the consolidation system. In the consolidation system, however, you import the newly developed software component[30] as a source file, as well as the used software components. New archives are created in CBS. You can carry out extensive tests in the consolidation system. QM team members can test the imported results if a runtime system is assigned to this phase. As the import is controlled by the administrator, the state can be retained until the tests have been completed.

Preparing shipment

4. **Assembly**

   The shipment version is created once the consolidation tests have been carried out. The shipment is created from imported and new archives, and from the source files, depending on the decisions made by management. Shipping source files is of course a prerequisite for

---

30 In DTR, the activities are integrated from the `dev active` to the `cons inactive` workspace.

modifications at the customer site. The corresponding setting in CMS enables or disables these modifications. The result of assembly is a deployable *Software Component Archive* (SCA).

5. **Testing**
Runtime objects that are included in the assembly step for SCAs are distributed in a central test system, if one has been defined. If not, this tab is not displayed.

6. **Approval**
The results of the assembly must now be approved. Approval for the shipment will, of course, depend on the SCA test results. The live runtime system is displayed here if it has been defined.

7. **Production**
This corresponds to the test system. Track connections can be used to connect several live systems that will be allocated the same version as the software.

8. **System state**
You can use this additional option to check the state of all systems at any time. Here, you see which version of the software is available in the different systems.

Checking the system states

Once you have carried out these steps, the development cycle is completed. No new physical systems need to be created for Support Packages, the next release or for a new product. You just need to define them in SLD and create new tracks in CMS.

Development Configurations

The creation of a new track results in two development configurations that describe the development and consolidation system. Each development configuration has an XML file. In addition to the information you specified when creating the track, this contains the following information you entered when defining the product release in SLD.

Defining developer access to central systems and resources

▶ **Information from SLD**
Above all, this includes the use dependencies between the software components. As already outlined in Section 10.2.1, *Component Model*, you can only use another software component for software components if this use has already been defined.

> ▶ **Information from CMS**
>
> As already outlined, this includes above all information on the using workspaces, the relevant buildspace, and CMS and test systems.

Example of development configuration

Figure 10.18 shows an example of a development configuration for the development state of Version 1.0 of the product **Online Sales**. The following information is displayed, which defines a developer's access to NWDI using SAP NetWeaver Developer Studio, and the objects managed in NWDI: The URL of the CBS, CMS, and Name Service used. You can see that the *Online Sales* software component uses the *Business Functions* and *TECH* software components. The DTR workspaces used are also displayed.

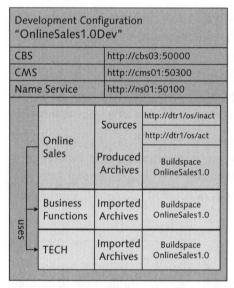

Figure 10.18 Development Configuration Online Sales — Defining Accesses to Source Files and Archives

The developer imports the XML file of each development configuration into SAP NetWeaver Developer Studio. This configures Developer Studio in such a way that it accesses only the objects required for the relevant development task. As described in Section 10.2.2 on DTR, the development configuration defines the DTR clients used to develop the product release.

10.2.5 Overview of the Development Process

We will now take a look at the entire development process contained in SAP NetWeaver Developer Studio and SAP NetWeaver Development Infrastructure. The effects of the described concepts have on the processes controlled by the developer will be focused on, which have not yet been discussed in detail.

Impacts of the component model and central system administration

A product release is defined with the corresponding software components and the track is stored in CMS. The development process starts when one of the development configurations is imported into SAP NetWeaver Developer Studio. Figure 10.19 shows the local development environment with the SAP NetWeaver Developer Studio interface — this is important, because the user interface displays a combined view of local and central objects, although the installation is local — and the central NWDI.

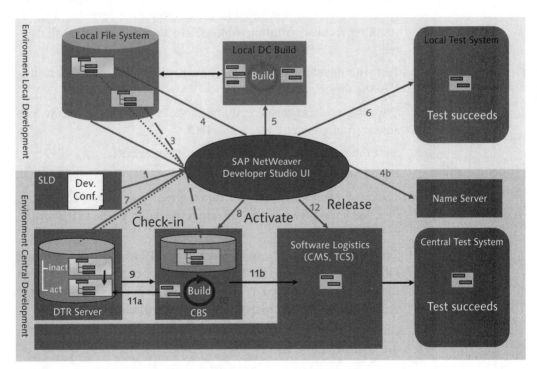

Figure 10.19 Development Process with SAP NetWeaver Developer Studio and SAP NetWeaver Development Infrastructure

513

Development steps For the developer, the development process covers the following steps:

1. Set up your environment: Use SLD to import a development configuration. To start, all you need is its URL and the name of the configuration.

2. Synchronize (download) the source files from DTR (Sync).

3. Synchronize (download) the archives from CBS (Sync).[31]

4. Make the required changes. New objects are now created, or existing objects are checked out and changed.[32] Name Service is called when new objects (development components or packages) are created, to ensure that the names assigned are unique.

5. Run the local build process: Start the local build of the development component in SAP NetWeaver Developer Studio. Source files and archives are retrieved from the file system. The new archives are built — the build tool is the same as the one in CBS — and the same checks are carried out, to build the development components. The resulting archives (runtime objects) are stored in the local file system.

6. Test your development. You can now deploy the archives for testing into the local Java EE Engine.

7. Once the test has run successfully, check in the new versions (which are saved in your activities), into DTR.

8. Start the central build process of your components.

9. Now activate your activity.

10. The new objects are retrieved from the `inactive` workspace. Source files that have already been built are retrieved from the `active` workspace.

11. The build starts with the source files from DTR and the archives from CBS. Activation is automatically triggered once the build has been successfully completed. The new archives are automatically deployed into the test system for the development phase.

12. Once the central test has been successful, release your activities for the next steps in CMS.

---

31 Steps 2 and 3 are automatically carried out when you create a project.

32 You need a project, to change existing development components during synchronization. You can carry out both steps together using Create Project in Developer Studio.

Once your objects have been released, your development work for this phase is complete. Further steps are carried out in CMS for consolidation, that is, the import into the consolidation system followed by the relevant tests.

The last phase of the process is comprised of *assembly* of the shipment and *approval*. The release cycle is then complete. The next cycle starts with the definition of the next release in SLD.

Steps after the development phase

10.3 New Features in SAP NetWeaver Development Infrastructure

SAP NetWeaver 7.0 Support Package Stack 13, which supports unrestricted development in SAP NetWeaver CE 7.1, contains a number of new and improved functions for SAP NetWeaver Development Infrastructure. It is recommended that you use this, or a more recent release, with SAP NetWeaver Composition Environment, as it is the first release that supports the management of deployment using the modified deployment tool of the new NWDI SAP NetWeaver release. In addition to improvements in general system performance, you can now configure the entire NWDI and availability of functions offered by individual components. The basic concepts of NWDI remain unchanged, and the NWDI version remains independent of the managed software states. The following sections provide a brief overview of new features, and provide experienced NWDI users with a quick guide to the changes that have been made.

10.3.1 Configuring the DI Usage Type After Installation

Just like previous versions, SAP NetWeaver 7.0 Support Package Stack 13 supports a Configuration Wizard, which guides you through the steps required to configure NWDI (and other usage types of SAP NetWeaver) after installation. This process is more flexible in Support Package Stack 13. When you enter changeable data, you can now change a number of different values during the configuration process. Up to now, you could only change passwords at this stage. The following values are interesting in this context:

Flexible configuration of NWDI

> ▸ You can enter the domain ID. The default value is the SID of the CMS installation.

> ▸ You can assign your own names to an initial track and the product, including the software component.

> ▸ A number of track templates are available. These can also be used once you have made the initial configuration settings for NWDI using this wizard. The required software components are stored in the track template.

10.3.2 New Features in Design Time Repository

Fusions — summaries of files for version creation units

In DTR, file versions are created across repository boundaries. During version creation, it is sometimes necessary to treat a group of files as one unit. In DTR, this unit is known as a *fusion*. In this case, there is only one version graph for the entire group. If a file is changed, the entire group is checked out of DTR.

If a group of this type is changed simultaneously by two users, a conflict will be reported even if the changes affect different files in the fusion (for more information on conflicts in DTR, see Section 10.2.2). Fusions are also used as units to propagate changes. In this context, only entire groups can be added to an activity, integrated into other workspaces, or exported to the file system. All of these features are used to put files, which belong together logically, under version control as a group. This is particularly useful in Web-Dynpro-based development, and allows you to logically group projects that contain manual and generated changes, so that the reconciliation of objects that are manually created and generated can be improved in modification scenarios.

Fusion scenario

In the example provided in Figure 10.20, there is no conflict at the file level:

> ▸ Phase 1: An application from files 1 and 2 is shipped.

> ▸ Phase 2: File 1* is produced in location A. File 2 is changed to 2* in location B.

> ▸ Phase 3: Shipment of the modified software

▸ Phase 4: Version 1* can be integrated without any conflict arising. However, its semantics do not necessarily match version 2*. Although there is no conflict at the file level, there is a logical conflict.

▸ As we can see in Figure 10.20, the group formed by files 1 and 2 is viewed as an entity in a fusion, and this type of conflict is therefore recognized.

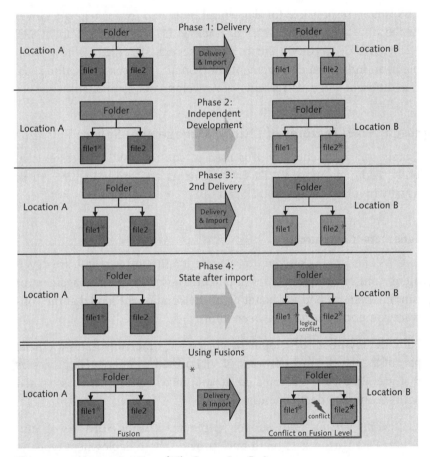

Figure 10.20 Version Creation of File Groups in a Fusion — Conflict Recognition Across File Boundaries

Fusions are primarily used in model-driven development. The use of fusions has already been implemented for Web Dynpro projects. Fusions are automatically created, if required. They prove particularly

Areas in which fusions are used

useful when reconciling the model. You may need to do this, for example, if iViews are added simultaneously by different users. As the conflict is automatically recognized, the merge is reliably detected, and more effective support provided.

10.3.3 New Features of Component Build Service

CBS is now responsible for the central build and for managing archives in the development process. Together with Developer Studio in SAP NetWeaver Composition Environment, several SDA files are now possible in an individual development component. This can be used to separate different language versions of a development component.

10.3.4 New Features of Change Management Service

Change Management Service is used to control NWDI processes centrally. Although most NWDI enhancements are visible in CMS, these usually involve changes in DTR and CBS.

Landscape Configurator

In CMS Landscape Configurator, you define the software you are developing, and determine the development landscape. The management of runtime systems and the handling of the component model at the software component level have been improved.

Deployment from NWDI tracks in runtime systems

Fully deploying all development objects on time constitutes a crucial part of the development process. NWDI provides deployment processes that are almost fully automated, to minimize the problems associated with incomplete deployment.

▶ Previous versions only support deployment using SDM. As of Support Package Stack 13, each track provides both deployment types — SDM and Deploy Controller.

▶ A configuration wizard allocates runtime systems to a track. It also identifies which deployment tool is available in the specified message server. To do this, it needs the server's HTTP port, which you can determine by selecting **Problem Management · Infrastructure Man-**

agement · Message Server · Show: Message Server Parameters · Parameter: ms/http_port in SAP NetWeaver Administrator, for example.

When you develop software based on the component model, you must take account of dependencies between software components. Maintaining this data is now easier and more flexible.

Dependencies between software components

▶ You can create temporary dependencies of the build time type directly in CMS, if it is currently not possible to reconcile elements with SDL data. The status of synchronization with SLD is displayed and can be carried out manually.

▶ Build variants can be defined for specific software components. In addition to the standard variants, other build variants can be defined, as can different system-specific standard variants with a variety of build options for development systems, consolidation systems, or all systems together. To save new build variants, they must be assigned to a software component. Section 12.3.4 provides a practical example.

CMS Transport Studio

The transports into the systems that you have previously defined are carried out in Transport Studio. The following improvements have been made:

▶ It is now easier to restore the state of CMS if the system fails unexpectedly. The status of import and assembly processes that are terminated is automatically set to `Failed`. It is now easier to view the system status, and no manual steps are required. CBS buildspaces are reset to `Open`, and all track and domain locks are released.

Increased robustness

▶ When you check in SCAs, you can now choose to search for SCA versions in a tree.

▶ An import check consists of a test import, which identifies any conflicts and import errors before the import is carried out. It may take some time to identify these problems.

▶ The SCA export directly provides SCAs for download using the Web user interface from each import queue.

▶ For development and consolidation systems, a snapshot of the active versions is used in each case. A consistent SCA version cannot be guaranteed.

▶ In the assembly step, the most recently assembled state of the software component is used.

Flexibility during assembly
▶ In the assembly step, you can specify whether the process will stop if an error occurs, and if so, for which type of error. You can also choose whether assembly will ignore inconsistent software components.

This option proves particularly useful if you assemble several software components at once. If problems are encountered with a software component, the entire process no longer terminates. Options include broken DCs (that reference a used public part that is incompatible, for example), dirty DCs (that still have to be built), or unresolved conflicts.

> **Note**
>
> This setting is an expert mode. The problems described should be resolved before the assembly step is actually carried out. Therefore, the default setting is that none of the problems are to be ignored. Figure 10.21 shows the dialog. 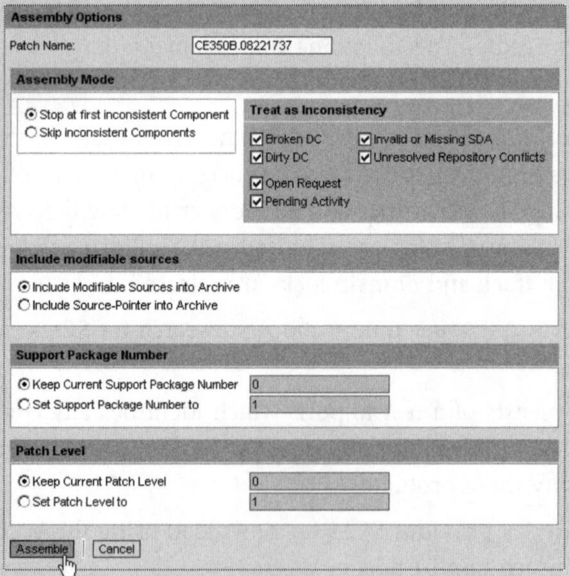
>
>
> **Figure 10.21** Assembly Dialog

▶ It is now considerably easier to update existing tracks in CMS, as an unnecessary rebuild of the buildspace is no longer triggered. Deletion and reimport in the development configuration settings in Developer Studio are no longer necessary.

Saving time when making track changes

▶ You can now create system messages for tracks or create development configurations that are displayed in Developer Studio and use the relevant systems.

▶ You can use the **advanced operations** of a deploy servlet (for more details, see Section 10.3.5, *Improvements in NWDI Logging*), to upgrade systems to a specific software release in a user-friendly manner.

Transporting XI objects, that is, objects with the usage type PI, is one of the tasks that can be carried out by an NWDI. This feature has also been improved. Now, change requests are transported directly from the consolidation system (CONS) to the approval stage. The assembly step is optional. This means that it is now also possible to transport change requests between tracks. You can use the **Import All Good** option, to have CMS import as many objects as possible. Only objects that contain errors will be kept in the import queue. In this context, we also recommend that you carry out the transport in this release in the extended ABAP Change and Transport System (for more information, see Section 11.3.4, *Non-ABAP-Based Transports in a Mixed System Landscape*).

Improvements to PI transports

10.3.5 Improvements in NWDI Logging

To effectively manage processes, it is crucial that you can track all steps. Improvements have, therefore, been made to the NWDI logging function. A deploy servlet is now available for *auto-deployment logging*. To call this servlet, go to *http://<host>:<port>/TCS/Deployer* (Figure 10.22). The following functions are available for displaying the status of development components.

Enhanced monitoring of buildspaces

▶ Testing the deployment status. This involves the following aspects:

▶ Transport Control System (TCS) reads a build request, including the follow-up requests, up to the deployable results. It displays these results with the return value.

▶ You can navigate directly to the deployment log files.

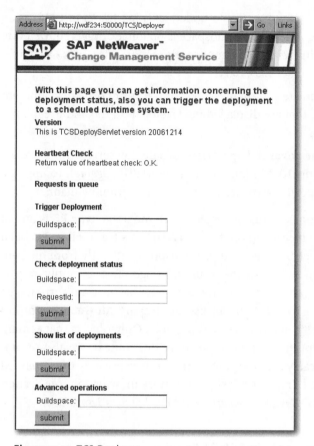

Figure 10.22 TCS Deployer

- ▶ Listing the deployments. This covers all deployments for any CBS buildspace and their results.

Additional deploy-ment options
- ▶ Advanced operations. These can only be used by users with extensive permissions. They include the following actions:
  - ▷ Interventions in the deploy queue of CBS buildspaces, in particular the deletion of deploy requests. This requires the new UME action TCS.CriticalFunctions.
  - ▷ The highest saved request number can be displayed. This can be used, for example, to control a CBS recovery or a CBS move.
  - ▷ Enhanced messages now differentiate between requests that do not exist in CBS, and requests that are not available.

10.3.6 New Features on the Interfaces

The interface design of SAP NetWeaver Development Infrastructure has been improved. For example, a clearer differentiation is now made between tracks, track connections, and domain data in Change Management Service tracks, and buttons are now available to toggle between change and display modes. Outgoing track connections are now displayed by default. The required software components are now displayed more clearly, as only direct dependencies are now displayed. You can now maintain track-specific permissions on the NWDI initial screen.

Differentiation between track and domain data

10.4 SAP NetWeaver Development Infrastructure and Component Model in Composition Environment

This book focuses primarily on the use of SAP NetWeaver Composition Environment 7.1. Therefore, a key question is whether SAP NetWeaver Development Infrastructure release 7.0 can be used in this environment? Yes, it can. As explained previously, NWDI is more or less independent of the version of the software being managed. This means that any NWDI version can basically contain CE tracks in addition to other tracks.

> **Note**
>
> One restriction does apply to earlier versions of NWDI, however. Not only does NWDI handle the saving of and access to source files and archives, it is also responsible for deployment to runtime systems in the development, consolidation, test, and production phases. The deployment tool called by NWDI has changed in SAP NetWeaver CE. In other words, Software Deployment Manager (SDM) has been replaced. The new deployment function can only run automatically in an NWDI, as was previously the case, as of SAP NetWeaver release 7.0, Support Package Stack 13. In Composition Environment, it is therefore recommended that at least this release of NWDI be used.

10.4.1 Scenarios for Component-Based Software Development in Composition Environment

As we have already seen, NWDI development is based on software components and development components that define the structure of all applications by determining mutual dependencies. Both the setting up of development landscapes for individual software projects and the development activities themselves — from the creation of new Eclipse projects to the local and central build process — follow the SAP component model.

Role of the component model in SAP-specific development

This is important to know, as it is possible to develop standard software on a non-component basis in SAP NetWeaver Developer Studio. This does have certain limitations, however, within the framework of the overall SAP environment. For example, it is difficult to draw up a modification concept for customers without using an NWDI- or component-based approach. Moreover, SAP-specific project types such as composite applications are based on the component model. (For more information, see Chapter 9, *Developing Composite Applications*.) If you do not use the component model in this context, two projects cannot use each other. The component model must be used for Web Dynpro projects that reuse elements in other Web Dynpro projects.

Before we look at scenarios, we will mention one more exception — the development of Guided Procedures.

Guided Procedures (GPs)

Exception in the development process

Guided Procedures are browser-based developments that are based on the component model. NWDI is integrated using a workaround that involves an export from the Guided Procedures Design Time. In Developer Studio, create a development component of the type **Content • Guided Procedure**, and copy the contents from the GP design environment using the copy and paste function. In this way, Guided Procedures can be shipped as SCAs. Check-in and activation are then carried out. The build process packs the GP objects into an SDA. The final steps then include release for transport, assembly, and, where applicable, automatic deployment.

Although NWDI developments are now entirely component-based, the component model can also be used without NWDI. Consequently, there are three scenarios for development using SAP NetWeaver Composition Environment:

▶ **Development that is not based on the component model and NWDI**
As described in the other chapters in this book, standard Java/J2EE applications can be developed without any restrictions. You have full control over version control, the build process, and deployment. DTR can be used for version control, in which case, DTR workspaces are created and managed manually.

Standard development only

▶ **Component-based development with local development configuration and optional external infrastructure**
All project types, including SAP-specific projects such as Web Dynpro, can be developed without any restriction. SLD is not used — you do not create products, you create software components and development components in SAP NetWeaver Developer Studio. Development components and software components (for example, the packing of development components into SCAs for shipment) are handled directly in Developer Studio or — particularly for team developments — using command line tools that are shipped with SAP NetWeaver Developer Studio. You can use SAP NetWeaver CE Developer Studio to create development configurations and distribute them as a file. You are free to choose tools, for version control, for example. Name reservation in an SLD is optional.

Standard and SAP development without development process requirements

Even if NWDI services are not used here, or are only used as an option or to some extent — the available command line tools and the Developer Studio functions described below are part of the development infrastructure.

▶ **Component-based development with NWDI**
All of the functions mentioned in the chapters on NWDI are available as described. This includes landscape configuration and software logistics in CMS, version control (including automated conflict control), modification-relevant mechanisms in DTR (including, for example, the use of fusions in Web Dynpro development), and the advantages of the CBS build process.

SAP development process

As far as NWDI usage is concerned, all concepts remain unchanged. SAP NetWeaver release 7.0 is still a satisfactory NWDI release. Support Package Stack 13 is required, due to the switchover to SAP NetWeaver CE in deployment. This ensures that you can avail of all functions outlined in the sections describing NWDI's improvements and new features. As applications developed on SAP NetWeaver CE platform require a different version of Java Development Kit than SAP NetWeaver 7.0 (1.5.xx instead of 1.4.xx), certain settings must be configured in NWDI, to use both variants. For more information on setting up a track for SAP NetWeaver CE, see Section 11.2.3, *Preparing a Track*.

Only the second scenario is of interest here. The third scenario is dealt with in the chapters on developing with NWDI (Chapters 10, 11, and 12), and almost all other chapters cover the first scenario.

10.4.2 Component-Based Development with a Local Development Configuration and Optional External Infrastructure

Minimal requirements for SAP-specific development

The scenario of component-based development with optional external infrastructure allows the development of all project types in the form of development components, without any restrictions. All concepts such as public parts and use dependencies work in the same way as for NWDI. This approach allows you the greatest flexibility when developing in Composition Environment, but does not ensure the integration of all steps, as is the case in NWDI. A modification concept is not available in the standard version of this scenario, but can be enabled, for example, if DTR is used by both the software vendor and customer, to manage source files in a more simple setting than the one described. We distinguish between two different levels:

▶ When developing software with a local development configuration on just one PC, the functions offered by Developer Studio and the file system are sufficient.

▶ For team-based developments, mechanisms are required, to synchronize work within the team. Shared access to a file system is the minimum requirement. To enable a central build and assembly process for components without NWDI, SAP also provides a command line tool in the Development Studio shipment.

Alternatively, you can integrate your own processes into this scenario. One example of this is when you use a system for version control.

Another example is the shared repository (part of the Visual Composer server), which provides check-in and check-out mechanisms.

Creating a local development configuration

You need a development configuration to work with the component model. If you do not use an NWDI, to generate the configuration centrally, you can create the configuration locally, that is, in Developer Studio of SAP NetWeaver Composition Environment. Just like an NWDI development configuration, you define the development framework, and your definition can be distributed to other team members. As the build process is carried out locally in Developer Studio or externally in a command line tool based on the component model, all dependencies must be dealt with in the same way as if you were using an NWDI. You are free to use an infrastructure for source file management and for the build process.

Local variants in the centrally controlled development landscape

In the **Component Browser** View of the **Development Infrastructure** Perspective, you can use SAP NetWeaver Composition Environment to create development components and development configurations. The following example shows a local development configuration of a pure standard development.

> **Note**
>
> For a development example, you also need the FRAMEWORK software component, if you want to work locally with the component model, to ensure that you can also use the SAP-specific DC type dictionary.

1. In the Component Browser context menu, select **New • Development Configuration** (Figure 10.23). The option Create DC is not offered as an option before a development configuration has been created.

2. Select create **from scratch**, enter a name, and from the list of available software components, select the software components you require that cannot be changed in this development configuration (Figure 10.24). Enter the URL of the name server, if you are using an NWDI, and choose **Finish**, to complete creation.

Defining the basis for a development

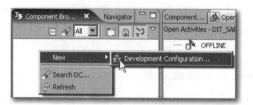

Figure 10.23 Creating a Development Configuration

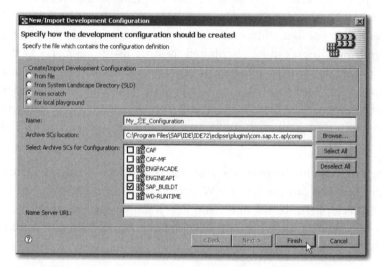

Figure 10.24 Creating a Development Configuration from Scratch

3. A local development configuration is generated. So far, it only contains the required software components that form the basis of the application. In the next step, you create the software component(s) that you wish to develop.

Defining the software to be developed

4. Create a new software component (Figure 10.25). In the Component Browser context menu, select **New • Software Component**.

Figure 10.25 Creating a New Software Component

5. On the screen that appears, enter the properties of the software components. A new screen appears (Figure 10.26).

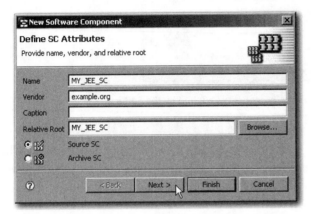

Figure 10.26 Properties of the New Software Component

Here, you enter the dependencies for the new software component, as follows:

▶ Enter a name (in upper case), and use your company's Internet ID as the vendor name.

▶ Enter a function description for the software component (optional).

▶ Create the software components that you wish to develop as the **Source SC**. Use the option **Archive SC** for software components that you wish to import from outside Developer Studio, to use them subsequently.

6. Accept your entries with **Next**.

7. In the new dialog box that appears (Figure 10.27), select the software components that you wish to use from the new software component. In this example, all of the software components used at the start are selected. However, you can also distribute these across two software components that you want to develop, or add dependencies to other new software components.

8. Select **Finish**, to complete the process.

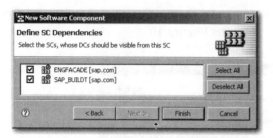

Figure 10.27 Software Components Required by the Software Component to be Developed

The development configuration is now ready for the development. The only difference between these development steps and the development steps for component-based development is that there is no communication with NWDI services.

The result of this development is a Software Component Archive (SCA file). This can be deployed, but can also be used or changed in a new development configuration. You can export your developments in this type of local development configuration as an SCA file.

Exporting a Software Component

Shipping the software

Start the export, to deploy or pass on your development.

1. To export a software component, select **Export** from the context menu of this component (Figure 10.28).

Figure 10.28 Exporting a Software Component from a Local Development Configuration

2. Enter information for the export, as shown in Figure 10.29. Information on the release, for example, can be changed. In this context, you

should exclude from the export development components that have the status Broken, and cannot be built.

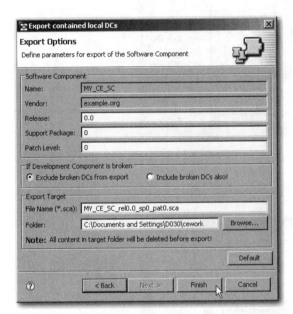

Figure 10.29 Information for Exporting a Software Component

3. The SCA files are located in the path in your PC's file system that has just been displayed (Figure 10.30).

Completed software package

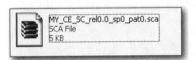

Figure 10.30 Software Component Archive File

Exporting a Development Configuration

Like software components, the local development configuration can also be exported. This is the first step for developing software in a team, to define the software components that are required and are to be developed, thereby ensuring that all team members start from the same basis.

Keeping team development simple

1. Select **Export as File...** in the context menu of a development configuration (Figure 10.31).

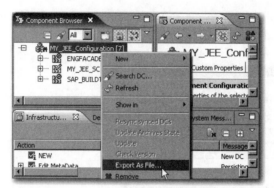

Figure 10.31 Exporting a Local Development Configuration

2. Save the **Export** file (Figure 10.32).

Figure 10.32 Export File of a Local Development Configuration

3. The SCA files are located in the displayed path in your PC's file system (Figure 10.33).

Figure 10.33 Export File of a Local Development Configuration

File-based distribution of the configuration among the team

4. From this directory, you can distribute the development configuration as a file among the team, using an email attachment or a file share.

5. You can use the **from file** import to load this development configuration to other Developer Studios.

Using the Command Line Tools

You can continue working on components using command line tools that are available in the Developer Studio installation directory under *\eclipse\tools\nwcetool*. Among other things, this allows you to build development components, and pack archives.

Extending the configuration in the team

1. This process is described in the SAP NetWeaver Developer Studio documentation for SAP NetWeaver Composition Environment 7.1. Go to *Composition Environment Command Line Tool* (Figure 10.34).

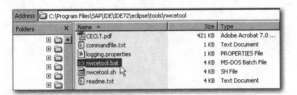

Figure 10.34 Calling the Command Line Tool

2. Set up access, as described in the tool (Figure 10.35).

```
Microsoft Windows XP [Version 5.1.2600]
(C) Copyright 1985-2001 Microsoft Corp.

C:\Program Files\SAP\IDE\IDE72\eclipse\tools\nwcetool>nwcetool.bat help
Incorrect usage, the following environment variables must be set:

NWCETOOLLIB:    must point to the "lib" folder that contains required Jars.
JAVA_HOME:      must point to the installation folder of a
                Java SDK installation

C:\Program Files\SAP\IDE\IDE72\eclipse\tools\nwcetool>_
```

Figure 10.35 Setting up the Command Line Tool

3. Configure the settings of the NWCETOOLLIB and JAVA_HOME variables, to finish configuring the command line tool. Figure 10.36 shows the available functions.

4. You can use this command to organize teamwork. Here are a few examples:

   ▶ The buildalldcs command can be used to build development components that are stored in a central directory.

   ▶ The importsca command can be used, to import a software component.

   ▶ The help <command> command provides a description of the relevant command for usage and syntax.

Figure 10.36 Functions of the Command Line Tool

Continuing on from Chapter 10, you will now learn more details concerning the configuration and administration of SAP NetWeaver Development Infrastructure. In addition to basic activities, we will discuss issues and recommendations related to track design, the modification of software, followed by reconciliation using the implementation of Support Packages, and the setting up of NWDI in ABAP/Java system landscapes and for global use.

11 SAP NetWeaver Development Infrastructure — Configuration and Administration

As you already know, SAP NetWeaver Development Infrastructure (NWDI) provides comprehensive functions that support you in developing and maintaining Java-based software using SAP NetWeaver Application Server Java. In this chapter, you will learn how to set up SAP NetWeaver Development Infrastructure, to develop an example project in this environment.

We will focus on the steps required to set up and configure NWDI, to ensure that a fully operational NWDI is installed on your PC by the end of this chapter. Theoretical explanations are given where they are most helpful. There are, of course, a few tasks that you have to execute repeatedly during the first setup and in your daily work.

Topics dealt with in this chapter

Here, however, we will only look at the setup process, and describe the administrative processes during development. An end-to-end practical example is provided in Chapter 12, *SAP NetWeaver Development Infrastructure — Developing an Example Application Step-by-Step.* General notes on other SAP Software Change Management mechanisms — that is, functions that allow you to manage software development and system states, set them up in large-scale development landscapes, and permit their interaction with NWDI — are provided at the end of the chapter.

11.1 Configuring SAP NetWeaver Development Infrastructure

SAP NetWeaver 7.0 DI and Composition Environment

SAP NetWeaver Development Infrastructure primarily is comprised of three building blocks, *Change Management Service* (CMS), *Design Time Repository* (DTR), and *Component Build Service* (CBS). There is also *System Landscape Directory* (SLD), which is used as the central information management system for the system landscape data of several other SAP NetWeaver components.

At the time of publication of this book, you will use SAP NetWeaver Composition Environment 7.1 together with an NWDI on SAP NetWeaver release 7.0, which fully supports this scenario, using Support Package Stack 13. For more information, see Section 10.3.4, *New Features of Change Management Service*.

NWDI as a component of SAP NetWeaver 7.0

With SAP NetWeaver release 7.0, NWDI is installed as an SAP NetWeaver *DI usage type* that requires the usage type *AS Java*. The configuration settings are made in the Configuration Wizard of SAP NetWeaver Administrator (NWA), which you can access from the SAP NetWeaver Application Server initial screen (which administrators can call using *http://<host:port>* of SAP NetWeaver AS). On this screen, choose **Deploy and Change**. Then select **Initial Setup of Functional Unit Development Infrastructure** (Figure 11.1), and follow the instructions that appear.

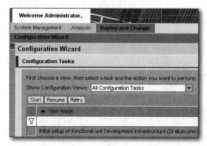

Figure 11.1 Configuration Wizard — DI Usage Type

The following sections describe the configuration steps you must carry out, to make retroactive changes and enhancements.

11.1.1 Java Development Landscape

From the point of view of system integration and administration, a Java development landscape is made up of SAP systems, each of which hosts one or more NWDI services (CMS, CBS, DTR), and of SLD, which although not a part of NWDI, plays a key role in the development process. A minimal development landscape requires one server on which an SAP NetWeaver Application Server Java runs with all building blocks of NWDI.

NWDI services

Figure 11.2 shows how NWDI and SLD systems interact with each other and with the runtime systems in the landscape on which new applications will eventually run.

NWDI and SLD

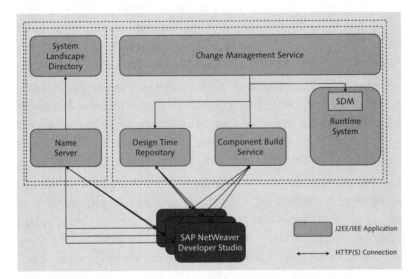

Figure 11.2 Landscape from the Point of View of System Integration and System Administrators

The arrows and boxes in Figure 11.2 can be interpreted as follows:

▶ System Landscape Directory and Name Service are two SLD roles that can either run on two separate servers or jointly on one server.

▸ The Development Infrastructure services that are implemented as J2EE applications are Change Management Service, Design Time Repository, and Component Build Service. All services can run on one or on separate servers. This also applies for DI services and System Landscape Directory.

▸ An NWDI can manage tracks for different development projects, even if these are for different target releases. This means that you can develop J2EE and JEE applications in parallel.

Functions of
NWDI services The basic functions of individual NWDI services are as follows:

▸ Change Management Service forms the central control unit of NWDI. It is responsible for the configuration of the development landscape and transport management. There is one CMS instance in each NWDI.

▸ Whereas Design Time Repository is responsible for managing source files and creating versions, Component Build Server is responsible for the central build of software components and managing all build results. You can install any number of systems as DTR and CBS servers in one NWDI. These servers are controlled by one CMS.

Note that availability demands on DTR systems are relatively high. They store the source files for your development projects. Hardware defects could result in source files being lost. Network accessibility is another important aspect in this context. Developers may not be able to continue their development work if network downtimes occur.

▸ The CBS server is the NWDI building block that requires most computing capacity. Whenever a developer activates an activity (change list), a central build process is triggered for all relevant development components. Each of these processes blocks a processor for the duration of the compilation. Each day, there are certain times when developers typically check in and activate their work. In this context, the CBS server is the bottleneck in NWDI. Inappropriate ratios between the number of processors and the size of development projects result in long waiting times for activation. SAP Note 737368 contains information on the size of NWDI systems.

▸ System Landscape Directory is used by NWDI for software component information and landscape configuration.

Several other SAP NetWeaver components use SLD to deliver information for landscape data. One IT system landscape requires exactly one SLD. If an SLD already exists in the system landscape, you do not need to install another one for NWDI.

▸ The Name Server is another SLD role, and is used in NWDI to avoid name conflicts among development objects. SAP NetWeaver Application Server provides a runtime environment for applications provided by different manufacturers. Therefore, if different manufacturers happen to name their development objects (such as database tables or Web application URLs) identically, these objects collide when used in the same runtime environment.

SAP has therefore developed a namespace concept, to ensure that the names of development objects created by different manufacturers are unique. (This concept has been — and will continue to be — used for ABAP development.) The Name Server in an NWDI ensures that developers can only create object names within the namespaces. Each object name can only be used once. The Name Server is a role in SLD. However, you do not need to run the Name Server and SLD on one SAP NetWeaver AS. To the contrary, it is recommended that you run these two functions on different servers.

SAP's namespace concept

▸ In addition to the systems that execute one or more NWDI services, *runtime systems* are usually also included in the development landscape for testing during development, consolidation, and testing before going live, and for production itself.

Runtime systems in the development landscape

Developers work locally with SAP NetWeaver Developer Studio, which is an integrated development environment that supports development work in NWDI, for example. Depending on the release used, each developer can choose to install a Java EE Engine or Java J2EE Engine at his/her local workplace for local tests.

As you can also see in Figure 11.2, all services (including SLD and the Name Server) communicate using *Hypertext Transfer Protocol* (HTTP). If necessary, the *Secure Socket Layer* (SSL) can be activated for HTTP in the relevant systems. An SAP protocol is used for communication between CMS and the runtime systems for testing and production.

As discussed previously, the server components of an NWDI may run in different systems. If developers work in NWDI, they require access to all systems. In other words, they need a user account in all systems.

To facilitate the logon procedure, developers in SAP NetWeaver Developer Studio must enter their own user name and password to log on to the central NWDI. This implies that their user names and passwords must be identical in all systems in a development configuration. To make it easier to maintain user data, we recommend that you set up a central user management system. This can either be a central directory service (for example, LDAP) or an ABAP system. *User Management Engine* (UME) of SAP NetWeaver Application Server supports both concepts.

An Example Landscape

The following sections describe the development process flow with NWDI and the component model, from a system administration point of view.

A system vendor wants to use the SAP NetWeaver technology platform to be used by different customers to develop an Internet application for online sales. Let's assume that the core of this application consists of two software components: the catalog server for a product search and the transaction server for handling orders. The Web user interface must be tailored to the individual needs of customers.

As we can see in Figure 11.3, CMS can be used to divide the development into different units (*tracks*): one unit each for the software components Catalog Server and Transaction Server. Each customer project forms its own development unit as a successor of these two tracks.

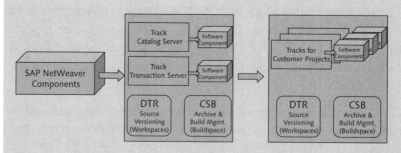

Figure 11.3 Example Development Landscape

In this case, NWDI consists of two DTR and CBS servers each, whose first pair is used for the standard development (catalog and transaction server). The second pair is needed for customer projects.

At the start of the development tracks for the catalog or transaction server, CMS is used to copy into the tracks any SAP NetWeaver components that are initially required. At the end of the two projects, stable versions of the software components have been created, which are used to deliver the customer project tracks under CMS control. This reduces the interweaving of development projects. Each project can be constructed on stable versions of the predecessors.

11.1.2 Setting Up an SAP NetWeaver Development Infrastructure

In this section, we will set up — that is, install and configure — an SAP NetWeaver Development Infrastructure. To keep things simple, we will set up a minimal implementation here, and run all services on a single AS Java system.

NWDI is installed by SAP NetWeaver as the *DI usage type*. It is integrated into the installation process, and the only prerequisite is that the AS Java usage type is installed.

Installing NWDI

After installation, you must configure NWDI. These steps are organized into the following categories:

- Creating global system parameters
- Setting up user authentication and authorization
- Starting up the SLD server, the Name Server, and the data supplier of SLD
- Configuring the DTR server
- Configuring the CBS server
- Defining a CMS domain and setting up a transport directory
- Creating a track

All of the previous steps are carried out in the **Configuration Wizard** of SAP NetWeaver Administrator, which guides you through the process. In this context, you configure the entire NWDI when all services have been installed on a server, or you configure the services (CMS, CBS, and DTR) separately. The following steps are therefore only required to retroactively optimize NWDI.

The system settings should also have been created in this context. Therefore, the following sections provide additional information. After installation, you should check the following two parameters:

▶ The parameter `idleStart` of CBS must be set to `false`. In this mode CBS is inactive, and CBS instances that are not required can be temporarily switched off, to conserve processors. This setting is available under *<drive>:\usr\sap\SID\JC00\j2ee\admin* in Visual Administrator, or in a pure Java installation under *<drive>:\usr\sap\SID\DVEB MGS01\j2ee\admin*. Select **Server • Services • Component Build Service/Properties**.

▶ Logging of the database must be tailored to meet requirements.

Global system parameters
:   Global settings include parameters of *Java Virtual Machine* (JVM), of SAP NetWeaver AS and the underlying database. Although these parameters are not application-specific, they do enable NWDI to operate more robustly and efficiently. In the following sections, we will discuss three important parameters: Heap size, JDBC connection pool size, and the maximum number of database accesses.

Heap size of JVM
:   Each server process of a Java system runs in a JVM. The memory required (heap memory) by JVM depends on the applications to the executed. For NWDI, it is advisable to set the maximum heap size of *all* server nodes of the Java system to at least 1.024 MB, by selecting **Config Tools** (Figure 11.4).

Figure 11.4 Maximum Heap Size for Java Virtual Machine

NWDI uses the database underlying SAP NetWeaver AS to save the source objects and binary archives. For certain processes (for example, the build process), NWDI needs a large number of simultaneous connections to the database. Use the Config Tool to set the JDBC parameter `sysDS.maximumConnections` to a higher value for each server node. The actual value depends on two factors:

JDBC connection pool size

▶ **Workload of the service**
Both the DTR server and the CBS server trigger a significant number of database accesses during operation. The workload depends on the scope of the development projects in an NWDI.

▶ **Number of server nodes**
This workload is actually distributed to the server nodes. As a general rule of thumb, the more server processes are running on a Java system, the lower the size of the connection pool required for each server node.

You can adjust this parameter as required, once you have implemented NWDI. For your NWDI, set the parameter so that there is a total of about 50 server node connections (Figure 11.5).

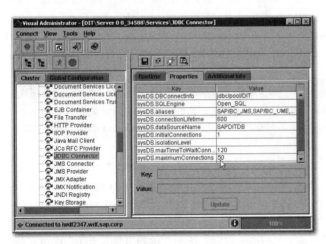

Figure 11.5 Connection Pool Size of the JDBC Driver

On the database side, you must also modify parameters, to allow you to use the connection pool sizes set for the JDBC driver. These parameters depend on the manufacturer, however. For MaxDB, for example, the

Maximum number of database accesses

543

value of the MAXUSERTASKS parameter must be slightly higher than the sum of all JDBC connection pool sizes.

Once you have set these parameters, remember to restart the database and the Application Server, to apply the new parameters.

Central User Management As already outlined, different server applications are involved in NWDI. These server applications can run on different systems. Users must log on to these systems to call NWDI services. To make it easier to maintain user data, we recommend that you set up a central user management system. This can be an ABAP system or an LDAP server. All Java systems involved in NWDI can connect to this system, to retrieve user data. This means that each user must only use one user account and password to log on to all participating systems.

Configuring Authorizations

Assigning authorizations Authorizations are required for different functions provided by the services. Depending on the user type (for example, developer, or quality manager) each user is granted different authorizations for the available services, allowing him or her to carry out his or her exact tasks. The users and authorizations listed here are created in the Configuration Wizard of SAP NetWeaver Administrator. However, knowledge of the mechanisms is very useful for running a live NWDI system.

> **Note**
>
> If NWDI is installed with the AS ABAP usage type, the users are created and managed in AS ABAP, but the group assignment is made as described below.

User roles and user groups To make it easier to allocate authorizations, we recommend that you set up one user group for each user type in the central user system. Authorizations can then be assigned once at the group level for all relevant systems. Users automatically receive the authorizations assigned to their group. Figure 11.6 shows how accesses are organized. Actions are assigned roles, which are allocated groups, to which users are then allotted.

SAP NetWeaver Application Server Java offers two concepts for user identification and authorization. The first adheres to the J2EE standard, to ensure that AS Java conforms with J2EE/JEE. The second is called *SAP*

User Management Engine (UME). UME uses a multi-layer authorization model to facilitate the integration of the Java and ABAP stack. The services always adopt one of these concepts.

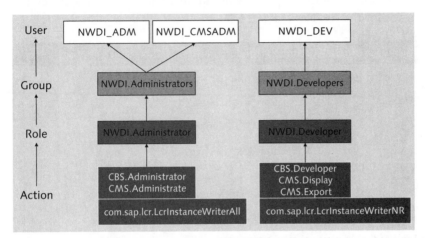

Figure 11.6 Actions, Roles, Groups, and Users in NWDI and SLD

Whereas CBS and CMS use the UME roles, SLD and the Name Server use the J2EE security roles for control access. Both security roles are linked to *actions* to be executed.

DTR manages source files of the development objects. For this reason, access to these objects is controlled by *Access Control Lists* (ACLs). ACLs work in the same way as security concepts for file systems at the operation system level. They are linked to the objects in DTR, and can also be managed centrally using track-specific authorizations in CMS.

Each building block also contains security roles, authorization objects, or access authorizations. For more details, see the product documentation. The following sections describe examples of the required authorizations using the most common user types in NWDI.

The daily work of a typical developer could include the following activities:

Authorizations for developers

- Creating and developing development objects
- Reserving object names during creation
- Checking source files in and out

▶ Activating changes to source files

▶ Releasing activities for transport

These tasks require the following authorizations, which a developer needs for the services (Table 11.1).

Building Block	Authorizations
Name Server	J2EE security role `LcrInstanceWriterNR`
SLD	J2EE security role `LcrUser`
CBS	UME action `CBS.Developer`
CMS	UME actions `CMS.Display` and `CMS.Export`
DTR	▶ Root directory: `read`, `write`, and `checkin` ▶ Project-relevant workspaces: `access`, `read`, `write`, and `checkin`

Table 11.1 Authorizations for Developers

Authorizations for project leaders

A project leader is usually responsible for the following tasks:

▶ Entering products to be developed in SLD

▶ Entering namespace prefixes reserved at SAP in the Name Server

▶ Defining and changing tracks for relevant projects in CMS

▶ Managing project-relevant tracks in CMS

To carry out these tasks, a project leader needs the authorizations shown in Table 11.2.

Building Block	Authorizations
Name Server	J2EE security roles `LcrInstanceWriterNR` and `LcrInstanceWriterCR`
SLD	J2EE security roles `LcrInstanceWriterCR` and `LcrInstanceWriterLD`
CBS	UME actions `CBS.Developer` and `CBS.QM`

Table 11.2 Authorizations for Project Leaders

Building Block	Authorizations
CMS	UME action `CMS.Administrate`
DTR	▸ Root directory: `read`, `write`, and `checkin` ▸ Project-relevant workspaces: All access authorizations

Table 11.2 Authorizations for Project Leaders (cont.)

NWDI administrators require the authorizations outlined in Table 11.3.

NWDI administrator

Building Block	Authorizations
Name Server	J2EE security role `LcrAdministrator`
SLD	J2EE security role `LcrAdministrator`
CBS	UME action `CBS.Administrator`
CMS	UME action `CMS.Administrate`
DTR	All access authorizations for all directory levels

Table 11.3 Authorizations for NWDI Administrators

Unlike the previous three user types, `NWDI_CMSADM-User` represents a single user. CMS uses this user for authentication in SLD, DTR, and CBS, to create workspaces in DTR and buildspaces in CBS during track definitions, and to transport changes to source files through the landscape. This is, therefore, an internal, technical user, and is not to be used for manual logon. It needs the authorizations shown in Table 11.4.

CMS user

Building Block	Authorizations
Name Server	None
SLD	J2EE security role `LcrIntanceWriterLD`
CBS	UME action `CBS.Administrator`
CMS	UME action `CMS.Administrate`
DTR	All access authorizations except `adminX` for all directory levels

Table 11.4 Authorizations for the CMS User

Creating
authorizations You will now set up the infrastructure user types of administrator and CMS user for your NWDI, to allow you to perform administrative tasks in the infrastructure at a later stage. The procedure for other user types is similar. Proceed as follows:

1. Log on as administrator to user management (*http://<host>:<port>/useradmin*). A screen appears (Figure 11.7).

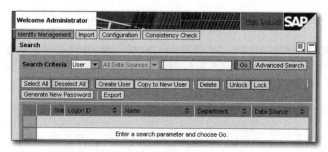

Figure 11.7 User Management Engine

2. On the left side, choose **Create User**, to create the users `nwdi_adm` and `nwdi_cmsadm`.

3. Use a different Web browser to log on with the newly created users and change their passwords. User management expects a user logging on for the first time to change the initial password. As this can only be done in the Web browser, this step is very important. Otherwise, the applications trigger unexpected errors if you try to log on to the system in the background with this user name.

4. On the left side, choose **Groups** from the dropdown box, and create a new group. Enter the group name "NWDI.Administrators" on the following screen.

5. Assign the user `nwdi_admin` to the group by selecting change mode, and choosing the required user from the list of all available users on the **Assigned Users** tab.

The roles and assigned actions are part of the shipment.

Allocating SLD
authorization You have now granted the required authorizations for CBS and CMS to your two users. Next, you must grant them authorizations for SLD and the Name Server. As both of these services use J2EE security roles, you will carry out the following steps in the **Config Tool**. SLD and the NWDI

Name Server run in one system, and you only need to grant authorizations for SLD once to the users or user groups, as SLD and the Name Server use the same piece of software in the system.

1. Log on as administrator in the Config Tool.

2. Choose **Cluster · Server * · Services · Security Provider · Runtime · Policy Configurations · Security Roles**.

3. In the **Components** area, choose the component `sap.com/com.sap.lcr*sld`, assign the role `LcrAdministrator` to the group `NWDI.Administrators`, and assign the role `LcrInstanceWriterLD` to the user `cms_user`.

4. You have now assigned authorizations to the users `nwdi_admin` and `nwdi_cmsadm` in NWDI.

Configuring System Landscape Directory

SLD is configured in NWA in SAP NetWeaver 7.0 (Figure 11.8).

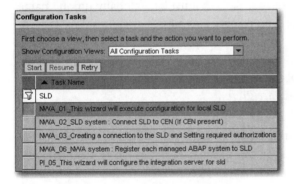

Figure 11.8 SLD Configuration Steps in NWA

System Landscape Directory (SLD) is the central unit for storing system landscape data of the SAP NetWeaver platform, and is increasingly used by various SAP tools for system management.[1] The basic concept of SLD is to provide a central unit for the entire system landscape, to reduce data redundancy brought about by distributed data management. Different applications can share data in SLD, and even store their data there to

The SLD server and data supplier

---

1 This includes, for example, SAP NetWeaver Process Integration and SAP Solution Manager.

make it available to other applications. SLD is used in several locations in NWDI.

If you already have an operational SLD, there is *no need to* set up an additional SLD for NWDI. For your NWDI, we will assume that you are using an island landscape, in other words, it is decoupled from its network neighbors. You, therefore, need your own SLD.

Activating SLD
SLD is installed, but not automatically activated, with each AS Java. You should only activate it in the system that acts as SLD in the system landscape. You use the NWDI system as an SLD server. As the first step in activation, you set some server parameters.

1. To do this, call the SLD Web interface (*http://<host>:<port>/sld*), and log on as administrator.

2. On the SLD initial screen, follow the **Administration** link.

3. On the following screen, select **Server/Profile**.

4. From the **Section** list, choose **Server Settings**, to set the server parameters. The parameter `Object Server` must be a globally unique name. SAP recommends that you reserve a namespace prefix at SAP (on SAP Service Marketplace *http://service.sap.com/namespaces*), to guarantee uniqueness. You can use this namespace prefix as a namespace for your development objects at a later stage. For more information, see Section 11.2.2, *Namespace Prefix*.

5. For your NWDI, assume you have already reserved the prefix "JBOOK" at SAP. You use this prefix as your object server name (Figure 11.9). Do not change the other parameters on this screen. Save your entries.

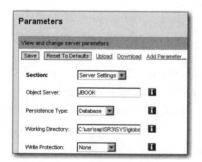

Figure 11.9 SLD Server Parameters

6. Once you save the parameters, go to the **Administration** screen again, and start the SLD server.

In the next step, import the *SAP Master Component Repository* data. This data includes, for example, information on all products, software components, and support packages shipped by SAP.

Initial data import in SLD

The initial data import is part of the SLD setup in SAP NetWeaver Administrator. If no data has been imported, the option **Import CR Content** is displayed under **Content/Import**. As component versions are continually updated, you must import new versions of CR content (and updated versions of SLD's CIM Model). You can download this data from SAP Service Marketplace. To copy them to SLD:

1. On the **Administration** screen, select the **Import** link.

2. On the **Content** page, choose the **Import** link. The import process may take up to 30 minutes.

3. This imported data represents just a snapshot of SAP products at a specific point in time. Information on products shipped by SAP after this time is provided by SAP in incremental updates of *Master Component Repository Data*.

SLD updates

You can download these updates from SAP Service Marketplace and import them into your SLD, to update the data stored there (Figure 11.10). You should carry out these updates in regular intervals, to keep the data in your SLD up-to-date. For the NWDI, you have already downloaded the updates from SAP Service Marketplace and imported them into SLD.

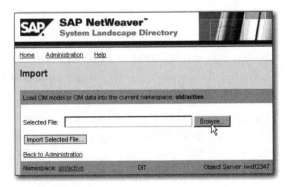

Figure 11.10 Data Import for SLD

You usually specify and import the updates on the **Import** screen. See Chapter 12, *SAP NetWeaver Development Infrastructure: Developing an Example Application Step-by-Step*, for more information on the SLD state you require to develop software for SAP NetWeaver Composition Environment.

The SLD data supplier and data supplier bridge

One key feature of SLD is that the systems in a system landscape automatically provide SLD with current system data at regular intervals. Therefore, SLD always contains a current picture of the entire landscape. The individual systems report their system data using *Data Supplier*. In each system, the data supplier is configured in such a way that it provides SLD with data at regular intervals. On the SLD server side, *Data Supplier Bridge* receives this data, converts it to the correct format, and inserts it into SLD.

1. To configure the Data Supplier Bridge for your development landscape, simply call the **Data Suppliers** link on the Administration screen.

2. Here, select the **Update Local Namespaces** parameter to the value `true`, and start the bridge.

3. You can set the data supplier in your system. To do this, call the Config Tool of the Java system.

4. Choose **Cluster** • **Server** • **Services** • **SLD Data Supplier**.

5. On the **HTTP Settings** tab, enter the host, the port, and the logon data (see Figure 11.11):

   ▸ The **host** is simply the PC name or the SLD server's Internet address.

   ▸ The **port** is the HTTP port of the Java system.

   ▸ To use the data supplier, you should create a new user. This **user** must have the J2EE role `LcrInstanceWriterLD` for the application component `sap.com/com.sap.lcr*sld`.

6. Once you have saved the setting, you can start data transfer to the SLD server manually by choosing the 🖥 icon. This triggers data transfer to System Landscape Directory (SLD). After a few seconds, a message should appear, telling you that data transfer has been completed successfully.

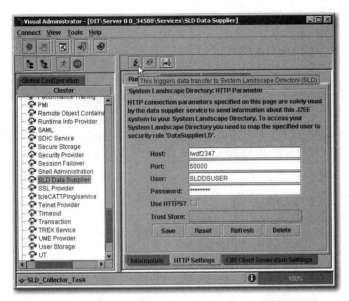

Figure 11.11 SLD Data Supplier for a Java System

7. Now you can check whether the data has really arrived in SLD. To do this, choose the **Technical Systems** link on the SLD initial screen. Enter "Web AS Java" as the **Technical System Type**.

Finally, register your SLD server in SLD. This means that you must enter the Java system on which the SLD server runs in SLD.

1. Call the **Landscapes** link on the SLD home page.

2. On the **Landscapes** screen which appears, choose **New Landscape...** (Figure 11.12).

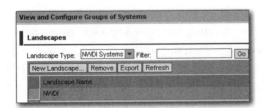

Figure 11.12 Landscape in the SLD Server

3. A wizard opens. Choose **NWDI System**, enter a name and choose **Create**.

Using the
Name Server

4. The Name Server is used in NWDI, to avoid name conflicts between development objects that may lead to objects overwriting each other during deployment. To activate the `Name Server` role, choose **Home • Name Reservation**.

Namespace
concept

SAP introduced the name reservation concept for ABAP development. In SLD, you enter prefixes in your Name Server. The owner's name (or Internet domain) also constitutes part of the name. You can then create development objects in the namespaces covered by these prefixes.

You will run the roles `Landscape Directory` and `Name Service` together in one system for your NWDI. You already made the required provisions when registering the SLD server. On the SLD name reservation screen, you can switch on and off the role `Name Server`.

Configuring Design Time Repository

Setting up the
DTR server

Setting up the DTR server is broken down into two parts: setting the URL for the Name Server and setting initial access authorizations.

As described previously, the names of the new development objects are entered in the Name Server, so that they cannot be used again. This avoids name conflicts. When a new development object (for example, a new database) is created, the developer uses SAP NetWeaver Developer Studio to provisionally reserve the name of the object in the name server. When the developer activates the new object, the DTR server finally reserves the name in the Name Server.

To do this, the DTR server must know the address of the name server. You can specify the Name Server and logon information on the **Name Server Configuration** screen, which you can open from the URL *http://<host>:<port>/dtr/sysconfig* by selecting the path **Support • Name Server Configuration**. The host and the port in the URL must be identical to the data you registered for the Name Server in SLD. The user that the DTR server uses to log on to the Name Server must have the J2EE security role `LcrInstanceWriterNR` in the Name Server for the application `sap.com/com.sap.lcr*sld`. For your NWDI, enter `nwdi_admin` and the relevant password, as this user has the superior authorization `LcrAdministrator`.

Before we focus on setting initial access authorizations in DTR, we will take a look at the concept of the *Access Control List* (ACL).

Access Control List

DTR development objects are stored as files in the database underlying SAP NetWeaver AS. The workspaces enable access. Unlike CMS and CBS, access to these objects is controlled by access authorizations linked to objects rather than by authorizations for specific actions. Nine access types are defined for each object or group of objects, that is, a directory. (These access types are access, read, write, checkin, import, export, integrate, adminA, and adminX. More details on the individual access types are contained in the product documentation.) You can grant or deny access authorizations for a particular object or directory to a specific Principal (either a user or a user group). For example, you can grant a user read authorization for an object, and deny the same user write authorization for this object.

Access authorizations from superior directory levels are inherited by inferior directory levels. This means that subdirectories take on the access definitions of superior directory levels, unless special access definitions are defined at the relevant levels. This saves the administrator from having to define access authorizations at all directory levels (whose depth cannot be foreseen). It is also possible to stop the inheritance of ACLs at any sub-directory level.

In addition to the two types of authorizations that control access already discussed — grant and deny — there is a third type finalDeny (irrevocable denial of access authorization). You can set the finalDeny of specific access authorizations for certain principals at a higher directory level, to irrevocably refuse these users or user groups access to the relevant access authorizations that they are granted at the structure's sub-directory levels. If, for example, you want to back up the DTR server database, you can temporarily set the finalDeny for write authorization for developers (or developer groups), for all workspace folders, to ensure that no one changes the database content during backup.

Remember to revoke the finalDeny after backup. Never set finalDeny for all users (this would include the administrator), for the root directory, or the subdirectory */ws/system*. If you do, it is possible that no one is able to revoke the finalDeny.

> **Note**
>
> An initial ACL is set when NWDI is being configured in the Configuration Wizard. This allows you to work in a functioning ACL.

Four priority rules

You may have noticed that contradictory access authorizations are sometimes possible. What happens if you grant read access to a user at the root level but deny this same authorization for a subdirectory? Does this user have read access to the subdirectory? To resolve these kinds of conflict, there are four priority rules that the DTR server uses in its evaluation:

- **finalDeny before subdirectories**
  You already know this rule. A `finalDeny` of an access authorization at a superior directory level overrules the granting of this authorization at the corresponding subdirectory levels. For example, a user can have read access for the *.../projects/app1* directory. This read access is no longer valid if a `finalDeny` of the read access is set for the *.../projects* directory.

- **Subdirectories before superior directories**
  This rule states that the definition of authorizations granted for subdirectories takes priority over contradicting definitions for superior directories. For example, you can deny a user write access for the *.../projects* directory, and simultaneously grant the same user write access for the *.../projects/app1* directory. This allows the user to write to this subdirectory and to all levels below it, but not to the superior directories. This rule enables you to restrict a developer's work to his or her project directory.

- **User before group**
  An authorization explicitly granted or denied to a single user always takes priority over the authorizations defined for the user's group at the same directory level or for the same object. For example, you can deny write access for the *.../project* directory to a group, but grant this authorization to a particular member of this group. This member is then allowed to write to this directory.

- **Deny before grant**
  Denying an authorization takes priority over granting the same authorization. For example, a user is a member of two different groups. If

read access for the .../*project* directory is granted to one group and denied to another, then the user has no read access to this directory.

These four rules are checked one after another in the order outlined above until one applies.

After deployment, only one access authorization is set in DTR, which grants all access types to all users, starting from the root directory. This is by no means adequate for a live version of NWDI. On the one hand, developers do not require administrator authorization, particularly not from the top directory level. On the other, there are some critical subdirectories to which all users should have access. For this reason, you should set at least the following access authorizations for each DTR server immediately after deployment:

Initial access authorizations for DTR

▶ **Root directory**
This is the highest directory level. All access authorizations set here are inherited by the subdirectories, unless other access authorizations are explicitly set in these subdirectories.

   ▶ Grant the access authorizations access, read, write, and checkin to all users. To work in NWDI, developers usually need these access types for their project directories. Thanks to the inheritance of access authorizations, project directories automatically receive these authorizations.

   ▶ Grant the group of Development Infrastructure administrators access to the root directory (and all directories below this).

   ▶ Grant all access types except adminX to the CMS user.

▶ **System directory /ws/system**
This directory contains the system settings such as the Name Server configuration. Only administrators should be allowed to access it. Note the following:

   ▶ Deny all kinds of access to all users.

   ▶ However, grant all kinds of access to at least one administrator.

   ▶ For all users, the DTR server provides an implicit user group <All Users>. If you grant access authorizations to administrators as a group (they belong to the <All Users> group), then the fourth priority rule (deny before grant) applies, which would deny these authorizations to the administrators as a group.

▶ **DTR configuration directory /sysconfig**
This directory contains all administration tools for the DTR server. Set the same access authorizations as you would for the */ws/system* directory.

You must now apply these initial access authorizations to your NWDI. To do this, use SAP NetWeaver Developer Studio.

DTR administration plug-in

SAP NetWeaver Developer Studio contains a DTR administration plug-in. Because only some users need this plug-in, it is initially deactivated when Developer Studio is installed.

1. To activate the plug-in, change the name of the file *plugin.xml.disabled* in the *<dev-studio-install-dir>/plugins/com.tssap.dtr.client.eclipse.admin* directory to *plugin.xml*. Change the name of the file *plugin.xml* in the same directory to *plugin.xml.disabled*. In SAP NetWeaver Developer Studio 7.1, after changing the file name, you need to use the option `-clean` to open Developer Studio, which triggers Developer Studio to read the changed file. Please remove this option once the developer has started to work on the new parameter to display the administrative features.

2. The plug-in is activated when you restart Developer Studio (in this context, you must specify the parameter `-clean` once, for example, in the shortcut to Developer Studio in the target line, to ensure that the system searches for new plug-ins).

DTR perspective

3. In Developer Studio, choose **Window • Open Perspective • Other • Design Time Repository** to open the DTR perspective.

4. You need a DTR client to connect to a particular DTR server. You can create any number of DTR clients for different servers in the DTR perspective, so you can manage different servers from one IDE instance. This is primarily important for administrators (for developers working in an NWDI environment, a corresponding client is part of each development configuration).

5. In the DTR perspective, select **DTR • Create Client**.

> **Note**
>
> You automatically receive a correctly configured DTR client when you load a development configuration. This sets a filter, so that you can only view and change suitable workspaces. In principle, therefore, only administrators who do not require a filter will want to create a client as demonstrated here.

6. On the **New DTR Client** screen, enter information for the new client, as shown in Figure 11.13. **Local Root** is the directory on the local PC in which the client stores the data downloaded from the server.

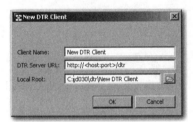

Figure 11.13 Creating a New DTR Client in Developer Studio

Creating a DTR
client manually

It is good practice to name the client and the local directory after the server name or system ID of the server system.

7. Once you have created the DTR client, you can log on to DTR as NWDI_ADM by selecting the **Log On** button (⬛) in the toolbar. (If you have saved your password and are working in a development configuration, you are automatically logged on. However, this logon may have filters set that prevent you from changing permissions.)

8. The node DTR_<SID> appears in the Repository Browser. This node is linked to the directory of the workspaces in DTR *http://<host>:<port>/dtr/ws*. Here, administrators can create workspace folders and workspaces (both actions are normally carried out automatically from CMS), and assign authorizations in DTR.

DTR administrator
plug-in

> **Note**
>
> To carry out this action in Developer Studio, and set the administrator status, the name of the file *plugin.xml.disabled* must be changed in the following directory in Developer Studio: *<Developer Studio installation directory>\SAP\ IDE\IDE72\eclipse\plugins\com.tssap.dtr.client.eclipse.admin*. The existing file with this name, which defines the developer status, must be deactivated.

Defining DTR accesses

9. To reach the access authorizations at any directory level, it is preferable to use the menu entry **Window • Show View • Other... • Design Time Repository • Permissions View** (Figure 11.14 — this view is only visible if you have activated the administrator plug-in as described previously).

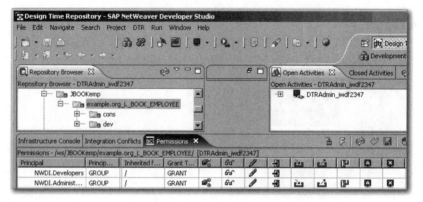

Figure 11.14 Permissions View of the DTR Administration Plug-in for the Example Software Component

In the title line of the **Permissions** view, you can also see the path of the directory currently displayed in the view. This is particularly helpful when you set access authorizations, as you can otherwise easily get lost in the directory structure, and assign access authorizations for the wrong directories, which could have serious consequences.

10. Now go to the root directory in the **permissions** view, by choosing **View Permissions for URL**. Enter the URL *http://<host>:<port>/dtr*.

Groups and users in DTR

11. Set the access authorizations specified in Table 11.5. In the context menu for the access authorization entries, you will find the items **Add Principal** (🖳), **Edit Principal**, and **Delete Principal** (🖳), which you need to set authorizations. You can only modify and delete entries if the relevant authorizations are set only for the current directory, and are not inherited from superior directory levels. You can determine this by looking at the **Inherited from** column.

12. Carry out the same process for the directories */ws/system* and */sysconfig*, using the entries shown in Table 11.6.

Make sure that you explicitly grant all authorizations to the user `nwdi_admin`. You already know the reason why. As of Support Package Stack 9 (SAP NetWeaver 2004, Support Release 1), there is a better option for setting access authorizations at the subdirectory levels. Because of this Support Package Stack, the DTR administration plug-in provides an extra feature that allows you to stop the inheritance of authorizations from superior directories. The **Ignore Inheritance** button (⬆) is available in the title line of the **Permissions** view.

Principal	Principal Type	Grant Type	access	read	write	checkin	import	export	integrate	adminA	adminX
\<All Users\>	All	Grant	✓	✓	✓	✓					
NWDI.Administrators	Group	Grant	✓	✓	✓	✓	✓	✓	✓	✓	✓
cms_user	User	Grant	✓	✓	✓	✓	✓	✓	✓	✓	

Table 11.5 Access Authorizations for the DTR Root Directory

Principal	Principal Type	Grant Type	access	read	write	checkin	import	export	integrate	adminA	adminX
\<All Users\>	All	Deny									
nwdi_admin	User	Grant	✓	✓	✓	✓	✓	✓	✓	✓	✓

Table 11.6 Access Authorizations for the /ws/system and /sysconfig Directories of DTR

When you have defined these access authorizations, you must transfer the new definition from the DTR client to the server, to enable the server to evaluate them.

1. The title line of the **Permissions** view contains the **Activate All Changes** (⊙) button, which transfers the changes to the server.

   The DTR server only reads the definition of the access authorizations in regular intervals. This means that the changes transferred to the server only apply after the server next synchronizes the access authorization definitions.

2. However, you can enforce the synchronization on the server side by navigating to *http://<host>:<port>/dtr/* in the Web browser, choosing **sysconfig · support · AclRefresh** and then selecting the **Refresh** button.

3. You can check that all access authorizations are set correctly. For example, log on as NWDI_ADM in the Web browser on the DTR server, so that you can navigate to the directories for which the access authorizations have been set.

Emergency user

4. If you have inadvertently locked all users (including nwdi_admin), use UME to create a user with the user ID superadmin (remember to switch to another browser to change the password for the new user before you continue), and log on as this user in Developer Studio. This user has all authorizations in DTR, so that you can delete the incorrect access authorizations.

Configuring Component Build Service

Configuration for the CBS server

Now let's look at the configurations required for the CBS server. Some parameters must be set for the CBS server for each of the system's server nodes. You must usually explicitly set four of these parameters before starting up the CBS server. You can do this manually, or in the Configuration Wizard, which is recommended:

Deactivating and activating CBS

▶ idleStart
This parameter tells you whether Component Build Service will be started in the respective server node. After deployment, it has the value true. If you set the value to false, CBS is also started in the corresponding node when you start up the system.

As you already know, all NWDI services are deployed in all systems when deploying the SCA files. Only set this parameter to false for those systems that you want to act as CBS servers, to activate CBS.

▶ threadPoolSize
This parameter sets the maximum number of build processes that can run in parallel.

CBS setting for CPU number of the server

The build processes use a great deal of the computing capacity (CPU and memory). Despite multitasking, a running build process actually blocks a processor. Therefore, set this parameter in such a way that the total of these parameters from all server nodes in one system instance does not exceed the number of available processors. This allows the computer to still have enough resources to execute other processes (such as monitoring the server) during the build processes. Take the number of processors and reduce it by one to determine this value (do not reduce the number if only one CPU is available).

▶ BUILD_TOOL_JDK_HOME

This parameter specifies which JDK version of CBS will be used to run the build tools.

You can install a number of JDK versions at the operating system level. CBS uses the version specified here to start the build tools. For example, this is necessary if you want to use CBS in parallel for SAP NetWeaver runtime system developments based on release 7.0 and 7.1. Figure 11.15 shows the enhancement of the parameters JDK_BUILD_HOME and JDK_HOME_PATH. For details on the track settings, go to the section *Creating Tracks for Development in SAP NetWeaver Composition Environment* in Section 11.2.4. The section *CBS Settings for JEE Version 5.0* in Section 12.3.1 outlines the step-by-step procedure.

CBS setting for different JDK versions

▶ JDK_HOME_PATHS

This parameter specifies all available JDK versions required by build tools to build software. Use a semi-colon to separate the versions (;).

Remember that contrary to the previous parameter, the JDK versions are called by the tools in this context. For example, you want to compile a particular software component using a specific Java compiler version (javac), which can differ from the version of JDK used to start the build tool. For more details, see Chapter 12.

Set the following parameters for your NWDI:

1. Call the Config Tool from *<Installation drive_of_NWDI>:\usr\sap\ <SID>\JC<instance number>j2ee\ configtool\confitool.bat*.

CBS setting — user interface

2. In the Config Tool, choose **cluster-data** • **Instance_ID<Number>** • **server_ID_<Number>** • **services** • **tc-CBS.Service**.

3. Set the four parameters in line with your specific system environment (for example, paths of JDK versions) for all server nodes.

4. When you have made these settings, start the nodes (Figure 11.15).

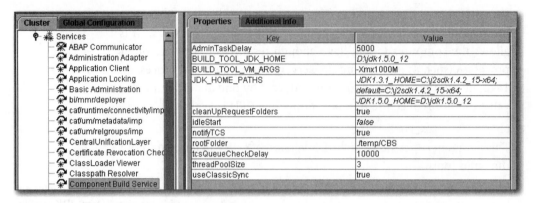

Figure 11.15 CBS Parameters

Configuring Change Management Service

CMS domain   We will now look at Change Management Service, which is the heart of NWDI. CMS is responsible for configuring the development landscape and controlling interaction between all services. All of these tasks are carried out in SAP NetWeaver Administrator. The following steps describe access to allow you to check the settings and change settings such as used SLD (for example, the domain can no longer be changed):

1. Configuration mainly involves defining a CMS domain. When you call the CMS Web interface for the first time after you deploy SCA files on the NWDI initial screen *http://<host>:<port>/devinf*, select the link to **Change Management Service**.

2. Choose the link to the domain. A domain represents a transport landscape. It consists of all tracks that are connected by one transport route.

Transport directory   3. CMS uses a transport directory to transport *Software Component Archives* (SCA files) between tracks. This directory stores the SCA files to be transported and, during the import, moves them into the follow-up tracks.

4. If you intend to use a network drive as a transport directory, make sure that this network drive is available to the CMS server at all times, and that the service user (SAPService<SID>) of the CMS system has write access to this drive.

5. This is where the CMS user comes in. CMS uses this user ID to com-   NWDI_CMSADM
municate with all services.

> ▸ As explained earlier, NWDI uses the SLD server in the system
> landscape to retrieve and store information. When creating a CMS
> domain, the SLD address is specified for later use.

> ▸ The domain ID identifies a CMS domain and, if you want to
> accommodate several CMS domains in your system landscape, it
> must be unique throughout the system landscape. This ID is
> stored in SLD. Call your CMS domain `ATP`.

6. Based on these descriptions, you should now be able to easily configure a CMS domain in NWDI. The URLs of the CMS and SLD server
take the form *http://<host>:<port>*. Simply use *<sap-dir>/jtrans* as the
transport directory (Figure 11.16).

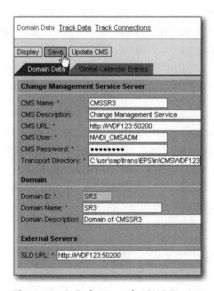

Figure 11.16 Definition of a CMS Domain

7. When you have saved the domain definition, switch to the operating
system level and look in the SAP directory *<sap-dir>*. Here, the transport directory *trans* is created with the subdirectory *CMS/inbox*.

8. The **Update CMS** button appears in different locations on the Web   Synchronizing CMS
interface of CMS. You can use this function to enforce an update of   with SLD data
temporarily stored SLD data (for example, software component data).

11.2 Administration of SAP NetWeaver Development Infrastructure

You have now installed SAP NetWeaver Development Infrastructure. In this section, we will look at administrative tasks in NWDI. As in the previous section, we will combine theoretical descriptions with practical administrative steps in NWDI. Screenshots for these processes (SAP NetWeaver release 7.0 Support Package Stack 13) are contained in Chapter 12.

11.2.1 Product Definition in System Landscape Directory

Products and their software components

Before you start to develop software in NWDI, you must define the software to be developed in System Landscape Directory. The aim is to register information on software products, such as version numbers, in SLD. If these products are deployed in the system landscape, SLD not only contains information on the systems in which the software is installed, it also contains information on the software itself. This allows you to organize software lifecycle management more methodically and with greater flexibility.

Instead of developing new software, in this chapter you will copy the Employee example from the previous chapters. In SLD, you define a software product called Employee, which contains the software component L_BOOK_EMPLOYEE 2.0. The vendor name is *example.org* (as if you were a new software manufacturer on the market named example.org) and the versions for both the product and the software component are 1.0.

1. Log on to SLD as NWDI_ADM, and select the **Software Catalog/Products** link on the SLD initial screen.

2. Select the **New Product Version** button, to start the definition of a product and the relevant software components. Make sure that you enter these names in SLD exactly as specified previously.

Reuse of software components

3. During software development, a component almost always needs other components. To develop your software component L_BOOK_EMPLOYEE, you need other SAP software components that provide basic libraries and tools for JEE applications. The use relationship between components is known as a *use dependency*.

4. Regardless of whether you have defined the product and the related software component in SLD or whether you have simply imported the definition as a file into SLD, use the Software Catalog to find the software component L_BOOK_EMPLOYEE Version 1.0, and select the **Dependencies** tab on the details page of this software component version.

5. Choose **Define Dependencies**, and select the software components shown in Figure 11.17 as the used software component versions. (Enter "7.10" in the **Filter** field, to restrict the search.)

Dependencies between software components

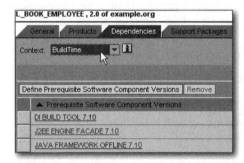

Figure 11.17 Software Component Versions Used in the Example Product

6. You have now finished defining the product for your development.

11.2.2 Namespace Prefix

A namespace prefix opens a theoretically unlimited space for subname spaces and object names. All users have to do is register the reserved prefixes in their Name Servers. The Name Servers then deal with the name reservation within the reserved namespace. Thanks to this procedure, neither SAP nor SAP users need to invest much time or effort in name reservation.

Reserving Namespace Prefixes in SAP Service Marketplace

On the first level of the two-level concept, you request a namespace prefix in SAP Service Marketplace. The quicklink */namespaces* opens the name reservation page on SAP Service Marketplace.[2]

Ensuring that names are unique

---

2 This page already existed for ABAP developments, and has been extended to include developments for the SAP NetWeaver platform.

1. A namespace prefix can have up to eight alphanumerical characters. Enter the prefix you want to request in the **Namespace** field.

2. Then activate the **SAP NetWeaver Name Server** option, to reserve the namespace for SAP NetWeaver objects.

3. In the **Name of Name Server** field, enter the Object Server Name of your Name Server. If you want to use the name to be reserved as the Object Server Name of a new SLD server or Name Server, enter this name in both the **Namespace** and **Name of Name Server** fields. You can also use the prefix you reserved for the Object Server Name for development objects (Figure 11.18 and SAP Note 84282).

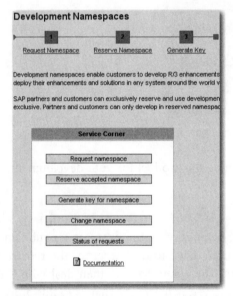

Figure 11.18 Requesting a Namespace Prefix in the SAP Service Marketplace

4. When you have requested a prefix, an asynchronous process is started. It may take up to three working days before you receive a positive reply. (A negative reply, for example, if the name has already been assigned, usually arrives faster, because the process is terminated immediately as soon as one condition is not met). A positive reply indicates that the desired prefix has not yet been assigned and that all other conditions for a reservation are met. To reserve the prefix, simply confirm the reservation.

You can also use a previously reserved ABAP name prefix for SAP NetWeaver development projects. To do this, simply declare the reserved prefix for the SAP NetWeaver Name Server in SAP Service Marketplace.

ABAP namespace

Registering Reserved Namespace Prefixes in the Name Server

The second level of the name reservation concept is to register the reserved namespace prefixes in your Name Server, so that your developers can create new development objects in the reserved namespaces.

Permitted namespaces for the development

> **Note**
>
> If the Name Service is activated, you need at least one entry for development components, to develop objects. This will also work — particularly if an application is solely for demonstration purposes — without having to carry out the reservation steps in SAP Service Marketplace.

NWDI knows eight development object types. To view and change these, log on as administrator to SLD, and select the **Name Reservation** link on the initial screen. We will now look at the most important types. The *x* in the examples represents a reserved namespace prefix (Figure 11.19).

Object types and namespaces

- **Application Context Root**

    This is the relative path under which Web applications in AS Java can be called, for example, *http://<host>:<port>/x/myapp*.

- **DB Object**

    Database objects are database tables and database indexes, such as X_MYTAB.

- **DB Pool**

    These are the aliases for the database connection pool. This type of alias has the format X/P_MYPOOL.

- **Development Component**

    Development components are the smallest units that can be built. Development component names have the format *<vendor>/x/mydc*.

- **Design Time Package**

    These are development packages of different programming languages, such as a Java package name. The names of the development packages follow the rules of the respective languages.

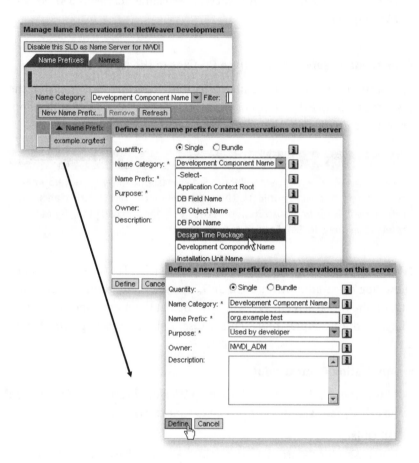

Figure 11.19 Defined DC Prefix and Creation of a Name Prefix for Design Time Packages

As presumed when we set up the Name Server and the SLD server, the JBOOK prefix is reserved for your NWDI. Now make this prefix available for the development in the Name Server.

1. On the Name Server initial screen, choose **Name Reservation • Define Namespace Prefix**.

2. Enter the data shown in Table 11.7.

Name Category	Namespace Prefix
Development Component Name	*example.org/test/**
Design Time Package	*org.example.**

Table 11.7 Name Category and Namespace Prefix

11.2.3 Preparing a Track

This section provides a general description of how to set up a development landscape. For a more detailed description of the track that you need to handle the example in the component model, see Section 12.3.4, *Creating, Configuring, and Preparing the Example Track*. Alternatively, without a server connection, you can carry out this process in a local development configuration, to allow you become more familiar with the component model. For more details, see Section 10.4.2, *Component-Based Development with a Local Development Configuration and Optional External Infrastructure*.

To recap: A track provides a development environment in which one or more versions of software components can be developed. A track defines the environment for up to four project phases: development, consolidation, quality assurance, and production. The following sections provide a general overview of how to create a track. For more details on the preparations required to create a track for an SAP NetWeaver CE environment, see *CBS Settings for JEE Version 5.0* in Section 12.3.1.

Project phases of a track

Defining Tracks

When you define a track, you specify the DTR and CBS servers to be used and the software component versions to be developed. CMS creates workspaces and buildspaces accordingly. These configurations are also stored in CMS as the development configuration, and are entered in SLD. Developers can use the IDE in SLD to search for the relevant configuration and then load this configuration from CMS into the IDE to create a real development context in the IDE (see Figure 11.20).

Defining a track

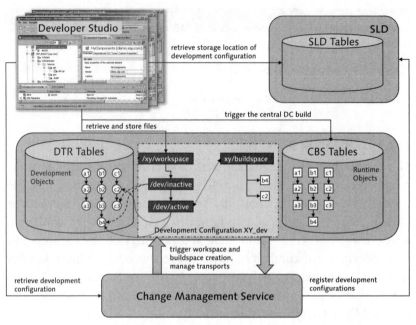

Figure 11.20 Generating Two Development Configurations when Defining a Track

Runtime systems

For each project phase in a track, you can choose to incorporate a runtime system that will serve as the test system for the corresponding phase.

Track templates — automated track definition

SAP NetWeaver 7.0 Support Package Stack 13 provides a user-friendly method for automatically creating tracks using specific templates. You do not have to know which standard SCAs are required to this end.

1. Open SAP NetWeaver Administrator and log on as an administrator.

2. Select **Deploy and Change**, and set a filter for "skeleton" in the configuration tasks (Figure 11.21).

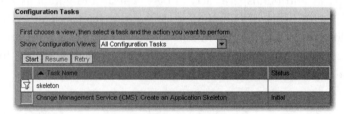

Figure 11.21 Creating an Automatic Track in NWA

3. Select **Start**, or choose **Resume** if you have already used the function (after a termination), or **Retry**.

4. On the next screen that appears, enter **CMS-URL** (if required). Enter the required password and choose **Next**.

5. The parameter screen for the track appears (Figure 11.22). Specify the following parameters:

   ▸ Track name

   ▸ Description

   ▸ Select the track template from the list. The software component dependencies are correctly set based on this template.

   ▸ You only have to change DTR and CBS-URL if you have several of these services.

   ▸ The transport directory may be changed, but the default entry can usually be used.

   ▸ The CMS name, domain, and host cannot be changed.

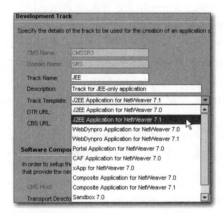

Figure 11.22 Selecting the Track Template

6. Choose **Next** and follow the wizard's instructions. The track is now available in CMS.

Defining Track Connections

You now know how to configure a track. In addition to development in a track, NWDI supports layered developments. This implies that a CMS

Transport route

573

domain represents a transport landscape. Tracks in a domain are inter-connected by supply dependencies. These connections between tracks are known as *transport routes*, as they are used to automatically deliver the released software component versions of a track — the results of this track — to the follow-up tracks.

There are two types of transport routes. The first is simply called *transport* and connects two tracks according to the supply dependency of these tracks. For example, the development in track B uses components developed in track A. Then the transport route from A to B is of the type *Transport*.

Maintenance tracks and back-ward transport

There is a different situation if track B is a maintenance track of track A. In track A, the development of a software application continues. In track B, a particular release state of track A is kept to correct any errors that are only discovered after the released version has been shipped. Support packages of this version are developed in track B. In this case, it is not sufficient to connect from A to B using a transport route of the type Transport to transport the release state into track B. We need an addi-tional transport route of the type Repair, which connects the two tracks from B to A. This is the way in which error corrections can (but do not necessarily have to) be integrated from the maintenance track back-wards into the original track. If you release an error correction in the maintenance track for transport, the transport request is not only included in the import queue of the next phase as usual, but the trans-port request is also added to the import queue of the development phase of the original track. The project leader decides whether to integrate these error corrections.

A backward transport of error corrections is not only carried out between two tracks connected by a Repair transport route. Backward transports also occur within a track between the consolidation and development phases. Errors detected early — that is before shipment — can still be eliminated in the consolidation phase. These error correc-tions can be integrated into the development phase using backward transports. Figure 11.23 illustrates both kinds of backward transports.

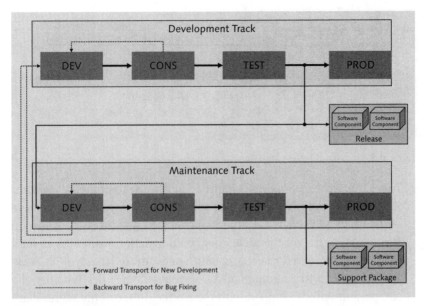

Figure 11.23 Transports Within a Track and Between a Development Track and a Maintenance Track

Let's return to NWDI, and create two tracks for development and maintenance.

Development and maintenance tracks

1. To do this, go to CMS **Landscape Configurator** and open **Track Data**.

2. If a track already exists, choose **New** to reset the input fields. Then enter data in the fields as shown in Table 11.8.

Repository Type	DTR
Track ID	\<maximum of eight characters>
Track Name	\<Name>
Track Description	\<Description>
Development Configuration Path	\<optional>
Design Time Repository URL	*http://\<host>:\<port>/dtr*
Component Build Service URL	*http://\<host>:\<port>*

Table 11.8 Data for the Development Track

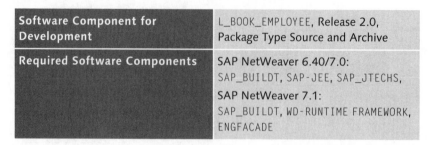

Software Component for Development	L_BOOK_EMPLOYEE, Release 2.0, Package Type Source and Archive
Required Software Components	SAP NetWeaver 6.40/7.0: SAP_BUILDT, SAP-JEE, SAP_JTECHS, SAP NetWeaver 7.1: SAP_BUILDT, WD-RUNTIME FRAMEWORK, ENGFACADE

Table 11.8 Data for the Development Track (cont.)

3. The software components required for the development (*Required Software Components*) are inserted automatically, because you have declared in SLD that the component JBOOK_EMPLOYEE depends on them. CMS retrieves this dependency information from SLD as soon as you have specified the component you want to develop. The **Package Type** of the component to be developed specifies whether the component will be shipped with the source files, or only with binary archives.

4. By saving the track definition, you trigger the track generation process. CMS now tries to create workspaces and buildspaces and to register the development configuration in SLD. This process can take several minutes.

5. In the DTR and CBS Web browser, check whether new workspaces and buildspaces have been created for your track. You can choose to define runtime systems. For more details, see Chapter 12.

Maintenance track   You can also create a maintenance track. Basically, the only difference between the maintenance track and the development track is, of course, that the track ID is different. Therefore, all you have to do is copy the definition of the development track.

1. To do this, choose **Save As**. Enter "Maintain" as the **New Track ID** and "Maintenance" as the **New Track Name**.

2. The **Track Description** is not mandatory, but you should still enter a descriptive text such as "Maintenance Track for...". This type of description can be very helpful in your daily work. Save your entries, to create a second tack as a maintenance track.

3. Once you have created the two tracks, you can connect them using transport routes. To do this, go to the **Track Connections** tab and create two transport routes, as described in Table 11.9.

Source Track	Target Track	Connection Type
Development	Maintenance	Transport
Maintenance	Development	Repair

Table 11.9 Transport Routes Between the Development Track and the Maintenance Track

4. You have now defined two tracks and identified the transport relationship between them.

Importing the Required Software Components into the Track

When you create a track, workspaces and buildspaces are created for the track in DTR and CBS. These workspaces and buildspaces are still empty, however.

References to source files are stored in the workspace. Depending on whether a track will be used for a new or a further development, the development starts either with completely empty workspaces, or with workspaces filled with the source files of the previous version. The buildspaces are usually filled with the required software components. The software component SAP_BUILDT is required for each component type, because it contains the build tools required for all supported component types. This is why the used software components, and maybe even the previous version of the software component to be developed, must be imported into the track before the actual development work can start.

The three used software components can be found in the *<sap-mnt>/ <SID>/<SYS>/global/CMS_CBS/plugins* directory. When the SCA file *SAP-BUILDT.SCA* is deployed, the components are copied into the file system. The version of the files here corresponds to the version of the target Java system. If you use this NWDI but want to develop software for

Providing a basis for development

AS Java with other versions, you must download the respective versions of the used software components from SAP Service Marketplace.

Checking in the software components into a track

There are only two tracks in our NWDI, where the first track development is located at the beginning of the transport landscape. This implies that it is not automatically supplied by other tracks. You must *check in* the required components into the import queue for the development phase of this track. In addition, you do not want to start a new development, but rather continue developing the Employee example from the previous chapters, so you must also insert this component with source files in the import queue.

> **Note**
>
> Chapter 12 describes how to create the Employee application from the very beginning. For more details on the actual source code, see the example for programming without components, as the development objects — for example, the classes — of this example do not change even if the component model is used.
>
> The exact commands and user interface elements are contained in the description of the example application provided in Chapter 12.

11.2.4 Development Steps

Sequence of activities for administrators and developers

The following development steps are required:

1. Set up your NWDI, as described, and save (at least) the required SCA files SAP_BUILDT, WD-RUNTIME FRAMEWORK, ENGFACADE of SAP NetWeaver CE 7.1 from the list on the DVD accompanying this book, into the subdirectory *CMS/inbox* of the transport directory:

   <sap-dir>/<SID>/<SYS>/global/CMS_CBS/plugins.

2. In the example, start with the definition of the software component *example.org~L_BBOOK_EMPLOYEE* and its dependencies.

3. On the left side of the Transport Studio, select the **Check-In** tab, and look for all SCA files that have already been developed. In this case, these are only the required SCA files. If an earlier version of the SCA to be developed is available, this can also be checked in and changed. Enter the file names in the **Archive Name** field, and select the **Check-In** button.

4. After you have added all the required packages to the import queue of the track, go to the **Development** tab. All packages should be displayed here.

5. Select all requests and choose **Import** to start the import process. It takes a few minutes to complete this process.

6. All imported archives of the required software components are now physically available in the buildspace for the track. Archives and any other software component source files that are to be developed may also have been copied to the buildspace, or the source files that contain this software component may have been integrated into the DTR_Workspace.

7. After the import into the development phase, go to the **Consolidation** tab. The SCAs now appear as well. Proceed as described for the development phase to import the packages into the consolidation phase.

8. The import of SCA files is made up of three steps, which are carried out consecutively:

What happens during the SCA import?

   ▶ **Repository Import**
   If an SCA file contains source files from the corresponding software component, these source files are first imported into the inactive DTR workspace.

   ▶ **Build**
   The source files imported in the previous step are now built in CBS. If the build is successful, they are activated, that is, they are integrated into the active workspace. The build creates binary build and deploy archives. If a package only contains binary archives, and does not contain any source files, these archives are loaded into the respective buildspace.

   ▶ **Deployment**
   The deploy archives contained in the SCA file, or the deploy archives created in the last step of the build, are deployed into the runtime system provided that a runtime system exists for the relevant project phase.

The import terminates immediately if one of these steps fails. Use the Web browser to check the state of DTR and CBS when the consolidation import is complete. If the workspaces and buildspaces of the Development track are filled with the correct content, you can start your actual development work.

Creating Tracks for Development in SAP NetWeaver Composition Environment

CE tracks

With SAP NetWeaver Composition Environment, tracks are created in exactly the same way as in all other releases. You can also use NWDI with release 7.0 (or even an earlier version). However, it is highly recommended that you use SAP NetWeaver release 7.0, Support Package Stack 13, because this is the first release to support automatic deployment using the new deploy tool in SAP NetWeaver Composition Environment. You only need to make the following changes:

SLD content

▶ Update the SLD content by downloading and implementing the most current content (as *CRDeltaXXX.zip*) from SAP Service Marketplace.

▶ Create a track for Composition Environment with at least the required software components SAP_BUILDT, ENGINEAPI, FRAMEWORK, and ENGFACADE on release 7.1 for development with IEE and Java Dictionary.

JDK version

▶ Enhance the CBS settings so that you can also use JDK 1.5 (you must restart CBS in the Config Tool when the settings have been changed):

  ▶ BUILD_TOOL_JDK_HOME
    Add the path for JDK 1.5

  ▶ JDK_HOME_PATH
    Enhance by defining a variable for JDK 1.5

Setting up the build option

▶ Add the following build option for the used build variant as described below (use the documentation to determine whether changes have been made):

```
<build-options>
  <build-option name="com.sap.sap.jdk.home_path_key">
    <option-value>JDK1.5.0_HOME</option-value>
  </build-option>
</build-options>
```

▶ Save the track. When you define the runtime systems, make sure that you choose the Option Deploy Controller instead of SDM, if your runtime systems are based on the CE release.

Chapter 12 describes in detail how to create this type of track with these settings.

Steps for the Developer: Changing an Application

Before you can continue to develop the Employee example in NWDI, you must perform two preparatory steps in Developer Studio.

1. First, open two perspectives: the **J2EE Perspective** and the **Development Infrastructure Perspective**. To do this, choose **Window • Open Perspective • Other** in the menu, and choose both of these perspectives.

   Central perspectives for the example

2. Now you must inform Developer Studio where it can find SLD, because this refers to the development configurations. In the menu, choose **Window • Preferences • Development Infrastructure • Landscape Directory**, and enter the SLD address in the **URL** field in the format *http://<host>:<port>*.

   SLD access

3. In **Preferences • Team • Ignored Resources**, select the objects of *.project* and *.classpath*, because these are not to be saved in DTR in NWDI-based developments.

   Files that are not to be saved

4. Go to the Development Infrastructure Perspective, and log on as `nwdi_dev` using the **Log on...** button (📲) in the toolbar.

   Importing the development configuration into the IDE

5. As you know, you need a development configuration to set the context for the development. Open the **Development Configuration Import** Wizard using the **New/Import Development Configuration** button (🎇), and activate the **remote** option.

6. A list of the development configurations that already exist appears in the bottom half of the dialog box. This list has been downloaded from SLD, which you have specified as the development configuration pool in Developer Studio. Choose a development configuration from this list, for example, `JBOOKemp_dev`, and choose **Next**.

7. The next screen displays details for this development configuration, for example, addresses of CBS, DTR, and the Name Server.

8. Choose **Finish**, to import the development configuration.

Overview of the software structure If you expand the **<track name>_dev** node in the **Component Browser** view using the *Inactive DCs* filter setting in the **Development Infrastructure** perspective, the software component `example.org/JBOOK_EMPLOYEE` appears, with four *development components* that you need to modify slightly in this track. If you expand the same node in the **Active DCs** view, the three standard components used by the development of your component will appear in addition to the component to be developed. Again, each of these components contains several development components (DCs).

Say, for example, you want to change the Web interface of the Employee example to suit your needs. To do this, you must load the `../employee/web` development component for the Web interface and the development component `../employee/ear` — which comprises all development components for a deployable and executable JEE application — as development projects into Developer Studio.

1. To change this part, select the menu items **Sync/Create Project · Create Inactive Project** from the `../employee/web` context menu.

2. In the dialog box that appears (Figure 11.24), the relevant development component `../employee/web` appears at the top of the list. Its source files are synchronized to the local PC because you want to change this development component.

3. The other development components in the list, including the two development components *../employee/dic* and *../employee/ejb*, which belong to the software component `example.org/L_BOOK_EMPLOYEE`, are synchronized to the local PC as binary build archives that are used by *../employee/web*. Select **OK**. The source files and build archives are downloaded to the correct versions.

4. Repeat the same steps for the `../employee/ear` development component, to generate the second DC project, which uses the changed Web module. The status `active` is sufficient here, because you do not want to directly change this development component.

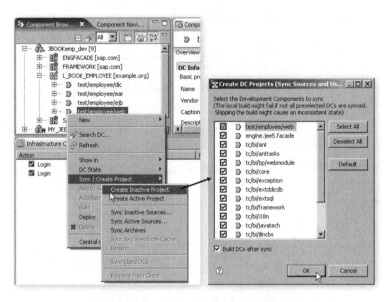

Figure 11.24 Synchronizing the DC Source Files and the Binary Archives of the Used Development Component

When the second development component has been synchronized, you can see that the development components either have a light green arrow or a dark green arrow in the **Inactive DCs** view. A light green arrow indicates that the inactive versions of the source files of the relevant development component can be edited on the local PC. This applies to the two development components for which you explicitly generated development component projects. A dark green arrow indicates that the active versions of the binary archives of the development component are available on the local PC. This applies to the other two development components, which have automatically been synchronized based on use dependencies.

When you generate a DC project in Developer Studio, source files of the development component and binary archives of the used development component are automatically synchronized on the local PC. All you actually did was set the SLD address in Developer Studio. In SLD you will find the development configurations that describe the development contexts. When you import one of these development contexts into the IDE, the IDE ensures that the file versions are correct.

Status of objects

Downloading archives and source files

Now you want to modify the Web interface.

1. Go to the **J2EE** perspective.

Changing files

2. In the **J2EE Project Explorer** view, expand the node for the Web project. The JSP file *index.jsp* is in the **WebContent** subfolder.

Managing changes in DTR — activities

3. In the context menu of this file, select **DTR • Edit**, and then create an activity. This displays a list of your changes. The activity name can be any text, for example "Change Web Interface".

4. Open the file, and display its source file in the **Source** view. Change the background color of this Web page. In the third line, overwrite the value of the `bgcolor` attribute with "**EFEFEF**":

```
<body style= "font-family:Arial;"  bgcolor="EFEFEF">
```

DC build

5. As soon as you have saved your entries, you can build the Employee example into a deployable and executable implementation. In the context menu of the `../employee/ear` development component project, select **Development Component • Build**.

6. The **Build DCs** Wizard is displayed. It automatically proposes all development component projects that have been changed since the last build and on which the `../employee/ear` development component depends (Figure 11.25).

Figure 11.25 Automatic IDE Proposals for Development Components That Must be Rebuilt Due to Modifications

7. Leave the proposed development components and let the wizard build the Enterprise Application development component. As you can

see, the wizard carries out its task to perfection. The result of the build is an enterprise archive for the Enterprise Application development component.

When the build has been successful, you can start deployment. Remember to first deploy the `../employee/dic` dictionary development component, because your application uses the database table in this development component. The easiest way to deploy the Dictionary development component is to use the **Inactive DC** view in the **Development Configurations** perspective.[3] Choose the **Deploy** menu item in the context menu for this development component. You can then use the same procedure to deploy the Enterprise Application development component. If everything went as it should, you should be able to call the application in the Web browser, with the new background color. Check that the namespace concept provided the URL with a prefix in the path. The URL is now *http://<host>:<port>/../employee/view*.

Deployment

You can now check in and activate your change.

Triggering the central build process

1. To do this, go to the **Activities** view in the **Development Infrastructure** perspective.

2. Under the workspace node, you will find the activity that you created to check out the JSP file. This file will probably be the only file contained in the activity unless you edited or added other files.

3. To check in the activity, choose **Checkin** from the context menu of the activity and confirm the subsequent check-in prompt.

4. Usually you will want to activate the changes to the source files directly after checking them in. The IDE, therefore, offers an activation option. Choose the **Activate** button to confirm **Activation** in the wizard.

5. You can monitor the status of the activation/build process either directly in the IDE or on the Web user interface of CBS. To monitor the status in the IDE, open the view **Activation Requests** during acti-

---

3 Usually, deploying the Dictionary DC in the **Dictionary** perspective, as described in the previous chapters, does not work here. To this end, the development component does not have to be changed. Therefore, only the binary archives of this development component have been synchronized to your PC. A development component project is not available in the **Dictionary** perspective.

vation, or using the **Window • Show View • Other...** menu. The view is available under **CBS Activation** in the **Show View...** dialog box.

6. As you know, the activation of changes in CBS triggers a build process. CBS also uses this number to identify the build process. In the **Activation Requests** view, the activation's identification number is displayed on the left side.

7. To query the current status, choose the view's **Refresh** function. For each activation request, the progress of activation is displayed (in the column with the ✿ icon, which displays the request status — Running, Succeeded or Failed) as is the deployment status (in the column with icon ♦). You can call the build log on the right side when the activation process has finished.

Follow-up requests 8. You cannot monitor *follow-up requests* in the **Activation Requests** view, however.

> ### What is a Follow-Up Request?
>
> If a changed development component is activated, it is rebuilt. We already know this much. What happens to the development components that depend on this development component? The changes may have a serious effect on syntax and semantics of these dependent development components. Therefore, they will be rebuilt and deployed based on the new build archives of the used development component. This is the only way to ensure that all development components of a software component remain consistent. CBS, therefore, triggers internal requests for all development components that depend on a changed development component.

To track these follow-up requests, you must switch to the Web user interface of CBS (*http://<host>:<port>/tc.CBS.Appl/CBS WebUI*).

9. Here, choose the **Requests** link using the ◔ icon.

10. The **CBS Request Information** screen appears. Here, you can search for the activation log and build request log assigned to a buildspace (Figure 11.26).

Automatic deployment
11. The build results are now available for both the test in the local installation of Java EE Engine (if available) and on a central runtime system, if specified by the track administrator for the development phase.

Figure 11.26 Activation Results

Steps to be Carried Out by the Administrator During Development — Checking the Application State

1. As administrator, check the state of the request directly in the CBS Web user interface.

2. To do this, open the NWDI initial screen, and log on as NWDI_ADM.

3. To view the request, select **Requests • Simple Search**, and enter the request number, or use the time interval, for example, in the **Advanced Search**.

4. The search result will contain a build request with the request ID displayed during activation. This build request will not be the last, however, but probably the next to last, even though you did not trigger any other activation (Figure 11.27).

CBS Web user interface

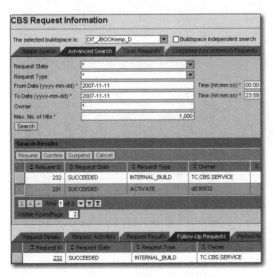

Figure 11.27 Request of JSP Change and Follow-Up Request

The **request type** of the last request is INTERNAL_BUILD. As **owner**, TC.CBS.SERVICE is specified. This is a follow-up request for your activation. You have changed and activated the Web development component ../employee/web. The activation request refers to this exact development component. The Enterprise Application development component ../employee/ear uses the Web development component, which is why it must be rebuilt by an internal build request and then deployed.

Checking the project status

As a project manager, you must monitor the statuses of the follow-up requests in this way, to determine whether the dependent development components are still syntactically correct despite changes to their used development components, and whether they can still be compiled. If they are syntactically correct, you must then test the newly built application in the runtime system to exclude any semantic inconsistencies. It is easier to check the buildspace state directly (Figure 11.28).

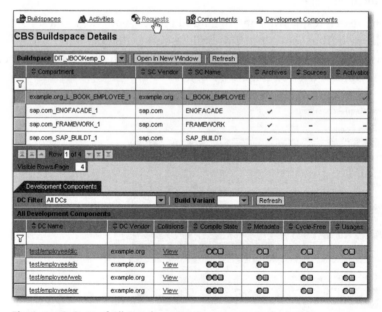

Figure 11.28 State of All Development Components in the Buildspace

5. In Component Build Service, select the buildspace (here <CMS>_JBOOKemp_D).

Steps to be Carried Out by the Developer After the Test — Releasing Changes

The last step you carry out in the IDE is to release the activity for transport. Transports import changes into the next project phase (for example, consolidation). Activities are placed as transport requests in the import queue of the next phase.

Releasing the transport

However, successfully activating the activity does not automatically release it for transport. Sometimes, several activities are required for one large change project. To be able to transport the related changes together and thus synchronously, you can release the respective activities collectively and create one joint transport request.

Now, release your activity for transport, to complete your development work.

1. Open the **Transport View** in Developer Studio by selecting **Window · Show View · Other... · CMS/Transport View** in the menu.

2. Expand the structure for the DTR workspace JBOOKemp_D.

3. You activity is located in the **Waiting** substructure. To release it for transport, select **Release** from the activity's context menu (Figure 11.29).

Figure 11.29 Releasing Changes

The activity moves to the **Released** substructure. It is now in the import queue for the consolidation phase of the track. If the QM team does not detect any problems in the consolidation or test system, your task as a developer is completed, and you can remove the development configuration from Developer Studio. If problems are detected, load the projects, and check out objects to be changed, and repeat the steps outlined previously.

Concluding the development phase

11.2.5 Consolidation Phase

Consolidating
software

Consolidation is the second project phase in a track. When developers have released their activities in the development phase for transport, the relevant transport requests are available in the import queue of the consolidation phase. Here you import the source files from the `active` workspace of the development phase. The source files are built and deployed (if you have defined a runtime system), and are available in an unchanged state for testing until the next import is carried out.[4]

Why has the consolidation phase been introduced? The activation concept can guarantee that activated changes are always syntactically correct. But how can you ensure that changes made by different developers match semantically? Before a software development is passed on to quality management, its functions are tested. At the same time, development may continue. To avoid the problem of new changes constantly invalidating the tests, you must save a particular state of the software and decouple testing from continuing development. This is where the consolidation phase comes in.

What happens with the errors detected during the tests in the consolidation state? Generally, there are two ways of correcting them. The first is to correct the errors in the development state and integrate the new version into the consolidation state. However, due to continuing development, an error may have become irrelevant in the development state or its correction may have become impossible. In this case, you must use the second method and correct the error directly in the consolidation state. The error corrections in the consolidation state are inserted backwards into the import queue of the development phase as soon as they have been released in the consolidation state. It is up to you to decide whether you want to integrate them into the development state.

For this development example in NWDI, you will not carry out any tasks in the consolidation phase. After all, you have not made any errors. Simply import the activity that you released in the development phase. After the import, make sure that your change has reached the active workspace in the consolidation.

---

4 Actions in the CMS user interface during consolidation and assembly are outlined in Chapter 12, which describes the example application.

11.2.6 Assembling the Software and Quality Assurance

After the consolidation phase, the software is assembled and passed on to quality assurance. Unlike the two previous phases, the software components are packed together as components during this stage. The results of the *assembly* process are *Software Component Archives* (SCA), which are deployed as packages into runtime systems. In the development and consolidation phases, only the development components affected by changes are rebuilt and deployed. Software components, and not the development components, are the units shipped to customers or installed in production systems.

Preparing Production Use and Shipment

The assembled software components are deployed to the runtime system for quality assurance and tested there. Generally, software products are tested by quality engineers before they are shipped.

You will now assemble the changed Employee example.

1. To do this, go to the **Assembly** tab. This tab contains all transport requests that have either been imported from development into consolidation or have been released in consolidation. During the assembly, all changes from both phases are packed together.

2. You will find only one request that results from the modification of the background color. From the **Select Component** dropdown list, select the software component to be assembled. In this case, you can leave the default setting **All Components**, because you are only developing one software component in this track.

3. Choose **Assemble Component(s)** to build a new version of the selected software component into an SCA file. The new SCA file is stored in the directory *<transport-dir>/CMS/archives*.

4. If you had defined a runtime system for the quality assurance phase during track definition, Transport Studio would contain a **Test** tab, and you could now deploy your software component as an SCA into the test system and test it.

Once you have successfully completed the test in the quality assurance system, the software can be shipped. This means that it can be shipped to customers or used in the company's own production system, if it is a

Final test

customer development. One formal step still has to be performed: the *approval* of the release for shipment.

1. To approve the release for shipment, go to the **Approval** tab.

2. In addition to the version of your software component that you have just built and tested, you will again see the three usual components.

   Why would you want to approve components that you have not developed? Because you use these components in your component. You have therefore developed your component version against the exact versions of the used components listed here. Approval of the used component versions means that your component version can only be used with these used component versions. Only this combination has been tested by quality assurance.

3. Select all listed components, and choose **Confirm**, to approve them.

11.2.7 Shipment to Customers

Shipment of SCA files

You can now ship your software. Or can you? There are three ways of shipping the software:

▸ As you are already aware, the packed software components are now SCA files in the *CMS/archives* subdirectory of the transport directory. These files are shipment units, which you can use for deployment in your production landscape, if you are not using automatic deployment, or transfer to your customer for installation.

▸ If the developed software is intended for use in your own company, you could include the production system in the track during track definition, so that a transport request is generated for deployment to this system after approval. To do this, go to the **Production** tab and trigger deployment.

▸ The third type of shipment involves supplying follow-up tracks. If your component is used by other components in other follow-up tracks, your new component version must be transported to the follow-up tracks. This also applies if a Support Package for a shipped software component version is to be developed in a maintenance track.

You have already defined a maintenance track and connected it to the development track. After release approval, transport requests are also included in the import queue of the development phase for the follow-up tracks. Go to the **Development** tab of the "Maintain" track. Here, four transport requests are waiting to be imported into the track, one for your component `demo.org/JBOOK_EMPLOYEE` and one each for the three standard required components.

You can now import these components into the maintenance track. Try to change your component in this track, as if you were developing a Support Package. Check whether the changes in the maintenance track are really transported back into the original track.

Other uses of SCA files

11.3 Software Change Management with SAP NetWeaver Development Infrastructure

Even this brief description of the development process uncovers an underlying problem during software development: The platform version changes continually. The problem is not serious if there is only one product version. However, a solution must be found if different versions are being maintained.

Maintenance problems

11.3.1 Managing Software Projects for Different Target Platform Releases

Replicating the entire environment, particularly the source files, to manage different software states (source code lines) is not an optimal solution, because this causes duplicate identical files, which again causes problems. NWDI development opted to take another route, and separate the management of development objects on the one hand from the physical development landscape on the other. This means that NWDI is able to simultaneously manage different releases of software in one NWDI instance. This is possible, because on the one hand, the database that contains the workspaces and buildspaces is not aware of the objects' version, and because the runtime systems that contain information is separated from NWDI, on the other.

Independence from development infrastructure and developed software

The connection between both poles is saved individually in the corresponding track for each software project. This fulfills the last basic requirement of an efficient development platform, and guarantees the use of new source files and archives in the next release and in other products (see Section 10.1, *Special Characteristics of Large-Scale Software Projects*). Note the following rules:

▶ Tracks are release-specific. Developer Studio, used archives and runtime systems must be based on the same release (this applies at the Support Package level).

▶ Runtime systems can be J2EE Engine instances on a physical server or on several servers. (Use of the server that contains NWDI itself is not recommended as a runtime system.)

▶ You could, of course, implement software components from different tracks in a shared runtime system, if all used software components have the same version.

▶ You should use one NWDI for all releases. In this context, we do recommend that you use the most current NWDI release.

11.3.2 Track Design and Further Development of Products

Regarding track design, if you have generated a version in a track, and this version is used in a production system, you can update the track with the used software component version of the next Support Package version or release when development of the first track has been completed, and develop further in the same track. It is important that you make a copy of the track, where the older version can be maintained.

Further development and maintenance of software

It is also important to remember that even if you develop further in the same release and Support Package version, you do change the state of the development and consolidation systems, so that you cannot directly maintain the state, as contained in the production system. For this reason, we recommend a track design as shown in Figure 11.30. The production state is always available in the COR track, to allow bugs to be fixed. The defined track connections automatically propagate changes between DEV and COR. In a track network, as displayed in Figure 11.30, an existing product is developed further. However, the version used in the production system is still available for urgent corrections in the COR track.[5]

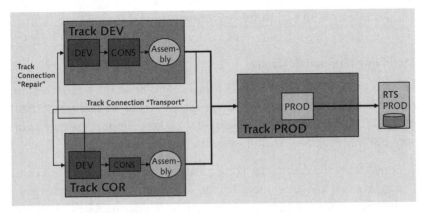

Figure 11.30 Track Network

11.3.3 Modification Concept of SAP NetWeaver Development Infrastructure

When you use SAP NetWeaver Development Infrastructure for your development, you can modify the Java-based software shipped by SAP. This software is available in SCAs, and in software that is a prerequisite for your development projects. You must reconcile your changes with later software states, which may be shipped in Support Packages, for example.

Prerequisites for Modification and Reconciliation

To carry out the steps described here, the software must have been developed with NWDI, the SCAs must have been shipped in source files, all the used SCAs must be available in the correct version, and you must use NWDI for your changes.

Use of NWDI at SAP, customers, and partners

The software version, and the dependencies, must be defined in your SLD. SAP ships this information as SLD content, for example. Alternatively, it can be entered manually in SLD. If you need to enhance SLD

---

5 This topic is discussed on SDN (*http://sdn.sap.com*), under the heading *Best Practices for NWDI: Track Design for Ongoing Development.*

content manually, and no other documentation is available for the software component used, as a workaround, information on the used software component versions is available as `ReqComp` in the file *SAP_Manifest.MF* in each software component archive.

Modifying Shipped Software

You can modify SCA files in NWDI tracks. This book only describes the reconciliation required at a later stage for the NWDI and Developer Studio steps. NWDI can also be integrated with Java Support Package Manager (JSPM), which is used for updating Java-based systems.

Creating a track for modifying software

1. Copy all involved software components (used components and components that are to be modified) as software component archives to the *Inbox* of the used Change Management Service (CMS). The version must correspond to the version specified in the description of the software component to be developed.

2. Create a track for your modification in CMS Landscape Configurator, and insert the software component(s) to be changed as a **Software Component for Development**. If use dependencies are defined between several software components, they must also be defined in SLD. The used software components are added automatically.

3. Check in all software components to be modified and all used software components into CMS Transport Studio and import all SCAs into this track. If this track is imported into an SAP NetWeaver Developer Studio, the development components of the software components to be modified and of the used software components are available.

4. Make the required changes by adding new or changing existing development components. After the steps from consolidation to approval have been carried out, a new version of the software component is available and can be used in the production system.

Reconciling modifications using Support Packages

Support Packages are shipped as SCAs. You can, for example, download them from SAP Service Marketplace, to use the most recent version. If you do this, and wish to keep some or all of your modifications, you must reconcile the versions. Using the *Global Version History* of all source files delivered from DTR, this can also be carried out after a transport into a new DTR. Reconcile the versions before you deploy the Support Packages into the production systems.

If you are using JSPM, the following enhancement must also be made: If a runtime system is controlled by NWDI, JSPM identifies whether a modified state is available when updating this system, and allows a modified version to be reconciled with the Support Package before a new state is deployed.

You copy the changes contained in the Support Package into the track in which you have made your modifications.

Transferring changes into the modification track

1. Copy the SCAs of the Support Packages into the CMS Inbox.
2. Check in the modified software component(s) into CMS Transport Studio, and import them into the track.
3. Import the SCAs. When you import file versions that have been modified in a different system — that is, they are neither predecessors nor successors of the existing modified version, which could be sorted into the version history — integration conflicts are generated. The DTR detects these conflicts.

A Quality Manager can search specifically for conflicts generated by the implementation of new versions, for example, using the DTR Web user interface.

Detecting conflicts

1. Open the Collision Search function on the DTR Web user interface. To locate this search, go to *<http://<host>:<port>/dtr* • **system tools** • **reports • Conflict Search**.
2. In the development configuration, select the inactive workspace of each software component affected by the Support Package.
3. Choose **Show**. You see the conflicts that result from importing a new version. The versions are compared as a resource and a **colliding version**.
4. Inform the *owners* of the development components of the colliding version, who must resolve the conflict. Developers can also view the conflicts directly in SAP NetWeaver Developer Studio.

Conflicts should be resolved by a developer responsible for the development components concerned, because the changes must be reconciled correctly at both the formal and semantic levels. Developers are

Resolving conflicts

informed in Developer Studio about the new version of the development configuration. All developers who work in this development configuration must remove the old version and import the new one.

1. The conflicts are displayed in the **Integration Conflicts** view. This is located in SAP NetWeaver Developer Studio under **Window • Show View • Other • Design Time Repository • Integration Conflicts**.

2. The developer of the relevant development component now resolves the conflicts. If the changes are implemented using a Support Package, no further conflicts arise when other Support Packages are imported.

3. The developer activates the changes and releases them.

4. Carry out the remaining steps up to approval of the software component.

Result   Your modifications are now available as an SCA and can be deployed into the production system.

This process is described for use of NWDI as a whole. If you only use DTR, files can be reconciled accordingly, as follows: After importing and integrating updates to software that was not developed based on the component model, carry out the steps to identify and resolve conflict. The prerequisite is that the development, modification, and update are carried out using Design Time Repository (DTR).

11.3.4   Non-ABAP-Based Transports in a Mixed System Landscape

Software change management for ABAP and Java   The software development process described previously can be used for all individual developments, including the modification of existing and externally developed applications. NWDI also provides options for transporting objects from other non-ABAP applications.

These options are provided by a separate track type for the SAP NetWeaver usage type PI (Exchange Infrastructure, XI). A description is also available for using NWDI for portal transports. In both cases, the quality of the processes was lacking. Whereas portal transports were not explicitly integrated, XI transports were integrated, but only for the Java part of this usage type, of course. Although the ABAP part was included in a transport system — ABAP Change and Transport System (CTS) —

the difficulty of synchronizing this type of transport remained unresolved. There were similar problems for other applications that consisted of ABAP and Java elements.

These problems have been resolved by improving the integration of both transport systems. In mixed landscapes, the enhanced version of Change and Transport System in the current SAP NetWeaver release, Support Package Stack 13, can transport practically any type of object, in addition to ABAP transports. In this context, the target systems for the transports may be from an earlier release. This is a significant advantage, particularly for the portal and XI transports mentioned at the start.

CTS can also transport SCAs from NWDI. This is useful in the following cases: First, in cases in which, as already mentioned, Java transports are to be carried out at the same time as ABAP transports, because these can be included in one transport request. Second, the supply of the test and production systems can be standardized. This offers the following advantages:

Integrating NWDI with CTS

▶ Any number of test and production systems can be supplied, which was previously only possible using track connections for production systems.

▶ A uniform process is used. An administrator with knowledge of ABAP can supply both systems in the same way, and in a synchronized manner, which helps reduce and better plan the time required to change the production system state.

▶ All tools for monitoring transports, in particular log files, are available equally for ABAP and Java transports.

In a system landscape with ABAP and Java systems, transports can be organized as follows (Figure 11.31): All development-related steps during development and consolidation in the Java development are carried out in NWDI, as was previously the case. When the development has been assembled in an SCA file, this file is exported from NWDI into CTS, and transported from there into test and production systems. XI and portal transports are carried out in CTS.

This new development does not undermine the significance of NWDI. The key functions for the development of Java-based applications have not been affected. The management of source files and archives in devel-

Role of NWDI

opment and consolidation systems and the control of build processes are still carried out in NWDI. The development of applications using NWDI is still a prerequisite for modifying Java software in the SAP environment. The new developments have simply enhanced, and not replaced, any existing functions.

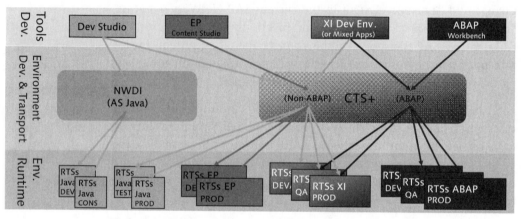

Figure 11.31 Combined Transport Landscape with NWDI and CTS

The described CTS enhancements also provide the technological basis for the Change Request Management scenario in SAP Solution Manager release 4.0, which is available as of Support Package Stack 12. This allows you to assign transport requests to specific changes, and track these requests throughout the transport landscape.

In addition to the advantages specified previously, which will primarily benefit providers with large system landscapes, one new feature will interest software companies that do not implement NWDI themselves, as their software does not need to be modified at customer sites. Using the enhanced version of CTS, Java applications that were not developed based on the component model can be distributed, for example, in at least one defined process in SAP system landscapes.

Options for Software Change Management

Based on current plans, the CTS enhancements are anticipated to include the following two options for defining the system landscape:

▶ **Setting up the Java development landscape in the form of a track in NWDI**

This is useful for customers that focus on Java development. This option can be combined with CTS to allow the more flexible design of transports in test and production systems.

▶ **Setting up a transport landscape using systems and transport routes in CTS**

In this context, NWDI only recognizes and manages individual systems. Transports between the systems are carried out exclusively in CTS. When future enhancements have been implemented, this scenario will be recommended for all landscapes that contain CTS.[6]

In SAP NetWeaver Composition Environment, you can also generate a local development configuration, and organize the transport of processes that you have implemented yourself. Section 10.4.1, *Scenarios for Component-Based Software Development in Composition Environment*, described how to create a local development configuration.

11.3.5 SAP NetWeaver Development Infrastructure in a Global System Landscape

NWDI is particularly suited to large development teams, as it allows distributed development. Distributed development is used between different companies (see Section 11.3.3, *Modification Concept of SAP NetWeaver Development Infrastructure*), in outsourcing scenarios and in companies in which the development departments are based in different locations.

Increased requirements of the development landscape

NWDI transport mechanisms — including the global version history, which is a part of all source file transports, and the option to set up identical development landscapes any number of times — support all of these scenarios. The following points must be taken into account to boost performance and ensure that work runs smoothly.

In principle, an NWDI server can also be used in a global environment for all development sites, even if these are in different locations. However, if these locations are too far apart, network effects can slow down

Network response times

---

6 This is also available in SAP Solution Manager 4.0, for example.

communication, as the request/response time increases (which are evident from the ping time). Therefore, as a basic rule of thumb, (at least) one instance should be available for each continent. In this context, exchanging data with DTR and CBS using connected Developer Studios accounts for the largest portion. Therefore, all NWDI installations can be independent of each other, or there can be a leading instance.

Process Types

Global development scenarios

There are different strategies for global development with NWDI. Choose the strategy that best suits your development scenarios.

▶ **Development of Joint Software Projects in Different Locations**
The central instance of NWDI is available for developing joint software projects in different locations. Although powerful systems are required, it is very easy to control the projects centrally. Objects can use each other seamlessly, and development objects are continually updated in tracks. Additional administrative tasks are not required.

To optimize central control, only one CMS is installed in this scenario. The network load is a lot less critical than for DTR and CBS. There are two options for managing source files and archives.

  ▶ CMS instances installed in the relevant location are not used, as a DTR will only be managed by a CMS. The central CMS is used for communication.

  ▶ DTR and CBS are also installed centrally. Developers use the *archive cache mechanism* (clones of the archives/source files are kept locally; available as of SAP NetWeaver 2004s Support Package Stack 8) to minimize the network load.

▶ **Distributed Development of (Relatively) Independent Software Projects**
There is no problem using several NWDI instances to this end. Layered development — that is, application components are built on lower layers — is handled by transporting software components. This strategy offers the greatest flexibility. Layered development, even if different layers are worked on simultaneously, is enabled by the transport of SCA versions. If interdependent layers are developed simultaneously, administrators must update the development envi-

ronment at regular intervals. DTR's version creation properties do not create any fundamental problems, however.

This strategy provides maximum flexibility for installation. Network requirements are low, as files are primarily transported in one direction instead of request/response cycles between Developer Studio and NWDI services. Centralized control and monitoring can be carried out at any stage using the NWDI Web user interfaces.

To ensure maximum flexibility and performance at any location, each location has a complete NWDI installation. Regarding the exchange of SCAs, cooperation between locations should be controlled centrally.

You do not have to decide immediately which scenario you will use. An NWDI installation can be tailored to meet increased requirements using additional installations. Initially, this can be done by adding CBS and then DTR servers, to extend a central instance of NWDI. Additional NWDI instances can also be installed, source files can be moved, and the required tracks set up again in the new location.

Deciding on scenarios

Runtime systems that support NWDI must have the same release/Support Package version as NWDI. Create tracks as described in the document *Best Practices for NWDI: Track design for ongoing development* (see *http://weblogs.sdn.sap.com/pub/wlg/3390*).

Runtime systems

NWDI and System Landscape Directory

NWDI should be integrated in your company's SLD concept (see *http://service.sap.com/SLD* • **Media Library** • **Planning Guide — System Landscape Directory**). In this context, you can only use a specific SLD for each NWDI. Ideally, this has the NWDI release state at the very least.

To make this assignment, use your own SLD for each NWDI instance, or use a shared central SLD for all NWDI instances (a mixture can be used). The Name Server role can also be assigned to a separate instance of an SLD.

Specific track information is provided for each location if several SLDs are used. As a result, each location can view the list of all tracks if a central SLD is used. If the latter case applies, you should use track-specific authorizations for the tracks to prevent incorrect accesses.

NWDI and an Enhanced Change and Transport System

Software Change Management in large-scale landscapes

As described in Section 11.3.4, *Non-ABAP-Based Transports in a Mixed System Landscape*, the enhanced version of Change and Transport System (CTS) contained in SAP NetWeaver AS ABAP can transport non-ABAP objects, as of SAP NetWeaver 7.0 Support Package Stack 12. This will impact on the transport landscape in very large system landscapes in particular. No existing transport scenarios will be rendered mandatorily invalid, however. Under no circumstances will these changes invalidate NWDI. Core functions such as setting up the development landscape, source files, and archive management, and synchronizing different development locations will continue to be carried out in NWDI. You should, however, take note of these changes, given the many advantages it will provide you when planning transport processes. The integration of both systems will be improved in the future.

You learned about SAP NetWeaver Developer Studio in the example in Chapter 3, the Employee Application. We will now use this example to illustrate development with NWDI, based on the SAP component model. Although you will create the same development objects, this time you will use software components and development components, and define public parts and use dependencies for development components. You will then check in your components into Design Time Repository (DTR) and activate them in Component Build Service (CBS), to make them available centrally. Finally, you will release your changes and complete the development.

12 SAP NetWeaver Development Infrastructure — Developing an Example Application Step-by-Step

To work with this chapter, it would help if you are familiar with Java and J2EE. More importantly, however, you should understand the concepts of the component model and its use in Developer Studio, as well as the interaction between Developer Studio and SAP NetWeaver Development Infrastructure (NWDI). Therefore, to gain most benefit from this exercise, you should have read Chapter 10, *SAP NetWeaver Development Infrastructure and the Component Model — Concepts*, and Chapter 11, *SAP NetWeaver Development Infrastructure — Configuration and Administration*, which describe the concepts and administration of NWDI and its services — DTR, CBS, and CMS. Before you can perform your steps as a developer, you must have executed the administrative steps of creating a user and a track. For more details, see the section on *Configuring Authorizations* in Section 11.1.2. Alternatively, you can simply use the NWDI_DEV user, which is created when NWDI is configured and installed.

Prerequisites

Objectives

This exercise is designed to show administrators the steps required to set up a development landscape for a specific development objective, and to give developers a feel for modularizing software into development components (DCs). You will also familiarize yourself with working in the central SAP NetWeaver Development Infrastructure in Java from a practical point of view. You will learn that by simply selecting a development component, you can configure your development environment — Developer Studio — for your development task, which in our case is the Employee application. All other steps will then be carried out in this configuration. Source files and archives are managed in NWDI. You can access only those objects that have been defined in the development configuration using the DTR workspaces and buildspaces.

Development process

The development process with Developer Studio and NWDI has been discussed in detail in Chapter 10, *SAP NetWeaver Development Infrastructure and Component Model — Concepts*, and Chapter 11, *SAP NetWeaver Development Infrastructure — Configuration and Administration*. Therefore, you already know that when you use NWDI, your local PC still plays a vital role. All existing source files and archives of the runtime objects are stored in the central systems of DTR and CBS. If you want to change them, you must download them to your local file system, check them out, and then make your changes locally. These changes are grouped into activities. You only make your changes generally available on the DTR server by checking in your activities once the local development component build has been successfully carried out (this corresponds to exactly one build in CBS) and tested in the local installation of J2EE Engine.

Tested archive state

Your source files are activated during the central build, that is, they are tested against the previously activated archives — and, as a result, against the archives added to central archive administration — and can be securely used by other developers. (By default, this happens outside of the group that develops a development component, only the activated versions can be used.) Once the centrally built archives have been successfully tested, you release your activities in CMS. SAP NetWeaver Developer Studio provides the user interface for all these steps.

12.1 Employee Example Application

We want to emphasize again that using NWDI does not affect the basic structure of development objects. However, some objects are added because the component model is used: All properties of the SAP component model — such as public parts and use dependencies — are added using the development component metadata. EJBs, JSPs, Java classes, and so on are not involved.

The component model and standard development

For our example application, this means that you can copy all specifications on the data model, persistency, business logic, the presentation layer, and Web service without changes. With NWDI, you will import the required development configurations and create all elements with unchanged source code. You still use Developer Studio to do so. However, it is now important that you create all projects as development components. The steps that follow are basically new: You define the DC-specific properties, which are the public parts and the use dependencies. You then make your objects available centrally by creating them centrally in DTR, creating the runtime objects in CBS, and releasing them in CMS.

The use of development components results in the structure shown in Figure 12.1. Here, you see the software component L_BOOK_EMPLOYEE with four development components displayed with their names and types. As part of the development components, you see the public parts and use dependencies between the development components and software components, based on the SAP component model. For the EMPLOYEE software component, the use dependencies to the imported software components SAP_BUILDT, FRAMEWORK, and ENGFACADE are displayed.

Structure of the example application

12.2 Working with SAP NetWeaver Development Infrastructure — Initial Steps

As mentioned previously, this example adheres very closely to the Employee application with which you are already familiar.[1] For this reason, the steps that do not change due to component-based development with NWDI will only be mentioned here, and will not be described again.

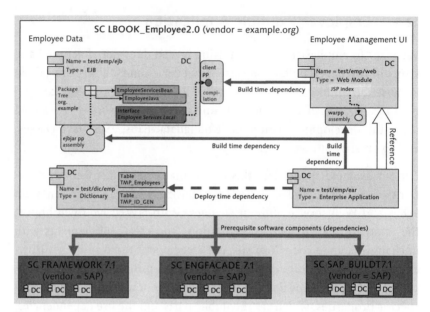

Figure 12.1 Structure of the Employee Application in the Component Model

Any changed or new steps will of course be explained in detail. Therefore, it makes sense at this point to run through the example again without using development components to familiarize you with the concepts of this development task and with Developer Studio. This also helps to emphasize the differences between the two development processes.

If you would only like to learn about DC-based development, you can view the details in the example of non–DC-based development, because the classes and tables, for example, are copied in an unchanged format.[2]

User management   In our example, NWDI uses SAP User Management Engine for user management. To be able to work with NWDI, you need a user account

---

1   Additional step-by-step descriptions are available in the SAP NetWeaver Developer Studio help documentation. To open these, choose **Help • Help Contents**. For more information on SAP NetWeaver Development Infrastructure, including the links to the SAP Help Portal for SAP and video demos in SDN (*http://sdn.sap.com*), go to **SAP NetWeaver Capabilities • Lifecycle Management • Software Logistics • Software Change Management**.

2   In many cases, you can use the copy and paste function, for example, in the Dictionary Explorer. However, make sure that table names are unique.

that grants developer authorizations for NWDI. The development process proposed by SAP contains the role NWDI.Developer. The actions CBS.Developer, CMS.Display, and CMS.Import are assigned to this role. The role itself is assigned to the group NWDI.Developers. All users in the role of an NWDI developer can now be assigned to this group. To maintain these settings, you need the group NWDI.Administrators with the role NWDI.Administrator, which contains the actions CBS.Administrator, CMS.Administrate, and CMS.Display.[3] You can also use the user of the demo installation, which has the role NWDI.Developer.

In the standard development process, an administrator must now define the product, the software component, and the dependencies between the software components in System Landscape Directory (SLD), to create the context for the new software development. For this example, a software component LBOOK_EMPLOYEE has been defined, which uses the software components ENGFACADE, FRAMEWORK, and SAP_BUILDT. This is the minimal configuration you require to generate the four DC types for the project. For example, you also need the software component WD-RUNTIME, to allow you to develop with Web Dynpro Java as well.

Preparing the development project

> **Note**
>
> If you use NWDI on SAP NetWeaver release 7.0, and do not yet have the required SCA files (release 7.10), you can download them from the DVD accompanying this book. They are located in the *CMS/inbox* subdirectory of the transport directory, in the directory *<sap-dir>/<SID>/<SYS>/global/ CMS_CBS/plugins*. Carry out this step (at least) for the required SCA files SAP_BUILDT, WD-RUNTIME, FRAMEWORK, and ENGFACADE of SAP NetWeaver CE, release 7.1. You can also download these files from SAP Service Marketplace (*http://service.sap.com*) under **Software Download • Download**.

Based on these prerequisites, at least one track must be created in CMS, which generates the development configurations for the development phases. To create a new development configuration, you can save one of the delivered development configurations under a new name, for example, JBookEmp, using **Save As** in CMS Landscape Configurator. (If this additional required software component is one of those listed, this does

Tracks and development configurations

---

3 In Visual Administrator, the settings LCRLcrInstanceWriterAll and LcrInstanceWriterNR must also be allocated for the roles NWDI.Administrator and NWDI.Developer.

not affect the process.) Finally, you must enter the used software components as SCAs on the **Check-in** tab, check them in, and select and import them on the **Development** tab (and possibly also choose **Consolidation**).

The tracks `Development` and `Maintenance` have been created for this example. Each of these tracks contains the development configurations for development and consolidation (`dev` and `cons`). You can also copy them and prepare them for the development by checking them in and importing them. In this example, we use the `JBookEmp` track.

12.3 Development Cycle Using the Employee Application

An example track allows the development of a software component using SAP NetWeaver Composition Environment, release 7.1, as the target platform in an NWDI on SAP NetWeaver 7.0 Support Package Stack 13. (If you use an existing NWDI, this will also contain tracks that are configured for development against release 7.0 runtime systems.)

12.3.1 Prerequisites for a Track Using SAP NetWeaver Composition Environment as the Target Platform

NWDI and
Composition
Environment

NWDI is more or less independent of the software version used. In the example, an NWDI is used on SAP NetWeaver release 7.0, Support Package Stack 13, which also supports deployment for SAP NetWeaver Composition Environment. The objects used must nevertheless be available in the correct version, and the track must be set up for a specific release, as follows:

▸ The content of SLD must correspond to that of the target platform.

▸ Preparatory steps must be carried out in CBS, to use JDK 1.5.0_xx.

SLD Update

Import the corresponding versions of the CIM model (an update to Version 1.4.30 is required, to allow you to update to Version 1.5; for more information, see SAP Note 907897) and of the CR content (at least CRDELTA1504xx; for more information, see SAP Note 669669). See *Configuring System Landscape Directory* in Section 11.1.2 for a more detailed description.

CBS Settings for JEE Version 5.0

Using several JDKs in CBS is a cross-track setting. To do this, the track that uses a variant other than the standard variant must be modified in each case. This is described in Section 12.3.4, *Creating, Configuring, and Preparing the Example Track*.

1. Start Visual Administrator under *<Drive>:\usr\sap\SID\JC00\j2ee\ admin* in a pure Java installation or under *<Drive>:\usr\sap\SID\ DVEBMGS01\j2ee\admin*.

2. Log on as **administrator**.

3. Select **Server • Services • Component Build Service/Properties**.

4. Assign the settings displayed in Figure 12.2 for BUILD_TOOL_JDK_HOME and JDK_HOME_PATHS.

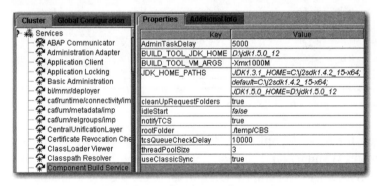

Figure 12.2 Visual Administrator CBS Settings for JEE Version 5.0

▶ BUILD_TOOL_JDK_HOME refers to the path of JDK_1.5=_xx.

▶ JDK_HOME_PATHS specifies the paths of all available JDK versions, each separated by a semi-colon.

JDK for Composition Environment

12.3.2 Creating a Product and a Software Component in System Landscape Directory

Application structure in the component model

As described in Section 10.2.1, *Component Model*, component-based development is always carried out in the context of software component and product. Therefore, as a first step, create new versions of these objects in SLD as an NWDI administrator (NWDI_ADM):

1. Log on as NWDI.Administrator to System Landscape Directory. The link is available on the NWDI initial screen under *http://<host:port>/devinf*.

2. Choose **Software Catalog · Products**, and create a new product by selecting **New Product Version** (Figure 12.3).

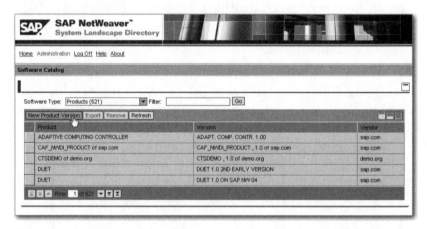

Figure 12.3 Creating a Product in SLD

Product parameters

3. Enter the **Name** "Employee", "example.org" for the owner's Internet domain (**Vendor**), and the **Version** "2.0" (Figure 12.4). Version 2.0 was selected, as an earlier version of this example was available in the first edition of this book. If you do not have this earlier version, you can start with version number 1.0.

4. Select **Create**.

Software unit

5. Create a new software unit called "Employee" (Figure 12.5). Software units are used to clearly structure products with several software components — for example, SAP NetWeaver.

▶ The product is the `Employee` product that has just been created (default entry in the field).

▶ Vendor is the Internet domain of the hypothetical company that owns the software. In our example, this is *example.org* (default entry in the field).

▶ The version is the product version.

▶ You can choose any name. In this case, select `Employee`.

Figure 12.4 Product Properties in SLD

Figure 12.5 Software Unit in SLD

6. Create the software component that you want to develop (Figure 12.6). **SC parameters**

▶ The product and unit are the ones that have just been created (default entry in the field).

▶ The vendor is the Internet name of the company that owns the software. In our example, this is *example.org*. (Default entry in the field.)

▶ You can choose any name. In this case, select `Employee`.

▶ The version is the product version.

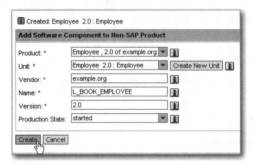

Figure 12.6 Software Component Properties in SLD

7. In the next step, select the software component, to define the dependencies of `L_BOOK_EMPLOYEE` to the required software components (Figure 12.7). In this case, the following software components are used:

▶ `DI_BUILD_TOOL 7.10 (SAP_BUILDT)`

▶ `J2EE_ENGINE_FACADE 7.10 (ENGFACADE)`

▶ `JAVA_FRAMEWORK OFFLINE 7.10(FRAMEWORK)`

This allows you to develop standard JEE projects (as development components), and to develop Dictionary development components for the database connection of your application.

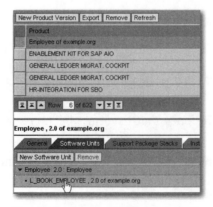

Figure 12.7 Selecting a Software Component for the Product

8. On the **Dependencies** tab of the SLD software component, select **Define Prerequisite Software Components**, and then choose **Build Time**. The **Define Prerequisite Software Components** screen appears (dependencies to the build time are mandatory; dependencies to the installation time are currently not evaluated).

Software component dependencies of the example application

9. Set a filter for ENGFACADE, and copy the software component in Version 7.10 using **Define Prerequisite Software Components** (Figure 12.8).

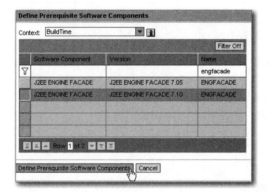

Figure 12.8 Defining a Build Time Dependency to the Software Component ENGFACADE

10. Repeat these steps for the software components SAP_BUILDT and FRAMEWORK. Your software component definition should be the same as the one shown in Figure 12.9.

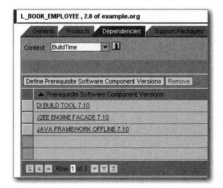

Figure 12.9 Dependencies of the Software Component L_BOOK_EMPLOYEE

12.3.3 Updating Change Management Service

SLD data forms the basis for defining tracks in CMS. You now have to load the new data from SLD.

1. Log on to CMS as NWDI_ADM. The link is available under *http:// <host:port>/devinf* on the NWDI initial screen.

2. Select **Landscape Configurator** and then **Domain Data** (Figure 12.10).

Figure 12.10 CMS Landscape Configurator/Domain Data

3. Select the **Change** mode, and start the update of CMS data from SLD by selecting the **Update CMS** button (Figure 12.11).

Figure 12.11 Updating CMS Data from SLD

12.3.4 Creating, Configuring, and Preparing the Example Track

Based on the structure defined in SLD for the Employee product, define the development landscape for the developer team.

1. In **CMS Landscape Configurator**, choose the link **Track Data** (Figure 12.12), and start to create a track by selecting **New** (Figure 12.13).

Figure 12.12 CMS Landscape Configurator/Track Data

Figure 12.13 CMS Landscape Configurator — Creating a Track

2. Assign the track data (Figure 12.14) and save your settings. Note that, when using these settings, L_BOOK_EMPLOYEE will contain source files and archives in the shipment.

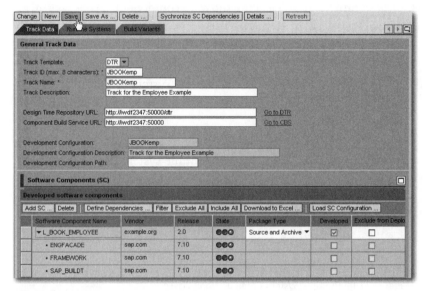

Figure 12.14 Settings in the Example Track

▶ The **Track ID** can have up to eight characters.

▶ The **Track Name** should be self-explanatory. As a track can be retained across several releases by implementing updates, release descriptions are not always recommended in this context.

▶ The **Track Description** should be self-explanatory.

▶ The **Design Time Repository URL** and **Component Build Service URL** are predefined; you are only required to change the default values if you are using more than one DTR or CBS system. If this is the case, you need to manually change the relevant URL or URLs in those tracks that do not use the DTR or CBS URL entered in the track by default.

▶ The **Development Configuration Path** allows you to define the hierarchy for displaying the list of available development configurations in Developer Studio during the import process (for example, Employee/1.0, Employee/2.0; both development configurations pairs — _dev and _cons from both releases — would then the displayed under the entry Employee, which you could then drill down).

SC dependencies

3. Choose **Add SC...**, to select the software component L_BOOK_Employee, which you wish to develop. The software components previously defined (for example, BUILDT, and FRAMEWORK) are automatically used, based on the dependency defined in SLD.

Assigning the run-time systems to the track

4. If you wish, you can now add a runtime system to the track. In CMS Landscape Configurator, choose the **Runtime Systems** tab and select **Consolidation**.

5. A wizard appears. Enter data in the fields **Host Name** and **HTTP Port of Message Server** of the relevant runtime system (Figure 12.15).

Figure 12.15 Runtime System Configuration Wizard

6. Enter data for the runtime system (Figure 12.16). The host and port entered may differ from those specified in Figure 12.16.

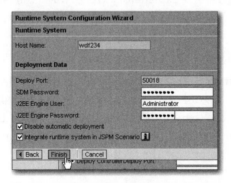

Figure 12.16 Properties of a Runtime System

7. Enter information for the use of the runtime system. In other words, specify if the system is to be used for the **Development**, **Consolidation**, **Test** or **Production** phase (Figure 12.17). Select the deploy

method **Deploy Controller** for SAP NetWeaver Composition Environment release 7.1 systems (**Deploy Host**, **Deploy Port**, **Deploy User**, **Deploy Password**).

8. Use the where-used list for runtime systems to determine whether this system is already being used for other phases. (Data would be overwritten if the system were used for several development phases of the same software components or even for different versions.)

Where-used list for runtime systems

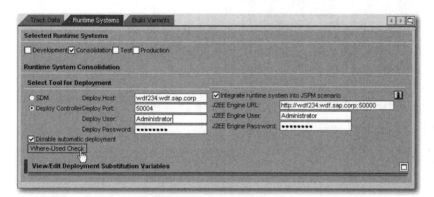

Figure 12.17 Where-Used List of the Runtime System

> **Note**
>
> If at all, you should only use the NWDI server as a runtime environment for tests in NWDI systems that are not used in a production environment. Otherwise, NWDI may not be available to resolve serious errors.

9. Finally, save your settings.

You must now modify the build variant of the track for JEE version 5.0.

Modifying a build variant

1. Select the **Build Variants** tab. Go to **Change** mode, select **Default**, and choose **Edit...** (Figure 12.18).

Figure 12.18 Editing the Build Variant

Setting the build
option for Compo-
sition Environment

2. Select **New** to create a new build option (Figure 12.19).

Figure 12.19 Creating a Build Option

JDK_1.5.0_Set
home parameter

3. Enter the following data (Figure 12.20):

> ▸ Enter: `com.sap.jdk.home_path_key`

> ▸ Enter the value `JDK1.5.0_HOME` — this variable contains the path to `JDK_1.5.0_xx` for CBS.

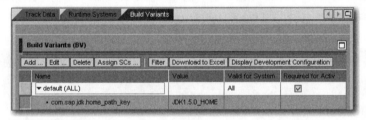

Figure 12.20 Build Option for Using JEE Version 5.0 for the Build Process

4. Save your entries.

Filling the
buildspace

DTR workspaces, CBS buildspaces, and the corresponding development configurations were generated when the track was saved. All other steps — to modify the track data if required — are carried out in **CMS Transport Studio**. Before development starts, you must fill the buildspaces with the archives that are initially available (development component of the used software components).

Checking in the
SCA version

When the versions are checked in, you define the Support Package version for the SCAs used. These should correspond to the release/Support Package version of the target platform for deployment.

1. Select **CMS Transport Studio**. The available versions of the software components in the track are displayed.

> **Note**
>
> If the list is empty, check the CMS Inbox directory, which is usually located under *D:\usr\sap\trans\EPS\in\CMShostSID\CMS\inbox*. Alternatively, configure the check-in for the directory in which your SCAs are located.

2. Select the required SCAs in Version 7.10 in the Support Package release of your Developer Studio and your target runtime system. Start **Check-In** (Figure 12.21).

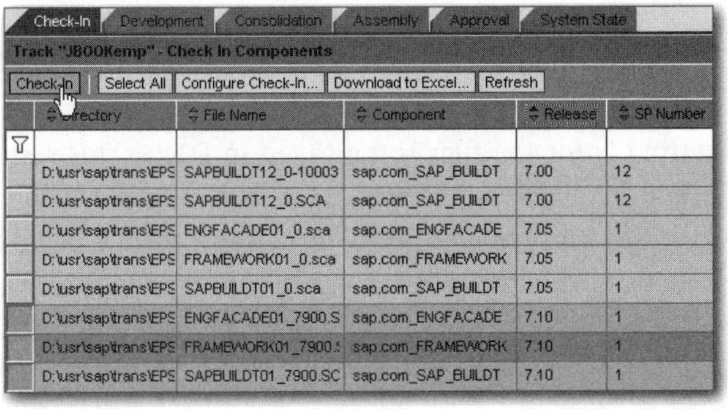

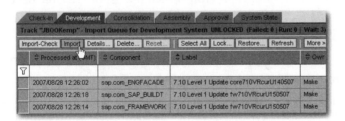

Figure 12.21 Check-In of Required SCAs in CMS Transport Studio

3. Import the checked-in SCAs one after another into the buildspaces of the development and consolidation system by choosing **Import** (Figure 12.22). If a version of the SCA to be developed is available, this can also be imported, along with the source files.

SC import to physically fill the development systems

Figure 12.22 Import of the Required SCAs

4. Repeat the import for the consolidation system.

12.3.5 Starting the Development Phase

When you have carried out these steps, the development landscape is configured. Inform your development team of the host and port of the SLD configured in NWDI (located under **CMS Domain**), the track name, and the version of the software component to be developed, if this is not already known.

Configuring the Developer Studio

Start parameters

Start SAP NetWeaver Developer Studio as you have previously. An Eclipse workspace is also required. However, now you must make or check some settings that are specific to NWDI development.

Window preferences settings

You also select your settings for working with NWDI under **Window · Preferences**. Note the following:

Defining file types that are not to be saved

▶ The first key setting is for the files to be saved in DTR.[4] This setting differs in different development scenarios. In our example, you use the entire NWDI and must select the relevant settings in Developer Studio. Ensure that all listed types including .project and .classpath are selected in the **Window · Preferences · Team · Ignored Resources** menu item. This means that they are not saved in DTR. If the entries do not appear in the list, you can add them using the same path by selecting **Add Pattern**, and then choosing the required entries.

Linking Developer Studio with SLD

▶ The second setting defines the system from which you retrieve the development configurations. Under **Window · Preferences · Development Infrastructure · Landscape Directory**, enter the URL of your NWDI's System Landscape Directory. This system defines the connection to CMS in your landscape, from which the list of available development configurations will be retrieved. Enter the server and port for your SLD here (*http://<server:port>*).

Because you often test your objects locally when you use an NWDI, make the settings for the local J2EE Engine as well.

---

4 Remember that, in the standard development process, only source files are saved in DTR. These include files that contain source code and files that contain metadata such as public parts or DC definitions. There are also files with information on the class path and the project. Whether these are stored depends on the development scenario. When using the entire NWDI, the latter two file types cannot be saved.

Importing a Development Configuration

To some degree, a developer's work with NWDI always starts with the import of the development configuration. This always defines the software component to be developed. It also determines the application's structure — that is, which software components can be used as a basis — and access to the correct logical systems — that is, the DTR workspaces and buildspaces. For a local development configuration, it describes the application's structure and the availability of local copies of the used SCs. You can also create development components outside of a *central* development configuration, but migrating them into NWDI will then require manual input. You can only check that a development component or package name is unique, as required, using NWDI.

Connection with central systems

Figure 12.23 shows the **Development Infrastructure** perspective. No development configuration has been imported. Local Development is a genuine test configuration that does not create a connection to central systems.[5] The cursor is already positioned on the icon for importing a development configuration.

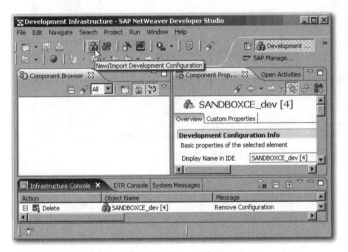

Figure 12.23 Perspective Development Infrastructure

1. Open the **Development Infrastructure** Perspective in Developer Studio.

---

5 Migration at a later stage is also not supported.

Importing development configurations

2. In the top function bar, select **New/Import Development Configuration** ( ).

3. In the **New/Import Development Configuration** Wizard, select **from System Landscape Directory (SLD)** (or create a local development configuration with these software components, but without access to the central server, as described in *Creating a Local Development Configuration* in Section 10.4.2, if you want to work without a server; all steps in Developer Studio — except for those related to activities, activation, and the release to CMS — remain the same).

Login

4. A list of the available NWDI development configurations, whose SLD you have specified in the preferences, now appears. Log on[6] to the central systems and select the development configuration for your tasks. In our example, this is the development configuration JBookEmp_dev[7] (Figure 12.24).

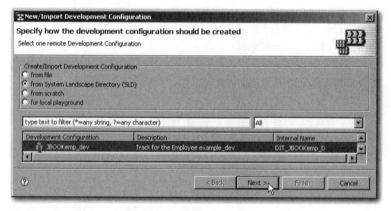

Figure 12.24 List of Development Configurations

5. Choose **Next** and **Finish**, to finish the import.

Storage location in the file system

The import automatically creates a folder in which the files created in this configuration are stored. By default, this folder is located under *<drive>:\Documents and Settings\<user>\.dtc\<development configuration name>*.[8]

---

6 If you do not have your own user for the NWDI.Developers group, you can use the NWDI_DEV user, which is created when you install and configure NWDI.

7 Here, specific details of the object names in the figures may differ from the text.

8 The Eclipse workspace references this directory.

Defining the Data Model

Compared to the non-component-based procedure, the data model of the Employee application remains unchanged. This means that you use the Java Dictionary to create the table for the management of persistent Employee data, and then add the required columns in the relevant editor.

To do this, you will now create a development component project that will produce a corresponding archive, which you will then deploy from Developer Studio, to convert your table definition, which initially only exists locally, into a physical representation on the database instance.

Creating a Dictionary DC Project

Dictionary projects are designed to create tables that, during design time, serve as containers for both Dictionary data types and data structure and for tables. You use a Development Component Wizard to create an initial project frame for the new Dictionary DC project.

After reading Section 10.2.2, *Design Time Repository*, and Section 10.2.3, *Component Build Service*, you should be familiar with the activation concept and understand that new development objects are always created with the status `inactive`.

Creating development components — a Dictionary DC project

1. In the **Component Browser** of the **Development Configuration** perspective, select the filter setting **All**, **Inactive** or **Local**. (You cannot create development components under **Active**.) Changeable software and development components are yellow. Required software components and active development components that cannot be changed at present are displayed in purple.

Component Browser

2. You see the compartment that contains your changeable software component, specifying the vendor[9] and name. In this example, this is `demo.org.JBOOK_EMP`.

3. To start the Development Component Wizard, select **Create New Development Component** in the context menu of your software component (Figure 12.25).

---

9 The vendor name is usually the vendor's Internet domain. For SAP software components, this is `sap.com`. In the screenshots, a different vendor name — `example.org` — is used.

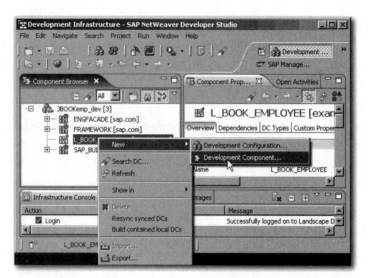

Figure 12.25 Creating a New Development Component (or a Local Development Configuration)

DC type 4. First, select the development component type. Each development component has a type, which is generated based on its structure. In line with the application structure, start with the basics, a **Dictionary** development component (Figure 12.26), which contains the required tables. Choose **Next**.

Figure 12.26 DC Types

5. The **New Development Component (Project)** Wizard appears.[10] Here, you define all key settings for your development component.

DC parameters

6. Set the following parameters (Figure 12.27):

   ▶ **Vendor**
   This is the owner of the development component. This value usually contains a default setting from SLD, in this case `example.org`.

   ▶ **Name**
   The name is made up of two parts:

   ▶ **Prefix**
   This is assigned in the Name Service. In our example, the prefix is `test`.

   ▶ **DC name**
   Call this Dictionary DC `employee/dic`.[11]

   ▶ **Caption**
   Enter a description for the development component.

   ▶ **Language**
   Define the language for the development component.

   ▶ **Domain**
   This is not the CMS domain. You can specify here the business environment to which your development component belongs. Select **Basis**.

   ▶ Do not change the setting for **Keep DC local for now…** (not selected). Only fill out **Support Component** for SAP components.

7. Now choose **Next**. You will now be prompted to select an activity (Figure 12.28).

Saving changes in activities

8. When creating a development component project using NWDI, source files that will be stored in DTR are generated. An activities selection screen appears.[12] Because you have not yet created an activ-

Creating an activity

---

10 You can also open this Wizard by choosing **File** • **New Project** • **Development Component** • **Next** • **<Development-Configuration>** • **SC** in the menu.

11 If more than one person implements this example on the same system, this name is reserved for the first person who creates it. In this case, add a suffix such as your initial directly to the `dic` part of the name.

12 You probably remember that all changes to objects in DTR are organized into activities.

ity for this development component, the list will probably be empty. Select **Create Activity** to generate a new activity.

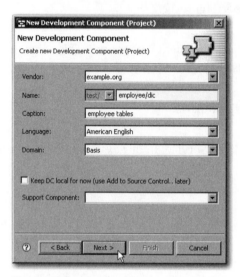

Figure 12.27 Properties of a New Development Component in the New DC Project Wizard

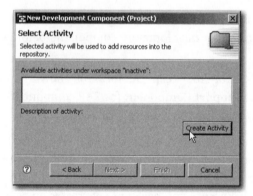

Figure 12.28 Creating a New Activity — First Step

9. Enter an unambiguous name, for example, `New dictionary DC <DC Name>`,[13] and a description (to allow you to easily recognize the development component at a later stage), and select **OK**, to confirm your entries. The activity is now available in the list.

---

13 If more than one person uses this example, you may add your initials as a suffix.

10. You will use this activity for all changes to this development component — right up to checking it in for the first time after a successful local test. This guarantees that all development component elements are in one group and can later be activated and transported together (Figure 12.29).

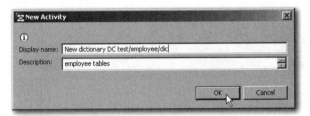

Figure 12.29 Creating an Activity — Assigning a Name and Description

11. Select the new activity from the list (Figure 12.30) and choose **Next** to confirm your entries. You can use this function if you are working on several tasks at once, for example, two development components, A and B. Make sure that related files are saved in the same activity. In other words, all files for DC A are stored in activity A, and all files for DC B are saved in activity B. (However, closely related changes to two DCs may be saved in one activity; mixing does not make sense.) Remember that activities are the units that propagate changes and provide content for the build process.

Assigning files to activities

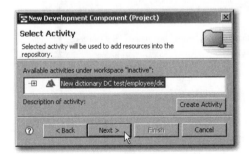

Figure 12.30 Selecting an Activity

12. The settings for the DC project now appear. Confirm these by selecting **Finish**.

DC properties 13. You now create the DC project structure. The relevant perspective appears automatically for the new development component (Figure 12.31). All development components share properties, the most important of which are **dependencies** and **public parts** (Figure 12.32).

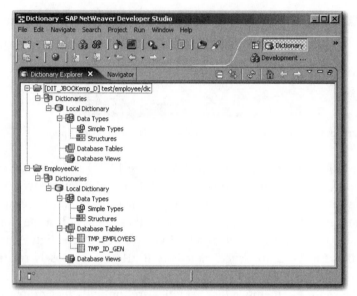

Figure 12.31 Structure of the Dictionary DC (test/employee/dic)

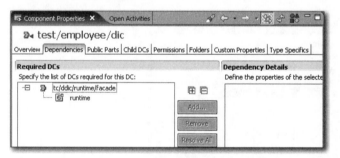

Figure 12.32 DC Properties

14. The other properties are the same as in the corresponding non-DC project. You can open the display of properties from the context menu of each development component by selecting **Show in · Component Properties**.

> **Note**
>
> In the **Navigator** view, you can copy the contents of the *packages* directory and insert them into the corresponding development component directory. All objects are added to the development component activity. Copying the contents in this way is a workaround. A function to transfer projects to the component model is to be developed but has not yet been implemented for all project types.

Defining an Employee Table

Now create the table for employee data as part of the DC project you have just created. Then add the required table fields as columns.

Table definition

1. Open the development component `employee/dic` in Dictionary Explorer, and create the tables as described in Chapter 3, *SAP NetWeaver Developer Studio — Step-by-Step to a Sample Application.*[14]

2. Select the same activity for all changes to your Dictionary DC to be able to check in all parts of this development component, and activate and transport them together at a later stage.

3. Create the table fields, as described in Chapter 3, and remember to set up a secondary index and buffering.

Table fields

4. Save your data. This is now available as a local project resource in the form of an XML file. Notice the following important result: Our table, as part of the Java Dictionary, has a database-independent definition.

Saving your entries

Defining the Public Parts of Development Components

You already know that you have to explicitly declare the use of components defined in line with the SAP component model. To recap: The use dependencies between software components are defined in SLD by the administrator. Use dependencies are parts of the metadata of almost all development components. In order for a development object to be used validly, this must be a component of a public part of the development

Public parts

---

14 The `JBOOK_` prefix must be defined in the SLD Name Service for data objects. If this has not been done, start the SLD user interface, select **Name Reservation • Define Namespace Prefix, Name Category = DB Object Name**, and assign the **Namespace Prefix**.

component to which it belongs. Depending on the purpose of the public part, we distinguish between the types `Compilation` and `Assembly`.

> **Note**
>
> If you use Java EE 5.0, which uses the new Java Persistence API (JPA), this step is no longer mandatory for the `Dictionary` DC type. We have included the description here, as you will need it if you do not use Java EE 5. Of course, you define a public part of the development component for earlier versions of Dictionary DCs and all other DC types — even in JEE 5.0.
>
> 1. In the **Component Browser**, double-click to select the development component.
> 2. Choose the **Component Properties** view, to enable you to maintain the **DC metadata** (under **Window • Show View... • Other... • Development Infrastructure • Component Properties**).
> 3. The **Dependencies** and **Public Parts** tabs are displayed (Figure 12.33). Earlier versions of Developer Studio contain the nodes **DC Definition** with the used development components and **Public Parts**.
> 4. It often makes sense to add public parts to the generated public parts.

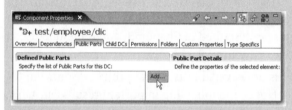

Figure 12.33 Creating a Public Part; No Longer Required with Java EE 5.0

You create public parts in **Component Properties**:[15]

Adding public parts to the development component

1. On the **Public Parts** tab, select the **Add...** button (Figure 12.33).
2. In the New Public Part Wizard, create the following parameters (Figure 12.34):

   ▶ **Name:** emp

   ▶ **Purpose:** COMPILATION

   ▶ **Caption:** Enter a description for the public part.

   ▶ **Description**: You can specify details for the public part here.

---

15 This public part is not explicitly required for this example application. However, it could be important for other uses and shows you how to create a public part manually.

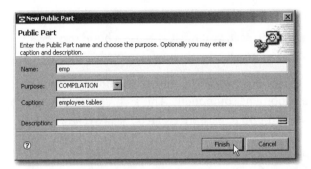

Figure 12.34 Public Part Properties

3. Add the public part to the activity that contains the definition for your Dictionary DC.

4. To add entities to the public part, choose **Manage Entities** in the context menu for the part.

5. On the wizard screen now displayed, select under **Entities**[16] the object types that will be published in the public part. Then create these objects under **Select Entities**.

Adding public part entities

6. In this example, find the **Dictionary Database Tables** TMP_ID_GEN and TMP_EMPLOYEES in the hierarchical structure (Figure 12.35).

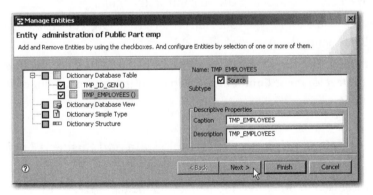

Figure 12.35 Public Part Entities

---

16 You can maintain the public part entities at any stage. Each public part contains the **Entities** node. To open the editor for the public part entities, select **Edit Entities...** in the context menu of this node. As this constitutes a change to the source files, the public part must be checked out at the very least, and you require an activity for the changes.

Building and Deploying Development Components

Generating a
dictionary archive As is the case for a local project, you must also use a build process to create an archive from a DC project, to obtain a deployable result.

1. To do this, select **Development Component · Build** from the context
   menu of the development component. The archives for the development component and public part are created locally (Figure 12.36).

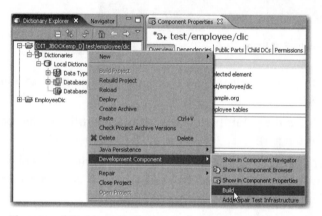

Figure 12.36 Build and Deployment of a Development Component

2. On the next screen, select **OK**, to confirm the build.

Preparing the
deployment 3. Because you should test your objects locally before you make them
   available centrally, start the local J2EE server.

4. To deploy the development component in the Dictionary Explorer,
   select **Development Component · Deploy** in the context menu of the
   DC node.

12.3.6 Implementing Access to Table Data and Business Logic

You can now create employee data in tables. The tables are filled and
data is accessed in other development components.

Creating an EJB Module Development Component

Creating develop-
ment components
— EJB DC project 1. In the **Component Browser**, create another development component
   of the type **J2EE · EJB Module**, using the following parameters. Then
   carry out the steps described in Chapter 3:

▶ **Vendor**

This is the owner of the development component.

▶ **Name**

The name is made up of two parts:

▶ **Prefix**

In our example, the prefix is `test`.

▶ **DC name**

Call the EJB development component `employee/ejb.ss`

▶ **Caption**

Enter a description for the development component.

▶ **Language**

Define the language for the development component. Choose **American English**.

▶ **Domain**

Choose **Basis**.

▶ Do not change the setting for **Keep DC local for now...** (not selected).

2. Choose **Next**.

3. In the **New Project** Wizard, leave **Java EE version 5.0**, and choose **Finish** to confirm your entries (Figure 12.37). This version must be available for CBS, and it must be used by the track. For more information, see Chapter 11.

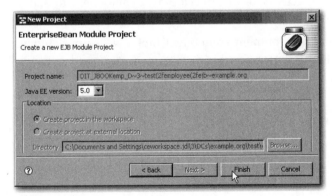

Figure 12.37 Properties of the EJB Module Development Component, Including the Java EE Version

Activity

4. For this development component, use a new activity, and call it "New EJB Module DC", for example. From this point on, you use J2EE DC Explorer as the basis for all other steps in EJB development.

5. The initial project structure already contains two deployment descriptors: the standard descriptor *ejb-jar.xml* and a server-specific descriptor called *ejb-j2ee-engine.xml*. In the next step, you add an entity bean to this project.

6. In this development component, define the following objects as described in the example in Chapter 3 and include all these objects in the new activity for the development component.

Automatic change of perspective

7. Use the function that appears on the screen, to go to the **J2EE** perspective.

> **Note**
>
> In the **Navigator** view, you can copy the contents of the *packages* directory and insert them in the corresponding development component directory. To do this, the contents of the *ejbModule* directory and its *com* subdirectories (including all content) and of *META-INF* (the file *persistence.xml*) are required. All objects are added to the development component activity.

Public parts of the EJB module development component

8. The public parts of this development component are generated automatically. The public parts `ejbjar` (type `Assembly`) and `client` (type `Compilation`) are located in your DC structure.

Local reference

9. As the local reference, select the **Employee Bean** from your EJB DC. Now use the activity of this development component to add your changes to DTR.

10. Execute the development component build. No extra deployment must be implemented for this development component. It will be deployed later in an Enterprise Application DC.

Creating a JSP-Based User Interface

Creating development components

To create a simple user interface for the Employee application, you need another development component that contains the Web resources.

1. Create a development component of the type **J2EE · Web Module**, using the following parameters:

   ▶ **Vendor**
   The name of the vendor is `example.org`.

   ▶ **Name**
   The name is made up of two parts:

   ▶ **Prefix**
   In this example, the prefix is `test`.

   ▶ **DC name**
   Call this Web module DC `employee/web`.

   ▶ **Caption**
   Enter a description for the development component.

   ▶ **Language**
   Select **American English**.

   ▶ **Domain**
   Choose **Basis**.

   ▶ Again, do not change the setting for **Keep DC local for now...** (not selected).

2. For the new development component, create an activity called **New Web Module**, in the same way as for the other development components. In the **New Project** Wizard, leave **Java EE version 5.0**, and choose **Finish**, to confirm your entries.

3. Go to the J2EE perspective, and carry out the following steps, as described for non-DC projects.

4. Error messages now appear for the JSP file in Developer Studio. These are shown in Figure 12.38. These messages tell you that you are not yet allowed to use the EJB DC. First, you must create a use dependency — only then are you allowed to use the released objects of another development component (public part entities).

   Adding a use dependency to the development component

5. Open your Web module DC in the **Component Properties** view (which you can access in the context menu of the development component, for example, by choosing **Development Component · Show in Component Properties**).

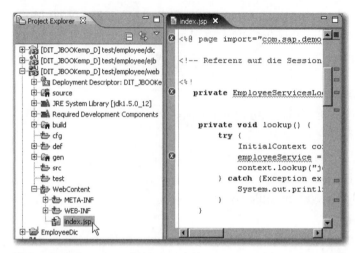

Figure 12.38 Error Caused by Unavailable Use Dependency when Importing in JSP

6. Under **Dependencies**, select the **Add...** button (Figure 12.39).

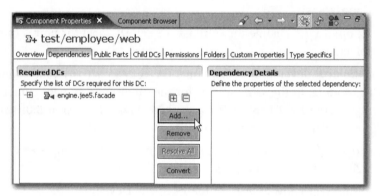

Figure 12.39 Creating a Use Dependency

DC Dependency Wizard

7. In the **Adding Dependencies** Wizard (Figure 12.40), select your software component from your development configuration. (Up to now, this was only available in the DTR workspace Inactive, because it has not yet been centrally built, that is, it has not been activated yet.)

Defining the DC dependency type

8. Navigate to the EJB DC employee/ejb to the public part ejbjar, and declare a use dependency of the **Build Time** dependency type (Figure 12.41).

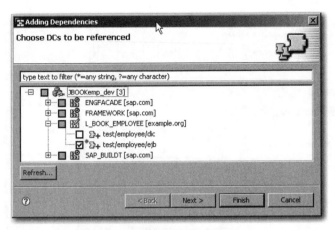

Figure 12.40 Creating a Use Dependency

Figure 12.41 Properties of a Use Dependency

9. Save your entries. The errors should have disappeared. Again, you use the activity of the development component whose metadata you change, that is, the one that declares the use dependency.

10. Implement the following steps as described for non-DC projects:

   ▸ Add a description to the *web.xml* deployment descriptor.

   ▸ Create a Web archive.

11. Finally, execute the DC build. A deployment is also not required here at this point of time.

12. When you have defined the use dependency, select **Validate** in the context menu of the Web module DC (Figure 12.42). The errors are eliminated.

Validating a DC project

639

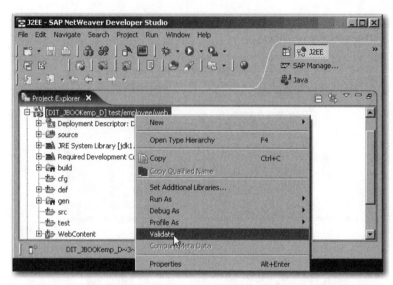

Figure 12.42 Checking the Consistency of a Development Component (Metadata is Complete)

Creating and Testing the Entire Application

Creating development components — Enterprise Application DC project

Now create a new development component of the type **J2EE · Enterprise Application**, which provides a framework for the entire application.

1. Use the following parameters:

   ▸ **Vendor**
   This is the owner of the development component.

   ▸ **Name**
   The name is made up of two parts:

   ▸ **Prefix**
   In our example, the prefix is test.

   ▸ **DC Name**
   The DC name is employee/ear.

   ▸ **Caption**
   Enter a description for the development component.

   ▸ **Language**
   Select **American English**.

> ▶ **Domain**
>
> Choose **Basis**.

> ▶ Do not change the setting for **Keep DC local for now...** (not selected).

2. Use a new activity for this development component, and call this "New Enterprise Application DC".

3. Then carry out the following steps, as described in the *Getting Started* section: To do this, select **Add Modules** in the development component context menu.

4. Select the two DC projects that are displayed on the screen.

5. Once you have defined the characteristics of the EAR DC, do not select **Finish**. Instead, choose **Next** again to add the Web module and the EJB DC directly (Figure 12.43).

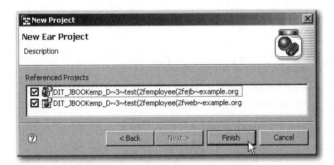

Figure 12.43 Choosing the Development Components to be Packed

Building, Deploying, and Testing the Enterprise Application

To deploy the application, build the EAR DC. The used development components are also built, if this has not already been done. You then continue to deploy and implement the Enterprise Application DC on the local J2EE Engine, as you have done before (Figure 12.44).

Deploying applications

Note
If an error appears during deployment, check whether a Web service that has not been implemented is specified in the source code. If this is the case, add a comment for this service in the object `EmployeeServicesBean.java`.

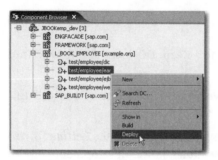

Figure 12.44 Deploying an Enterprise Application

Test the application by entering the vendor name in the browser, as follows:

Calling the application in the browser

*<Protocol>://<host:port>/<vendor>~<DC name Part 1>~<Part 2>~
<Part n>/<file name>*, for example: *http://abc123:50000/
example.org~test~employee~web/index.jsp*

Making Development Objects Available Centrally

After you have successfully created, built, and tested the application locally, you must now make your development objects centrally available.

Checking in source files and activating all development components

Your activities contain all file versions that you have created. When a successful test has been carried out, you know that they contain a complete version of your development components. To store these versions in the DTR database, check in your changes as follows:[17]

1. Navigate to the **Development Configuration** perspective. By default, this contains the **Open Activities** view. In this view, you see your open (local) activities in the context of your DTR workspace.

Checking in changes

2. In the context menu of the activity[18] that you created first, select **Checkin** (Figure 12.45). With this step, you make all versions in these activities available in Design Time Repository.

---

17 When you work on a development component for a long time, there is always a risk of data loss. Checking in the data stores them securely, but you should still only check in completed changes. The **Upload of Changes** function allows you to store changes on the server without checking them in.

18 This contains no dependencies to development components that were created at a later stage, and should therefore be checked in and activated first.

Figure 12.45 Open Activities in the Open Activities View — Check-In

3. During check-in, the **Activation** Wizard opens automatically. If you want to use this function, it is important to check in used development components before using development components.

Triggering the central build

4. You build your development component centrally in Component Build Service. Select **Activate with all Predecessors** in the **Activation-Wizard**.

5. When your build is successful, your development component becomes visible in the **Active DCs** view.[19]

6. When you choose **Open Request View**, you can see the result of the build process and display a log file, if errors occurred. Figure 12.46 shows the activation dialog that automatically appears when an activity is checked in. You can monitor the central build process in CBS in the **Activation Requests** view of Developer Studio (Figure 12.47).

Monitoring the central build in Developer Studio

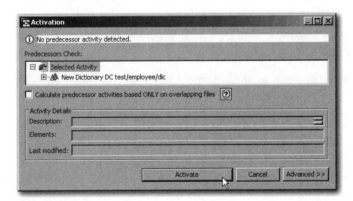

Figure 12.46 Activating an Activity

---

19 By default, this is the only place from which it can be used by users other than the group that develops the development component, because the central build guarantees that all objects are up-to-date.

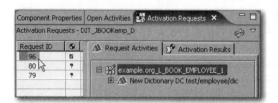

Figure 12.47 Predecessor Check and the Relevant Build Request

Activation
Requests View —
CBS user interface
for developers

As you can see, developers can also use the **Activation Requests** view to monitor the CBS central build process. You will also find the request and build logs here that help you to analyze errors if build problems occur. One possible error, for example, is that you have built against the public part of a development component created by one of your colleagues, and this colleague has since changed the component so that it is no longer compatible. As a result, your version no longer suits the one available centrally. (You may recall that in such a case, the changes are not activated. Make the required changes in a new activity, and activate both at the same time. The first activity is identified as the predecessor activity during activation.[20])

Releasing Changes

Transferring devel-
opment to admin-
istration and QM

If the central build was also successful, your work as a developer is finished for the time being. Your application is now complete, from the database to the user interface. Figure 12.48 shows the result in the **Component Navigator**.

Subsequent steps (such as the transport into the consolidation system, further tests, and assembly) are carried out by the quality management team, and are controlled by Change Management Service.

---

20 When a development component is changed and you use its public part, available versions of your development component are automatically built by CBS to keep the buildspace up-to-date. If the files used contain incompatible changes, the build will fail, and your development component will have the status Broken. For more information on how to deal with this, see *https://www.sdn.sap.com/irj/sdn/go/portal/prtroot/docs/library/uuid/30b7c94e-fc6b-2910-30b8-d34a7b51309e* (*CBS Secrets Unveiled — Understanding Broken and Dirty DCs*).

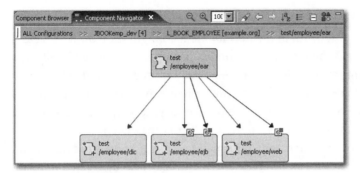

Figure 12.48 Structure of the Employee Application in the Component Model

1. To release your objects for subsequent steps, select the **Transport** view in the **Development Configuration** perspective. If you do not see this view, carry out the usual steps to add and display it.

2. Open the **Waiting** node. All activated activities are displayed.

3. In the context menu for your activities, choose **Release** (Figure 12.49). Once you release your activities, your work as a developer is finished.

Releasing activities — CMS user interface for developers

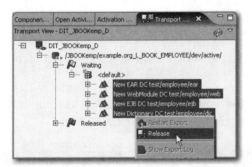

Figure 12.49 Releasing a List of Activities

When you have released your activities, these are available for import into the consolidation system. If no errors occur during testing, you have completed your work as a developer. If the QM team discovers errors in the consolidation system, you can, if necessary, correct these errors in this system by loading the corresponding development configuration. However, you will usually check out and edit the objects in the development system again, and transport the changes in the same way as new objects. For more details on further steps to be taken, see Chapter 11.

645

12.3.7 Steps in CMS After Development

Consolidating applications, preparing and testing transport, and releasing for production

Developers now work in the development configuration of the development system. When the application has been built and tested locally, the activities are released. These are imported into the consolidation system where they are tested. If they do not contain any errors, they are assembled into an SCA, changed again if necessary, tested, and are available for import to the production system (if one has been defined) or for shipment to customers. All information on the software component, such as the owner, can be accessed. An SCA can also be created immediately and downloaded (Figure 12.50).

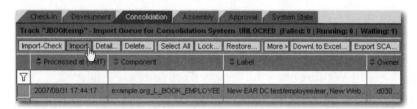

Figure 12.50 Importing a List of Activities into the Consolidation System

Import into the consolidation system

With the import, the application that was transported in the activities in the form of its source files is automatically built, and deployed into the connected runtime system. It is assumed that the test does not identify any errors.

Assembling development components into software components

1. Now carry out assembly (**Assemble Component(s)...**), to compile the software component into a shippable SCA (Figure 12.51).

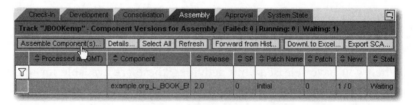

Figure 12.51 Assembling a Software Component

Determining the Support Package and patch level

2. Determine the patch level and the Support Package for the new SCA. To do this, use the radio button in the dialog box that appears (Figure 12.52) to specify whether you want to keep the number last selected or increase it by one digit.

3. After assembly, automatic deployment runs in the `Test` runtime system, if it has been defined.

Final test of software components

4. When the test is successful, the quality of the software is confirmed (*approval*).

5. Open the **Approval** tab, and release the software component by choosing **Approve** (Figure 12.53).

Releasing software components

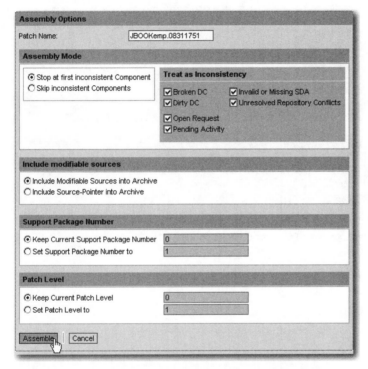

Figure 12.52 Patch Level and Support Package for the New SCA

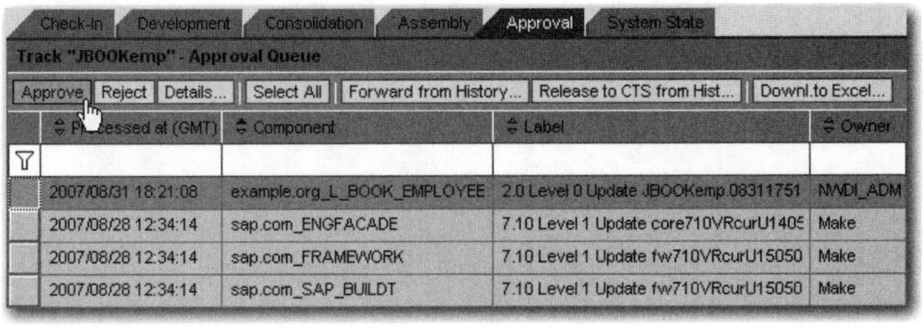

	Processed at (GMT)	Component	Label	Owner
	2007/08/31 18:21:08	example.org_L_BOOK_EMPLOYEE	2.0 Level 0 Update JBOOKemp.08311751	NWDI_ADM
	2007/08/28 12:34:14	sap.com_ENGFACADE	7.10 Level 1 Update core710VRcurU1405	Make
	2007/08/28 12:34:14	sap.com_FRAMEWORK	7.10 Level 1 Update fw710VRcurU15050	Make
	2007/08/28 12:34:14	sap.com_SAP_BUILDT	7.10 Level 1 Update fw710VRcurU15050	Make

Figure 12.53 Approval for the New SCA

6. When the SCA has been approved, it is available for import into a production system, if one has been defined. You can also send the SCA
files from the *CMS\archives* folder in the transport directory.

7. In the history of the approval queue in the new transport scenario for
non-ABAP objects, you can also export the SCA into CTS by selecting
Release to CTS... (Figure 12.54).

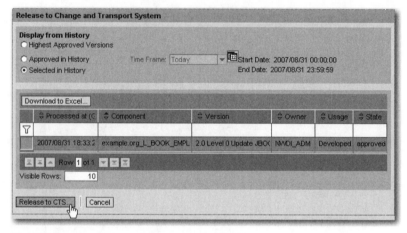

Figure 12.54 New Transport Connection in NWDI

The SAP NetWeaver Application Server Java has a sophisticated design that allows you to run multiple instances allocated to several servers and to balance the workload in an efficient way. This chapter focuses on the cluster and runtime architecure of SAP NetWeaver Application Server Java. The cluster architecture builds the foundation of a coherent, consistent, and scalable platform for enterprise solutions on top.

13 SAP NetWeaver Application Server Java — Architecture

SAP NetWeaver Application Server Java is part of the SAP NetWeaver Application Platform. It provides the complete infrastructure for deploying and running Java applications. The Application Server Java is optimized to run mission-critical business applications and provides many new concepts and enhanced features, such as:

Complete
Infrastructure

- ▸ Increased robustness and stability of the server infrastructure and applications
- ▸ Simplification of server infrastructure and improved supportability
- ▸ Advanced administration capabilities provided by the Zero Administration concept
- ▸ Enhanced monitoring and easy access to all monitoring data
- ▸ Integration of SAP Java Virtual Machine with additional capabilities
- ▸ Central cache management and session management

13.1   Cluster Architecture of SAP NetWeaver Application Server Java

Reliable
System

The AS Java cluster is a set of processes that work together to build a scalable and reliable system. The cluster architecture is transparent to the client and appears to it as a single server unit.

An AS Java cluster consists of several types of instances, all of which have an instance number and can be started, stopped, and monitored separately (Figure 13.1). They are:

▶ **Central services instance**
The central services instance consists of a Message Service and Enqueue Service. They are responsible for lock administration, message exchange, and load balancing within the Java cluster.

▶ **One or more Java instances**
A Java instance consists of an Internet Communication Manager (ICM) and one or several server processes. The ICM handles requests coming from clients and dispatches them to the available server processes that actually process the requests.

▶ **One or several databases**
The database stores system and application data.

Layered
Architecture

An appropriate cluster setup is one of the main prerequisites for the efficient performance of your system. You can scale the Java cluster by installing additional Java instances to your system, or by adding server processes to an already existing Java instance. For high availability reasons, the different instances can be split up among different physical machines.

A minimum AS Java cluster installation consists of a central services instance, one Java instance with one server process, and a database. A larger AS Java installation can have several Java instances with more than one server process each, a central services instance, and one or several databases.

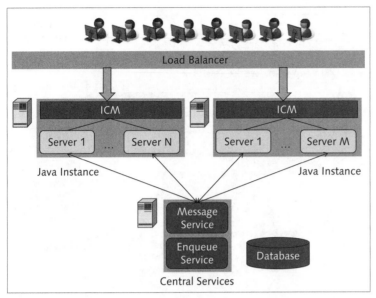

Figure 13.1 Java Cluster Topology in SAP NetWeaver Composition Environment

13.1.1 Java Instance

A Java instance is a unit in the Application Server Java cluster that is identified by its instance number. The elements that form an instance run on one physical machine. Also, it is possible to run several instances on one physical machine, but it is recommended that you split the different instances among different physical machines.

A Java Instance consists of:

▶ Internet Communication Manager (ICM)

▶ One or several server processes

13.1.2 Internet Communication Manager

The Internet Communication Manager (ICM) is an element of the Java instance that handles requests coming from clients and dispatches them to the available server processes. Data is transferred from the ICM to the server processes and vice versa using the Fast Channel Architecture (FCA), which allows fast and reliable communication between them (Figure 13.2).

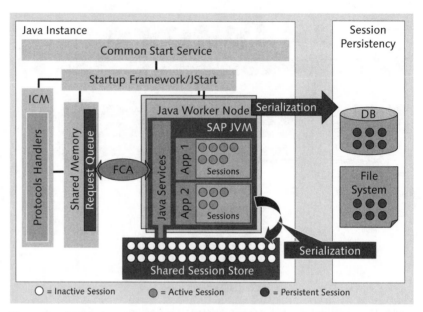

Figure 13.2 Java Instance Architecture in SAP NetWeaver Composition Environment 7.1

Communication

▶ The ICM reads the request from the TCP/IP stack into the FCA, decides which server process should handle the request (load balancing), and then sends the requests directly to the individual process. The required information for load balancing is retrieved by the ICM from the Message Service.

▶ When a server process has sufficient resources to consume a request, it takes it out of the FCA queue, processes it, and writes it back into the queue so it is returned to the originator of the request.

▶ The server processes of the AS Java actually execute the Java application. They are responsible for processing incoming requests that are assigned to them by the ICM.

▶ Each server process is multi-threaded, and can therefore process a large number of requests simultaneously. When more than one server processes run inside a Java instance, all of them have the same capabilities.

▶ During installation, the installation procedure configures the optimal number of server processes in an instance based on the available hardware resources. You can add more server processes to an existing Java instance.

▶ Server processes in an instance have a shared memory that enables much faster interaction. In the shared memory, server processes and the ICM store all their monitoring information, which can be used for detailed analysis of the current internal status of each Java instance. Figure 13.3 shows the management console for a Java instance.

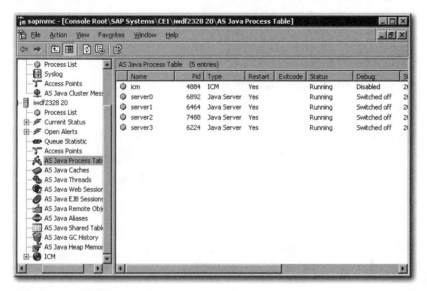

Figure 13.3 SAP Management Console

All VMs in the instance have access to a shared memory area used as a session store, which is also a safeguard against VM failures. This is enabled by the use of SAP's own implementation of a Java Virtual Machine.

13.1.3 Central Services Instance

Central services form the basis of communication and synchronization for the AS Java cluster. They are responsible for lock administration, message exchange, and load balancing within the cluster.

Enqueue Server, Message Server, Workload Balancing

Central services run on one physical machine and constitute a separate instance. They comprise:

The Message Service keeps a list of all server processes in the AS Java cluster and provides information about their availability to the ICM. It also represents the infrastructure for data exchange between the participating server processes.

Tasks
The Message Service is responsible for the following tasks in the AS Java cluster:

▸ Notification of events that arise in the cluster, for example, when a service is started or stopped

▸ Communication between different services

▸ Forwarding of messages and requests to all participants

▸ Guaranteed message transmission

▸ Exchange of cache information in the cluster

Applications can lock objects and later release these locks again. The Enqueue Service manages logical locks. It has the following tasks:

▸ Internal synchronization within the AS Java cluster

▸ Servicing of lock requests and management of the lock table with the existing locks

The central services are always required when an AS Java cluster is installed. The central services instance has its own instance number.

When central services are running, the other Java instances are started with the program `JControl`. `JControl` reads profile parameters and makes sure that the server environment is initialized according to the current profile settings.

13.1.4 SAP Java Virtual Machine

AS Java uses SAP JVM as its runtime platform. The SAP JVM is based on the Hotspot Java VM provided by Sun Microsystems but it also possesses some additional features, such as:

▸ **Memory analysis**
Easier detection of out-of-memory situations and analysis of memory footprint due to memory debugging features embedded into the VM.

▶ **Robustness**

Due to fast session failover based on shared memory.

The robustness concept is based on two main ideas: fewer active user requests per VM and a VM independent safe storage of inactive user sessions. More than one VM can run on each machine to reduce the amount of parallel processed user requests per VM. Inactive user sessions are separated from the VMs and stored in a shared memory region.

Stability and Robustness

Figure 13.4 shows how the SAP Java VM increases the robustness of SAP NetWeaver 7.1 in comparison with the architecture of SAP NetWeaver 7.0. While a user session failure in SAP NetWeaver 7.0 can bring down a complete server node (thereby affecting all other user sessions associated with the same node) all sessions are held in shared memory as of release 7.1. The number of sessions per VM instance is kept small so that only few sessions are affected in case of a failure.

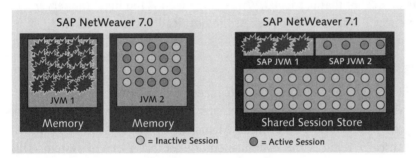

Figure 13.4 Robustness of SAP Java VM

13.2 Runtime Architecure of SAP NetWeaver Application Server Java

The AS Java runtime architecture provides the core functions of the system. It is made up of several low-level subsystems containing manager components that provide the infrastructure and runtime to support the upper layer of the AS Java system components.

Core functions

The Java enterprise runtime provides a number of key concepts that significantly enhance the robustness, stability, and supportability of the AS Java, such as central cache management and session management.

13.2.1 Cluster Communication

Coordination of
Messages Flow

AS Java cluster elements communicate via *cluster messages*. The system is able to send messages to one cluster element, to a group of elements, or to all elements in the cluster. Cluster elements use messages to broadcast notification events. The Cluster Manager is responsible for managing this communication.

There are several types of cluster communication depending on the abilities they provide for transferring messages. The type of cluster communication that is used when processing one message is determined by the Cluster Manager and is transparent for the cluster elements.

The successful message delivery is guaranteed, except in cases when the corresponding element stops or is timed out. In this case, the corresponding exception occurs and can be handled by the sending party. The ability of a server element to process a notification depends on the load level of that particular VM — if the load is too high, the server element will not be able to process the notification immediately.

13.2.2 Cache Management

Memory Reduction

The AS Java uses a central cache management to better control the memory consumption of the components' caches. It provides a complete cache framework — the Cache Management Library (CML) — which drastically reduces the overall memory footprint of the system. This lower memory footprint results in the capability of running more VMs.

Cache management has the following features:

- One cache implementation is used by all layers to reduce redundancies.
- Central cache configuration for all system caches.
- Advanced monitoring and administration of the whole cache landscape.
- Optimizations and tuning of the cache can be done on a higher level and therefore more efficiently.
- Cluster-wide invalidation of cache entries is possible.

13.2.3 Session Management

The SAP NetWeaver Application Server Java has a central session management that provides the following features:

Basic Functions

- ▶ Enhanced control of the sessions in the server
- ▶ Enables a session failover safety mechanism

In general, sessions are used to keep the state of a user accessing an application between several requests. The AS Java architecture provides a reduced number of sessions per VM, which is achieved through separating the inactive user sessions from the active user sessions and reducing the number of sessions stored in a VM.

An active user session is a session that is currently bound with a request that is processed by the server, while an inactive user session is currently not bound with a request. Active user sessions are stored inside the memory space of the VM, while inactive user sessions are stored in a shared memory region that is not damaged if the VM crashes due to certain problems such as Out of Memory errors, JVM bugs, and so on. In case of failure, the inactive user sessions stored in the shared memory region remain unaffected, and they can be mapped to a different VM process when a request for that session needs to be processed.

13.2.4 Thread Management

The AS Java thread management system provides common handling, maintenance, configuration, error processing, and monitoring for the thread resources used for execution of parallel system and application requests. The thread management system is comprised of two thread managers that handle the system and application operations separately. The Thread Manager supplies threads for the AS Java system operations such as framework tasks, system events handling, and services management, while the Application Thread Manager supplies threads for application requests processing.

Shared Monitoring

Thread management controls the thread usage in the system and ensures that the overload on one AS Java component cannot deplete the thread resources and leave the other components blocked due to lack of threads. This is achieved by effective load control for application requests, optimal resource management, low synchronization level, and high degree of isolation.

Manager   The managers that constitute the subsystems of Java Enterprise Runtime are listed in the following. All managers can be configured with the Config Tool (Figure 13.5), so you can finetune the application server:

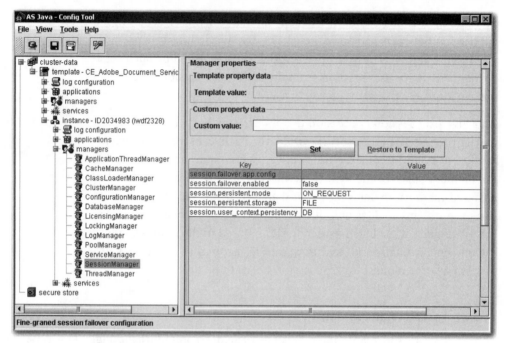

Figure 13.5 Config Tool for the Configuration of the Managers of SAP NetWeaver Application Server

▶ **ApplicationThreadManager**
The ApplicationThreadManager handles threads in which client applications' source code is executed.

▶ **CacheManager**
The CacheManager provides a centralized cache management infrastructure that consolidates caches used by various components within the system.

▶ **ClassLoaderManager**
The ClassLoaderManager is responsible for registering and removing loaders and references between them.

- **ClusterManager**

  The ClusterManager manages communication between elements in the AS Java cluster. It updates the information about the status of each cluster element and the services running on it.

- **ConfigurationManager**

  The ConfigurationManager manages the process of storing and reading of persistent configuration data to and from a relational database.

- **DatabaseManager**

  The DatabaseManager provides a pooling functionality for database connections.

- **LicensingManager**

  The LicensingManager handles SAP licenses.

- **LockingManager**

  The LockingManager handles locking as an interface to the Enqueue Service.

- **LogManager**

  The LogManager manages the process of logging system events.

- **PoolManager**

  The PoolManager manages the process of pooling Java objects.

- **ServiceManager**

  The ServiceManager manages the lifecycle of AS Java system components and acts as a container in which all services in the cluster work.

- **SessionManager**

  The SessionManager manages the lifecycle of user sessions and provides failover capabilities.

- **ThreadManager**

  The ThreadManager handles threads in which the AS Java system operations are executed.

Supportability is a major factor when assessing a software product. Having a robust and easy to use supportability infrastructure could greatly reduce the total cost of ownership. In this chapter, the tools available to operate the SAP NetWeaver Composition Environment will be detailed.

14 Supportability of the SAP NetWeaver Composition Environment

For a product to be supportable, it must allow its users to operate in an efficient way to guarantee the well-being of the system. To be able to achieve supportability, they need some tools to continually check the status of the system as well as tools to influence the behavior of the system in order to adjust it to specific requirements. In addition, from time to time administrators might face some extraordinary situations in which parts of the system do not react as expected or show significant performance degradation. In cases like these, tools that go into more details should be at hand to quickly allocate the reason for the problem.

Checking the status of tools

The requirements listed above define three major areas in the field of supportability that will be covered in the paragraphs that follow:

▶ Monitoring (see Section 14.1)

▶ Administration (see Section 14.2)

▶ Troubleshooting (see Section 14.3)

14.1 Monitoring

The monitoring infrastructure in the SAP NetWeaver Composition Environment provides the users with an overall picture of the well-being of the system. Thus, it is a crucial part of the process to ensure high availability and high performance of the product.

14.1.1 JMX Infrastructure

Monitoring in SAP NetWeaver Composition Environment is based on the open standard Java Management Extensions (JMX). On the one side, this ensures clear logic and architectural structure built on proven concepts; on the other side, it allows for easy integration with other existing management solutions.

JMX organizational model
The organizational model defined by the standard specifies three layers that are highly independent of each other and allow for building flexible and loosely coupled solutions, which is especially important when managing huge systems consisting of heterogeneous modules.

▶ In the first layer, called instrumentation layer, the managed resources are situated. Their role is to provide management interfaces called *MBeans*, via which they expose some management or monitoring information.

▶ In the second agent layer is the JMX agent, called MBean server. The MBean server acts as an intermediator in the communication between the managed resources and the managed system, thus preventing any direct communication that could lead to dependencies on class level. The MBean server also cares about the lifecycle of the MBeans registered by the resources.

In addition to the MBean server in the agent layer, a set of more services are defined. They provide useful functionality, such as the possibility to define relations between the resources, loading of classes from remote locations, timeout events, and so on.

▶ In the third layer, called distributed services layer, we have the clients that retrieve and process the information together with the connectors and protocol adaptors provided by the infrastructure. The clients of the management and monitoring information could be various — from browsers to complex management systems built on proprietary technologies. Depending on their nature, they use different techniques to connect to the MBean server. Nevertheless, the means to

connect could be sorted in two major groups — connectors and protocol adaptors.

▶ Connectors are modules that consist of a client part used by the
management system and a server part deployed at the MBean
server.

▶ Protocol adaptors allow for more generic access to the MBean
server by transforming the calls over another protocol like http
into JMX calls.

Figure 14.1 shows the cooperation between the three layers of the JMX   Cooperation
organizational model.

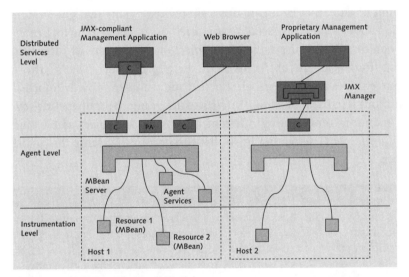

Figure 14.1 JMX Organizational Model

In SAP NetWeaver Composition Environment, the JMX infrastructure is
exposed via a dedicated service called JMX service that also cares about
the distribution of the requests in the cluster and is able to perform security checks on the incoming calls.

14.1.2 Monitors

The monitoring framework in SAP NetWeaver Composition Environ-   Monitoring
ment is a pluggable framework that utilizes the existing JMX infrastruc-   framework

ture. It allows different resources to register as providers of monitoring data. The data collected from the resources is then processed by the monitoring framework and visualized in the SAP NetWeaver Administrator tool coming with the Composition Environment. Typically, a resource that registers and provides monitoring data to the monitoring framework is either a JEE application or a service that is part of the Java Server.

Monitoring tree The monitoring infrastructure structures the data in a tree of monitors (below this is called *monitoring tree*). A monitor is an entity that cares about the communication with a single monitored resource and processes data collected from it. Typically a monitor represents a small amount of data, that is, it contains a simple type value that gives information about a single aspect of a monitored object. For example, a monitor could represent the name of an object or the number of successful transactions with an object but not the object itself. That's why a resource that works with a logical object and wants to provide information about it in the monitoring infrastructure would typically define several monitors representing different aspects of the object and would then group them semantically so that the group represents the whole object.

> **Example**
>
> Let's take for example a JEE application that cares about the proper functioning of a bank. In this case, the resource that provides monitoring data is the application and the logical object could be the bank. The name, the average number of transactions, or the daily cash flow could be different monitors representing the bank.

A monitor is always part of a certain group of monitors describing an object. The objects themselves can be further logically grouped inside the monitoring tree in entities called *summaries* and the summaries on their turn can be grouped together with other summaries and objects in summaries again. Thus, the hierarchical structure of the tree follows the semantics of the objects being monitored. In the monitoring tree, the leaves are always monitors, the nodes in the first level above the leaves are objects, and the nodes in the upper levels are summaries. The summaries from the first level below the root are predefined.

The monitoring infrastructure supports several types of monitors. Some of them represent a simple counter while others model more complex scenarios as cache access or session duration. Depending on the type of the monitor, it is possible to define thresholds of critical values. When such a critical value is reached, the monitor is able to signalize an alert. The monitors also keep persistent history so that a user is able to analyze how the system has behaved in the past. Customization of the time frame, over which the history is kept, allows for analysis in a broader scope of time.

Figure 14.2 gives an idea about the structure of the monitoring tree.   **Structure**

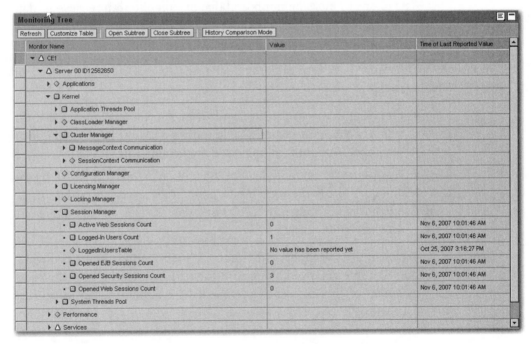

Figure 14.2 Monitoring Tree

14.1.3 Adding New Content in the Monitoring Framework

As mentioned previously, the monitoring framework is open for new resources to plug in. To do this they have to fulfill two tasks.

▶ The first task is to define the monitors, the objects, and the summaries that have to be created inside the monitoring tree for them. This is done declaratively via an XML file that is packed in the deliverable archive (SDA) of the resource. The monitoring framework takes care to retrieve the xml file after the deployment of the resource, to parse it, and to install the entities described there in the monitoring tree.

▶ The second task is to provide resource MBeans. The resource MBeans (also called runtime MBeans) are used by the monitors to retrieve the monitoring data at runtime. All the communication between the monitors and the resource MBeans at runtime is done over JMX.

The relation between the resource MBeans and the monitors is one to many. This means that one resource MBean can provide monitoring data to one or more monitors and that one monitor can retrieve its data from one resource MBean only (that is because a monitor typically represents a single attribute of a resource).

Methods for providing data The resource MBeans can provide the monitoring data either actively or passively.

▶ Providing data actively (data pushed by the resource) means that the resource MBean is responsible to initiate a change in the monitor by sending a JMX notification with the updated value.

▶ Passive provisioning of data on the other hand (data is polled by the monitor) forces the monitor to periodically check the value of the monitored attribute. In this case, the changes of the value are detected automatically.

Which of the two modes a monitor will use is defined in the configuration XML file deployed along with the resource. Figure 14.3 shows an overview of the different components the monitoring infrastructure consists of.

14.1.4 Java System Reports

The standard way to view the monitoring data is via the Java system reports within the SAP NetWeaver Administrator. This tool allows for correlation of different monitoring values in order to analyze specific problems.

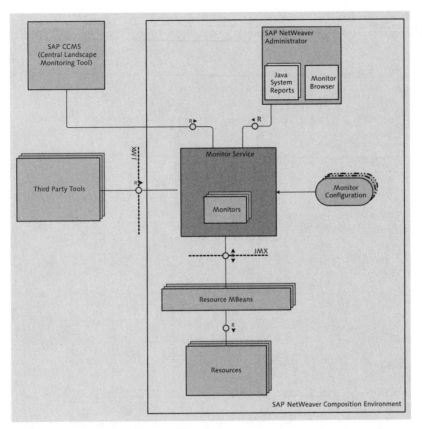

Figure 14.3 Monitoring Infrastructure

Different monitors from the generic monitoring tree can be combined and displayed together in a chart that shows their values over a configurable time period. In addition charts are further combined in reports, which represent several charts side by side, thus allowing the user to build dashboards showing different aspects of the system together.

Monitoring charts and reports

By default, the SAP NetWeaver Composition Environment comes with several predefined reports that cover problems such as Capacity Planning, Activities Overview, System Health, and others (Figure 14.4). The user is free to define further chart and reports, selecting monitors to be tracked from the monitoring tree, according to specific use cases. The monitor browser report is a special report representing all the monitors in a generic manner.

Monitor browser

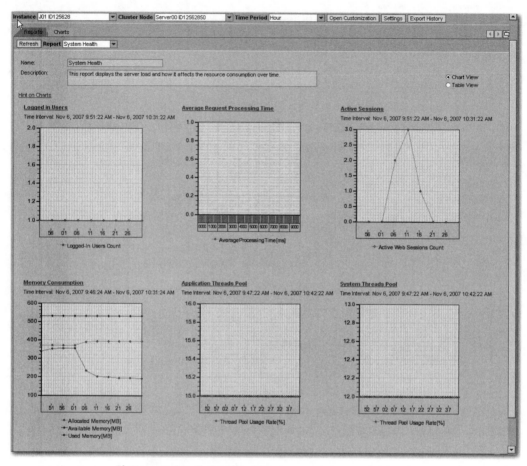

Figure 14.4 Java System Reports

14.2 Administration

The administration infrastructure of the SAP NetWeaver Composition Environment allows its users to configure and control the product in a way that best suits their needs. Administration of the SAP NetWeaver Composition Environment is also based on JMX. This makes the infrastructure highly extensible and open for integration with other management solutions.

14.2.1 SAP NetWeaver Administrator

Valuable tool

SAP NetWeaver Administrator (Figure 14.5) is a Web-based tool that covers various management aspects of the SAP NetWeaver Composition Environment. Designed as a single entry point to a variety of administrative use cases, it is a valuable tool for the daily operation of the system.

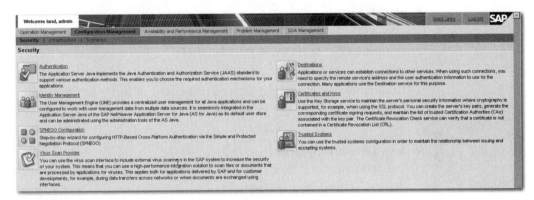

Figure 14.5 SAP NetWeaver Administrator

From an architecture point of view, SAP NetWeaver Administrator consists of three layers:

▶ **Resource layer**
This layer includes the major components of the SAP NetWeaver Composition Environment by exposing some management functionality.

▶ **Model layer**
All the management functionality, provided be the Composition Environment components, is structured in a harmonized model, access to which is done via JMX.

▶ **UI layer**
Built using the Web Dynpro technology, the UI layer provides a consistent look and feel to the user, based on well-established UI patterns.

SAP NetWeaver Administrator comes together with the SAP NetWeaver Composition Environment and is ready to be used out of the box, after the Composition Environment has been installed.

SAP NetWeaver
Administrator —
Work Center These are some of the most frequently used administration work centers:

▶ **Identity Management**
Used for configuration of the User Management Engine (UME), this work center allows for creation of new users, configuration of roles, and permissions.

▶ **Start & Stop**
This work center is the main entry point for restarting Composition Environment instances, as well as separate services or applications.

▶ **Destinations**
Destination configuration is frequently used in order to set up connections required for Composition Environment to consume services from a landscape of systems.

▶ **Java System Properties**
This work center allows viewing and modifying of some basic configuration settings (whenever online modifiable) of the Java System such as service properties, VM parameters, and so on.

▶ **Licences**
Using this work center, an administrator is able to apply or modify system licenses.

▶ **SOA Management**
This set of work centers contains everything around Webservices configuration, such as endpoint configuration and WS client configuration.

14.2.2 Other Administrative Tools

As SAP NetWeaver Administrator is an online, Web-based tool, a prerequisite for its operation is that the system is already up and running. However, in several cases, an administrator needs tools also when the system is stopped or only parts of it have been started. SAP NetWeaver Composition Environment provides two useful tools for situations like these.

▶ **SAP Management Console**
The SAP Management Console (Figure 14.6) is a tool, which allows for basic administration and monitoring of the system. As it requires

only small part of the kernel to be started, it is able to cover also many bootstrapping scenarios, when the system is only partially started, in addition to normal operation.

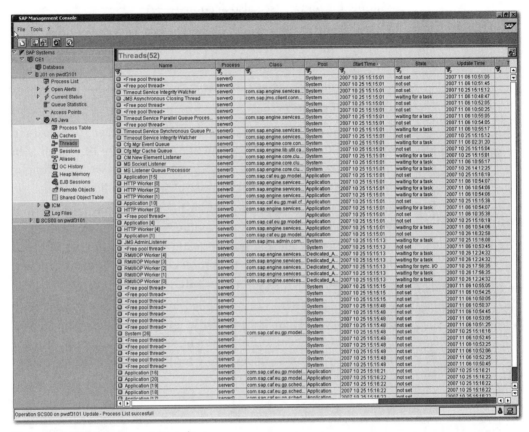

Figure 14.6 SAP Management Console

Some of the major capabilities provided by the SAP Management Console include:

SAP Management Console — main function

- ▶ Starting and stopping of Composition Environment instances and the system itself
- ▶ Detailed view on process list, communication queues, and access points
- ▶ Session overview

> ▶ Detailed view on Java Server Runtime, including information on threads, cache usage, Java garbage collection activities, and cluster messaging

> ▶ Simple log viewer (see also Section 14.3.1)

SAP Management Console can be started as a Java applet or as a plugin in the SAP NetWeaver Development Studio. Because it connects remotely and is able to display several systems side by side, it could be used for basic landscape overview as well.

▶ **Offline Configuration tool**

Yet another useful tool that comes with SAP NetWeaver Composition Environment is the Offline Configuration tool (Figure 14.7). This is an expert tool, which is typically used in emergency cases, for example, when the system cannot start because of wrong configuration.

The Offline Configuration tool works directly with the database, so it does not need a running Composition Environment to perform its tasks. Some of the most important features in it are the possibility to edit various Java settings for the processes running in the cluster and to add or remove nodes from the cluster.

Changes in the system can be applied to the complete system or to different instances within it. Different capabilities of the SAP NetWeaver Composition Environment, as configuration inheritance and parametrization of values, allow for flexible and adaptive configuration with minimum effort.

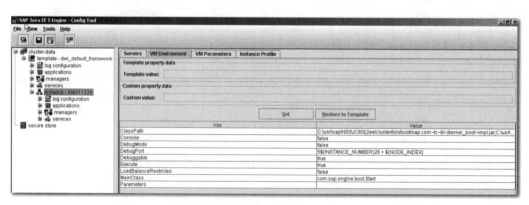

Figure 14.7 Offline Configuration Tool

In SAP NetWeaver Composition Environment, there are also several low level console-based administration tools that can be used via telnet. They require proficient knowledge of the system architecture to be used and will not be covered in this book.

14.3 Troubleshooting

Logging is a very popular and straightforward way to provide information about the status of the system and to troubleshoot unexpected behavior. It is used to denote significant events in the lifecycle of the server, so that they could be analyzed in the order in which they happened.

14.3.1 Logging and Tracing

The logging infrastructure provided by SAP aims at providing this basic functionality and at the same time meeting the different configuration requirements that might appear in the broad variety of scenarios executed in the SAP NetWeaver Composition Environment. The log records produced by the system are grouped in problematic areas (called categories) such as `/System/Database`, `/System/Server`, `/System/Security` and so on, which helps the user to quickly get a grasp about the relevance of the respective message. This concept, however, could be expanded in a way that the category could be defined more precisely, for example `/System/Server/Connectivity`. Thus, the problematic areas are structured hierarchically.

Logging infrastructure

When the system is running, the user is free to configure the logging infrastructure in a way that suites his needs best. Typically, this means changing the severity level for a problematic area in order to get more or less information about it. In the hierarchical structure of categories, the more specific problematic areas inherit the configuration of their parents. If we take the previous example, this means that assigning a specific severity to the messages produced by the category `/System/Server` will also have effect on the messages produced by the category `/System/Server/Connectivity`. In this way, the user has more flexibility and could manipulate the configuration at different levels of granularity.

Log configuration in SAP NetWeaver Composition Environment is performed using the log configuration work center in the SAP NetWeaver Administrator tool (Figure 14.8).

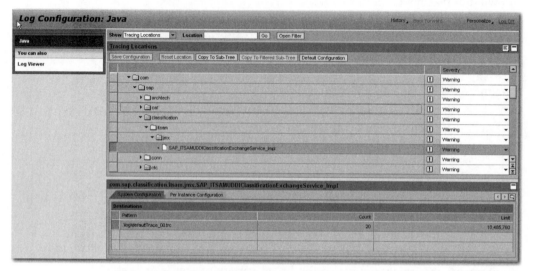

Figure 14.8 Log Configuration Work Center in SAP NetWeaver Administrator

Tracing
In addition to the log messages, the logging infrastructure produces additional trace messages that are targeted at more experienced users. These messages are typically switched off. They could be used in extreme situations when certain misbehavior has been detected. The trace messages usually depict the program flow and are grouped by the software component that produced them. As software components are denoted by the Java packages from which they consist (e.g., com.sap.engine.services or com.sap.portal), they are also structured in a hierarchical way. Thus, the user can configure the traces at a greater or at a more fine-grained scale.

Log and trace messages often need to be analyzed together. Typically, when a certain problem occurs, the system administrator would detect it using the logs and then switch on the traces for more details. The logging infrastructure connects the related log and trace messages using message identificators. These identificators allow the user to verify that a certain trace message belongs to a certain problematic area.

Along with the message, each log record contains additional information that helps the user to find the context in which the message has been produced. This information includes the name of the application that has been requested, the user that is executing the request, the session identificator, and so on.

Log and trace messages can be viewed using the log viewer work center in the SAP NetWeaver Administrator (Figure 14.9). It comes with a wealth of features that allow sorting, filtering, and searching the contents, based on various search criteria. Physical files are automatically merged and some predefined views, displaying the messages from the last 24 hours or all the errors, are provided. This enables the administrator to quickly browse through the messages he is interested in. Additional views, based on customized filter criteria can be defined and saved for further reuse.

Log Viewer

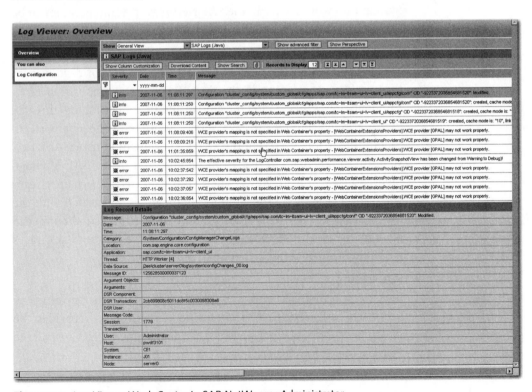

Figure 14.9 Log Viewer Work Center in SAP NetWeaver Administrator

A simplified version of the log viewer is available also within the SAP Management Console. It can be used to view the log and trace information when the SAP NetWeaver Composition Environment is not started.

14.3.2 Troubleshooting Scenarios

While logging and tracing provide generic means to analyze problems on the system, some examples of typical problem analysis scenarios follow, which show how other tools can be efficiently used to troubleshoot the SAP NetWeaver Composition Environment.

▸ **Acquiring information about the installed components**
Unexpected behavior is sometimes a result of missing deployments or inconsistent versions of the components deployed. In order to get the full list of the deployed components, along with their versions, the System Info work center in the SAP NetWeaver Administrator can be used.

▸ **Analyzing deadlocks**
A user might experience hanging of screens because of deadlocks in the applications running in the SAP NetWeaver Composition Environment. Cases like that typically result in long running threads, which are detected by the Java Server Runtime of the Composition Environment and are red in the SAP Management Console. As a first step, the problematic threads can be analyzed in the SAP Management Console thread view, where the executed task name, user, application class, and other important attributes, associated with the different threads, are displayed. Subsequently, a full thread dump can be triggered via the SAP Management Console, so that the stack traces of the threads could be further analyzed.

▸ **SQL tracing**
Inefficient database access can be the reason for various performance problems. SAP NetWeaver Composition Environment provides the means to analyze such problems via the Sap Open SQL Engine and the SQL tracing technology.

SAP Open SQL engine copes with the variety of database management systems and SQL dialects by providing a unified portable solution for all components in the SAP NetWeaver Composition Environment that need relational persistence. That is why analyzing the Open SQL layer gives important information about application behavior.

SQL tracing is a technique that uses events from the Open SQL engine to record the SQL statement, duration, application name, and other useful data for each database query that has been executed. It does not require additional instrumentation from the application developer and could be switched on and off dynamically. The information gathered can later be displayed via the Open SQL Monitors work center in the SAP NetWeaver Administrator.

Further tools for problem analysis can be found in the SAP NetWeaver Administrator work center **Problem Management**, as well as in the SAP Management Console.

The Authors

Alfred Barzewski (*alfred.barzewski@sap.com*) joined SAP in 1997 as a member of the Product Management group for ABAP Workbench. Initially, he was responsible for Information Development in various areas of the SAP technology. These areas included Remote Communication, Non-SAP Accesses using BAPIs, RFC Programming, and ABAP Development. Most recently, he has focused on Java technologies in the environment of the SAP NetWeaver Application Server. Alfred publishes articles about Java Programming with SAP NetWeaver on a regular basis.

Carsten Bönnen (*carsten.boennen@sap.com*) received his M.A. in computer linguistics and artificial intelligence in 2001. In the same year he started his career at SAP, first as a Java developer and as an instructor, later in the role of a consultant. At the end of 2002, he became Product Manager for the SAP NetWeaver Portal. In 2003, he took over Product Management responsibility for a new tool called *GUI Machine*, today known as Visual Composer. Today Carsten Bönnen works as Product Manager for the SAP NetWeaver UI strategy.

After his position as software trainer, **Bertram Ganz** (*bertram.ganz@sap.com*) came to SAP in 2002. Since then, he has worked as part of the development team on Web Dynpro Java Runtime. The main focus of his work is on the following topics: knowledge transfer, rollout, and documentation. Bertram regularly publishes articles on Web Dynpro in the context of the SAP NetWeaver Application Server.

Wolf Hengevoss (*wolf.hengevoss@sap.com*) finalized his studies at the University of Kaiserslautern. He began his employment in Product Management at SAP in 1999. He has worked in the Basis group on R/3 topics such as Computer-Aided Test Tool and Business Address Services. In the early development stages of the Exchange Infrastructure, he took on topics from the Java environment. Today, his work focuses on the rollout of the Java Development Infrastructure of SAP NetWeaver.

Karl Kessler (*karl.kessler@sap.com*) came to SAP in 1992 as a computer scientist. After his initial experience with the modeling of the Basis technology, he switched to Product Management for ABAP Workbench, where he was responsible for the rollout of SAP technology at various conferences. In 2003, he assumed responsibility for Production Management of the SAP NetWeaver Technology Infrastructure, with a focus on SAP NetWeaver Application Server Java and ABAP. Today, he focuses on how SAP NetWeaver builds the foundation for SAP ERP and the SAP Business Suite.

Markus Küfer (*markus.kuefer@sap.com*) studied Medical Information Technology at the University of Heidelberg. In 2000, he joined SAP. He was responsible for the JDO server integration and represented SAP AG in the expert group for the JDO specification (JSR 243). Markus participated in patents for JDO und EJB 3.0 and has influenced the design of SAP's EJB 3.0 implementation. Today, he is a solution architect of the Global Ecosystem and Partner Group and leads projects in the area of enterprise SOA and SAP NetWeaver Composition Environment at the interface between SAP development and partners.

Anne Lanfermann (*anne.lanfermann@sap.com*) joined SAP AG in 1992 as an instructor in the training department. Since 1996, she has been a member of the Product Management team focusing on documentation and knowledge transfer. Her area of expertise is Process Integration and Enterprise Services.

Miroslav Petrov (*miroslav.petrov@sap.com*) studied Information Technology at the University of Sofia, Bulgaria. In 2000, he began working at SAP Labs Bulgaria. Since 2001, Miroslav has led a development team in the area Java Administration and Monitoring. He is also a development architect in the area of SAP NetWeaver Lifecycle Management.

Susanne Rothaug (*susanne.rothaug@sap.com*) joined SAP AG in 2001 as a member of the SAP NetWeaver Product Management team responsible for e-learning in the Web services area. During the last four years, Susanne worked as a Product Manager for Web services und Enterprise Service-Oriented Architecture.

Dr.-Ing. **Oliver Stiefbold** (*oliver.stiefbold@sap.com*) studied Engineering at the University of Stuttgart and received a Ph.D. at the University of Karlsruhe. In 1998, he started his career with SAP AG in the development area of ERP Manufacturing. Afterwards, he worked for three years as a consultant for Internet solutions. Since 2001, he has been a member of Product Management for the Java development environment of the SAP NetWeaver Portal. In 2006, he turned his focus onto SAP NetWeaver Java EE Server and the SAP NetWeaver Developer Studio.

Volker Stiehl (*volker.stiehl@sap.com*) studied Computer Science at the Friedrich Alexander University of Erlangen-Nürnberg. In 2004, he started to work at SAP AG focussing first on presales activities around the Java EE stack of SAP NetWeaver Application Server. In 2005, he moved to the Product Management of the Composite Application Framework where he was in particular responsible for the guidelines and methodology of writing composite applications. With the introduction of SAP NetWeaver Composition Environment, his area of responsibility was extended to cover the design and architecture of composite applications and their implementation based on the composition tools, the Composite Application Framework, the Guided Procedures framework, or the SAP NetWeaver Visual Composer. Volker is a regular speaker on architecture and development of composite applications at conferences such as SAP TechEd, SAPPHIRE, or JavaOne.

Index

E

X

New 2nd Edition of the bestselling programmers' guide — fully updated and expanded

New sections on architecture, integration topics, and migrating legacy applications

Up-to-date for SAP NetWeaver 7.1

550 pp., 2007, 2. edition, 69,95 Euro / US$ 69.95
ISBN 978-1-59229-092-5

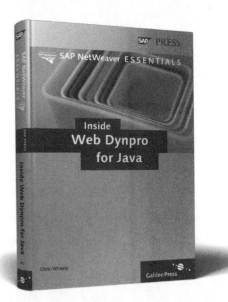

Inside Web Dynpro for Java

www.sap-press.com

Chris Whealy

Inside Web Dynpro for Java

This updated and completely revised second edition of "Inside Web Dynpro for Java" covers everything you need to know to leverage the full power of Web Dynpro for Java — taking you well beyond the standard drag and drop functionality.
Benefit from expert guidance on how to create your own Web Dynpro applications, with volumes of practical insights on the dos and don'ts of Web Dynpro Programming. The author provides you with detailed sections on the use of the Adaptive RFC layer, as well as Dynamic Programming techniques, to name just a few. This exceptional book is complemented by an in-depth class and interface reference, which further assists readers in their efforts to modify existing objects, design custom controllers, and much more.